Adam Westra
The Typic in Kant's *Critique of Practical Reason*

Kantstudien-Ergänzungshefte

Im Auftrag der Kant-Gesellschaft
herausgegeben von
Manfred Baum, Bernd Dörflinger
und Heiner F. Klemme

Band 188

Adam Westra

The Typic in Kant's *Critique of Practical Reason*

Moral Judgment and Symbolic Representation

DE GRUYTER

ISBN 978-3-11-057824-9
e-ISBN (PDF) 978-3-11-045593-9
e-ISBN (EPUB) 978-3-11-045515-1
ISSN 0340-6059

Library of Congress Cataloging-in-Publication Data
A CIP catalog record for this book has been applied for at the Library of Congress.

Bibliographic information published by the Deutsche Nationalbibliothek
The Deutsche Nationalbibliothek lists this publication in the Deutsche Nationalbibliografie; detailed bibliographic data are available on the Internet at http://dnb.dnb.de.

© 2016 Walter de Gruyter GmbH, Berlin/Boston
This volume is text- and page-identical with the hardback published in 2016.
Printing and binding: Hubert & Co. GmbH & Co. KG, Göttingen

♾ Printed on acid-free paper
Printed in Germany

www.degruyter.com

To my brother, Evan

Acknowledgements

I would like to express my heartfelt thanks to the following people:
Mon amour, Clara Dupuis-Morency, for her caring, passion, and inspiration;
My awesome brother, Evan, to whom the book is dedicated;
My wonderful parents, Haijo and Monique Westra, for their infinite, loving support;
My favourite Auntie, Claudette Reich, for a thousand things;
Sonia Mansour and Philippe Robaey, for their generosity, guidance, and humour;
My friends, in Canada and in Europe, for their advice, encouragement, and companionship: Mark & Nataly Westby, Stephen Bank, Jen Spiegel, Olivier Huot-Beaulieu, Maude Forget-Chiasson, Olivier Contensou, Rebecca Dolgoy, Zoë Robaey, Alexandre Robaey, Manuel Roy, Tobias Leßmeister, Anna Wehofsits, David Löwenstein, Alice Cugusi, Agnès Grivaux, Sara Reichert, and Ida Lohse.

This book is a revised version of my PhD dissertation of the same title, which I defended at the Université de Montréal on 18 September, 2014. I would therefore like to acknowledge the people who gave me so much knowledge and guidance during my time as a graduate student. Claude Piché, my supervisor, for his boundless support and enthusiasm over the years, and for having shown me what it means to be a gentleman and a scholar. His many comments and suggestions have greatly improved the book. Holm Tetens, for so kindly hosting me from 2010 to 2013 as a *Gastwissenschaftler* at the Institut für Philosophie, Freie Universität Berlin, and for including me in his *Forschungskolloquium*. The administrative staff of the Département de philosophie, Université de Montréal, especially Pierrette Delisle, for shepherding me through my *doctorat*. The staff of the libraries in which I spent so many hours: Bibliothèque des lettres et sciences humaines, Université de Montréal (special thanks to Nino Gabrielli); Bibliothèque et Archives Nationales du Québec, Montréal; Humanities and Social Sciences Library, McGill University; Taylor Family Digital Library, University of Calgary; St. Mary's University College Library, Calgary; KUB Nord, Copenhagen; Philologische Bibliothek, Freie Universität Berlin; and especially my beloved 'Stabi' (Staatsbibliothek zu Berlin), where the bulk of the book was researched, written, and later revised.

My doctoral studies were made possible by several generous scholarships: Joseph-Armand Bombardier Canada Graduate Scholarship and Michael Smith Foreign Study Supplement, Social Sciences and Humanities Research Council of Canada; Financement intégré, Département de philosophie, Université de Montréal; Bourse de fin d'études doctorales, Faculté des études supérieures et postdoctorales, Université de Montréal.

Adam Westra   Montréal, 2016

Contents

Method of citation and list of abbreviations —— XIII

Introduction —— 1
1 The Typic chapter in the *Critique of Practical Reason* —— 1
2 Need for the present study —— 3
2.1 Obscurity of the primary text —— 3
2.2 Conflicting interpretations in the secondary literature —— 4
3 Goals of the present study —— 6
4 Approach and methodology —— 7
4.1 General approach —— 7
4.2 Specific methodology —— 9
4.3 On the selection of texts —— 11
5 Overview —— 12
5.1 Part One. Commentary —— 12
5.2 Part Two. The typic's place in Kant's theory of symbolic representation —— 15

Commentary

Chapter 1. The task —— 19
1.1 Objects of pure practical reason and the concepts of good and evil —— 19
1.2 Moral appraisal —— 22

Chapter 2. The 'particular difficulties' —— 27
2.1 Construals of the problem in the secondary literature —— 28
2.1.1 Natural necessity vs. freedom —— 28
2.1.2 Is vs. ought —— 32
2.1.3 Concrete vs. abstract —— 34
2.1.4 Matter vs. form —— 35
2.1.5 Subjective ends vs. objective ends —— 36
2.2 The representational mismatch: sensible intuitions vs. supersensible Ideas —— 37
2.2.1 From 'the very same difficulties' as theoretical judgment to the 'particular difficulties' of practical judgment —— 37

2.2.2　Reason and finitude —— 38
2.2.3　Sensible intuitions vs. supersensible Ideas —— 42

Chapter 3. The resources —— 45
3.1　　The schematism and the imagination —— 45
3.1.1　Nature and function —— 45
3.1.2　Two problems with the schematism —— 46
3.2　　The 'schema of a law itself' —— 50
3.3　　The law of nature and the understanding —— 53

Chapter 4. The solution —— 59
4.1　　Overcoming the 'particular difficulties' —— 59
4.1.1　Type$_1$: the law of nature as the 'type' of the moral law —— 59
4.1.2　Type$_2$: *Natura formaliter spectata* as the type of supersensible nature —— 63
4.2　　Accomplishing the task —— 75
4.2.1　The typic-procedure —— 75
4.2.2　The typic-procedure's place in Kant's ethics —— 89
4.2.3　The typic-procedure in the secondary literature —— 96

Chapter 5. The outcome and effectiveness —— 117
5.1　　The Typic's heuristic effectiveness for the 'common understanding' —— 117
5.1.1　The common understanding's moral discernment —— 117
5.1.2　An 'example in a case of experience' —— 119
5.1.3　Isolation and amplification —— 124
5.2　　The typic's protective functions —— 125
5.2.1　Guarding against empiricism —— 126
5.2.2　Type$_3$ —— 130
5.2.3　Guarding against mysticism —— 131

The Typic's Place in Kant's Theory of Symbolic Representation

Chapter 6. The typic and symbolic hypotyposis —— 140
6.1　　The symbolist interpretation of the Typic chapter —— 140
6.1.1　The task —— 140
6.1.2　The 'particular difficulties' —— 142
6.1.3　The resources —— 143
6.1.4　The solution —— 144

6.1.5	The outcome and effectiveness —— 147	
6.2	Critical assessment of the symbolist interpretation —— 148	
6.2.1	The task —— 148	
6.2.2	The 'particular difficulties' —— 151	
6.2.3	The resources —— 152	
6.2.4	The solution —— 152	
6.2.5	The outcome and effectiveness —— 168	
6.3	Against aestheticizing the Typic —— 170	
6.3.1	Two agendas —— 170	
6.3.2	Betting on the wrong horse —— 173	
6.4	Conclusion —— 179	

Chapter 7. The typic and symbolic anthropomorphism —— 180
- 7.1 'Symbolic anthropomorphism' in the *Prolegomena* —— 181
- 7.1.1 Merely symbolic, as opposed to absolute —— 182
- 7.1.2 Analogical —— 185
- 7.1.3 Non-sensible —— 189
- 7.1.4 Permitted and required —— 191
- 7.1.5 Sufficient —— 191
- 7.1.6 Protective —— 193
- 7.2 Symbolic anthropomorphism and Aquinas' doctrine of analogical predication —— 195
- 7.3 Symbolic anthropomorphism and symbolic hypotyposis —— 198
- 7.4 Symbolic anthropomorphism and the typic —— 203
- 7.4.1 Merely symbolic, as opposed to absolute —— 203
- 7.4.2 Analogical —— 204
- 7.4.3 Non-sensible —— 209
- 7.4.4 Permitted and required —— 209
- 7.4.5 Sufficient —— 211
- 7.4.6 Protective —— 211
- 7.5 Conclusion —— 213

Conclusion —— 215
- 1 Summary of Part One —— 215
- 2 Summary of Part Two —— 221
- 3 The Typic in the evolution of Kant's thought —— 228
- 3.1 Symbolic representation —— 228
- 3.2 The relation between nature and morality —— 231

Works Cited —— 237
    Primary sources —— 237
        Immanuel Kant's works in German —— 237
    Secondary sources —— 238

Appendices

Appendix I : German text of the Typic chapter —— 251

Appendix II: English translation of the Typic chapter —— 255

Index of names —— 259

Subject index —— 260

Method of citation and list of abbreviations

Method of citation:
Kant's works are cited in-text by an abbreviated title, followed by the volume and page number in the *Akademie-Ausgabe* (Ak) (e.g., *KU* 5: 351), with the exception of the *Kritik der reinen Vernunft*, which is cited by the pagination of the first (A) and second (B) editions (e.g., *KrV* A689/B717). The *Vorlesungen* are cited by the name of the note-taker, followed by the Ak volume and page number (e.g., *VE Collins*, 27: 1428). The *Reflektionen* are identified by a four-digit number and cited by the Ak volume and page number (e.g., *Refl* 7260, 19: 296). Letters from Kant's correspondence are cited by Ak volume and page number.

The German text of Kant's major works is from the *Philosophische Bibliothek* edition, published by Felix Meiner Verlag (Hamburg); the text of minor works and *handschriftlicher Nachlass* is from the complete electronic edition of Kant's works, *Kant im Kontext III*, produced by Karsten Worm InfoSoftWare (Kant 2007a). The Karsten Worm edition retains earlier orthographic conventions than the Meiner edition; as a result, there are occasionnally minor spelling variations in the German (e.g., *Urtheilskraft* vs. *Urteilskraft*). The German text of the Typic chapter is from the Karsten Worm edition and is reproduced in full in Appendix I. Throughout the book, the German original always accompanies quotations from the Typic chapter; for other texts, it is provided only when relevant.

Unless otherwise indicated, all English translations of Kant's works are from the Cambridge Edition, sometimes with modifications. Appendix II contains the English translation of the Typic chapter used in this book.

The secondary literature is cited in footnotes. Unless otherwise indicated, all English translations of the secondary literature are my own.

List of abbreviations:
Ak   *Immanuel Kants Schriften*. Ausgabe der Königlich Preussichen Akademie der Wissenschaften (Berlin: de Gruyter, 1902–).
Ca   Cambridge Edition of the Works of Immanuel Kant, edited by Paul Guyer and Allen Wood (New York: Cambridge University Press, 1992–).
ANTH   *Allgemeine Naturgeschichte und Theorie des Himmels* (1755), Ak 1
       Universal Natural History and Theory of the Heavens, Ca Natural Science
APH   *Anthropologie in Pragmatischer Hinsicht* (1798), Ak 7
       Anthropology from a Pragmatic Standpoint, Ca Anthropology, History and Education
B   *Beobachtungen über das Gefühl des Schönen und Erhabenen* (1764), Ak. 2
       Observations on the Feeling of the Beautiful and Sublime, Ca Anthropology, History and Education

BB	Bemerkungen zu den *Beobachtungen über das Gefühl des Schönen und Erhabenen*, Ak 20
	Notes on the *Observations on the Feeling of the Beautiful and Sublime*, Ca Notes and Fragments
ED	*Das Ende aller Dinge* (1794), Ak 8
	The End of All Things, Ca Religion and Rational Theology
EEKU	'Erste Einleitung' in die *Kritik der Urteilskraft*, Ak 20,
	'First Introduction' to the *Critique of the Power of Judgment*, Ca Critique of the Power of Judgment
EF	*Zum ewigen Frieden: Ein philosophischer Entwurf* (1795), Ak 8
	Toward Perpetual Peace: A Philosophical Project, Ca Practical Philosophy
FM	*Preisschrift: Welches sind die wirklichen Fortschritte, die die Metaphysik seit Leibnitzens und Wolff's Zeiten in Deutschland gemacht hat?* (1804), Ak 20
	Prize Essay: What Real Progress Has Metaphysics Made in Germany since the Time of Leibniz and Wolff?, Ca Theoretical Philosophy after 1781
G	*Grundlegung zur Metaphysik der Sitten* (1785), Ak 4
	Groundwork of the Metaphysics of Morals, Ca Practical Philosophy
I	*Idee zur einer allgemeinen Geschichte in weltbürgerlicher Absicht* (1784), Ak 8
	Idea toward a Universal History with a Cosmopolitan Aim, Ca Anthropology, History and Education
JL	*'Jäsche-Logik'* (1801), Ak 9
	'Jäsche Logic', Ca Lectures on Logic
KK	*Versuch über die Krankheiten des Kopfes* (1767), Ak. 2
	Essay on the Maladies of the Head, Ca Anthropology, History and Education
KrV	*Kritik der reinen Vernunft* – first edition (A) 1781, Ak 4; second edition (B) 1787, Ak 3
	Critique of Pure Reason, Ca Critique of Pure Reason
KpV	*Kritik der praktischen Vernunft* (1788), Ak 5
	Critique of Practical Reason, Ca Practical Philosophy
KU	*Kritik der Urteilskraft* (1790), Ak 5
	Critique of the Power of Judgment, Ca Critique of the Power of Judgment
M	*De Medicina Corporis, quae Philosophorum est* (1786), Ak 15
	On the Philosophers' Medicine of the Body, Ca Anthropology, History and Education
MS	*Metaphysik der Sitten* (1797–1798), Ak 6
	Metaphysics of Morals, in Ca Practical Philosophy
O	*Was heißt: Sich im denken orientieren?* (1786), Ak 8
	What does it Mean to Orient Oneself in Thinking?, in Ca Religion and Rational Theology
P	*Prolegomena zu einer jeden künftigen Metaphysik, die als Wissenschaft wird auftreten können* (1783), Ak 4
	Prolegomena to any Future Metaphysics, Ca Theoretical Philosophy after 1781
R	*Religion innerhalb der Grenzen der bloßen Vernunft* (1793–1794), Ak 6
	Religion within the Boundaries of Mere Reason, Ca Religion within the Boundaries of Mere Reason
Refl	*Reflexion* (note) from Kant's *handschriftlicher Nachlass* (handwritten literary remains)
	A selection of *Reflexionen* are translated in Ca Notes and Fragments
SF	*Streit der Fakultäten* (1798), Ak 7
	Conflict of the Faculties, Ca Religion and Rational Theology

TG	*Träume eines Geistersehers, erläutert durch Träume der Metaphysik* (1766), Ak 2
Dreams of a Spirit-Seer, Elucidated by Dreams of Metaphysics, Ca Theoretical Philosophy, 1755–1770
TP	*Über den Gemeinspruch: Das mag in der Theorie richtig sein, taugt aber nicht für die Praxis* (1793), Ak 8
On the Common Saying: That May Be Correct in Theory But It Is of No Use in Practice, Ca Practical Philosophy
UB	*Von der Unrechtmäßigkeit des Büchernachdrucks* (1785), Ak 8
On the Wrongfulness of Unauthorized Publication of Books, Ca Practical Philosophy
VA	*Vorlesungen über Anthropologie*, Ak 25
Lectures on Anthropology, Ca Lectures on Anthropology
VE	*Vorlesungen über Ethik*, Ak 27
Lectures on Ethics, Ca Lectures on Ethics
VL	*Vorlesungen über Logik*, Ak 9, 24
Lectures on Logic, Ca Lectures on Logic
VP	*Pädagogik* (1803) Ak 9
Lectures on Pedagogy, Ca Anthropology, History and Education
VpR	*Vorlesungen über die philosophische Religionslehre*, Ak 28
Lectures on the Philosophical Doctrine of Religion, Ca Religion and Rational Theology
WA	*Beantwortung der Frage: Was ist Aufklärung?* (1784), Ak 8
An Answer to the Question: What is Enlightenment?, Ca Practical Philosophy

Introduction

1 The Typic chapter in the *Critique of Practical Reason*

How can we represent a universal moral principle so as to apply it to concrete cases? This problem takes on a particularly acute form in the moral philosophy of Immanuel Kant (1724–1804), since he holds that the moral law refers to freedom, a 'supersensible' form of causality that is radically different from the natural causality that governs the sensible world in which we act. Kant's theory of *moral judgment* stands or falls with this problem, since one must apply the moral law to particular actions in order to determine them as morally good or evil. More precisely, the "pure practical power of judgment" must subsume actions, as cases *in concreto*, under the moral law, as a rule *in abstracto*. This task raises particular difficulties, however, because it evokes a conflict in the constitution of humans as finite rational beings. As beings possessed of reason, we represent the moral law as a *supersensible Idea*, but as finite, sensible beings, we represent actions in the physical world via *sensible intuition*. Given that these two species of representations are totally heterogeneous, it seems "absurd" to subsume the latter under the former (*KpV* 5: 68).

This representational mismatch between sensible intuitions and the supersensible Ideas of morality gives rise to two opposing dangers that threaten the very heart of Kant's moral philosophy.[1] On the one hand, if Kant were to admit that the Ideas of morality cannot be applied to actions at all, then he would have to concede that these Ideas are empty of significance, that moral appraisal is futile, and that practical reason is bankrupt – in a word, he would have to capitulate to the objection of empty formalism. On the other hand, presenting the supersensible Ideas directly in sensible intuition would denature them beyond recognition, for no concrete *image* can ever be commensurate with the pure universality of the rational Idea.

Furthermore, any solution to these difficulties must harmonize with Kant's philosophical outlook and principles. Consequently, two escape routes – if such they are – must be debarred from the outset. Kant cannot grant that the significance of the Ideas could be intuited independently of sensibility (e.g., through intellectual intuition or mystical illumination), for then he would have to recant his fundamental position that human beings are radically finite. Nor can he posit, *à la* absolute idealism, that the moral Ideas manifest their signifi-

---

[1] For an excellent presentation of the philosophical issues at stake in the Typic, see Renaut, 1997, p. 301–313.

cance directly in the world in virtue of an underlying ontological identity between the rational and the real; such a transcendent assertion would "tear down the boundary posts" erected by the critical philosophy (*KrV* A296/B352–3). In a word, Kant cannot take refuge in the metaphysics of immediacy or of identity. Rather, the *dualism* between Ideas of reason and sensibility is a fundamental tenet of his critical rationalism, and he must therefore find a way to *mediate between them* so as to enable moral judgment, yet without denaturing the supersensible Idea of the moral law by turning it into an image. Thus, the viability of Kant's moral philosophy, particularly his theory of moral judgment, depends on finding a way to 'present the unpresentable'.

Kant raises this complex representational problem, and proposes a solution to it, in a remarkable chapter of the *Critique of Practical Reason* entitled "On the Typic of the Pure Practical Power of Judgment [*Von der Typik der reinen praktischen Urteilskraft*]" (*KpV* 5: 69–71).[2] Given that the moral law, as a supersensible Idea of reason, cannot be applied directly to actions that present themselves in sensible intuition, Kant resorts to a particular form of indirect, *symbolic representation*. His ingenious solution is to provide the power of judgment with a "type [*Typus*]," or formal analogue, of the moral law (*KpV* 5: 69). This type is the law of natural causality: *qua* law, it serves as a formal standard for assessing the universalizability of maxims; *qua* law *of nature*, it can also be applied to any and every action in experience. With this type in hand, one can perform moral appraisal by means of a thought experiment in which one asks oneself if one could will to be part of a counterfactual nature in which one's maxim were a universal law. This thought experiment functions as a "test [*Probe*]" of the universalizability of maxims and thereby of the moral status of actions (*KpV* 5: 69–70). Kant maintains that, as a matter of fact, everyone, "even the most common understanding," judges the moral status of actions in this manner. Finally, he adds that this "typic [*Typik*]"[3] serves a critical, protective function insofar as it guards against two threats to his rationalist ethics, namely empiricism (i.e., consequentialism) and mysticism.

---

[2] The German text is reproduced in Appendix I; the English translation used in the present study appears in Appendix II.

[3] When uncapitalized in English, the word "typic" shall refer to Kant's *concept* (more precisely, to the procedure for using the "type"); when capitalized, it shall refer to the *text*, as in "the Typic chapter." This convention is analogous to the practice of using "the schematism" to refer to the procedure for using schemata, and "the Schematism" to designate the corresponding chapter in the first *Critique*.

Thus, the typic should be recognized as a fundamental component of Kant's practical philosophy, as several scholars have argued.[4] Indeed, it is truly *indispensable* to Kant's theory of moral judgment, as Henry Allison has aptly noted:

> for purposes of practical judgment, we can consider a universalized maxim as if it were a law of nature and by this means judge its conformity (or lack thereof) with the imperative. Indeed, according to Kant, not only can we do this, we *must*, if were are to apply the moral law to particular cases; for this is the only way in which we can bring the law, as a product of pure practical reason, to bear on such cases.[5]

What is more, studying the Typic chapter, situated at a crucial juncture in Kant's system, will shed light on the critical philosophy as a whole. Indeed, this intriguing text promises "to elucidate and give meaning to the themes and features that distinguish Kant's view," as John Rawls has suggested, and thereby "bring to life and make intelligible Kant's characteristic and deeper ideas."[6]

2 Need for the present study

2.1 Obscurity of the primary text

Most readers, from Kant's contemporaries to present-day scholars, have found the Typic chapter difficult to understand (even by Kantian standards). For instance, in 1789, a year after the publication of the *Critique of Practical Reason*, Gotthard Ludwig Kosegarten, an earnest reader of Kant's philosophy, reported his struggles in a letter to the author:

> Dearest Kant, I am still a long way from being able to pride myself on having grasped and worked through your thought so completely that I could then acclaim you with completely unreserved applause. The deduction of the pure dynamical principles is still somewhat obscure, but perhaps only to my eyes. The transcendental 'I' is an abyss that I have yet to fathom. But as for this 'type' by means of which actions in the sensible world are to be subsumed under the totally heterogeneous moral law – I can't make head or tail of it [*der Typus ... ist mir unbegreiflich*].[7]

---

[4] See Bahr 2004, p. 276; Cassirer 1987, p. 259; Cassirer 2001, p. 249; Grondin 2000, p. 394; Irrlitz 2010, p. 316, 331; Krüger 1931, p. 83; Rawls 2000, p. 163–164; Renaut 1997, p. 297–302.
[5] Allison 2011, p. 178.
[6] Rawls 2000, p. 163–164.
[7] Letter to Kant, 4 June 1789 (11: 340, my translation). Unfortunately, there is no record of Kant's reply, if there was one.

The fact that Kosegarten found the Typic chapter even less comprehensible than the notoriously obscure Transcendental Deduction testifies to the text's difficulty. And Kosegarten was not alone: even a reader as acute and sophisticated as Jacob Sigismund Beck wrote to Kant in 1792 to express his puzzlement over the Typic.[8] More recently, several scholars have remarked that this text presents considerable hermeneutical challenges.[9] The text is highly condensed (only four pages long in the Akademie edition) and contains technical, even unusual vocabulary. For example, the key term "typic [*Typik*]" is practically a *hapax legomenon* in the corpus, occurring only within the Typic chapter itself, while the term "type [*Typus*]" remains absent from Kant's subsequently published works, reappearing (in the relevant sense) only in a single letter.[10] What is more, the text's philosophical content is undeniably difficult: the problem is technical and formidably complex; Kant's proposed solution is abstract, even counter-intuitive; and his highly condensed reasoning remains largely implicit. Moreover, Kant's theory of symbolic representation, while crucial to understanding the typic's nature and function, is nowhere near as fully and explicitly developed as many of his other doctrines.[11] More generally, we will see that the Typic chapter is a microcosm of Kant's philosophical system, requiring comparisons with principles, concepts, and problems from his *moral philosophy* (the moral law, maxims, the will, universalization tests), *theoretical philosophy* (the imagination, the schematism, the understanding as the law-giver of nature), *philosophy of religion* (the critique of mysticism, symbolic anthropomorphism), and *aesthetics* (symbolic hypotyposis, the sublime, aesthetic ideas).

2.2 Conflicting interpretations in the secondary literature

In 1969, Paul Dietrichson made the following observation about the state of the secondary literature on the typic: "It is surprising that Kant's commentators and critics have not devoted more attention to the typic. Its nature and function is not explained satisfactorily in any work on Kant I am familiar with."[12] Almost half a century later, the same can be said of the current state of research.

---

[8] Letter to Kant, 31 May 1792 (11: 340).
[9] Bielefeldt 2003, p. 6; Irrlitz 2010, p. 316; Reath 2010, p. 34; Renaut 1997, p. 309.
[10] Letter from Kant to Jacob Sigismund Beck, 3 July 1792 (11: 348).
[11] Bielefeldt 2003, p. 5–6, 180.
[12] Dietrichson 1969, p. 168.

Often, the Typic chapter is not regarded as an object of study in its own right, but instead as a "minor appendix."[13] Many general works on Kant's ethics, including some devoted primarily to the *Critique of Practical Reason*, mention the Typic chapter only in passing or disregard it altogether.[14] The same neglect can be observed in studies of directly related topics, such as moral judgment,[15] the concept of the "type" in philosophy,[16] and symbolic representation.[17] When the Typic is mentioned within a more general work, it is most often dispatched with a footnote or a quick summary.[18] One possible explanation for this cursory treatment is that the typic tends be overshadowed by its precursor, the Formula of the Law of Nature (FLN), just as the second *Critique* as a whole tends not to receive as much attention as the *Groundwork of the Metaphysics of Morals*. This is a regrettable oversight, however, as the typic performs different functions from FLN and is in fact considerably more sophisticated.[19] Moreover, the tendency to summarize the Typic chapter, rather than interpret it in depth, may result from what could be called an exegetical illusion: Kant's succinct, step-by-step exposition can give the impression that it explains itself and therefore requires no more than a summary. In reality, the text requires extensive commentary to be properly understood, as it is highly condensed and contains many obscurities.

Some studies of the Typic chapter do exist, but they are few and far between. The past century of Kant scholarship has only produced, on a generous count, just under thirty studies touching on the Typic.[20] But none of these is book-

---

13 Zimmermann 2001, p. 51.
14 Little more than a page is devoted to the Typic in Reath 2010. The Typic is completely absent from Philonenko 1981.
15 E.g., Sullivan 1989; although the book deals extensively with Kant's theory of moral judgment, the index contains only two references to the Typic.
16 Bergfeld's 1933 study does not deal with Kant's conception; the Typic is mentioned only once in Showler 2008, p. 28.
17 For instance, Sebastian Maly excludes the Typic from his otherwise excellent study of symbolic hypotyposis, on the grounds that it presents the interpreter with special challenges, Maly 2012, p. 14–15.
18 E.g., Delbos 1969, p. 374–376.
19 See section 4.2.2.1. of the Commentary.
20 Beck 1960, p. 154–163; Bielefeldt 2001; Bielefeldt 2003; Castillo 2007, p. 29–40; Cohen-Halimi 2004, p. 81–108; Elton Bulnes 1989; Grandjean 2004; Grapotte 2015; Green 1982; Grondin 2000; Höffe 2012, p. 108–112; Johnson 1985; Konhardt 1979, p. 287–306; Krüger 1931, p. 79–89; Luf 1975; Marty 1955; Marty 1997, p. 247–266; Mumbrú Mora 2009; Paton 1947, p. 157–164; Pieper 2011, p. 108–116; Pieper 2009; Rawls 1999, p. 118n; Rawls 2000, p. 162–180; Recki 2001, p. 247–252; Renaut 1997, p. 298–313; Schwartländer 1968, p. 154 ff.; Schwartländer 1981; Shell 1980, p. 81–91; Silber 1966; Silber 1974; Zimmermann 2011, p. 50–63.

length; in fact, most of them are merely sections of chapters and are under twenty pages long. Tellingly, not one of these studies is cited in the (very brief) article on the Typic in the forthcoming *Kant-Lexikon*.[21] One can appreciate how little research has really been done on the Typic chapter when one considers how much more attention has been given to its two 'sister chapters' in the first and third *Critiques*. The Schematism chapter, in the *Critique of Pure Reason*, and § 59, "On beauty as a symbol of morality," in the *Critique of the Power of Judgment*, have been studied in countless monographs, dissertations, and articles. Moreover, it will be shown that many of the studies nominally devoted to the typic in fact overlook its specific nature and function because they wrongly assimilate it to concepts from other parts of Kant's corpus (especially the notion of "symbolic hypotyposis" in § 59 of the *Critique of the Power of Judgment*).

But the most serious lacuna in the current state of research on the Typic chapter is the near total absence of scholarly discussion and debate. Generally, scholars who have written on the Typic chapter do not cite each other – no doubt because the existing studies are so few in number and are scattered across different time periods, scholarly traditions, and languages. As a result, each commentator must start from scratch, with very little input or feedback from other scholars. Not surprisingly, the resulting interpretations, when viewed all together, appear disparate, inconsistent, and sometimes arbitrary. Indeed, the lack of consensus is striking, at times even bewildering. It will be shown, for example, that commentators have proposed *four* main interpretive approaches to the universalization test that the typic provides for moral judgment, *six* different interpretations of the "particular difficulties" that the typic is designed to overcome, and no less than *ten* different construals of the analogy between the moral law and its "type," the law of nature. And while the existing scholarship does contain many valid explanations and insights, no cumulative knowledge, much less consensus, can be attained until the alternative hypotheses are compared and critically evaluated within a truly *comprehensive* study of the Typic.

3 Goals of the present study

This study will provide the first comprehensive, book-length treatment of the Typic chapter. Three main goals will be pursued:

---

[21] Willaschek et al. forthcoming.

1. To provide a unified, coherent and comprehensive exegesis of the Typic chapter in the form of a commentary that elucidates its central concepts and inner logic together with its presuppositions, principles, and philosophical significance within Kant's system.
2. To characterize the typic as a mode of symbolic representation by situating it, both historically and conceptually, within Kant's theory of symbolic representation, notably by comparing and contrasting it with "symbolic hypotyposis" in the *Critique of the Power of Judgment* (1790) and "symbolic anthropomorphism" in the *Prolegomena* (1783).
3. To foster a scholarly discussion about the Typic by integrating the existing secondary literature into the study and critically engaging with it throughout.

4 Approach and methodology

4.1 General approach

The present book is an exegetical study in the history of philosophy. An exegesis, or what Dieter Schönecker has called a "*kommentarische Interpretation*," treats the text as an end in itself.[22] It enjoins the scholar to understand the text's meaning, inner logic and coherence in relation to the author's presumed intention (or intentions). Indeed, it is this particular *attitude* vis-à-vis the text, rather than any specific methodological tools, that distinguishes the exegetical approach. It requires the interpreter to read the text patiently, attentively and persistently. One must carefully analyze every paragraph, every sentence, every word; establish their interconnections, parallels and contrasts; and fix their respective places in the structure of the whole, which is gradually reconstructed from the parts. The resulting interpretation typically takes the form of a *commentary*, which may be compared to a seventeenth-century Dutch still-life, in which meticulously painted individual elements are combined, through overlaps, reflections, and transparencies, to form an interconnected and coherent composition. Moreover, this thorough way of working through the text presents the considerable advantage of making the genesis of the interpretation itself fully transparent and thereby comprehensible, or *nachvollziehbar*. Throughout the exegetical process, the interpreter must entertain and test alternative interpretive hypotheses, weigh the

---

[22] Schönecker 2001. This entire paragraph and the following one are based on the lucid explanation of this approach by Maly 2012, p. 6–12.

evidence for and against each one, determine the best fit, and make the necessary adjustments. Moreover, this transparency of the exegetical approach reflects the responsibility of the individual commentator towards the subject-matter as well as towards other scholars. Indeed, transparency is an appropriate epistemic ideal for a study of Kant, who held that all scholarship worth the name must be presented "before the entire public of the *world of readers*" (*WA* 8: 37).

In this study, I do not prioritize the 'systematic' approach, which uses the text as a *means* for thinking through contemporary philosophical problems and proposing solutions to them. Nor do I purport to evaluate the philosophical plausibility or usefulness of Kant's doctrines from the perspective of any particular contemporary theory. Instead, what I offer is a *lectio benevolentiae* that provides a maximally coherent interpretation of the Typic *within* Kant's philosophical system, *assuming* its specific principles, concepts, and constraints. Indeed, I believe that systematic assessments should be preceded by an understanding of Kant's thought on his own terms, as Lewis White Beck declares in the Preface to his *Commentary on Kant's Critique of Practical Reason*:

> But the first task is to find out what Kant said, how he said it, and why. Only then can evaluation have before it a firm object, not an amorphous mass that varies in shape with the degree of sympathy or hostility with which it is approached; too often in the past, debates on whether Kant was right or wrong have been vitiated by lack of the most rudimentary agreement as to what he actually said and meant."[23]

Indeed, the need to determine precisely "what Kant said, how he said it, and why" is especially pressing for the Typic chapter. As was mentioned above, most readers, from Kant's contemporaries to present-day scholars, have found the Typic difficult to decipher. Moreover, the danger of misrepresentation against which Beck warns is very real in this case. In the absence of a clear, faithful and generally accepted account of what Kant actually meant in the Typic chapter – and, conversely, of what he did *not* mean – some theory-driven interpreters have wilfully distorted the text, sometimes to the antipodes of Kant's considered views. Consequently, one of my main tasks throughout this study will be to expose, criticize and counteract this tendency.

---

23 Similar arguments to this effect have been advanced by several noted scholars: Ameriks 2001, p. 12 ff.; Schönecker 2001, p. 171 f.; Wood 2001, p. 277–280.

4.2 Specific methodology

Throughout the book I make extensive use of philological analysis to provide detailed glosses of particular passages or expressions in their immediate context. I therefore devote considerable attention to the precise phrasing of the German original, which accompanies most quotations (in brackets or in footnotes). In some cases, it is necessary to examine the etymology of certain terms (e. g., Kant's term *Typus*, which is derived from the ancient Greek word *túpos*), or their usage beyond the Kantian corpus (e. g., the many uses of "*Symbol/symbolisch*" in eighteenth-century German).

Of course, Kant's philosophy is made not only out of words, but out of concepts and principles. Accordingly, throughout the study I employ conceptual analysis to characterize particular concepts as well as to trace their logical, justificatory, and functional relationships to each other and to more general principles. These concepts and principles are duly situated within the overall structure of Kant's architectonic.

Another general characteristic of the interpretation is that it is diachronic, rather than synchronic. That is, the evolution of Kant's thought over time strongly informs the analysis; conversely, I take care to avoid anachronistically reading later texts back into earlier ones. These historical considerations exert a decisive influence on the analysis and overall argument of Part Two.

The secondary literature is integrated throughout the exposition. This method provides an overview of the current state of research which clearly shows the precise points where the existing scholarship converges or diverges. In places where there is considerable disagreement, I lay out the various interpretations that have been proposed and conduct a critical assessment of the alternatives. My aim is thereby to arrive at the most plausible gloss, but I also leave some questions about the text open.

Furthermore, Part One and Part Two each has some methodological particularities worth noting here. Part One provides an exegesis of the Typic chapter in the form of a Commentary. The most conspicuous and consequential feature of the Commentary is its overall organization. While the exposition is meant to be read as a continuous whole, it is sub-divided into five chapters, each of which corresponds to a stage in the progressive resolution of a problem: there is a *task* to be accomplished; an *obstacle,* which Kant refers to as "particular difficulties," standing in the way; a certain number of *resources* that present themselves; a *solution* that resolves the difficulties and accomplishes the task; and finally an assessment of the *outcome* and *effectiveness* of the proposed solution.[24] This analytical framework performs three important exegetical functions. Firstly, it largely matches the structure and sequential order of the Typic chapter, thereby carving the text at its joints. Secondly, this analytical scaffolding serves to 're-verse-engineer' the typic, so that the reader can understand it as a carefully designed solution to a well-defined problem. Thinking the problem through – assuming the particular resources and constraints of the Kantian system – not only elucidates the typic's specific nature and function, but also contributes to a greater appreciation of the ingenuity, even audacity, of Kant's strategy as well as the remarkable coherence and complexity of his system as a whole. Thirdly, the exposition is *transparent* insofar as it clearly shows the logic underlying each and every step of the interpretation; there are no dubious 'leaps of genius', to paraphrase Kant. By the same token, the clearly articulated structure of the Commentary contributes to the goal of fostering scholarly discussion and debate by facilitating targeted comparisons and contrasts between different interpretations. For instance, the "symbolist interpretation" presented in Part Two, Chapter 6, can be compared, point by point, with the exegesis proposed in the Commentary.

The business of Part Two is to shed more light on the concept of the 'typic' by characterizing it as a mode of symbolic representation. Indeed, Kant provides a valuable clue to the nature and function of the typic when he indicates that it functions not as a schema, but "serves only as a symbol" (*KpV* 5: 70–71). I take this brief remark as a point of departure for situating the typic, both historically as well as conceptually, within Kant's theory of symbolic representation. This is achieved by means of a comparative analysis: I examine the typic's continuities and divergences with the notions of "symbolic hypotyposis," presented in the *Critique of the Power of Judgment* and other texts, and "symbolic anthropomorphism," presented in the *Prolegomena*. Consequently, Part Two is broader than the Commentary, both philologically as well as philosophically: it goes beyond the Typic chapter proper to examine other texts in detail; and it extends beyond the sphere of Kant's moral philosophy to aesthetic and epistemological contexts. Another distinguishing feature of Part Two is that the investigation requires more analysis of a conceptual and formal nature, notably of the roles played by *analogy* in the various forms of symbolic representation. Finally, Part Two gives a strong impetus to scholarly debate by first, in Chapter 6, unifying and elaborating a favoured yet hitherto scattered interpretation of the typic (as a form of symbolic hypotyposis), then challenging this interpretation, and finally, in Chapter 7,

---

[24] This framework was inspired by an empirical study of analogical reasoning by Chen 2002.

suggesting a new alternative (namely, that the typic bears greater affinities to symbolic anthropomorphism).

4.3 On the selection of texts

The central primary text is, naturally, the Typic chapter, entitled "On the Typic of the Pure Practical Power of Judgment [*Von der Typik der reinen praktischen Urteilskraft*]" (*KpV* 5: 69–71). The German original is reproduced in Appendix I; the English translation used in this study appears in Appendix II. In addition, references are made to the entire Kantian corpus, including major and minor published works, the *Nachlass*, and the lectures. Of these additional primary texts, the following receive the most attention:

- *Critique of Practical Reason* (1788): "On the Deduction of the Principles of Pure Practical Reason" (*KpV* 5: 42–50); "On the Concept of an Object of Pure Practical Reason" (*KpV* 5: 57–67).
- *Groundwork for the Metaphysics of Morals* (1785): the Formula of the Law of Nature (*G* 4: 421–425, 436–437).
- *Critique of Pure Reason* (1781/87) "Transcendental Deduction of the Pure Concepts of the Understanding," B version (*KrV* B129–169); "On the Schematism of the Pure Concepts of the Understanding" (*KrV* A137–147/B176–187).
- *Prolegomena* (1783) "On Determining the Boundary of Pure Reason" (*P* 4: 350–365, §§ 57–59)
- *Critique of the Power of Judgment* (1790) "On Beauty as a Symbol of Morality" (*KU* 5: 351–354, § 59)
- *Nachlass*: Letter from Jacob Sigismund Beck to Kant, 31 May 1792 (esp. 11: 340); letter from Kant to Beck, 3 July 1792 (esp. 11: 348).
- *Lectures on Ethics* (*Vorlesungen über Ethik*, Ak 27)

The secondary literature includes Kant scholarship, studies of topics related to the Typic chapter (e.g., analogy), and works by other philosophers. I was able to consult studies written in English, German, French or Spanish; research in other languages is unfortunately not included here. Unless otherwise indicated, all English translations of the secondary literature are my own.

5 Overview

The book is divided into two main parts. Part One offers a comprehensive exegesis of the Typic chapter. This 'Commentary' is a single, continuous exposition, sub-divided into five chapters which (unlike conventional book chapters) vary considerably in length and complexity. Part Two situates the typic in Kant's theory of symbolic representation by comparing it with two other modes of symbolic representation in the corpus. Part Two is divided into two chapters. Chapter 6 compares the typic with *symbolic hypotyposis* as described in the *Critique of the Power of Judgment*, mostly stressing the differences. Chapter 7 compares the typic with *symbolic anthropomorphism* as described in the *Prolegomena*, mostly stressing the similarities. The general Conclusion provides summaries of both Parts as well as an analysis of the Typic's particular relevance to the evolution of Kant's conception of the symbolic relation between nature and morality.

5.1 Part One. Commentary

As mentioned above, the Commentary is organized into five chapters that correspond to the progressive stages of the resolution of a problem.

Chapter 1. The task
The *task* to be accomplished is a particular exercise of the "pure practical power of judgment [*die reine praktische Urtheilskraft*]" that Kant terms "moral appraisal [*die moralische Beurtheilung*]" (*KpV* 5: 67, 69). Moral appraisal consists in judging particular actions as morally good or evil with respect to the moral law. More precisely, it is a matter of *subsuming* particular actions *qua* cases *in concreto* under the two "concepts of an object of pure practical reason" (*KpV* 5: 67) namely "the morally good [*das sittlich Gute*]" and "the morally evil [*das sittlich Böse*]" (*KpV* 5: 57 ff.). Both of these concepts derive *a priori* from the moral law, conceived as an abstract rule that determines actions as good or evil depending on whether they were willed according to "the representation of a law in general and its form" (*KpV* 5: 68), i.e., according to formally universalizable maxims.

Chapter 2. The 'particular difficulties'
However, this task entails "particular difficulties [*besondere Schwierigkeiten*]" (*KpV* 5: 68) for the pure practical power of judgment because of a mismatch be-

tween the cases and the rule under which they are to be subsumed. I examine and criticize a number of interpretations of this mismatch that have been proposed by commentators. I then proceed to make the case that the mismatch is representational in nature: on the one hand, actions in the physical world present themselves to us in *sensible intuition*; on the other hand, the moral law is a *supersensible Idea* of reason to which no sensible intuition can correspond. The total heterogeneity between these two kinds of representation threatens to prevent subsumption and thereby impede moral appraisal.

Chapter 3. The resources

The next stage of the problem is to determine which *resources* in Kant's conceptual repertoire could serve to resolve these difficulties and accomplish the task.

The first possibility that suggests itself is the transcendental *schema*, introduced in the *Critique of Pure Reason* as a mediating representation that the theoretical power of judgment employed for overcoming the heterogeneity between the pure concepts of the understanding and sensible intuition. Despite its usefulness in the first *Critique*, the schema is unsuitable for solving the particular difficulties of the pure practical power of judgment, for two reasons: firstly, as a product of the sensible imagination, it would contaminate the supersensible moral Ideas; secondly, it does not represent actions in a manner that would be relevant to moral appraisal.

On the other hand, the assessment of the transcendental schema opens up a "favourable prospect [*eine günstige Aussicht*]" (*KpV* 5: 68). Kant indicates that we should look for a representation that performs an *analogous function* to that of the schema – i.e., mediation between heterogeneous representations in order to enable the subsumption of cases under a rule – while avoiding the characteristics of the transcendental schema that do not fit the "particular difficulties" of the pure practical power of judgment. What is needed, Kant hints, is a "schema (if the word 'schema' is appropriate here) of a law itself" (*KpV* 5: 68). I propose an interpretation of this peculiar expression as a formula encapsulating *four criteria* that describe the right tool for overcoming the particular difficulties and accomplishing the task, namely (1) a sensibly uncontaminated representation of (2) the form of universal lawfulness that (3) can mediate the subsumption of particular actions given in sensible intuition under the supersensible moral law and (4) provide an effective procedure for moral appraisal.

I then offer a characterization of the universal law of natural causality (i.e., 'the law of nature') and of *natura formaliter spectata*. These pure representations of formal lawfulness produced by the understanding's intellectual synthesis are promising resources for satisfying the four criteria.

Chapter 4. The solution

Kant's original *solution* is to employ the law of nature as the "type [*Typus*]," or formal analogue, of the moral law for the purposes of moral appraisal (*KpV* 5: 69–70). As a pure representation of universal lawfulness, the law of nature – more precisely the *form* of this law – can be analogically substituted for the supersensible moral law without contaminating it with sensible intuition.[25] And as a law *of nature*, its application to any and every action in sensible intuition is assured by the schematism. Thus the law of nature is well suited to functioning as a type that can mediate the subsumption of actions in sensible intuition under the supersensible moral law despite the heterogeneity between the two species of representations – a process I term "typification." Finally, the type also provides an appropriate standard against which to test the formal universalizability that the moral law demands of all maxims.

Before elaborating on this last point, I investigate Kant's remark that "it is also permitted to use the nature of the sensible world as the type of an intelligible nature" (*KpV* 5: 70). I offer an interpretation of the source, nature, and function of this second, more general formulation of the type ('Type$_2$'), which I then compare with other interpretations in the secondary literature. Starting from the etymology of the ancient Greek word "*túpos*," I propose that Kant conceives of Type$_2$ as the abstract form shared by *natura archetypa* and *natura ectypa*, namely the understanding's purely conceptual representation of nature's universal lawfulness (*natura formaliter spectata*). Type$_2$ mediates between reason's Idea of a supersensible 'nature' under the law of freedom and the sensible nature in which we live and act, thereby providing a regulative horizon for our moral vocation that heeds the strictures of Kant's critical rationalism.

Moral judgment is performed by means of a thought experiment that I term "the typic-procedure": the agent asks herself if she can both conceive and will herself as a part of a (counterfactual) nature in which the maxim of her action were a universal law. This is a decisive "test" or "trial" (*Probe*) of the formal universalizability of a maxim and thereby of its moral possibility. I offer an analysis of this thought experiment based on the fundamental principles of Kant's moral philosophy, proposing that the typic-procedure be understood as a new way of operationalizing the "canon of moral appraisal" first introduced in the *Groundwork* (*G* 4: 124). In addition, I bring out the specificity of this procedure in Kant's moral philosophy and in his theory of moral judgment in particular. Also, I evaluate the exegetical strengths and weaknesses of the consequentialist, teleological, logical, and 'rational agency' interpretations of the typic-procedure.

---

[25] I spell out this analogy in more detail in Ch. 7, section 4.2.

Chapter 5. The outcome and effectiveness

Lastly, I examine the *outcome* and *effectiveness* of Kant's proposed solution. I explain Kant's claim that the typic-procedure is widely and effectively employed by "even the most common understanding" to make accurate, even subtle, moral judgments with ease (*KpV* 5: 70). This explanation involves an analysis of the Typic's heuristic efficacy, in particular the way in which it provides "an example in a case of experience" (*KpV* 5: 70).

I also discuss why and how the typic guards against two dangers to morality, empiricism (i.e., consequentialism) and mysticism. The typic's formal, *a priori*, and strictly universal standard for moral appraisal prevents empiricism's grave error of turning moral appraisal into a self-interested, probabilistic calculus and thereby protects the purity of moral motivation from being corrupted by the heteronomous ideal of happiness. Indeed, Kant even hints at a way of transforming the principle of happiness into a purely formal type of the Idea of the morally Good ('Type$_3$'). In addition, the typic's strictly analogical representation of the moral law in the *pure form* of the law of nature provides a properly rationalist alternative to mysticism's tendency to denature the supersensible Ideas by a transcendent pseudo-schematization with ostensibly "real but non-sensible intuitions of a kingdom of God" (*KpV* 5: 71). In sum, the typic is presented as the instrument *par excellence* of "the rationalism of the power of judgment [*Rationalism der Urtheilskraft*]."

5.2 Part Two. The typic's place in Kant's theory of symbolic representation

Kant states that the typic "served only as a symbol [*nur als Symbol diente*]" (*KpV* 5: 70), which suggests that the typic is a particular mode of *symbolic representation*. Among interpreters, the symbolic dimension of the typic has proven to be a central – and contentious – issue. Part Two investigates this question in depth by comparing the typic with two other notions in Kant's theory of symbolic representation, namely symbolic hypotyposis and symbolic anthropomorphism. While many scholars interpret the typic in light of the former, I argue instead that it shares greater continuities with the latter.

Chapter 6: The typic and symbolic hypotyposis

Many commentators affirm that the typic is a form of "symbolic hypotyposis" as defined in § 59 of the *Critique of the Power of Judgment*. Yet as I mentioned above, these commentators generally do not cite each other; as a result, my first task is to weave their studies together in order to present a unified and complete interpretation of the Typic chapter. I then critically examine the resulting 'symbolist interpretation', arguing extensively that it is anachronistic, inaccurate and arbitrary. The type is not a symbol in the sense of § 59, I argue, nor does typification function in the same manner as symbolic hypotyposis. Furthermore, I contend that the tendency to assimilate the typic with symbolic hypotyposis is not only mistaken, but misguided. Indeed, many such attempts are motivated by a desire to *aestheticize* the typic, and with it, Kant's moral philosophy as a whole. But this enterprise is ill-advised, even from an aesthetic point of view: I show that the *sublime* and the *aesthetic idea* respectively produce far more powerful and poetic expressions of the moral Ideas than symbolic hypotyposis could ever provide.

Chapter 7: The typic and symbolic anthropomorphism

Next, I pursue a hitherto unexplored avenue of research by comparing the typic with the concept of "symbolic anthropomorphism" that Kant had developed in the *Prolegomena*, five years before the *Critique of Practical Reason*. I first bring out the characteristic features of symbolic anthropomorphism by means of a close textual analysis of §§ 57–59 in the *Prolegomena*. An important result of this analysis is that Kant consistently imposes a series of restrictions on this mode of "only [*nur*]" or "merely [*bloß*]" symbolic representation: it is a non-absolute, non-sensible, and strictly analogical procedure in accordance with the restrictions imposed by Kant's critical rationalism. In addition, I provide some historical background to Kant's conception of symbolic anthropomorphism by investigating its continuities and discontinuities with the influential doctrine of analogical predication proposed by St. Thomas Aquinas. Next, I identify and illustrate the key differences between symbolic anthropomorphism and the notion of symbolic hypotyposis as presented later on in the third *Critique*. In the former, the determining power of judgment employs analogy only to provide a conceptual grasp of abstract relations; in the latter, the reflecting power of judgment employs analogy in order to furnish an "indirect presentation [*indirekte Darstellung*]" of an abstract concept in the form of a symbol in sensible intuition (*KU* 5: 351). Finally, I carry out a systematic and detailed comparison between symbolic anthropomorphism and the typic. I endeavour to show, through numerous correspondences, that the typic is also a *merely* symbolic – i.e., strictly analogical – form of representation, and furthermore that this analogical character is the source of the legitimacy and efficacy of both procedures, each of which, in its respective sphere, gives us a conceptual grasp of the supersensible while preserving its purity. In the course of this comparative analysis, I also propose a precise model of the complex, implicit analogy underlying $Type_1$ and $Type_2$.

Commentary

Chapter 1.
The task

> Dearest Kant, I am still a long way from being able to pride myself on having grasped and worked through your thought so completely that I could then acclaim you with completely unreserved applause. The deduction of the pure dynamical principles is still somewhat obscure, but perhaps only to my eyes. The transcendental 'I' is an abyss that I have yet to fathom. But as for this 'type' by means of which actions in the sensible world are to be subsumed under the totally heterogeneous moral law – I can't make head or tail of it.
> – Gotthard Ludwig Kosegarten[26]

The general purpose of a moral theory is to tell us how we ought to act. In the *Critique of Practical Reason*, Kant maintains that the concepts of the morally good (*das sittlich Gute*) and morally evil (*das sittlich Böse*) respectively determine which actions ought to be performed or avoided. Yet Kant's moral theory would be otiose if it did not also provide a *decision procedure* for ascertaining whether a particular action is, was, or would be either good or evil. And since Kant holds that these concepts are determined by a practical *rule* (namely the moral law), the problem becomes that of ascertaining whether a particular action is *a case falling under this rule*. This is a particular problem of moral judgment, to which Kant refers more specifically as "moral appraisal [*die moralische Beurtheilung*]." Moral appraisal is the main *task* set for the "pure practical power of judgment [*die reine praktische Urtheilskraft*]" (*KpV* 5: 67). The present chapter examines in detail what this task consists in.

1.1 Objects of pure practical reason and the concepts of good and evil

The Typic chapter opens by succinctly recapitulating the main results of the immediately preceding chapter, entitled "On the concept of an object of pure practical reason" (*KpV* 5: 57–67):

---

[26] My translation of Kosegarten's letter to Kant, 4 June 1789 (11: 340): "*Ja, theuerster Kant, noch fehlt viel daran, daß ich Sie ganz zu fassen, zu durchdringen, folglich mit ganzem uneingeschränkten Beyfalle zu umfangen, mich rühmen dürfte. Die Deduction der reinen dynamischen Grundsätze hat noch immer einige vielleicht nur subjective Dunkelheit für mich. Das transscendentale Ich ist ein mir noch unergründeter Abgrund. Der Typus, vermöge dessen erscheinende Handlungen unter das ganz heterogene moralische Gesetz subsumirt werden sollen, ist mir unbegreiflich.*"

> The concepts of good and evil first determine an object for the will. They themselves, however, stand under a practical rule of reason which, if it is pure reason, determines the will a priori with respect to its object (*KpV* 5: 67).[27]

All of these points are taken for granted in the subsequent development of Kant's exposition; therefore we need first to clarify what the concepts of good and evil are and how they determine an object for the will according to a 'practical rule of reason'.

Kant defines the concept of an "object" of practical reason *in general* as the representation of "an object as a possible effect through freedom" (*KpV* 5: 57). This definition is broad: "freedom" refers to the generic freedom of choice (*Willkür*);[28] and the term "object" refers loosely to an action or to an object produced by an action.[29] In other words, an object of practical reason in general is anything the existence of which we could voluntarily produce in the world. The definition of an object of *pure* practical reason is more specific: it refers to *an action considered in light of its moral possibility*. In order to determine whether a given action is an object of pure practical reason, accordingly, "the *moral possibility* of the action must come first [*die moralische Möglichkeit der Handlung* [*muss*] *vorangehen*]" (*KpV* 5: 58); that is, moral evaluation must precede the question of the *physical possibility* of executing the action, which is a matter of experience (*KpV* 5: 57–58). Accordingly, an object of pure practical reason is an action that we "may will [*wollen dürfen*]" in accordance with the moral law (*KpV* 5: 57–58). As is well known, Kant holds that the will of an agent possessed of pure practical reason, i.e., a free, morally responsible will (*Wille*), is subject – or better, subjects itself – to the moral law; indeed, the capacity of the will to determine itself by the *representation of laws* is just what characterizes it as a will (*Wille*), in contradistinction to a generic faculty of volition (*Willkür*) (*G* 4: 414). In short, an object of pure practical reason is a morally possible action, i.e., one that a free rational agent could permissibly will in accordance with the moral law.

A morally possible action is *good*; a morally impossible action is *evil*.[30] Accordingly, the class of "good" actions in this sense is broad: it includes those

---

27 [*Die Begriffe des Guten und Bösen bestimmen dem Willen zuerst ein Object. Sie stehen selbst aber unter einer praktischen Regel der Vernunft, welche, wenn sie reine Vernunft ist, den Willen a priori in Ansehung seines Gegenstandes bestimmt.*]
28 Beck 1960, p. 130.
29 Beck 1960, p. 129 f. As Beck also notes, Kant seems to use the terms "*Objekt*" and "*Gegenstand*" interchangeably in this context.
30 A disadvantage of Kant's formulation is that it seems to imply that evil actions cannot possibly be objects of the will at all, in which case it is hard to see how one could choose to do evil;

that are permitted (*erlaubt*) as well as those that are obligatory (*obligatorisch, verpflichtet*), i.e., commanded (*befohlen*) by the law. The class of "evil" actions includes only those actions that are unpermitted (*unerlaubt*), i.e., forbidden (*verboten*) by the moral law. Accordingly, the concepts of "the morally good" (*das sittlich Gute*) and "the morally evil" (*das sittlich Böse*) apply primarily to *actions*: "Thus good or evil is, strictly speaking, referred to actions [*Das Gute oder Böse wird eigentlich auf Handlungen ... bezogen*]" (*KpV* 5: 60). These moral concepts characterize actions adverbially, so to speak, according to the way in which the latter are willed vis-à-vis the moral law: an action is *good* (i.e., is a morally possible object of pure practical reason) if and only if *it is willed in a morally good way*, that is, if the will is permitted or commanded by the moral law to realize the action (*G* 4: 373n); an action is *evil* (i.e., a morally impossible object of pure practical reason) if and only if it is willed *in a morally bad way*, that is, if the moral law forbids the willing of the action (*G* 4: 373n; *KpV* 5: 68). Kant also notes that good actions are what the will would desire, and evil actions, those that the will would avoid, if it were entirely and exclusively determined by pure practical reason (*KpV* 5: 57). More generally, Kant proposes this construal of the concepts of good and evil in opposition to the conception of them in terms of their beneficial or deleterious effets on our empirical state and hence as equivalent to "*well-being* or *ill-being* [*das* Wohl *oder* Übel]," which "always signif[y] only a reference to our state of *agreableness* or *disagreeableness*, of gratification and pain" (*KpV* 5: 60). This distinction is fundamental, for the latter way of framing the concepts of good and evil underlies "the empiricism of practical reason" – a philosophical position that Kant will fiercely oppose in the Typic chapter (*KpV* 5: 70–71).[31]

We are now in a position to understand the opening statements of the Typic chapter quoted above. The concepts of good and evil "first determine an object for the will [*bestimmen dem Willen zuerst ein Object*]" (*KpV* 5: 67) by instructing it, when it entertains a possible particular action, whether it should make that action its object (i.e., desire to realize it): "What we are to call good must be an object of the faculty of desire in the judgment of every reasonable human being, and evil an object of aversion in the eyes of everyone" (*KpV* 5: 61). The rule mediated by the concepts of good and evil can be formulated as follows: *For any particular action, it should be desired if it is good, and avoided if it is evil*. Furthermore, the statement that the concepts of good and evil "themselves

---

however, there is no contradiction, for while evil actions are impossible objects for a *Wille* determined exclusively by pure practical reason, they remain possible objects of sensibly conditioned *Willkür*.

31 See below, section 5.2.1.

stand under a practical rule of reason which [...] determines the will *a priori* with respect to its object" (*KpV* 5: 67) refers to their being derived *a priori* from the moral law. Indeed, Kant's key philosophical move in the "Concept of an object of pure practical reason" chapter was to explain and justify this apparent "paradox of critical method," which consists namely in deriving good and evil from the moral law, rather than, as other moral philosophers have done, deriving the law from a prior determination of the good (*KpV* 5: 62–63). In the Typic, however, Kant stresses not the methodological, but rather the logical aspect of this dependency: the application of the concepts of good and evil (i.e., good and evil actions) must be determined with respect to the *rule* articulated by the moral law. What does this "rule" state? In the *Groundwork*, dedicated to the identification and exposition of "the supreme principle of morality," Kant explains that, for finite rational beings such as us, the moral law is represented as a Categorical Imperative. This abstract rule is essentially a law of lawfulness; empty of determinate empirical content, it prescribes that maxims conform to the universal form of a law as such:

> But when I think of a Categorical Imperative I know at once what it contains. For, since the imperative contains, beyond the law, only the necessity that the maxim be in conformity with this law, while the law contains no condition to which it would be limited, nothing is left with which the maxim is to conform but the universality of a law as such; and this conformity alone is what the imperative properly represents as necessary [*so bleibt nichts als die Allgemeinheit eines Gesetzes überhaupt übrig, welchem die Maxime der Handlung gemäß sein soll, und welche Gemäßheit allein der Imperativ eigentlich als notwendig vorstellt*]. There is, therefore, only a single Categorical Imperative and it is this: *act only in accordance with that maxim through which you can at the same time will that it become a universal law* (*G* 4: 420–1; cf. *KpV* 5: 30).

Accordingly, the good will ought to determine itself according to the form of "universal lawfulness in general [*die allgemeine Gesetzmäßigkeit überhaupt*]" (*G* 4: 402), or, as Kant puts it in the Typic, "merely through the representation of a law in general and its form [*blos durch die Vorstellung eines Gesetzes überhaupt und dessen Form*]" (*KpV* 5: 68). Hence, if an action is willed through a maxim that accords with this rule, then it is good; if it is willed through a maxim that violates this rule, then it is evil.

1.2 Moral appraisal

Despite the fact that the chapter's title is often garbled in translation, and occasionally even in German, as "The Typic of Pure Practical *Reason*," the Typic properly concerns the "Pure Practical *Power of Judgment* [*die reine praktische* Urtheilskraft] (*KpV* 5: 67 my emphasis)."[32] Indeed, appreciating this faculty's role is essential to understanding the text. Kant defines the power of judgment in general as "the faculty of *subsuming* under rules, i.e., of determining whether something stands under a given rule (*casus datae legis*) or not" (*KrV* A133/B172). The ability to conjugate general rules and particular cases is so indispensable for our thinking that the power of judgment lies at the root of the "sound understanding" shared by all human beings (*KU* 5: 169), although its acuity may vary between individuals (*KrV* A133–134/BB172–173; *TP* 8: 275–276). At the time of writing the *Critique of Practical Reason*, Kant held that the power of judgment could be exercised theoretically or practically: the *theoretical* power of judgment subsumes appearances under the categories and concepts of the understanding;[33] the *practical* power of judgment subsumes actions and maxims under moral principles. Kant assigns the pure practical power of judgment the task of "moral appraisal [*die moralische Beurtheilung*]," namely, determining which particular actions fall under the concepts of the morally good and evil. And since, as we just saw, the concepts of good and evil derive *a priori* from the moral law, the pure practical power of judgment must determine whether or not each particular action is a case falling under this law (*casus datae legis*): "Now, whether an action possible for us in sensibility is or is not a case that stands under the rule concerns the practical power of judgment, by which what is said in the rule universally (*in abstracto*) is applied to an action *in concreto*" (*KpV* 5: 67).[34] Further on, Kant specifies that moral appraisal therefore involves the "[s]ubsumption of an action possible to me in the sensible world under a pure practical law [*die Subsumtion einer mir in der Sinnenwelt möglichen Handlung unter einem reinen praktischen Gesetze*]" (*KpV* 5: 68, my emphasis), whereby, as Beck explains, "subsumption may mean the estimation of a particular action in the light of a general rule or the decision that a particular action would satisfy the rule and should, therefore, be performed."[35] In short, an action that can be subsumed under the "rule" articulated by the moral law is *good*; one that cannot is *evil*.

Some additional remarks are necessary in order to properly situate moral appraisal within Kant's theory of judgment. Firstly, the relation between an abstract rule and the particular representations falling under it can be conceived in two

---

32 This recurring mistake has been noted by Renaut 1997, p. 306f.
33 See the "Analytic of Principles" (*KrV* A137–235/B176-B294).
34 [*Ob nun eine uns in der Sinnlichkeit mögliche Handlung der Fall sei, der unter der Regel stehe, oder nicht, dazu gehört praktische Urtheilskraft, wodurch dasjenige, was in der Regel allgemein (in abstracto) gesagt wurde, auf eine Handlung in concreto angewandt wird ...*]
35 Beck 1960, p. 156.

directions, as it were, whereby the power of judgment is called determining or reflecting, respectively:

> The power of judgment in general is the faculty for thinking of the particular as contained under the universal. If the universal (the rule, the principle, the law) is given, then the power of judgment, which subsumes the particular under it ... is *determining*. If, however, only the particular is given, for which the universal is to be found, then the power of judgment is merely *reflecting* (KU 5: 179).

Moral appraisal is an exercise of the *determining* power of judgment. We must *determine* unequivocally whether a particular action is good or evil through a judgment "by which what is said in the rule universally (*in abstracto*) *is applied* to an action *in concreto*" (KpV 5: 67, my emphasis). Here, the rule is given – indeed, the moral law imposes itself on us as an indisputable "fact of reason [*Faktum der Vernunft*]" (KpV 5: 31) – and the particular case must be subsumed under it. As Beck has, I believe, rightly concluded, "in the *Critique of Practical Reason*, Kant is concerned exclusively with determinative judgment: the principle being given, find the case to which it applies."[36]

In contrast, some commentators have suggested that moral appraisal is instead an exercise of the *reflecting* power of judgment. For instance, Longuenesse claims that moral judgments concerning the derivation of duties ('What should I do?') are *determining* while moral appraisals ('Is this action good or evil?') are *reflecting*, with the hedge that her characterization of moral appraisal as "reflecting" – which, she admits, Kant never explicitly makes in the text – should be taken in a "distinctively practical meaning," viz. that one must look for the practical rule under which an action has been performed.[37] This gloss does not hold up to scrutiny, however. To begin with, it is clearly anachronistic, given that Kant did not introduce the notion of reflecting judgment until the *Critique of the Power of Judgment* in 1790, two years after the publication of the second *Critique*. What is more, the characterization that Kant later offers of reflecting judgment conflicts with his characterization of moral appraisal. In the First Introduction he explains that, in contradistinction to determining judgment, "*to reflect* (to consider) [*Reflectiren (überlegen)*] however, is to compare and to hold together given representations either with others or with one's faculty of cognition, *in relation to a concept thereby made possible* [*in Beziehung auf einen dadurch möglichen Begrif*]" (EEKU 20: 211, my emphasis). But this is not at all what Kant is suggesting in the second *Critique*. On the contrary, the concepts of good and evil

---

[36] Beck 1960, p. 154n
[37] Longuenesse 2005, p. 237–238n; Granja 2010, p. 131–144.

and, *a fortiori*, the moral law, are given *a priori* (*KpV* 5: 57 ff.); there is absolutely no need to 'first make them possible' by comparing many actions amongst themselves and extracting a common rule by reflection. Indeed, Kant views the idea of *inventing* a new moral principle as preposterous: "But who would even want to introduce a new principle of morality and, as it were, first invent it? [*und diese gleichsam zuerst erfinden?*]" (*KpV* 5: 8n).[38] Clearly, moral appraisal is not an exercise of the reflecting, but of the determining power of judgment.[39]

Secondly, moral appraisal is a *pure*, rather than an *applied* employment of moral judgment. As the title of the Typic chapter already makes explicit, moral appraisal pertains to the "*pure* practical power of judgment [*der reinen praktischen Urteilskraft*]" (*KpV* 5: 67, my emphasis) for the determination of the *pure* concepts of good and evil, insofar as it consists in evaluating the moral possibility of actions with respect to an *a priori* rule (the moral law) (*KpV* 5: 62). Therefore, moral appraisal in the strict sense does *not* involve, as has been suggested, "moving rationally from the formulation of a supreme moral principle to specifying particular imperatives as they apply to the messy and intricate circumstances of our lives."[40] This is a mischaracterization, for two reasons. First of all, while Kant believes that maxims can and must be *appraised a priori* with respect to the moral law, he does not claim that particular maxims can be fully *specified* or *deduced a priori* from the moral law.[41] Moreover, in moral appraisal we take a particular action and its corresponding maxim *as given* and then evaluate its moral possibility according to an *a priori rule*.[42] By contrast, fine-tuning one's maxims to the "messy and intricate circumstances of our [human] lives" is an *applied*, fine-grained use of the power of practical judgment – a kind of *phronêsis* that requires extensive empirical knowledge of what Kant calls "anthropology" (psychology, pedagogy, etc.) and of other aspects of the actual situation in which we act (e.g. particular social mores and cultural practices). But as Otfried Höffe and others have emphasized, these two forms of moral judgment should not be confused, since the "pure practical power of judgment" that Kant introduced in the Typic chapter represents a distinctive *philosophical innovation* vis-à-vis Aristotle's influential notion of *phronêsis*.[43] It is crucial to keep this pure, limited function of moral appraisal in mind, for it

---

38 Cf. Beck 1960, p. 154n.
39 I will argue below that what I term the 'typic-procedure' for moral appraisal is strictly determining as well, see section 4.2.2.4.
40 Johnson 1985, p. 266; cf. von Wolff-Metternich 2004.
41 Dietrichson 1969, p. 169–70.
42 See Schwartz 2006, p. 121–122.
43 Höffe 2012, p. 107; Höffe 1977, p. 364ff.; Zimmermann 2011, p. 52.

would be misguided to expect the *typic* – which, as we will see next, is designed to enable moral appraisal – to serve as a comprehensive guide to all aspects of moral judgment, whereas it in fact serves only to enable the strictly delimited task of mediating the subsumption of actions in sensibility under the pure concepts of good and evil.

A final point to note is that moral appraisal presupposes what could be called the *volitional finitude* of human beings – i.e., the "subjective imperfection" of our will vis-à-vis the moral law. Indeed, it only makes sense to distinguish good actions from evil ones if we do, or at least can, perform actions of both kinds. For angels, say, who supposedly have perfect, "holy wills" and accordingly never do – and never *can* do – anything wrong (*G* 4: 414, 439), moral appraisal would be a vain exercise. Lamentably, our species is not so constituted that we automatically do whatever the law prescribes; rather, the law has to *command* our morally deficient wills to do the good (*G* 4: 414; *KpV* 5: 19–20). Accordingly, moral appraisal is needed to evaluate whether the performance of a particular action in a certain situation either complies with or violates a moral command.

Chapter 2.
The 'particular difficulties'

We have just seen that the *task* of the pure practical power of judgment is moral appraisal: the subsumption of actions under the pure moral concepts of good and evil. When the pure practical power of judgment undertakes this task, however, it becomes "subject to particular difficulties [*besonderen Schwierigkeiten unterworfen*]" (*KpV* 5: 68). Kant states the problem in three key passages:

> But a practical rule of reason *first*, as *practical*, concerns the existence of an object, and *second*, as a *practical rule* of pure reason, brings with it necessity with respect to the existence of an action and is thus a practical law, not a natural law through empirical grounds of determination but a law of freedom in accordance with which the will is to be determinable independently of anything empirical (merely through the representation of a law in general and its form); however, all cases of possible actions that occur can only be empirical, that is, belong to experience and nature; hence, it seems absurd to want to find in the sensible world a case which, though as such it stands only under the laws of nature, yet would admit of the application to it of a law of freedom and to which there could be applied the supersensible Idea of the morally good, which is to be exhibited in it *in concreto* (*KpV* 5: 67–68).[44]

> On the other hand, the morally good as an object is something supersensible, so that nothing corresponding to it can be found in any sensible intuition; and the power of judgment under laws of pure practical reason seems, therefore, to be subject to special difficulties having their source in this: that a law of freedom is to [be] applied to actions *qua* events that take place in the sensible world and so, to this extent, belong to nature (*KpV* 5: 68).[45]

---

44 [*Weil aber eine praktische Regel der reinen Vernunft erstlich, als praktisch, die Existenz eines Objects betrifft und zweitens, als praktische Regel der reinen Vernunft, Nothwendigkeit in Ansehung des Daseins der Handlung bei sich führt, mithin praktisches Gesetz ist und zwar nicht Naturgesetz durch empirische Bestimmungsgründe, sondern ein Gesetz der Freiheit, nach welchem der Wille unabhängig von allem Empirischen (blos durch die Vorstellung eines Gesetzes überhaupt und dessen Form) bestimmbar sein soll, alle vorkommende Fälle zu möglichen Handlungen aber nur empirisch, d.i. zur Erfahrung und Natur gehörig, sein können: so scheint es widersinnisch, in der Sinnenwelt einen Fall antreffen zu wollen, der, da er immer so fern nur unter dem Naturgesetze steht, doch die Anwendung eines Gesetzes der Freiheit auf sich verstatte, und auf welchen die übersinnliche Idee des sittlich Guten, das darin in concreto dargestellt werden soll, angewandt werden könne.*]

45 [*Hingegen ist das sittlich Gute etwas dem Objecte nach Übersinnliches, für das also in keiner sinnlichen Anschauung etwas Correspondirendes gefunden werden kann, und die Urtheilskraft unter Gesetzen der reinen praktischen Vernunft scheint daher besonderen Schwierigkeiten unterworfen zu sein, die darauf beruhen, daß ein Gesetz der Freiheit auf Handlungen als Begebenheiten, die in der Sinnenwelt geschehen und also so fern zur Natur gehören, angewandt werden soll.*]

But no intuition and hence no schema can be put under the law of freedom (as that of a causality not at all sensibly conditioned), nor consequently under the concept of the unconditioned good, for their application *in concreto* and [the power of judgment] under laws of pure practical reason seems, therefore, to be subject to special difficulties (*KpV* 5: 69).[46]

Needless to say, these passages are quite complex and have consequently elicited many different interpretations. Yet it is essential to understand precisely what these '*particular [besondere]* difficulties' consist in, as the *particular* role of the *typic* will be to overcome them and thereby enable the task of moral appraisal to be performed. Fortunately, the analysis of the previous chapter provides a guiding thread: given that moral appraisal (like all exercises of determining judgment) consists in *subsuming* particular *cases* under an abstract *rule*, we can expect that the obstacle to this subsumption should take the form of a *mismatch between the case and the rule* – here, a mismatch between actions and the moral law. I will begin by presenting and critically examining various construals of this mismatch that have been proposed by commentators. Although some adduce relevant aspects of the problem, none of them quite hit the nail on the head. In the following section I will go on to propose my own characterization of the mismatch.

2.1 Construals of the problem in the secondary literature

Commentators have interpreted the mismatch between the case and the rule in terms of five dichotomies: natural necessity vs. freedom; is vs. ought; concrete vs. abstract; matter vs. form; and subjective ends vs. objective ends. Here I present and critically assess each interpretation in turn.

2.1.1 Natural necessity vs. freedom

The passages previously quoted readily invite the interpretation that the mismatch between actions and the moral law consists in a *metaphysical dichotomy*, between natural necessity and causality through freedom. Longuenesse advances an interpretation along these lines:

---

46 [*Hingegen ist das sittlich Gute etwas dem Objecte nach Übersinnliches, für das also in keiner sinnlichen Anschauung etwas Correspondirendes gefunden werden kann, und die Urtheilskraft unter Gesetzen der reinen praktischen Vernunft scheint daher besonderen Schwierigkeiten unterworfen zu sein.*]

Kant is mostly concerned with explaining the fundamental difficulty we encounter in attempting to think the relation between the moral law (which depends on the faculty of reason alone, and thus on our belonging to a purely intelligible world) and actions that unfold in the sensible world and are thus causally necessitated. *This metaphysical difficulty is according to Kant the root of the difficulty of moral judgment*, evaluating an action or the will of the subject that performs the action (is it a good will or not?).[47]

On the one hand, all actions belong to *nature*. In the Transcendental Analytic of the *Critique of Pure Reason*, Kant establishes that nature is the sum of all sensible appearances under laws prescribed by the understanding, such that everything that happens within nature must be empirically determined by a cause preceding it in time (*KrV* A542/B570). In general, "the sensible world is nothing but a chain of appearances connected in accordance with universal laws [*Die Sinnenwelt ist nichts als eine Kette nach allgemeinen Gesetzen verknüpfter Erscheinungen*]" (*P* 4: 354) and every particular action constitutes merely a "link in the chain of nature [*ein Glied der Naturkette*]" (*KrV* A544/B572). Accordingly, a person acting within nature exercises her causality by setting certain events in motion, yet she is always determined to do so by previous links in the causal nexus of which she forms a part. Actions *qua* sensible appearances are *events* within the unbroken causal chain of natural necessity; they not only cause succeeding events in time, but are themselves caused by preceding events in time – as Kant puts it in the Typic, they are brought about "through empirical grounds of determination [*durch empirische Bestimmungsgründe*]" (*KpV* 5: 68; cf. *KrV* A543/B571). In other words, there is nothing new under the sun:

> all the actions of the human being in appearance are determined in accord with the order of nature by his empirical character and the other cooperating causes; and if we could investigate all the appearances of his power of choice down to their basis, then there would be no human action that we could not predict with certainty, and recognize as necessary given its preceding conditions. Thus in regard to this empirical character there is no freedom ... (*KrV* A549–550/B578–9).

On the other hand, the concepts of good and evil derive from a law of *freedom*. As we have seen, they flow *a priori* from a practical rule of reason, which, when applied to a particular action, instructs us whether or not we should desire to perform it. As Kant stresses in the Typic chapter, this rule is a *practical law* insofar as it represents the actual realization of good actions as *necessary* effects of *freedom*:

---

[47] Longuenesse 2005, p. 237 (my emphasis).

> But a practical rule of reason *first*, as *practical*, concerns the existence of an object, and *second*, as a *practical rule* of pure reason, brings with it necessity with respect to the existence of an action and is thus a practical law, not a natural law through empirical grounds of determination but a law of freedom in accordance with which the will is to be determinable independently of anything empirical (merely through the representation of a law in general and its form) (*KpV* 5: 67–8; cf. *KpV* 5: 31).[48]

By characterizing the moral law here as a law of *freedom*, Kant is recalling the key result of the first main chapter of the second *Critique*, namely that "[t]he moral law is, in fact, a law of causality through freedom ... [*Das moralische Gesetz ist in der Tat ein Gesetz der Kausalität durch Freiheit* ...]" (*KpV* 5: 47). Rational beings exercise causality through freedom – i.e., exercise free will – *positively* insofar as they autonomously determine themselves to act according to the moral law, which in turn presupposes *negative,* or "transcendental," freedom, i.e., the capacity to determine one's will completely independently from sensible determination (*KrV* A533–534/B561–562; *G* 4: 446; *MS* 6: 213). Freedom is therefore "a causality not at all sensibly conditioned [*eine gar nicht sinnlich bedingt[e] Causalität*]" (*KpV* 5: 69), as Kant puts it in the Typic. Actions brought about through freedom can be called freely willed, or free actions. Finally, as Kant stresses in many contexts, the law of freedom can only be conceived as the law of the *supersensible, intelligible* or *noumenal* realm, separated by a great gulf from the realm of sensible appearances.

This stark metaphysical dichotomy apparently creates a grave predicament for *moral appraisal*. On the one hand, the actions under appraisal belong to the sensible world; as such, they are in the first instance events determined through and through by *natural law*. On the other hand, appraising actions as good or evil presupposes their being *freely caused* by the agent, for insofar as they are morally appraisable, they must be entirely imputable to the agent's will, to the exclusion of other causes (negative freedom); furthermore, the action is judged *qua* effect of a will that determines itself by the moral law (positive freedom). The problem is, no "link in the chain of nature [*Glied der Naturkette*]" (*KrV* A544/B572) *as such* can be represented as freely caused and hence, as Kant writes in the Typic, "it seems absurd to want to find in the sensible world a case which, though as such it stands only under the laws of nature, yet would admit

---

48 [*Weil aber eine praktische Regel der reinen Vernunft erstlich, als praktisch, die Existenz eines Objects betrifft und zweitens, als praktische Regel der reinen Vernunft, Nothwendigkeit in Ansehung des Daseins der Handlung bei sich führt, mithin praktisches Gesetz ist und zwar nicht Naturgesetz durch empirische Bestimmungsgründe, sondern ein Gesetz der Freiheit, nach welchem der Wille unabhängig von allem Empirischen (blos durch die Vorstellung eines Gesetzes überhaupt und dessen Form) bestimmbar sein soll.*]

of the application to it of a law of freedom … [*so scheint es widersinnisch, in der Sinnenwelt einen Fall antreffen zu wollen, der, da er immer so fern nur unter dem Naturgesetze steht, doch die Anwendung eines Gesetzes der Freiheit auf sich verstatte …*]" (*KpV* 5: 68, my emphasis). It therefore seems that moral appraisal must inevitably run into "particular difficulties" because it requires a *metaphysical impossibility*, namely that actions be both naturally and freely caused.

However, *this* problem cannot constitute the 'particular difficulties' in the Typic for the simple reason that *it is not a difficulty at all* – at least not in Kant's eyes, as he considers himself to have satisfactorily resolved the matter beforehand. Indeed, it is the *solution* to this problem that constitutes the ontological backdrop to the Typic. Kant takes himself to have already demonstrated, in the *Critique of Pure Reason*, that natural necessity and causality through freedom *are metaphysically compatible*, even with regard to the very same action:

> Yet the problem which we had to solve … was only this: Do freedom and natural necessity in one and the same action contradict each other? And this we have answered sufficiently when we showed that since in freedom a relation is possible to conditions of a kind entirely different from those in natural necessity, the law of the latter does not affect the former; hence each is independent of the other, and can take place without being disturbed by the other (*KrV* A557/B585; cf. *P* 4: 356).

As far as Kant is concerned, then, moral appraisal implies no metaphysical contradiction or impossibility. If a person tells a lie, for example, her action can be viewed as freely caused through her intelligible character even though it is at the same time the necessary product of her empirically determined character; accordingly, the lie *qua* free act can be morally condemned and the liar can be held morally responsible for his action (*KrV* A554–556/B582–4). And whereas in the first *Critique* Kant defended the compatibility of natural necessity with transcendental freedom as a mere possibility from a theoretical point of view while abstaining from asserting freedom's reality, in the second *Critique* he goes one step further by proving the reality of freedom from a practical point of view through the moral law, which is in turn an indisputable 'fact' of reason (cf. *KpV* 5: 70). So by the time we get to the Typic chapter, *the metaphysical stage has already been set* for moral appraisal: actions are the sensible effects of free wills that can determine themselves according to the law of free causality. We must therefore conclude that the metaphysical construal of the mismatch between the case and the rule, while alluded to in the language of the Typic and relevant to its problematic, nevertheless does not constitute the 'particular difficulties' of moral judgment per se.[49]

2.1.2 Is vs. ought

Other commentators, notably Beck and Pieper, trace the special difficulties of the pure practical power of judgment to a *conceptual* mismatch, namely "the conceptual gap between what ought to be and what is."[50] On the one hand, moral appraisal invokes normative predicates – good and evil – belonging to the conceptual domain of what "ought to be" (*das Sollen*). As we have seen, moral appraisal consists in determining an action's moral possibility, i.e., whether or not one may will to bring it into existence as an "object of pure practical reason" in accordance with the moral law. In other words, we have to consider whether or not the action could be regarded as an effect consonant with "a law of what ought to be," regardless of whether or not the action actually exists, and even independently of its physical possibility. We appraise actions solely with respect to what we ought to do (*sollen*) and what we are permitted to will (*wollen dürfen*). On the other hand, the actions we are to appraise belong to the conceptual domain of what is (*das Sein*). We conceptualize them as events in the natural world, determined by the law of natural necessity. Accordingly, we must describe every action as just another link in an unbroken causal chain; everything that happens must have a preceding physical cause that brings it into existence according to 'a law of what is.' From this point of view, the description of human action is not qualitatively different from that of other events in the physical universe (*KrV* A550/B579). All that we can meaningfully say, under these conditions, concerns what is (*sein*), can (*können*), or must (*müssen*) be the case according to natural laws. In Kant's thought these two conceptual domains – *das Sollen* and *das Sein* – constitute incommensurable spheres of meaning:

---

[49] I fully concur with Giovanni Sala's reading here: "Obwohl Kant im ersten Absatz vom "Gesetz der Freiheit" einerseits und von einer "Sinnenwelt ... die unter dem Naturgesetz steht" andererseits spricht, geht es hier nicht (zumindest nicht in erster Linie) um die Frage nach der Anwendbarkeit des Sittengesetzes als eines Gesetzes der Freiheit auf eine Natur, in der ein lückenloser Determinismus herrscht. Dieses Problem wurde bereits im Rahmen der dritten Antinomie der *KrV* behandelt und kommt zwar an mehreren Stellen der *KpV* zur Sprache, vor allem in der "Kritischen Beleuchtung der Analytik der reinen praktischen Vernunft" (A 167–191), aber ist hier nicht gemeint." Sala 2004, p. 153f.
[50] Beck 1960, p. 157.

> The *ought* expresses a species of necessity and a connection with grounds which does not occur anywhere else in the whole of nature. In nature the understanding can cognize only *what exists*, or has been, or will be. It is impossible that something in it *ought to be* other than what, in all these time-relations, it in fact is; indeed, the *ought*, if one has merely the course of nature before one's eyes, has no significance whatever. We cannot ask at all what ought to happen in nature, any more than we can ask what properties a circle ought to have; but we must rather ask what does happen in nature, or what properties the circle does have (*KrV* A547/B575, trans. mod.).

Therefore, the attempt to import concepts from one domain into the other would be a formidable leap (*metábasis eis állo génos*), and hence "absurd" or "nonsensical" – which is exactly what Kant asserts in the Typic chapter. (*KpV* 5: 68).

Beck and Pieper argue that this is the mismatch that creates the 'particular difficulties' of pure practical reason. Beck declares that the very intelligibility of moral appraisal crucially depends on surmounting this conceptual divide: "unless some way is found to "bridge the conceptual gap between what ought to be and what is so that the concepts of the former may be applied in a definite way to ... the latter," he maintains, "the normative-descriptive distinction, upon which Kant lays such enormous weight, marks an uncrossable chasm."[51] Similarly, Pieper locates the special difficulties of pure practical reason in what she calls "das Problem der Sein-Sollens-Differenz."[52] Natural necessity (*das Sein*) and free causality (*das Sollen*) constitute two entirely heterogeneous rule systems, and consequently one *cannot make valid inferences* from one to the other: "No 'is' can be derived from an 'ought' and no 'ought' can be derived from an 'is'. How then can practical judgment ... [avoid – A.W.] committing the 'naturalistic fallacy'?"[53] That is, from the fact that something *does happen* according to the law of physical causality, one cannot infer that it *ought to happen* according to the law of free causality; conversely, from the moral law's command that something *ought* to happen, one cannot infer that it *will* also occur through physical law. Either way, then, moral appraisal would seem to involve an invalid, "absurd" *inference* between what ought to be and what is.[54] Overcoming this logical gap, Pieper suggests, constitutes the special difficulty that the typic must solve.

Now, while Beck and Pieper are correct to note that Kant laid great weight on the normative-descriptive distinction, assigning natural and free causality to mu-

---

51 Beck 1960, p. 157.
52 Pieper 2011, p. 109; cf. Pieper 2009, p. 189. (The second reference is an English translation of Pieper's original German article.)
53 Pieper 2011, p. 189f.; Pieper 2009, p. 110.
54 Other scholars have also framed the difficulty in these terms: Höffe 2012, p. 111; von Wolff-Metternich 2004, p. 743.

tually irreducible rule systems (cf. *VE Vigilantius*, 27: 488), I do not think that their logico-conceptual interpretation of the 'particular difficulties' is entirely apt. There is no talk in the Typic chapter about the problem of *making inferences* between two systems of rules; rather, the task set for the pure practical judgment consists in simply *subsuming* individual cases under a rule.[55] Indeed, the task of *making inferences* does not belong to the power of judgment at all, but rather belongs to the logical use of *reason* (*KrV* A303–305/B359–361). And as we will see in more detail below, it is an essential feature of the mismatch that it involves *two different species of representations*; consequently, it cannot consist in a merely logical difference between two *concepts* or two *systems of rules*.[56]

2.1.3 Concrete vs. abstract

François Marty submits that the purpose of the typic is to resolve an incongruity between a *concrete* action belonging to space and time on the one hand and an *abstract* rule of reason on the other: "But the action is realized in space and time, it belongs to sensibility. On the other hand, reason presents itself as independent of any particularity, and hence as 'general' and abstract. And so we face the problem of the typic of pure practical judgment."[57] Dietrichson construes the problem along similar lines: "So the important problem [is] how we are to go about applying the purely formal, abstract, existentially indeterminate moral law as a criterion for evaluating the *material maxims of our particular actions in the concretely existing phenomenal world*" (original italics).[58]

However, the "problem" described by Marty and Dietrichson is not a *particular difficulty*, but simply the *task* of moral appraisal just as it is described in the Typic: the subsumption of an action *in concreto* under a practical rule *in abstracto* (*KpV* 5:67). Moreover, bridging the gap between the abstract and concrete, as such, is not *particular* to moral appraisal or even to moral judgment: *every* determining exercise of judgment involves applying an abstract rule to a concrete particular (*KrV* A133/B172). Tellingly, by framing the difficulties of the *practical* power of judgment in these terms, Dietrichson can no longer distinguish them in any relevant way from those of the *theoretical* power of judgment, which he characterizes in exactly the same terms: "A schematization had to be worked out in order to explain how the purely *abstract*, existentially indeterminate cat-

---

[55] For similar criticisms, see Zimmermann 2011, p. 57 ff.
[56] See section 2.2.3.
[57] Marty 1997, p. 248.
[58] Dietrichson 1969, p. 167 f.

egories could be applied to *concrete* individual sensory contents ..." (my emphasis).[59] But as we will see, Kant states that the practical power of judgment faces particular difficulties that it *doesn't* share with the theoretical power of judgment (*KpV* 5: 68). In short, the abstract-concrete dichotomy cannot be the *particular* difficulty we are seeking, for it is not *specific* to the present context.

2.1.4 Matter vs. form

According to other scholars, the problem arises from a mismatch between "form" on the one hand and "matter," or "content," on the other. According to Johnson, it appears difficult, if not impossible, to subsume "material content" (i.e., actions) under a "purely formal principle that abstracts from all material content."[60] Interpreters have framed two variants of this dichotomy, depending on whether they construe the "material content" as actions or as maxims. On the first view, the problem is how to apply the unconditioned form of the moral law to the determinate contents of the will: "How is it possible," asks Gerhard Luf, "to determine the unconditioned *form* of a universal law and to apply it to particular, finite *contents* derived from the objects of the faculty of desire?"[61] On the second view, the mismatch takes the following form:

> The *moral law* (the law of pure practical reason) is an empirically empty principle, a purely formal principle, namely a norm prescribing that I should always act on such a maxim that I could also consistently want a universal law to become modeled on it. A *maxim*, on the other hand, is an empirically determinate principle, a *material* principle, namely a specific subjective rule of action in the phenomenal world. ... It is obvious that the completely formal (empirically empty) law of pure practical reason is not a standard of evaluation that can be applied directly to our material (empirically determinate) rules of action.[62]

The Typic chapter itself offers little textual basis for either construal of the problem, however. Firstly, Kant simply does not employ the terms "content [*Inhalt*]" or "matter/material [*Materie/materiell*]" at all. Secondly, actions are never characterized as "contents" of a formal principle, but rather as "cases [*Fälle*]" (*KpV* 5: 68) of a rule. Thirdly, maxims are not mentioned in the passage where the 'particular difficulties' are presented (*KpV* 5: 67–8); and when they do come into play, it is always with reference to their *form*, rather than to their status as 'ma-

---

59 Dietrichson 1969, p. 172.
60 Johnson 1985, p. 270.
61 Luf 1975, p. 58.
62 Dietrichson 1969, 173 f.; cf. Reath 2010, p. 35.

terial' principles, as in the following passage: "If *the maxim* of the action is not so *constituted* that it can stand the test as to *the form of a law of nature in general*, then it is morally impossible [Wenn *die Maxime* der Handlung nicht *so beschaffen ist*, daß sie an der *Form* eines Naturgesetzes überhaupt die Probe hält, so ist sie sittlich unmöglich]" (*KpV* 5: 69 – 70).[63] Either way, Kant *does* tell us, at least in principle, how it is possible to apply the formal principle to actions *qua* contents, namely *mediately*, by imparting the *maxim* (the subjective principle through which the action is willed) with "the form of lawfulness in general" – that is just what the Universal Law Formula of the Categorical Imperative states. Furthermore, this very requirement clearly presupposes that *maxims* have both a matter and a form: while they are *material* insofar as they make reference to concrete actions in the empirical world, they also have a *formal* dimension, insofar as they are *principles* or *rules* of action (*G* 4: 436). So the supposed incongruity between the formal law and the "material" maxim is a false problem: the *formal* law applies not to the matter of the maxim, but to its *form* – and that is both the source of moral obligation and the corresponding criterion of moral judgment (*KpV* 5: 27–28). This is not a *special difficulty*, but just the *task* of moral appraisal. The problem specific to the typic is therefore not 'Is this determination possible?' but rather 'How is it done?'

2.1.5 Subjective ends vs. objective ends

It has also been suggested that there is an incongruity between the kinds of *ends* respectively referred to by maxims and by the moral law, namely subjective and objective ends (or ends in themselves). This apparent mismatch leads Mark Johnson to ask: "How can a particular maxim that specifies subjective ends [...] be evaluated by a moral principle [...] that does not depend on subjective ends?"[64] But ends – whether subjective or objective – are not germane to the special difficulty that makes the typic necessary. Again, this ostensible problem has already been answered (at least in principle) by a formula of the Categorical Imperative, namely the Formula of Humanity: a maxim is wrong if it involves treating another person as a mere means to a subjective end and not also at the same time as an end in itself (*G* 4: 436). In any case, it seems implausible that the typic's purpose should be to resolve some particular difficulty with the application of the Formula of Humanity, which is never mentioned. Indeed, in the Typic

---

[63] I will of course return to this key statement in more depth below, in section 4.2.
[64] Johnson 1985, p. 270.

chapter Kant makes no mention of *ends* at all, whether subjective or objective; as we will see, he is concerned instead with the strict universalizability of maxims, a criterion that abstracts from ends altogether.[65]

2.2 The representational mismatch: sensible intuitions vs. supersensible Ideas

2.2.1 From 'the very same difficulties' as theoretical judgment to the 'particular difficulties' of practical judgment

Since none of the interpretations examined above proved entirely satisfactory, let us return to the primary text. A valuable hint as to the true nature of the problem is Kant's indication that, in at least one important respect, "the power of judgment of pure practical reason is subject to *the very same difficulties* as those of pure theoretical reason [*Also ist die Urtheilskraft der reinen praktischen Vernunft* eben denselben Schwierigkeiten *unterworfen, als die der reinen theoretischen*]" (*KpV* 5: 68). Accordingly, determining what these "very same difficulties" consist in will allow us to establish the backdrop against which the "particular difficulties" of the *practical* power of judgment should come into focus.

In the Schematism chapter of the *Critique of Pure Reason*, Kant describes how the power of judgment must *subsume empirical cases (sensible appearances) under the a priori rules defined by the pure concepts of the understanding, or categories*. Let us recall that subsumption operates on *representations*: 'subsuming an object under a concept' is really shorthand for subsuming the *representation* of the object under the *representation* of the concept. Furthermore, these two levels of representation must be "homogeneous [*gleichartig*]," that is, representationally compatible (*KrV* A157/B176). On the other hand, the pure concepts of the understanding are, by definition, "totally unhomogeneous [*ganz ungleichartig*]" vis-à-vis the empirical intuitions to which they are to be applied (*KrV* A137/B176). Thus, the "difficulties" of pure theoretical judgment stem from a mismatch between pure concepts and sensible intuitions *qua* representations. I will call this the *theoretical heterogeneity problem*.

Are these the "very same difficulties" faced by pure practical judgment? Not entirely. Practical judgment does not apply pure concepts of the understanding to sensibility in order to obtain theoretical cognition; rather, it applies concepts of practical reason in order to appraise actions morally. So the "very same diffi-

---

[65] See below, section 4.2.3.2.

culties" must be less specific than those described in the Schematism. If we recast the theoretical heterogeneity problem more generally, *in terms of judgment as such,* we can say that *subsumption is hindered by a representational mismatch: the representation of the case is heterogeneous vis-à-vis the representation of the rule.* I will refer to this more general and abstract formulation of the difficulty as the *general heterogeneity problem.* Accordingly, Kant's hint that pure practical judgment faces "the very same difficulties" as pure theoretical judgment should be understood as referring to the *general heterogeneity problem* rather than to the specifically theoretical form of the problem. That is, both theoretical judgment in the context of possible experience and practical judgment in the context of moral appraisal face the common general problem of subsumption's being hindered by a representational mismatch between the case and the rule.

Conversely, what distinguishes the "*particular* difficulties" the pure *practical* power judgment is that they refer to the particular form that the general heterogeneity problem assumes regarding moral appraisal. I will call this the *practical heterogeneity problem:* the representation of a particular action (the case) is heterogeneous vis-à-vis the representation of the moral law (the rule). On my view, the 'particular difficulties' confronting pure practical judgment should be spelled out in terms of *the heterogeneity between the specific representations involved in moral appraisal.* In the rest of this chapter, I will further characterize the source and nature of this problem.

2.2.2 Reason and finitude

In order to understand the source of the 'particular difficulties' posed by moral appraisal, it is essential to consider *who* is doing the appraising. Although Kant emphasizes that the moral law applies in principle to "all rational beings as such [*alle vernünftigen Wesen überhaupt*]" (*G* 4: 408), he specifically states that *the typic* is employed by the ordinary *human* mind (which he calls "the common understanding") (*KpV* 5: 69–70). Thus it is *we human beings* who must overcome a certain obstacle in order to exercise *our power of judgment* in *our* moral life – and this, in spite of a deep tension between our *finitude,* linked to *sensibility,* and our *reason,* linked to the *supersensible.*[66]

Our epistemic finitude stems from the "particular constitution of our faculties of cognition [*die eigentümliche Beschaffenheit unserer Erkenntnisvermögen*]"

---

[66] The importance of finitude for understanding the Typic is emphasized by Renaut 1997, p. 300 ff.

(*KU* 5: 402, 408). As Kant explains in the famous opening paragraph of the Transcendental Aesthetic (*KrV* A19/B33), all cognition must relate to objects, and the only way it can relate to them immediately is through intuition. Intuitions only arise if the objects are "given" to the cognizing subject in some way. While in theory a divine being could spontaneously produce the objects of its intuition (*intuitus originarius*), such a feat, "at least for us humans," is impossible; instead, our finite mind must first be *affected* by objects (*intuitus derivatus*) (*KrV* B72). More particularly, we can only be affected by objects *via our senses*, and consequently all of our intuition is sensible: "It comes along with our nature that *intuition* can never be other than *sensible*, i.e., that it contains only the way in which we are affected by objects [*Unsre Natur bringt es so mit sich, daß die* Anschauung *niemals anders als* sinnlich *sein kann, d.i. nur die Art enthält, wie wir von Gegenständen affiziert werden*]" (*KrV* A51/B75). It follows from this contingent particularity of human nature (*P* 4: 350–1) that all of our thought must ultimately relate to sensible intuition in order to acquire significance: "But all thought, whether straightaway (*directe*) or through a detour (*indirecte*), *must ultimately be related to intuitions, thus, in our case, to sensibility [zuletzt auf Anschauungen, mithin, bei uns, auf Sinnlichkeit beziehen]*" (*KrV* A19/B33, my emphasis). Two consequences entailed by this epistemic "receptivity" of our mind are especially significant to the Typic:

1. Sensibility acts as a "restricting condition [*restringierende Bedingung*]" (*KrV* A146/B186) on our thought: all of our concepts must relate to sensibility in order to acquire meaning (*Bedeutung*) (*KrV* A146/B185). So while our understanding can frame empirical concepts of varying degrees of generality (e.g., 'dog') as well as engender pure concepts not drawn from experience (e.g., 'substance'), these concepts can acquire meaning only if they are ultimately *presented* or *exhibited* (*dargestellt*) in sensible intuition (*KU* 5: 351). Without a sensible presentation, the concept remains, at best, a pure form of logical synthesis through which we can *think* objects, or, at worst, an empty thought-entity (*Hirngespenst*) devoid of objective reference.

2. Not only must we exhibit all our concepts sensibly, *but we cannot do it in any other way than sensibly*. Just as a monitor can display information only in pixels, a radio only in soundwaves, so can the human mind exhibit concepts only in sensible intuition, according to Kant. We have no other medium, as it were, for exhibiting abstract concepts *in concreto*; our capacity for presentation, i.e., our imagination, can only present concepts in intuition, which (whether pure or empirical) is always sensible. Correspondingly, Kant denies that non-sensible, "intellectual intuition" is available to human beings (*KrV* B307, B159), dismissing "supersensible intuition" and other forms of ostensible insight into the intelligible realm as *Schwärmerei*, variously translated

as "mysticism," "fanaticism," or "enthusiasm" (*KpV* 5: 70–1, 135–6, 146; *KU* 5: 459; *SF* 7: 45).[67] For human beings, therefore, all "hypotyposis [*Darstellung, sujectio sub adspectum*]" is limited to "sensible rendering [*Versinnlichung*]" (*KpV* 5: 351).

These two consequences of our epistemic finitude – our *need* to exhibit our thoughts in sensible intuition and our *inability* to exhibit them any other way – are two sides of the same coin. Together, they constitute a more specific limitation of the human mind that I will refer to as *representational finitude*.

On the other hand, humans beings also possess reason (*Vernunft*), a faculty that spontaneously engenders *supersensible* representations that are not limited by sensibility: "pure concepts of reason [*reine Vernunftbegriffe*]," or "Ideas [*Ideen*]." It is in virtue of this capacity to engender Ideas that Kant sometimes characterizes reason as a 'productive' or 'poietic' faculty (*Verstandes-Dichtungskraft, facultas fingendi*).[68] Accordingly, reason can be considered an 'in-finite' representational faculty that surpasses even the pure understanding:

> Now, a human being really finds in himself a capacity by which he distinguishes himself from all other things, even from himself insofar as he is affected by objects, and that is *reason*. This, as pure self-activity, is raised even above the *understanding* by this: that though the latter is also self-activity and does not, like sense, contain merely representations that arise when we are *affected* by things (and are thus passive), yet it can produce from its activity no other concepts than those which serve merely *to bring sensible representations under rules* and thereby to unite them in one consciousness, without which use of sensibility it would think nothing at all; but reason, on the contrary, shows in what we call "Ideas" a spontaneity so pure that it thereby goes far beyond anything that sensibility can ever afford it ... [*weil die Vernunft unter dem Namen der Ideen eine so reine Spontaneität zeigt, daß sie dadurch weit über alles, was ihr Sinnlichkeit nur liefern kann, hinausgeht ...*] (*G* 4: 452).

Since the notion of "supersensible representations" will play a crucial role in what follows, let me take a moment to define it. Representations can be called "supersensible" in two regards:

1. Representations can be deemed "supersensible" in virtue of their *objective referents*. In contradistinction to empirical concepts like "dog" or "table," which refer to perceivable objects in the sensible world, Ideas of reason are special concepts that refer to objects in the intelligible, noumenal, or *supersensible* realm that is ontologically distinct from the world of sensible appearances. Take, for example, the Idea of God as the wise architect of the

---

[67] See below, section 5.2.3.
[68] See Piché 1984, p. 24–31.

physical cosmos. No referent can be found in the sensible world for this Idea of reason because it refers to a supersensible object, which is "something *completely heterogeneous which cannot be an object of the senses* [etwas ganz Ungleichartigem, was gar nicht ein Gegenstand der Sinne sein kann]" (*P* 4: 355, my emphasis).

2. Ideas are also "supersensible" with respect to their *subjective quality as our representations*. The moral law and associated concepts of reason have no sensible content, nor are they derived from sensation through composition or abstraction. Due to our representational finitude, however, we cannot display them adequately in sensible intuition. As I already mentioned, although Kant raises the merely hypothetical possibility of a supersensible *intuition*, which would produce an immediate presentation of an intelligible object designated by an Idea, he strictly denies that human beings possess any such thing (*KrV* B307, B159). We representationally finite beings enjoy no direct representational access to intelligible objects; at best, we can *think* – i.e., logically determine – Ideas through the abstract concepts of the understanding. Thus, the Ideas of the morally good or the moral law are super-sensible representations (*Vorstellungen*) insofar as they transcend our finite capacity for giving them direct sensible presentations (*Darstellungen*). In this respect, the Ideas of reason consequently differ in kind from the *concepts of the understanding*, which can be exhibited in sensible intuition through *examples* (in the case of empirical concepts) or *schemata* (in the case of pure concepts) (*KpV* 5: 351): "*Ideas*, however, are still more remote from objective reality than *categories*; for no appearance can be found in which they may be represented *in concreto*" (*KrV* A567/B595; *P* 4: 452).

Consequently, the term "supersensible" can be ambiguous with respect to the Ideas: it can pertain either to their objective referents or to their subjective quality as representations. In order to prevent confusion, I will reserve the term "*intelligible*" for talking about the *objective referents* of the Ideas (i.e. the intelligible realm or *mundus intelligibilis* as a whole, its objects or its laws) and keep "*supersensible*" for their *subjective quality* as rational Ideas intrinsically heterogeneous from sensible intuitions.

In sum, the finite rationality of human beings entails a deep tension with regard to our representational capacity. On the one hand, insofar as we are representationally finite, we need sensible, and only sensible, exhibitions of our concepts; on the other hand, insofar as we possess reason, we produce supersensible Ideas that transcend all sensibility and can never be exhibited within it.

2.2.3 Sensible intuitions vs. supersensible Ideas

Crucially, this particular constitution of ours as finite rational beings results in 'particular difficulties' because moral appraisal provokes a conflict between our ability, as beings endowed with reason, to produce *supersensible* representations and our inability, as finite beings, to furnish *sensible* exhibitions of such concepts.

Let us recall that all exercises of determining judgment involve *subsuming* particular cases *in concreto* under a pre-given rule *in abstracto* – more precisely, subsuming the *representations* of the cases under the *representation* of the rule (*KrV* A68/B93). Accordingly, moral appraisal consists in subsuming our representations of particular actions under our representations of the moral law and the morally good. On the one hand, actions present themselves to us as events in nature, and as a consequence of our epistemic finitude, we can only become acquainted with such events via our sensible intuition, i.e., as "objects *of sensible intuition* [*Gegenstände sinnlicher Anschauung*]" (*KpV* 5: 68, my emphasis). On the other hand, in the Typic, Kant repeatedly refers to the moral law and the morally good with the term "Idea," thereby characterizing them as a supersensible *representations* produced by reason. But the total heterogeneity between these two kinds of representations makes direct subsumption impossible. Kant expresses this problem by saying that it is impossible to *exhibit* or *apply* the moral Ideas in sensible intuition:

> hence, it seems absurd to want to find in the sensible world a case ... to which there could be applied the supersensible Idea of the morally good, which is to be exhibited in it *in concreto* (*KpV* 5: 68).[69]

> But no intuition and hence no schema can be put under the law of freedom (as that of a causality not at all sensibly conditioned), nor consequently under the concept of the unconditioned good, for their application *in concreto* and [the power of judgment] under laws of pure practical reason seems, therefore, to be subject to special difficulties (*KpV* 5: 69).[70]

To my eyes, these passages strongly suggest that the 'particular difficulties' of the pure practical power of judgment are representational in nature. More precisely,

---

[69] [so scheint es widersinnisch, in der Sinnenwelt einen Fall antreffen zu wollen, der, ... die Anwendung eines Gesetzes der Freiheit auf sich verstatte, und auf welchen die übersinnliche Idee des sittlich Guten, das darin in concreto dargestellt werden soll, angewandt werden könne.]

[70] [Hingegen ist das sittlich Gute etwas dem Objecte nach Übersinnliches, für das also in keiner sinnlichen Anschauung etwas Correspondirendes gefunden werden kann, und die Urtheilskraft unter Gesetzen der reinen praktischen Vernunft scheint daher besonderen Schwierigkeiten unterworfen zu sein.]

2.2 The representational mismatch: sensible intuitions vs. supersensible Ideas

they consist in a mismatch between *sensible intuitions* by which actions are represented and the *supersensible Ideas* of the moral law and the morally good (i.e., the practical heterogeneity problem).[71] Moreover, this construal of the *particular* difficulties makes sense against the backdrop of the *common* difficulties that the pure practical power of judgment shares with the theoretical power of judgment: in both cases the power of judgment faces *a subjective obstacle to subsumption*, namely the heterogeneity between the representations to be subsumed. The *specific difference* that gives rise to practical judgment's *particular* difficulties, therefore, is that the *subjective quality* of the representations in each case are different: for theoretical judgment, the mismatch exists between sensible intuitions and *pure concepts of the understanding*; for practical judgment, between sensible intuitions and *supersensible Ideas of reason*.

By contrast, it has also been argued that the "particular difficulties" of pure practical judgment involve an incompatibility between the case and the rule due to their respective *objective referents* rather than an incompatibility with respect to their *subjective quality* as our representations. According to this reading, the problem stems from the *ontological* deficiency of actions qua objects in the sensible world to serve as adequate counterparts to the *intelligible objects* that we are referring to in moral appraisal. Grandjean frames the problem in this way, rejecting any "merely subjective" construal of the problem.[72] In my view, this incompatibility at the objective, ontological level is presupposed, however it only becomes relevant to the particular problematic of the Typic *insofar as it results in 'particular difficulties' for us at the subjective, representational level*. And the text seems to confirm this reading. If we look more closely at the passage where Kant mentions the good's objective, intelligible referent, "as an object something supersensible [*etwas dem Objecte nach Übersinnliches*]," the *problem* that Kant identifies as such is not the good's objective, ontological incongruity with *an object of the sensible world per se*, but rather the consequent impossibility – for us, as representationally finite beings – of furnishing a *presentation* of it: ".... nothing corresponding to it can be found *in any sensible intuition* [in keiner sinnlichen Anschauung]... " (*KpV* 5: 68, my emphasis).

Crucially, the representational mismatch between sensible intuitions and the supersensible Ideas of morality gives rise to two opposing dangers that threaten the very heart of Kant's moral philosophy.[73] On the one hand, if Kant were to admit that the supersensible moral Ideas cannot be applied to actions in sensi-

---

[71] Renaut and Ware also construe the problem in these terms. See Renaut 1997, p. 301, 307; Ware 2010, p. 120.
[72] Grandjean 2004, p. 46. This interpretation is disputed in Ch. 6, section 2.2.
[73] This paragraph is based on the exposition in Renaut 1997, p. 301–313.

ble intuition at all, then he would have to concede that the moral Ideas are devoid of significance and that moral appraisal is an empty, formalistic exercise. But on the other hand, presenting the supersensible Ideas directly in sensible intuition is no solution either, as it would defigure them beyond recognition, for no concrete *image* can ever be commensurate with the purity and universality of the rational Idea. Next we will see how Kant navigates between this Skylla and Charybdis by inventing a 'presentation of the unpresentable'.

Chapter 3.
The resources

So far, we have identified the *task* – successfully carrying out moral appraisal by subsuming particular actions under the moral law – and the *'particular difficulties'* – the representational mismatch between actions in sensible intuition and the supersensible Ideas of the moral law and the morally good. Now it is time to take stock of the *resources* available for an eventual solution. Which faculties and representations does Kant have at his disposal? Which ones does he presently need? Which ones can he suitably use?

3.1 The schematism and the imagination

3.1.1 Nature and function

Kant recalls that the *theoretical* power of judgment has a "means at hand [*ein Mittel zur Hand*]" for overcoming its representational difficulties, namely the schematism:

> Thus the power of judgment of pure practical reason is subject to the very same difficulties as those of pure theoretical reason, though the latter had means at hand for getting out of these difficulties, namely that with respect to its theoretical use it depended upon intuitions to which pure concepts of the understanding could be applied, and such intuitions (though only of objects of the senses) can be given a priori (as *schemata*) conformably with pure concepts of the understanding (*KpV* 5: 68).[74]

Kant introduced the schematism in the *Critique of Pure Reason* as a procedure for overcoming the heterogeneity between the pure concepts of the understanding and sensible intuition. As we saw above, this difficulty consists in a mismatch between two kinds of representations: the pure concepts of the understanding are "totally unhomogeneous [*ganz ungleichartig*]" vis-à-vis the *sensible* intuitions

---

74 [*Also ist die Urtheilskraft der reinen praktischen Vernunft eben denselben Schwierigkeiten unterworfen, als die der reinen theoretischen, welche letztere gleichwohl, aus denselben zu kommen, ein Mittel zur Hand hatte: nämlich da es in Ansehung des theoretischen Gebrauchs auf Anschauungen ankam, darauf reine Verstandesbegriffe angewandt werden könnten, dergleichen Anschauungen (obzwar nur von Gegenständen der Sinne) doch a priori, mithin, was die Verknüpfung des Mannigfaltigen in denselben betrifft, den reinen Verstandesbegriffen a priori gemäß (als Schemate) gegeben werden können.*]

to which they are to be applied (*KrV* A137/B176). In order to mediate between these representations, the power of judgment employs a "third thing [*ein Drittes*]," namely a *transcendental schema*. The schema assumes the form of a *transcendental time-determination* sketched by the imagination. It serves as a "mediating representation [*vermittelnde Vorstellung*]" (*KrV* A138/B176) insofar as it is "homogeneous [*gleichartig*]" with each of the two poles – on the one hand, with the pure concept of the understanding insofar as it expresses a universal, *a priori* rule and, on the other hand, with the manifold of sensible intuition insofar as time is the pure form of the latter (*KrV* A138–9/B177–8). While the individual pure concepts cannot be exhibited directly by individual intuitions, the schematism nevertheless enables judgment to *subsume* all sensible intuitions under the former through the mediation of their schemata, i.e., the *a priori* rules that determine the order and mutual connection of all sensible intuitions in time (*KrV* A145/B184–5).

3.1.2 Two problems with the schematism

Crucially, Kant insists that the *practical* power of judgment *cannot rely on a schema* to get out of its own difficulties (*KpV* 5: 69). It is essential to understand why the schematism is the *wrong* tool for the job here, as this will allow us to spell out what the *right* tool must be like. In the Typic chapter Kant adduces two problems with the schematism. The first problem reflects its ineffectualness for overcoming pure practical judgment's particular difficulties, while the second problem reflects its unsuitability for performing the task of moral appraisal.

3.1.2.1 Sensible contamination
The first problem is that no transcendental schema could resolve pure practical judgment's particular difficulties because it would inevitably denature the supersensible representations of the moral law and the morally good.

In the *Critique of Pure Reason*, Kant defined a *schema* in general as the "representation of a general procedure of the imagination for providing a concept with its image [*Die Vorstellung ... von einem allgemeinen Verfahren der Einbildungskraft, einem Begriff sein Bild zu verschaffen*]" (*KrV* A140/B179–80). Transcendental schemata, while they do not match each pure concept of the understanding with a single intuition or "image [*Bild*]," nevertheless translate the former's logical structure into a sensible structure, namely a transcendental determination of time, thereby *applying – and restricting – the categories to sensible intuition:* "although the schemata of sensibility first realize the categories, yet they likewise also restrict them, i.e., limit them to conditions that lie outside the understanding (namely, in sensibility)" (*KrV* A146/B185–6). By contrast, the Ideas of reason tolerate no such sensible restriction; they cannot be schematized. And significantly, Kant repeats several times in the Typic chapter that the schematism can yield exhibitions only in *sensible intuition:*

> ... such intuitions (though only of objects of the senses) can be given a priori (as schemata) [*dergleichen Anschauungen (obzwar nur von Gegenständen der Sinne) doch a priori ... (als Schemate) gegeben werden können*] (*KpV* 5: 68).

> ... it belongs to the theoretical use of reason to appraise that possibility in accordance with the law of causality, a pure concept of the understanding for which reason has a *schema* in sensible intuition. [... *denn die gehört für die Beurtheilung des theoretischen Gebrauchs der Vernunft nach dem Gesetze der Causalität, eines reinen Verstandesbegriffs, für den sie ein Schema in der sinnlichen Anschauung hat*] (*KpV* 5: 68).

> Physical causality, or the condition under which it takes place, belongs among [the] concepts of nature, whose schema transcendental imagination sketches. [*Die physische Causalität, oder die Bedingung, unter der sie stattfindet, gehört unter die Naturbegriffe, deren Schema transscendentale Einbildungskraft entwirft*] (*KpV* 5: 68).

> To a natural law, as a law to which objects of sensible intuition as such are subject, there must correspond a schema, that is, a universal procedure of the imagination (by which it presents a priori to the senses the pure concept of the understanding which the law determines) [*Dem Naturgesetze als Gesetze, welchem die Gegenstände sinnlicher Anschauung als solche unterworfen sind, muß ein Schema, d.i. ein allgemeines Verfahren der Einbildungskraft (den reinen Verstandesbegriff, den das Gesetz bestimmt, den Sinnen a priori darzustellen), correspondiren*] (*KpV* 5: 69).

> ... a schema of sensibility [*ein Schema der Sinnlichkeit*] (*KpV* 5: 69).

These passages also highlight the fact that all schemata originate in the imagination (*die Einbildungskraft*). Indeed, if the schematism gives only sensible output, it is because the faculty that produces it, the imagination, is constrained by human sensibility:

> Now since all of our intuition is sensible, the imagination, on account of the subjective condition under which alone it can give a corresponding intuition to the concepts of the understanding, belongs to *sensibility* [*so gehört die Einbildungskraft ... zur Sinnlichkeit*] (*KrV* B151–2).

In the second edition of the *Critique of Pure Reason*, Kant acknowledges the imagination's spontaneity, however he strictly confines its field of action to sensibility. Bounded by our representational finitude, the imagination can only produce sensible output – including schemata – through its "figurative synthesis (*synthesis speciosa*)" (*KrV* B 151, A145–6/B185).

But there's the rub: if we were to feed supersensible Ideas into the schematism, it would invariably produce the wrong kind of output; consequently, it cannot be employed to solve the practical heterogeneity problem. Supersensible Ideas of reason, to be adequately presented, would require supersensible intuitions. But representationally finite human beings do not possess a faculty of supersensible intuition; instead they possess only the schematism, which, as a procedure of the sensibly limited imagination, yields only sensible intuitions and therefore cannot fully and adequately exhibit the Ideas. And it is primarily for *this* reason that Kant rules out the schema as a potential type for the moral law: "*But no intuition and hence no schema* can be put under the law of freedom (as that of a causality not at all sensibly conditioned), nor consequently under the concept of the unconditioned good, for their application *in concreto* [*Aber dem Gesetze der Freiheit (als einer gar nicht sinnlich bedingten Causalität) mithin auch dem Begriffe des unbedingt Guten* kann keine Anschauung, mithin kein Schema *zum Behuf seiner Anwendung in concreto untergelegt werden*]" (*KpV* 5: 69).

3.1.2.2 Irrelevance

The second problem is that the schematism, on its own, does not provide the pure practical power of judgment with a suitable procedure for appraising actions from a moral point of view. As Kant explains in the first *Critique*, the schematism is a procedure that the theoretical power of judgment employs to subsume all cases of experience under the laws of possible experience. And since "all cases of possible actions that occur can only be empirical, that is, belong to experience and nature [*alle vorkommende Fälle zu möglichen Handlungen aber nur empirisch, d.i. zur Erfahrung und Natur gehörig, sein können*]" (*KpV* 5: 68), the schematism automatically assigns all actions a determinate order, duration, etc. in the spatiotemporal nexus of experience. In so doing, however, the schematism represents human actions no differently from any other event in nature, like an apple falling from a tree or a planet orbiting a star. As far as the theoretical power of judgment is concerned, all events must be indifferently subsumed under the (schematized) law of physical causality.[75]

The *practical* power of judgment cannot content itself with this procedure, however, as it views actions from a radically different perspective. When it engages in moral appraisal, it regards every particular action as a freely caused, morally imputable *deed:* "An action is called a *deed* [*That*] insofar as it comes under

---

75 On the relevance of this point, see Konhardt 1979, p. 289.

obligatory laws and hence insofar as the subject, in doing it, is considered in terms of the freedom of his choice" (*MS* 6: 223). In the Typic chapter Kant draws a sharp contrast between theoretical and practical judgment's respective interests with regard to actions:

> Subsumption of an action possible to me in the sensible world under a *pure practical law* does not concern the possibility of the *action* as an event in the sensible world; for, it belongs to the theoretical use of reason to appraise that possibility in accordance with the law of causality, a pure concept of the understanding for which reason has a *schema* in sensible intuition. Physical causality, or the condition under which it takes place, belongs among the concepts of nature, whose schema transcendental imagination sketches. Here, however, we have to do not with the schema of a case in accordance with laws but with the schema of a law itself (if the world 'schema' is appropriate here), since the *determination of the will* (not the action with reference to its result) through the law alone without any other determining ground connects the concept of causality to conditions quite other than those which constitute natural connection (*KpV* 5: 68–9).⁷⁶

In other words, the practical power of judgment does not aim to subsume actions *qua events* under the law of nature, but rather to subsume actions *qua deeds* under "a law of freedom in accordance with which the will is to be determinable independently of anything empirical (merely through the representation of a law in general and its form) [*ein Gesetz der Freiheit, nach welchem der Wille unabhängig von allem Empirischen (blos durch die Vorstellung eines Gesetzes überhaupt und dessen Form) bestimmbar sein soll*]" (*KpV* 5: 68). When we morally appraise an action, we are not interested primarily in its *physical* possibility, but rather in its *moral* possibility; in other words, we are not interested in investigating which physical forces could bring about a particular event, but rather whether we are "allowed to will [*wollen dürfen*]" a particular action as an "object of pure practical reason" (*KpV* 5: 57–67).⁷⁷ (For example, consider euthanasia: the *theoretical* question as to which particular method would be the most humane way to end a

---

76 [*Es ist bei der Subsumtion einer mir in der Sinnenwelt möglichen Handlung unter einem reinen praktischen Gesetze nicht um die Möglichkeit der Handlung als einer Begebenheit in der Sinnenwelt zu thun; denn die gehört für die Beurtheilung des theoretischen Gebrauchs der Vernunft nach dem Gesetze der Causalität, eines reinen Verstandesbegriffs, für den sie ein Schema in der sinnlichen Anschauung hat. Die physische Causalität, oder die Bedingung, unter der sie stattfindet, gehört unter die Naturbegriffe, deren Schema transscendentale Einbildungskraft entwirft. Hier aber ist es nicht um das Schema eines Falles nach Gesetzen, sondern um das Schema (wenn dieses Wort hier schicklich ist) eines Gesetzes selbst zu thun, weil die Willensbestimmung (nicht die Handlung in Beziehung auf ihren Erfolg) durchs Gesetz allein, ohne einen anderen Bestimmungsgrund, den Begriff der Causalität an ganz andere Bedingungen bindet, als diejenige sind, welche die Naturverknüpfung ausmachen.*]
77 As explained above, in Ch. 1.

human being's life is a technical problem for theoretical judgment to solve scientifically, and is obviously distinct from the properly *moral* question as to whether the action of deliberately cutting short a suffering person's life should be deemed good or evil.) It follows from all this that the "schema of a case [i.e., an event – A.W.] according to [physical] laws," while indispensable for theoretical cognition, is nonetheless inappropriate for the purposes of moral appraisal. While all human actions are in fact realized in the sensible world in accordance with natural causality, when we engage in moral appraisal we nevertheless consider actions not under the aspect of nature, but rather under the aspect of freedom: "the determinations of a practical reason can take place ... conformably with the categories of the understanding, but not with a view to a theoretical use of the understanding ..." (*KpV* 5: 65).

3.2 The 'schema of a law itself'

The schema is the wrong tool for the job, "[b]ut here again a favourable prospect opens for the pure practical power of judgment [*allein hier eröffnet sich doch wieder eine günstige Aussicht für die reine praktische Urtheilskraft*]" (*KpV* 5: 68). That is, if we articulate the criteria with respect to which the schematism was found wanting, we can form a precise idea of what the *right* tool would be. Indeed, in the very passage where Kant rejects the schematism, he provides an enigmatic yet valuable hint as to what kind of tool could overcome the latter difficulty: "Here, however, we have to do not with the schema of a case in accordance with laws but with the schema of a law itself (if the world 'schema' is appropriate here) [*Hier aber ist es nicht um das Schema eines Falles nach Gesetzen, sondern um das Schema (wenn dieses Wort hier schicklich ist) eines Gesetzes selbst zu thun*]" (*KpV* 5: 69). The expression "the schema of a case according to laws" refers to theoretical judgment's subsumption of events under the law of nature by means of transcendental time-determinations – but what does the expression "the schema of a law itself" mean?

This unusual expression can be parsed into four points. First, Kant's qualified use of the word "schema" – "(if the word 'schema' is appropriate here [*wenn dieses Wort hier schicklich ist*)]" (*KpV* 5: 68) – reflects the need to find a 'schema' in a *generic, functional* sense which can be spelled out as follows:

> The schema presents itself as a 'third thing,' i.e., as a 'mediating representation' between the rule (or the concept) and the concrete instance. The most general characterization of a schema that we can obtain, then, consists in the mediation between a rule and the cases of

its application; therefore, the schema does not necessarily have to be a product of the sensible imagination.[78]

In the Typic chapter, accordingly, Kant cannot employ a 'schema' in the specific sense of the first *Critique*, but he can employ a 'schema' in the generic sense of a representation that would play a functional role in the practical heterogeneity problem *analogous* to the functional role played by the transcendental schema in the theoretical heterogeneity problem, namely a mediating representation (*vermittelnde Vorstellung*) or 'third thing' that enables subsumption between a general rule and particular cases despite their heterogeneity. But given the supersensible nature of the moral Ideas, the sought-after 'schema' must achieve a presentation without any direct temporalization or sensible rendering (*Versinnlichung*).[79] Second, the "law itself" referred to here is of course the *moral law*, with respect to which we appraise moral actions. Now, the moral law determines the will not by commanding particular actions per se, but rather by commanding *the universally lawful form of maxims*, the subjective principles according to which actions are willed (*G* 4: 420–1). Accordingly, a schema of the moral law itself would have to be a representation that captures *the form of lawfulness in general* to which maxims and actions ought to conform. Third, as Beck and others have noted, there is an *functional analogy* between the schema in the theoretical context and the 'schema' in the practical context insofar as both perform a mediating role: "a schema of a case occurring according to a law is necessary for knowledge of the case, while a schema of the law itself is necessary to connect, in practice, possible events in sense experience with a cause under a law which is not a law of natural connection."[80] Fourth, just as the theoretical power of judgment employs the schematism as a "procedure [*Verfahren*]" (*KrV* A140/B180) for achieving its own theoretical task (i.e., experiential cognition), so, *mutatis mutandis*, should the pure practical power of judgment employ its "schema of a law itself" in a *procedure* for achieving its task (i.e., moral appraisal).

Based on this analysis, I want to suggest that the expression "the schema of a law itself [*das Schema ... eines Gesetzes selbst*]" (*KpV* 5: 68) can be understood as a *formula* encapsulating a number of *criteria* for the right tool for overcoming the particular difficulties of the pure practical power of judgment and enabling

---

[78] Piché 1984, p. 106.
[79] Cf. Renaut 1997, p. 308–9.
[80] Beck 1960, p. 158; cf. Delbos 1969, p. 374; Grandjean 2004, p. 44; Kant 1994, p. 194n-195n.

moral appraisal. I propose to articulate the criteria that the required representation must meet as follows:
1. It must be a pure, non-sensible representation.
2. It must be a representation of the moral law insofar as the latter determines the will, i.e., "the representation of a law in general and its form [*die Vorstellung eines Gesetzes überhaupt und dessen Form*]" (*KpV* 5: 68) that prescribes the "the *form of lawfulness* in general [*die bloße Gesetzmäßigkeit überhaupt*]" (*KpV* 5: 70). This form of lawfulness must have strict universality.
3. It must serve as a third thing, or 'schema' in a functional sense, i.e., as a mediating representation (*vermittelnde Vorstellung*) that can overcome the heterogeneity between the case and the rule and thereby enable the subsumption of the former under the latter.
4. It must ultimately give the pure practical power of judgment a *procedure* by which actions and maxims can be appraised with respect to a morally relevant criterion, namely conformity with universal law (*Gesetzmäßigkeit*).

Lastly, we can confirm that these are indeed the relevant criteria by using them to explain retrospectively why Kant excluded the imagination's schematism as an instrument for applying the moral law:
1. The schema fails to meet the first criterion because, as a product of the imagination's figurative synthesis, it is a sensible representation and would therefore contaminate the supersensible Ideas with sensible content (as in the first problem adduced above).
2. Likewise, the transcendental schema cannot meet the second criterion: it does not represent the pure form of lawfulness, but instead 'intuitivizes' (*veranschaulicht*) the laws articulated by the pure concepts of the understanding by converting them into 'temporal laws' of appearances (*KrV* A145/B184–185).[81]
3. The schema does function as a mediating representation; nevertheless, it does not meet the third criterion, for it performs this function only within the parameters of the theoretical heterogeneity problem, not the practical heterogeneity problem. In other words, while it can successfully mediate between pure concepts of the understanding and sensible intuition, it cannot mediate between supersensible Ideas of reason and sensible intuition.
4. The schema fails to meet the fourth criterion because it fails to provide a relevant procedure for judging actions from a properly *moral* point of view (as in the second problem adduced above).

---

[81] See Tetens 2006, p. 127.

Given these shortcomings, it is no surprise that Kant rules out the imagination and turns instead to the understanding:

> Thus the moral law has no cognitive faculty other than the understanding (*not the imagination*) by means of which it can be applied to objects of nature ... [*Folglich hat das Sittengesetz kein anderes die Anwendung desselben auf Gegenstände der Natur vermittelndes Erkenntnißvermögen, als den Verstand* (nicht die Einbildungskraft) ...] (*KpV* 5: 69, my emphasis).

But what makes the understanding a better option than the imagination? What are its particular capacities? Which particular representation could it produce that would meet the four criteria for a 'schema of the law itself'? To answer these questions, we must now examine Kant's conception of the understanding as the "law-giver of nature."

3.3 The law of nature and the understanding

As is well known, in the *Critique of Pure Reason* Kant identifies the understanding and sensibility as the two "fundamental sources of the mind [*Grundquellen des Gemüts*]" (*KrV* A50/B74). Kant's critical model posits a fundamental separation between the two faculties as well as between their respective kinds of representations:

> If we will call the *receptivity* of our mind to receive representations insofar as it is affected in some way *sensibility*, then on the contrary the faculty for bringing forth representations itself, or the *spontaneity* of cognition, is the *understanding*. It comes along with our nature that *intuition* can never be other than *sensible*, i.e., that it contains only the way in which we are affected by objects. The faculty for *thinking* of objects of sensible intuition, on the contrary, is the *understanding*. Intuitions and concepts therefore constitute the elements of all our cognition (*KrV* A51/B75).

From the outset, the understanding is characterized negatively as "a non-sensory faculty of cognition [*ein nichtsinnliches Erkenntnisvermögen*]" (*KrV* A67–8/B92), yet it also performs a range of positive functions, such as forming concepts and formulating logical rules. I will focus on its positive *transcendental* use, namely prescribing "laws ... insofar as they are related to objects *a priori*" (*KrV* A57/B82). To this end, I will follow the guiding thread of the Transcendental Deduction in the second edition of the *Critique of Pure Reason*, which, being written just before or even concurrently with the *Critique of Practical Reason*, I regard as the most relevant and authoritative source for interpreting Kant's conception of the understanding in the Typic chapter.

Kant opens the B Deduction by identifying the understanding's particular transcendental function as "combination [*Verbindung*]," through which it spontaneously effects a synthesis of a manifold of intuition in general, and this, independently of sensibility:

> ... the *combination* (*conjunctio*) of a manifold in general can never come to us through the senses, and therefore cannot already be contained in the pure form of sensible intuition; for it is an act of the spontaneity of the power of representation, and, since one must call the latter understanding, in distinction from sensibility [*zum Unterschiede von der Sinnlichkeit*], all combination, whether we are conscious of it or not, whether it is a combination of the the manifold of intuition or of several concepts, and in the first case either of sensible or of non-sensible intuition, is an action of the understanding [*Verstandeshandlung*], which we could designate with the general title *synthesis* in order at the same time to draw attention to the fact that we can represent nothing as combined in the object without having previously combined it ourselves, and that among all representations *combination* is the only one that is not given through objects but can be executed only by the subject itself, since it is an act of its self-activity [*ein Actus seiner Selbsttätigkeit*] (*KrV* B129–130).

The understanding effects this combination of the manifold according to certain general forms of pure synthesis, namely the pure concepts of the understanding (*KrV* A78/B104). The *categories* are "concepts of an object in general, by means of which its intuition is regarded as *determined* with regard to one of the *logical functions* for judgments" (*KrV* A94/B128). For example, to the logical functions of relation (categorical, hypothetical, and disjunctive) there correspond three categories, i.e., forms of pure synthesis of intuitions in general: Inherence and Subsistence (substance and accident), Causality and Dependence (cause and effect), and Community (reciprocity between agent and patient).[82]

Crucially, Kant stresses in the B Deduction that this "combination of the understanding [*Verstandesverbindung, synthesis intellectualis*]" (*KrV* B151) *operates completely independently from sensibility*. Firstly, it is a spontaneous, original act of the understanding, a faculty that is radically separate from sensibility. Secondly, combination cannot possibly originate in sensibility: "the *combination* (*conjunctio*) of a manifold in general can never come to us through the senses, and therefore cannot already be contained in the pure form of sensible intuition" (*KrV* B129–1130).[83] Thirdly, all of the *representations* originally produced by this "intellectual synthesis without any imagination merely through the understand-

---

[82] See the first chapter of the Analytic of Concepts, "On the Clue to the Discovery of all Pure Concepts of the Understanding" (*KrV* A66 ff./B91 ff.).
[83] [*Allein die Verbindung (conjunctio) eines Mannigfaltigen überhaupt, kann niemals durch Sinne in uns kommen, und kann also auch nicht der reinen Form der sinnlichen Anschauung zugleich mitenthalten sein.*]

ing [*der intellektuellen Synthesis ohne alle Einbildungskraft bloß durch den Verstand*]" (*KrV* B152) – notably the pure concept of causality – are distinct and independent from sensible intuition: "the concept of cause itself ... is always found *a priori* in the understanding, even independently of any intuition" (*P* 4: 49; cf. *KpV* 5: 56). Fourthly, intellectual synthesis has no intrinsic link to sensible intuition as such: combination applies *a priori* to a manifold of intuition *in general*, of which *sensible* intuition is just one parameter, as it were, from a range of other types of intuition (which could conceivably include non-sensible ones) (*KrV* B153–154). Finally, while the understanding's synthesis can ultimately be applied to sensible intuition, it does not thereby lose its purely conceptual, intellectual character. In effect, the categories, generated by a purely intellectual synthesis, are *subsequently applied* to the manifold of sensible intuition by the transcendental synthesis of the imagination *on behalf of* the understanding. In contrast to the A Deduction, in the B version Kant sharply distinguishes the two forms of synthesis from each other and orders them in a definite hierarchy – the sensible synthesis of the imagination is subordinated to the intellectual synthesis of the understanding insofar as the former serves as the mere "effect [*Wirkung*]" and "application [*Anwendung*]" of the latter:

> The *synthesis* of the manifold of sensible intuition, which is possible and necessary *a priori*, can be called *figurative* (*synthesis speciosa*), as distinct from that which would be thought in the mere category in regard to the manifold of intuition in general, and which is called combination of the understanding (*synthesis intellectualis*) ... the imagination is to this extent a faculty for determining sensibility *a priori*, and its synthesis of intuitions, *in accordance with the categories*, must be the transcendental synthesis of the *imagination*, which is an effect of the understanding on sensibility and its first application to objects of intuition that is possible for us. As figurative, it is distinct from the intellectual synthesis without any imagination merely through the understanding (*KrV* B151–2).[84]

In other words, the understanding doesn't get its hands dirty, but instead delegates the application of the categories to the imagination.

---

84 [*Die Synthesis des Mannifaltigen der sinnlichen Anschauung, die a priori möglich und notwendig ist, kann figürlich (synthesis speciosa) genannt werden, zum Unterschiede von derjenigen, welche in Ansehung des Mannigfaltigen einer Anschauung überhaupt in der bloßen Kategorie gedacht würde, und Verstandesverbindung (synthesis intellectualis) heißt ... so ist die Einbildungskraft so fern ein Vermögen, die Sinnlichkeit a priori zu bestimmen, und ihre Synthesis der Anschauungen, den Kategorien gemäß, muß die transzendentale Synthesis der Einbildungskraft sein, welches eine Wirkung des Verstandes auf die Sinnlichkeit und die erste Anwendung desselben (zugleich der Grund aller übrigen) auf Gegenstände der uns möglichen Anschauung ist. Sie ist, als figürlich, von der intellektuellen Synthesis ohne alle Einbildungskraft bloß durch den Verstand unterschieden.*]

The Deduction culminates with the revolutionary idea that the understanding lays down the conditions of a *possible experience in general* and thereby acts as the "lawgiver" of nature:

> Categories are concepts that prescribe laws *a priori* to appearances, thus to nature as the sum total of all appearances (*natura materialiter spectata*) … i.e., they … determine *a priori* the combination of the manifold of nature without deriving from the latter. … all appearances of nature, as far as their combination is concerned, stand under the categories, on which nature (considered merely as nature in general) depends, as the original ground of its necessary lawfulness (as *natura formaliter spectata*) (*KrV* B163, B165)

Let me unpack the different concepts of "nature" mentioned in this dense passage:

- Nature in the *material* sense (*die Natur in materieller Bedeutung, natura materialiter spectata*) is the 'stuff' experience is made of (*P* 4: 318), namely the sum of spatio-temporal appearances.
- Nature in the *formal* sense, or formal nature (*die Natur in formeller Bedeutung, das Formale der Natur, natura formaliter spectata*) refers to the universal and necessary lawfulness of appearances in general, as articulated by the general conditions of the possibility of experience in general (the categories): "formal nature … is derived from the laws of the possibility of experience in general and is fully identical with the mere universal lawfulness of experience [*die (formale) Natur … ist mit der bloßen allgemeinen Gesetzmäßigkeit der letzteren völlig einerlei*]" (*P* 4: 319).[85]

---

[85] Since this notion will figure prominently in my exegesis (esp. section 4.1.2. below), I will quote some additional passages in which it is described: "the understanding itself is the source of the laws of nature, and thus of the formal unity of nature [*der Verstand ist selbst der Quell der Gesetze der Natur, und mithin der formalen Einheit der Natur*]" (*KrV* A127–8). "The formal in nature … is therefore the conformity to law of all objects of experience, and, insofar as this conformity is cognized a priori, the necessary conformity to law of those objects [*Das Formale der Natur … ist also die Gesetzmäßigkeit aller Gegenstände der Erfahrung und, sofern sie a priori erkannt wird, die nothwendige Gesetzmäßigkeit derselben*]" (*P* 4: 296). "How is nature possible in the formal sense, as the sum total of the rules to which all appearances must be subject if they are to be thought as connected in one experience? The answer cannot come out otherwise than: it is possible only by means of the constitution of our understanding, in accordance with which all these representations of sensibility are necessarily referred to one consciousness, and through which, first, the characteristic mode of our thinking, namely by means of rules, is possible, and then, by means of these rules, experience is possible [*Wie ist Natur in formeller Bedeutung, als der Inbegriff der Regeln, unter denen alle Erscheinungen stehen müssen, wenn sie in einer Erfahrung als verknüpft gedacht werden sollen, möglich? Die Antwort kann nicht anders ausfallen als: sie ist nur möglich vermittelst der Beschaffenheit unseres Verstandes, nach welcher alle jene Vorstellungen der Sinnlichkeit auf ein Bewußtsein nothwendig bezogen werden, und wodurch aller-*

- The concept of *nature, or order of nature, in general* (*die Natur überhaupt, die Naturordnung überhaupt*) represents the conjunction of the two, that is, the sum of all spatio-temporal appearances (material nature) under universal and necessary laws (formal nature); however, Kant sometimes uses the expression to refer to the *formal* lawfulness of nature (e.g., *KpV* 5: 43).
- Nature in general, as *possible* experience, is to be distinguished *from a particular, or determinate, nature* (*eine bestimmte Naturordnung*), i.e., a particular constellation of nature at a particular time, with particular empirical laws (*P* 4: 320).[86]

Regarding the laws of nature, Kant distinguishes between the *pure*, or *universal*, laws of a nature in general, prescribed by the understanding to nature *a priori*, and the *empirical* laws of a particular nature, which, while they necessarily conform to the universal laws of nature, must nevertheless be investigated and discovered *a posteriori* (e.g., 'Light travels at a constant speed of 299 792 458 m/s'): "There are therefore certain laws, and indeed *a priori*, which first make a nature possible; the empirical laws can only obtain and be found by means of experience, and indeed in accord with its original laws, in accordance with which experience itself becomes possible" (*KrV* A216/B263; cf. *KrV* A126–8, B165; *P* 4: 320).[87] Among the universal laws of nature, pride of place belongs to *the law of cause and effect*, which states that for every alteration that occurs in time (i.e., every event), "something *must* have preceded it, upon which it *necessarily followed, that is, it must have a cause*" (*KpV* 5: 51). Indeed, Kant will often refer to it in the singular as *the* law of nature (*das Naturgesetz*), as it is this fundamental law of the understanding that first constitutes a "nature" (in the formal sense):

> The law of nature that everything that happens has a cause [*Das Naturgesetz, daß alles, was geschieht, eine Ursache habe*], that since the causality of this cause, i.e., the *action*, precedes in time and in respect of an effect that has *arisen* cannot have been always but must have *happened*, and so must also have had its cause among appearances, through which it is determined, and consequently that all occurrences are empirically determined in a natural order – this law, through which alone appearances can first constitute one *nature* and furnish objects of one experience [*dieses Gesetz, durch welches Erscheinungen allererst eine Natur ausmachen, und Gegenstände einer Erfahrung abgeben können*], is a law of

---

erst die eigenthümliche Art unseres Denkens, nämlich durch Regeln, und vermittelst dieser die Erfahrung, welche von der Einsicht der Objecte an sich selbst ganz zu unterscheiden ist, möglich ist.]" (*P* 4: 318).

86 The latter distinction may sound odd, but it will become relevant to an interpretive point discussed below, in section 4.2.3.4.

87 Cf. Cassirer 1920, p. 37–8.

the understanding [*Verstandesgesetz*], from which under no pretext can any departure be allowed or any appearance be exempted ... (*KrV* A542/B570, B163, B165; *Prol* 4: 320).[88]

Lastly, this universal law of nature has two aspects – form and matter – analogous to the formal and material aspects of nature discussed above. As the supreme *law* of nature, its form consists in a universal and necessary rule articulated by the faculty of rules, the understanding (*KrV* A126). As a law *of nature*, its matter consists of the sum of sensible appearances (i.e., nature in the material sense).

In summary, the understanding, in its role as the law-giver of nature, spontaneously produces purely conceptual representations of universal lawfulness (*allgemeine Gesetzmäßigkeit*): the universal laws of nature, notably the law of physical causality prescribe the lawfulness of appearances in general; together, these laws make up an even more universal representation of lawfulness as such, namely formal nature, or the form of nature (*das Formale der Natur, natura formaliter spectata*) which constitute the universal and systematic lawfulness of all appearances. These representations are purely conceptual, formal, and extremely abstract, yet they can nonetheless be applied to appearances in sensible intuition by means of the schematism.

---

88 Note that Kant clearly emphasizes that this law is universal, admitting of no exceptions. See below, section 4.2.1.3.

Chapter 4.
The solution

So far, we have been analyzing the Typic chapter within a global problem structure. In Chapter 1, we identified the *task*, namely moral appraisal, which consists in subsuming particular actions under the moral law, thereby determining them as either good or evil "objects of pure practical reason." In Chapter 2, we identified *'particular difficulties'* hindering this task, namely the heterogeneity between actions in sensible intuition on the one hand and the supersensible Idea of the moral law on the other. In Chapter 3, we considered the available *resources* that might be used for overcoming these difficulties: the schema produced by the imagination, and the law of nature produced by the understanding. This examination led to the rejection of the transcendental schema, yet it also revealed a "favourable prospect" for the pure practical power of judgment: it needs a 'schema' (in a generic sense) of the moral law. We have now arrived at the *solution*, the general principle of which can be articulated in terms of the four criteria adduced above:

> Find and employ (1) a sensibly uncontaminated representation (2) of the form of universal lawfulness (3) that can mediate the subsumption of particular actions given in sensible intuition under the supersensible moral law and (4) provide a procedure for moral appraisal.

The business of this chapter, sub-divided into two main sections, is to explain Kant's strategy for overcoming the particular difficulties (4.1.) and for subsequently performing the task of moral appraisal (4.2.).

4.1 Overcoming the 'particular difficulties'

4.1.1 Type$_1$: the law of nature as the 'type' of the moral law

Kant's original strategy is to employ the law of nature as the "type [*Typus*]" of the moral law:

> Thus the moral law has no cognitive faculty other than the understanding (not the imagination) by means of which it can be applied to objects of nature, and what the understanding can put under an idea of reason is not a *schema* of sensibility but a law, such a law, however, as can be presented *in concreto* in objects of the senses and hence a law of nature, though only as to its form; this law is what the understanding can put under an idea of

reason on behalf of the power of judgment, and we can, accordingly, call it the *type* of the moral law (*KpV* 5: 69).[89]

Several "universal laws of nature" flow from the categories (*KrV* A216/B263; *P* 4: 320), but here Kant is specifically referring to *the* universal law of nature *par excellence*, namely the law of "physical causality [*die physische Causalität*]" (*KpV* 5: 68), which states that for every alteration that occurs in time (i.e., every event), "something *must* have preceded it, upon which it *necessarily followed, that is, it must have a cause*" (*KpV* 5: 51; cf. *KrV* A542/B570; *G* 4: 421). But what exactly does Kant mean by calling the law of nature the "type [*Typus*]" of the moral law? I will analyze this new, unusual term below, in section 4.1.2. For now, I will assume that the "type" is functionally equivalent to a 'schema of a law itself' as characterized above (section 3.2.) and show, on the basis of the Typic chapter, that Kant selects *the law of nature* to serve as the type of the moral law because it satisfies the corresponding four criteria.

(1) Non-sensible:
In the passage quoted above (*KpV* 5: 69), Kant clearly emphasizes that the law of nature has a non-sensible nature and origin. He underlines that the type can *only* come from the understanding, *not* from the imagination. Correspondingly, the "type" that the understanding supplies is "not a *schema* of sensibility but a law [*nicht ein Schema der Sinnlichkeit, sondern ein Gesetz*]" (*KpV* 5: 69). And as we have seen, the universal law of nature is a pure product of intellectual synthesis, free of sensible contamination – just as required by the first criterion.

(2) The form of lawfulness:
The law of nature has a form and a matter. Its *form* prescribes universal conformity to the law of causality and thereby functions as the constitutive unifying principle of nature's formal lawfulness (*natura formaliter spectata*) (*KrV* A227–228/B280).[90] Its *matter* consists of the entities that it governs, namely the sum of sen-

---

[89] [*Folglich hat das Sittengesetz kein anderes die Anwendung desselben auf Gegenstände der Natur vermittelndes Erkenntnißvermögen, als den Verstand (nicht die Einbildungskraft), welcher einer Idee der Vernunft nicht ein Schema der Sinnlichkeit, sondern ein Gesetz, aber doch ein solches, das an Gegenständen der Sinne in concreto dargestellt werden kann, mithin ein Naturgesetz, aber nur seiner Form nach, als Gesetz zum Behuf der Urtheilskraft unterlegen kann, und dieses können wir daher den Typus des Sittengesetzes nennen.*]
[90] As explained above, in section 3.3.

sible appearances (i.e., material nature, *natura materialiter spectata*). In the passage just quoted, Kant explicitly appeals to this distinction, specifying that the type is "a law of nature, though only as to its form [*ein Naturgesetz, aber nur seiner Form nach*]" (*KpV* 5: 69). From that point onwards in the Typic chapter, he repeatedly specifies that *only the law of nature's form serves as a type of the moral law:* he refers to "the form of a law of nature in general [*der Form eines Naturgesetzes überhaupt*]" (*KpV* 5: 70) and the "formal rule of a law of nature in general [*der formalen Regel eines Naturgesetzes überhaupt*]" (*KpV* 5: 71). Thus, the form of the law of nature provides an impeccable representation of the form of universal lawfulness – and that is exactly what the second criterion calls for.

(3) Mediation ('typification'):
Kant selects the law of nature as the type of the moral law in order to serve as a 'third thing' or 'schema' (in the broad sense) for mediating between the supersensible representation of the moral law and the sensible representations of actions – just as the third criterion requires.

On the one hand, the law of nature considered 'only as to its form' is a sensibly uncontaminated representation of universal lawfulness, and to that extent it is compatible with the supersensible representation of the moral law, which also contains the form of universal lawfulness (*G* 4: 401–402, 420–421; *KpV* 5: 29, 33). In this respect, the two laws are *formally analogous* to each other in spite of the radical metaphysical difference between their respective "determining grounds," namely natural causality and free causality, respectively: "for to this extent laws as such are the same, no matter where they derive their determining grounds from [*Denn Gesetze als solche sind so fern einerlei, sie mögen ihre Bestimmungsgründe hernehmen, woher sie wollen*]" (*KpV* 5: 70).[91]

On the other hand, situating the type at such a high level of abstraction and universality raises the question: Can the type be brought back down to earth and applied to particular actions (*qua* events) represented in sensible intuition? As a law *of nature*, it can indeed, for as such its applicability to sensible intuition is guaranteed by the schematism (as was already established in the first *Critique*): "To a natural law ... there must correspond a schema, that is, a universal procedure of the imagination (by which it presents a priori to the senses the pure concept of the understanding which the law determines) [*Dem Naturgesetze als Gesetze ... muß ein Schema, d.i. ein allgemeines Verfahren der Einbildungskraft (den reinen Verstandesbegriff, den das Gesetz bestimmt, den Sinnen a priori darzustell-*

---

[91] I spell out this analogy in Ch. 7, section 4.2.

en), correspondiren]" (*KpV* 5: 69). Accordingly, if Kant selects the law of nature to serve as a type for the moral law, it is because he needs "a law ... [that] can be presented *in concreto* in objects of the senses and hence a law of nature [*ein Gesetz, aber doch ein solches, das an Gegenständen der Sinne in concreto dargestellt werden kann, mithin ein Naturgesetz*]" (*KpV* 5: 69). Correspondingly, all actions given in sensibility can be subsumed under the type "as a law to which objects of sensible intuition as such are subject [*als Gesetze, welchem die Gegenstände sinnlicher Anschauung als solche unterworfen sind*]" (*KpV* 5: 69).

Thus, the form of the law of nature occupies an intermediary position as a 'third thing' between the supersensible moral law and actions *qua* events in sensible intuition. The *process of mediation*, which I will call "typification," occurs in two stages:

1. The form of the law of nature is analogically *substituted for* the supersensible moral law, as its type.
2. The type is then applied, via the schematism, to actions given in sensible intuition, all of which *eo ipso* fall under the law of nature.

In this way, actions are subsumed under a formal rule that serves as an adequate *proxy* for the moral law's demand of conformity to universal law; conversely, the supersensible moral law receives a *Darstellung* without a (direct) *Versinnlichung*, insofar as it is applied to concrete cases through the mediation of a pure, formal representation produced by the understanding.[92]

(4) A procedure for moral appraisal:

Finally, Kant maintains that employing the law of nature as the type of the moral law provides an effective *procedure* for moral appraisal – just as required by the fourth criterion. The law of nature functions as a formal standard for testing the universalizability of maxims through a *thought experiment* in which one asks oneself if one could will one's maxim to become a universal law of a counterfactual nature to which one would belong oneself (*KpV* 5: 69–70). This procedure for evaluating maxims is complex and controversial, however, so I will treat it separately in section 4.2. But first, I propose to examine a second formulation of the type in order to extend and clarify the interpretation proposed here.

---

[92] This point is well explained in Renaut 1997, p. 308 ff.

4.1.2 Type₂: *Natura formaliter spectata* as the type of supersensible nature

In a seldom noticed passage of the Typic chapter, Kant states that "it is also permitted to use the nature of the sensible world as the type of an intelligible nature [*Es ist also auch erlaubt, die Natur der Sinnenwelt als Typus einer intelligiblen Natur zu brauchen*]" (*KpV* 5: 70). The expression "it is *also* permitted" at the head of a fresh paragraph, signals a separate, additional element in Kant's exposition. And as Marty has aptly pointed out, this second formulation of the type is significantly *more general* than the first: here, the "nature" of the sensible world as a whole is a type of the "nature" of the intelligible world as a whole, whereas the first formulation of the type involves only *a single law* – the law of nature – serving as the type for the (one and only) moral law.[93] Thus it appears that Kant in fact introduces a *second formulation of the type,* or even a *second type* (henceforth "Type₂"), in addition to the law of nature (henceforth "Type₁"). Here I offer an exegetical account of the source, nature, and function of Type₂, which I then compare with other interpretations in the secondary literature.

4.1.2.1 The source of Type₂

This second, more general type relates directly to an earlier passage from the "Deduction of the Principles of Pure Practical Reason" in which Kant characterizes the moral vocation of human beings. In this rich and quintessentially Kantian passage, we are told that the moral law commands us, as finite rational beings, to impart the world in which we live and act – i.e., sensible nature – with the form of a purely intelligible moral order – i.e., supersensible nature:

> This law [i.e., the moral law – A.W.] is to furnish the sensible world, as a *sensible nature* ... with the form of a world of the understanding, that is, of a *supersensible* nature ... Now, nature in the most general sense is the existence of things under laws. ... The supersensible nature of [rational] beings ... is their existence in accordance with laws that are independent of any empirical condition and thus belong to the *autonomy* of pure reason. ... This law of autonomy, however, is the moral law, which is therefore the fundamental law of a supersensible nature and of a pure world of the understanding, the counterpart of which is to exist in the sensible world but without infringing upon its laws. The former could be called the *archetypal world* (*natura archetypa*) which we cognize only in reason, whereas the latter could be called the *ectypal world* (*natura ectypa*) because it contains the possible effect of the idea of the former as the determining ground of the will (*KpV* 5: 43).

---

[93] Marty 1997, p. 252.

This passage is the only place in the *Critique of Practical Reason* where Kant employs a vocabulary that bears a direct etymological relation to the key terms "*Typus*" and "*Typik*": here, Kant speaks of a "*natura archetypa*" and a "*natura ectypa*" (*KpV* 5: 43). It is significant that Kant felt the need to supply these *Fremdwörter* in addition to their German counterparts ("*urbildliche Welt*" and "*nachgebildete Welt*"), for it suggests that he deemed them necessary for his philosophical purposes.[94] Indeed, the words themselves tell an illuminating story. While Kant indicates the terms in Latin, the family of words related to *Typus* originally stems from ancient Greek. Kant was doubtless aware of this fact, for if there was one valuable thing that he acquired as a youth from his despised school in Königsberg, the *Collegium Fredericianum*, it was an excellent command of the ancient languages, including ancient and Biblical Greek. Originally, the ancient Greek word "*túpos*" (τύπος), deriving from the verb forms meaning 'to strike' (τύπτω) or 'to stamp' (τυπόω), had three related meanings: (1) that which stamps, impresses, or imprints; (2) that which is stamped, impressed or imprinted; and (3) the relationship between two things.[95] After the classical period, the more univocal composite words 'archetype' (*archetupos*, ἀρχέτυπος) and 'ectype' (*ectupos*, ἔκτυπος) were coined to denote, respectively, (1) the original, impressing model and (2) the shape that is imprinted or copied.[96] Although these coinages did not entirely supplant the wide application of 'type', they did allow its third sense to emerge more sharply, as from then on 'type' *tout court* could be used to refer more precisely to what the arche-*type* and the ec-*type* have in common, namely (3) a shared relation, pattern, outline, or form (without

---

[94] Compare, for instance, Kant's remarks in the *Critique of Pure Reason* on the importance of the original (Platonic) meaning of the term "Idea" (*KrV* A312ff./B369ff.). In addition, scholars have brought out the deep conceptual and philosophical import of other deliberately employed non-Germanic words such as "*Deduction*" and "*Factum*" in their respective contexts – see Henrich 1989; Kleingeld 2010.

[95] "Die Bezeichnung [Typus] geht auf griech. týpos zurück; im profanen wie im biblischen griechischen Sprachgebrauch verweist sie auf das Prägende (Prägestempel, Prägeform, Vorlage) wie auf das Geprägte (Siegelabdruck, Prägung, Kopie, Münzbild, Gestalt, Form, Muster), also (auch) auf eine Beziehung zwischen zwei Dingen" – see "Typologie" 2009, p. 843.

[96] "Im Griechischen von τύπτω 'schlagen' bzw. τυπόω 'prägen' abgeleitet, bedeutet Typus im handwerklich-künstlerischen Bereich die 'prägende Form' (Hohlform, Skizze) wie das 'Geprägte (Relief, Statue, eingravierter Buchstabe, allgemein auch 'Abdruck', z.B. eines Siegelringes oder Münzstempels. Weiter finden sich die Bedeutungen 'Umriß', 'Gestalt', 'Form' und 'Art'. Als 'Vorbild' und 'Muster' steht T[ypus] dem Begriff παράδειγμα ('Paradigma') nahe und wird im nachklassischen Zeit meist durch die in diesem Sinne eindeutigeren Komposita ἀρχέτυπος ('Archetyp') oder πρωτότυπος ('Protoyp') ersetzt. Als 'Abbild' tritt T[ypus] wie ἔκτυπος ('Ektyp')" – see "Typos; Typologie" 1998, p. 1587.

the matter).⁹⁷ I want to suggest that these three root meanings respectively inform Kant's concepts of an "archetypal nature (*natura archetypa*)," "ectypal nature (*natura ectypa*)," and "type (*Typus*)."

4.1.2.2 The nature of Type₂
In Kant, the expressions "*natura archetypa*" and "*natura ectypa*" designate a correlative pair of concepts, each of which is a hybrid, so to speak, containing both ontological and moral elements. Kant characterizes the intelligible world as an "archetypal nature (*natura archetypa*)": it constitutes a *nature* "in the most general sense [of] the existence of things under laws" insofar as all rational denizens of the noumenal realm are governed by the law of autonomy (*KpV* 5: 43); and it represents a pure rational *archetype* of moral order that is to be copied in the sensible world. Correlatively, Kant characterizes the sensible world as an "ectypal nature (*natura ectypa*)": it constitutes an ordered, lawful *nature* insofar as all spatio-temporal objects within it obey the law of natural causality; and from a practical point of view, it can be regarded as an *ectype* insofar as it represents a potential 'counterpart' or 'copy' (*Gegenbild*) of the archetypal moral cosmos – or, as Kant puts it, "because it contains the possible effect of the idea of [archetypal nature] as the determining ground of the will." Introducing these two concepts allows Kant to articulate the practical vocation of finite rational beings as the task of instituting a systematic moral order here on Earth, which amounts to copying, or as it were 'imprinting', the *universal lawful form* of supersensible nature onto sensible nature by systematically performing morally good actions.

Kant does not introduce Type₂ in the Deduction passage (*KpV* 5: 43), but only later, in the Typic chapter proper (*KpV* 5: 70). Assuming that the Typic chapter is to the second *Critique* what the Schematism chapter is to the first *Critique*, we can expect Type₂ to be a special representation that will mediate between, on the one hand, the *representation* of "archetypal nature" *as a supersensible Idea* produced by reason, and on the other hand, the *representation* of "ectypal nature" *as the sum of sensible intuitions* that compose phenomenal experience. In other words, we are looking for a 'schema' – in a generic, functional sense – that can form a bridge between two heterogeneous representations (cf. *KpV* 5: 68).

Type₂ is the understanding's representation of the pure form of nature, or *natura formaliter spectata* (*KpV* 5: 70). This corresponds to the narrow sense of the

---

97 Liddell and Scott 1996, p. 1835, list "form," "pattern" and "outline" as meanings of the term.

word "*túpos*" in ancient Greek as the *abstract form* shared by the arche-*type* and ec-*type*. Indeed, what supersensible nature and sensible nature share, in spite of their specific differences, is *the form of "nature" itself* (*natura formaliter spectata*): "Natural (*formaliter*) means what follows necessarily according to laws of a certain order of whatever sort, hence under the moral order as well as the physical order" (*ED* 8: 333n, trans. mod.).[98] In other words, nature in a formal sense is "the form of universal lawfulness in general" (*P* 4: 318–320; *G* 4: 37), and therefore it inheres in both supersensible nature and sensible nature *qua* representations of 'nature' i.e., insofar as each constitutes a lawful and ordered universe (albeit in different spheres). And it just so happens that we already possess a representation of this formal lawfulness *a priori*, since, as established in the *Critique of Pure Reason*, the form of nature is produced transcendentally by the understanding (*KrV* B163, B165). Thus "reason is entitled and even required to use nature (in the understanding's pure form of nature) [*die Natur (der reinen Verstandesform derselben nach)*] as the type of judgment" (*KpV* 5: 70, my emphasis). This abstract conceptual form is shared by – and can thereby mediate between – the supersensible representation of archetypal nature and the sensible representation of ectypal nature, as shown here:

---

natura archetypa
"supersensible nature [*die übersinnliche Natur*]"
(i.e., the rational Idea of a perfect moral order in the intelligible realm)
natura 'rationaliter' spectata
|
Type$_2$
"nature (in the understanding's pure form of nature)
[*die Natur (der reinen Verstandesform derselben nach)*]"
(i.e., the purely conceptual form of lawfulness in general
prescribed to experience by the understanding)
natura formaliter spectata
|
natura ectypa
"sensible nature [*die sinnliche Natur*]"
(i.e., nature as the sum of sensible intuitions & schematized categories)
natura materialiter spectata

It is indeed this *formal* representation of nature that Kant has in mind when he states in the Typic chapter that the power of judgment can "use *the nature of the*

---

98 [Natürlich (*formaliter*) heißt, was nach Gesetzen einer gewißen Ordnung, welche es auch sei, mithin auch der moralischen (also nicht immer bloß der physischen) nothwendig folgt.]

sensible world as the *type* of an *intelligible nature*" (*KpV* 5: 70). The formulation is confusing: at first sight, "the nature of the sensible world" seems to correspond to "sensible nature" rather than to the "understanding's pure form of nature"; however, this would imply that sensible nature is at once the type *and* the ectype of archetypal nature, which is absurd. Despite their similarity, the expressions "sensible nature" and "nature of the sensible world" are not in fact synonymous in this context. On the one hand, "sensible nature [*die sinnliche Natur*]" designates the sum of sensible intuitions and schematized categories making up phenomenal experience and which Kant calls "nature in the material sense" or "*natura materialiter spectata*" (*P* 4: 318); it is the ectype vis-à-vis archetypal nature. On the other hand, the "nature *of* the sensible world [*die Natur* der *Sinnenwelt*]" designates "the understanding's pure form of nature," i.e., the pure "form of lawfulness in general" (*KpV* 5: 70) which the understanding *thinks into* sensible nature *a priori* and which the power of judgment then *extracts from* sensible nature in order to use it as a type: "the power of judgment […] *takes from sensible nature* nothing more than what pure reason can also think for itself, that is, *conformity with law,* [von der sinnlichen Natur *nichts weiter* nimmt, als was auch reine Vernunft für sich denken kann, d.i. die Gesetzmäßigkeit] and transfers [it] into the supersensible" (*KpV* 5: 71).[99]

What *kind* of representation is Type$_2$? *Natura formaliter spectata* is a formal matrix composed of all the *a priori* rules (laws) of possible experience; it is a fabric woven from purely conceptual threads (*P* 4: 318). Type$_2$ is thus an abstract, formal, and purely conceptual representation produced by the intellectual synthesis (*synthesis intellectualis*) (*KrV* B151) of the understanding – "a non-sensory faculty of cognition" (*KrV* A67–8/B92). As such, it belongs to the same representational genus as Type$_1$, which is a pure *Verstandesgesetz* (*KrV* A542/B570). And while in this respect Type$_2$ is extremely abstract, Kant emphasizes that the form of lawfulness in general is nevertheless a concept that "occurs even in the most common use of reason" (*KpV* 5: 70). The original representation of the form of lawfulness is not abstracted from experience through conscious inquiry, but is rather a transcendental condition of the possibility of experience and can therefore be presupposed *a priori* in every normal subject.

In summary, Type$_2$ is an *a priori*, purely conceptual representation of the abstract form of nature's universal lawfulness, which is the pattern, or "type," shared by the representations of archetypal nature and ectypal nature.

---

99 Cf. Renaut 1997, p. 309.

4.1.2.3 The function of Type$_2$

To recall, we expect the type to perform a function analogous to that of the schema, i.e., mediating between heterogeneous representations, with the difference that the type should mediate between *Ideas* and intuitions rather than between *categories* and intuitions. Like Type$_1$, Type$_2$ performs its mediating function through a process that I term *typification*, whereby a conceptual representation of the understanding is "transferred" or "transposed" (*übertragen*) between supersensible Ideas and sensible intuitions despite their representational heterogeneity, as explained in the Typic chapter:

> Hence it is also permitted to use *the nature of the sensible world* as the *type* of an *intelligible nature*, provided that I do not carry over into the latter intuitions and what depends on them but refer to it merely the *form of lawfulness* in general (the concept of which occurs even in the most common use of reason ... For to this extent laws as such are the same, no matter where they derive their determining grounds from. ... [T]he power of judgment ... takes from sensible nature nothing more than what pure reason can also think for itself, that is, conformity with law [*Gesetzmäßigkeit*], and transfers into the supersensible nothing but what can, conversely, be really exhibited by actions in the sensible world in accordance with a formal rule of a law of nature in general (*KpV* 5: 70 – 71, trans. mod.).

On the one hand, in virtue of its purity as a non-sensible, conceptual representation of formal lawfulness, Type$_2$ can be referred to the supersensible Idea of *natura archetypa* without contaminating it; Type$_2$ thereby gives us a conceptual grasp of the formal architecture of the archetypal world and hence of a lawful moral order while preserving the purity of the supersensible Idea. On the other hand, Type$_2$ is compatible with the sensible representation of ectypal nature: *natura formaliter spectata*, as the blueprint of the *a priori* laws of sensible nature, *can be schematized within sensible experience*, as the first *Critique* proved, and can thus be applied to all actions and agents within it. In addition, because Type$_2$ is a produced representation produced *a priori* by the understanding, it is available to everyone: "This is how even the most common understanding judges [*so urtheilt selbst der gemeinste Verstand*]" (*KpV* 5: 70). Thus Type$_2$ allows a presentation without sensible rendering, or a '*Darstellung* without *Versinnlichung*', of the supersensible moral order while guarding against the dangers of "empiricism" and "mysticism," which unduly sensibilize this Idea (*KpV* 5: 70 – 71).[100]

Also like Type$_1$, Type$_2$ ultimately enables *a specifically practical task*, yet the latter's function is more general than the former's. Type$_1$ provides a precise procedure for morally appraising concrete actions one at a time by means of a

---

[100] Cf. Renaut 1997, p. 309 – 310.

thought-experiment that tests whether each individual maxim could be universalized as a law of nature (*KpV* 5: 69).[101] Type$_2$'s function is more general, even holistic – it serves as a regulative "pattern [*Muster*]" for moral appraisal, deliberation and action by facilitating the coordination of maxims in general:

> ... [W]e are conscious through reason of a law to which all our maxims are subject, as if a natural order must at the same time arise from our will. This law must therefore be the idea of a nature not given empirically and yet possible through freedom, hence a supersensible nature ... The most ordinary attention to oneself confirms that this idea is really, as it were, a sketch of the *pattern* for the determinations of our will [*Daß diese Idee wirklich unseren Willensbestimmungen gleichsam als Vorzeichnung zum Muster liege*] (*KpV* 5: 44, trans. mod.).

In other words, employing *natura formaliter spectata* as the type of a perfect moral order allows the moral agent to anticipate the form that all of her own maxims, and indeed everyone's maxims taken together, ought to collectively constitute: a system that has "the form of nature," i.e., a system that is unified, ordered, and lawful (*gesetzmäßig*). And this, Kant avers, functions as a reliable and recognizable guide judging the universalizability of maxims in general.

4.1.2.4 Type$_2$ in the secondary literature
I will now compare my interpretation of Type$_2$ with some other accounts that have been proposed in the secondary literature. Type$_2$ has been variously characterized as a *sensible image* or *symbol*, as a *teleological realm*, as the *intelligible world* per se, and as a *fiction*.

a) Type$_2$ as a "sensible image" or "symbol"
My interpretation of Type$_2$ as a pure, formal, and abstract representation goes against the thesis put forward by some scholars, notably Susan Shell, that the term "*Typus*" here signifies a 'sensible image' (*Sinnbild*). Shell bases her gloss on the etymology of Kant's term:

> The typic expresses the abstract and objective moral law in terms subjectively concrete and comprehensible. Like the *túpos* or stamp, which translates force into image, the typic translates the moral law, which 'forces itself' on our consciousness, into a figure we can 'see' or 'imagine' (*einbilden*) ... [t]he archetype (*Urbild*) and ectype (*Nachbild*) are connected by a kind of visible construction (*Bild*).[102]

---

101 See below, section 4.2.1.4.
102 Shell 1980, p. 82, 86.

However, the suggestion that Kant's type is a picture, or image, that we can "imagine (*einbilden*)" is directly contradicted by the text of the Typic chapter, which clearly states that "the moral law has no cognitive faculty other than the understanding (not the imagination) [*nicht die Einbildungskraft*] by means of which it can be applied to objects of nature" (*KpV* 5: 69). Moreover, Shell's etymological gloss of the term "*Typus*" as a stamp or image (*Bild*) is too concrete: as we have seen, in ancient Greek the word "*túpos*" already admitted of a more *abstract* sense of a shared formal relation between two terms. In the context of the *Critique of Practical Reason*, it is all the more necessary to recognize that what Kant calls a "type" is not literally, or even metaphorically, a physical object or image, but rather a *representation of an abstract relational structure* (i. e., 'the form of lawfulness in general').

In a similar vein, Paton proposed that Kant's term "type" be understood as a particular kind of *Sinnbild*, namely the kind of symbolic prefiguration that has played such an important role in Scriptural exegesis.[103] In his interpretation of the Typic chapter, he observes: "The word 'type' is commonly used in theology in more or less the same way as Kant uses the word 'symbol': it is that by which something is symbolised or figured. Thus the people of Israel are said to be a type of God's people, and the Paschal lamb is said to be a type of Christ. Kant's application of the word to the law of nature is a natural extension of this usage."[104] It should be clear by now, however, that the two contexts could not be more different. Kant's technical philosophical usage of the term "*Typus*" to denote an austere, formal representation produced by the understanding's intellectual synthesis is anything but a "natural extension" of Biblical symbolism.[105] More generally, although the interpretation of the type as a symbol

---

103 "*Die idee in concreto ist das Urbild in rationalem Verstande. Die Regel in concreto ist das Beyspiel. Das analogon des Urbildes ist das Sinnbild (typus), das des Beyspiels ist Gleichnis.*" (*Refl* 4983, 18: 51).
104 Paton 1947, p. 160.
105 The difference becomes immediately clear when one considers some concrete examples of the nature and function of typology in Scriptural exegesis: "The Church fathers often justify figural interpretation on the basis of certain passages in early Christian writings, mostly from the Pauline Epistles. The most important of these is I Cor. 10:6 and 11, where the Jews in the desert are termed *typoi hemon* ("figures of ourselves"), and where it is written that *tauta de typikos synebainen ekeinois* ("these things befell them as figures"). Another passage often adduced is Gal. 4:21–31, where Paul explains to the freshly baptized Galatians, who, still under the influence of Judaism, wished to be circumcised, the difference between law and grace, the old and the new covenant, servitude and freedom, by the example of Hagar-Ishmael and Sarah-Isaac, linking the narrative in Genesis with Is. 54:1 and interpreting it in terms of figural prophecy. Still others are Col. 2:16f., saying that the Jewish dietary laws and holidays are only the shadow

is relatively popular among commentators, it has serious flaws, as I argue more extensively in Chapter 6.

b) Type₂ as a teleological "realm"

Many scholars, starting with Paton, have given Type₂ a teleological gloss. Based on the *Groundwork*, they identify "intelligible nature" with the "kingdom of ends [*Reich der Zwecke*]" whose counterpart – read: type – is the "kingdom of nature [*Reich der Natur*]" (*G* 4: 438 f.). For example, Ernst Cassirer writes: "But the 'nature' meant here [in the Typic chapter – A.W.] is not the sensuous existence of objects, but the systematic interrelation of individual ends and their harmonious composition in a 'final end.' It is a model, a type, against which we measure every particular determination of the will ..."[106] Indeed, some scholars have gone so far as to argue that *only* a teleological interpretation of the Typic chapter is tenable.[107]

This interpretation is problematic, however. On the one hand, the *kingdom of nature* is a teleological conception of nature as a harmonious and hierarchical whole (*G* 4: 436n) "insofar as and because it has reference to rational beings as its ends" (*G* 4: 438); the *kingdom of ends* is conceived, by analogy, as a lawful and harmonious noumenal community of rational beings *qua* ends in themselves, united under God, conceived as a "sovereign [*Oberhaupt*]" (*G* 4: 438 – 9). On the other hand, neither teleological hierarchies nor anything like a "sovereign" have any place whatsoever in "the understanding's pure form of nature," (*KpV* 5: 70) which is merely the abstract conceptual representation of lawful order that the understanding – the faculty of *rules*, not of *ends* – imposes on phenomenal experience *a priori:* "The understanding ... in its transcendental legislation for nature ... takes into consideration *only* the conditions of the possibility of an experience in general *as far as its form is concerned*" (*EEKU* 20: 210, my

---

of things to come, whereas the body is Christ; Rom. 5:12 ff. and I Cor. 15:21, where Adam appears as the *typos* of the future Christ, and grace is opposed to the law; II Cor. 3:13, which speaks of the veil (*kalymnos*) that covers the Scritpure when the Jews read it; and finally Heb. 8:11 ff., where the sacrifice of Christ's blood is represented as the fulfillment of the high priest's sacrifice in the Old Testament." Auerbach 1984, p. 49 – 50.

106 Cassirer 1987, p. 259; Cassirer 2001, p. 250. See also Beck 1960, p. 158 – 160; Bielefeldt 2003, p. 181 f.; Cohen 1910, p. 277; Grondin 2000, p. 394; Shell 1980, p. 88.

107 Aune 1979, p. 51 ff.; Konhardt 1979, p. 295 ff.; Paton 1947, p. 149 ff. By contrast, Lewis White Beck proposes a more moderate version of the teleological interpretation in Beck 1960, p. 154 – 163.

emphasis).[108] Kant reiterated this point in a letter to his friend Jacob Sigismund Beck, where he took pains to emphasize that Type$_2$ *abstracts* from everything except the mere form of lawfulness of a natural order in general: "But there is in that type only *the form of a natural order in general*, that is, the contexture of actions as events under *moral laws* just as under natural laws *qua* universal [*Aber es ist in jenem Typus nur die Form einer Naturordnung überhaupt d.i. der Zusammenhang der Handlungen als Begebenheiten nach sittlichen Gesetzen gleich als Naturgesetzen blos ihrer Allgemeinheit nach*]."[109] Finally, the teleological interpretation of Type$_2$'s mediating function turns out to be incoherent even on its own terms. If archetypal nature and Type$_2$ are both conceived as teleological representations produced by reason, then *ipso facto* they must share *the very same rational order* – but then, they appear to be indistinguishable. This problem becomes especially evident in Aune's gloss, which begins as follows:

> The laws of freedom define a possible 'order' of rational wills. As imperfectly rational natural beings, our only available *model* for such a rational order is nature 'as regards its form', that is, as a system of natural laws. These natural laws are to be understood teleologically: they describe a world in which each element has a natural place or function and in which everything that happens contributes to some supreme end.... In conceiving of nature this way we are imposing a rational order on it; we are conceiving it as a fundamentally rational system. As so conceived, the formal structure of natural laws is not just analogous to the formal structure of rational laws: the formal structure is the *same* in both cases.[110]

Then, in an endnote appended to this passage, Aune recognizes that this way of interpreting the text is problematic: "A problem worth thinking about arises here: If we need the typic for the moral law because we have no direct access to the domain of perfectly rational beings, how can Kant's typic, which requires us to view nature as a rational system, possibly be comprehensible to us?"[111] In other words, by construing the Type$_2$ as *identical* with what it is supposed to typify, i.e., supersensible nature, the teleological interpretation makes the typic seem useless.

---

108 Incidentally, Kant's explicit identification of Type$_2$ with "*the understanding's* pure form of nature" directly contradicts Konhardt's argument that the "form of lawfulness" in question is a teleological representation proper to the *power of judgment*; see Konhardt 1979, p. 297.
109 Letter to Jacob Sigismund Beck, 3 July 1792 (11: 348, trans. mod.).
110 Aune 1979, p. 58–60.
111 Aune 1979, p. 204n.

c) Type₂ as "intelligible" nature

We encounter a similar conflation of type and archetype in Grondin's interpretation of the Typic. While Grondin correctly identifies Type₂ as *natura formaliter spectata*, he goes on to identify this *intellectual representation* produced by the understanding with the *intelligible world* on the basis of the ostensible synonymy of the expressions "*Verstandeswelt*," "*intelligible Welt*" and "*intellectuelle Welt*."[112] This leads Grondin to declare that Kant's typic is otiose: if the type is an 'intelligible nature' infinitely remote from sensibility, then we would need an additional typic for employing it.[113] Grondin then goes on to propose that the typic's "great renunciation" to mediate the moral law must give way to an alternative, "phenomenological" mode of presentation, namely the mystical experience of "awe [*Ehrfurcht*]" inspired by "the miracle of moral elevation above and beyond the sensible world [*das Wunder der sittlichen Erhebung über das Sinnliche hinaus*]."[114]

However, the terms "intellectual [*intellectuell*]" and "intelligible [*intelligible*]" are not in fact synonymous. In the passage cited by Grondin, Kant does seem to use the terms in a loose way (*G* 4: 451 ff.), yet in other passages (including one from the second edition of the *Critique of Pure Reason*, written only a year before the Typic), Kant carefully distinguishes them: "For the *cognitions* through the understanding are *intellectual* [*intellektuell*], and the same sort of cognitions also refer to our sensible world; but *intelligible* [*intelligibel*] means *objects* insofar as they can be represented *only through the understanding*, and none of our sensory intuitions can refer to them" (*P* 4: 316n; cf. *KrV* B312n.). Accordingly, the understanding's *intellectual* representation of nature (*natura formaliter spectata*) is *not* identical with the *intelligible* world, and therefore the alleged uselessness of the type does not follow. Type₂ is not an infinitely remote *intelligible* object, but rather an *intellectual* representation which can "also refer to our sensible world" (as the a priori form of its universal lawfulness); indeed, this representation "occurs even in the most common use of reason" (*KpV* 5: 70).

---

112 Grondin 2000, p. 393–394.
113 "Hat die Typik ihre Aufgabe einer Vermittlung zwischen dem Sittengesetz und der Sinnenwelt schließlich gelöst? Im Grunde genommen: Nein, aber in diesem großartigen Verzicht ist die Typik vielleicht doch ihrem unmöglichen Ziel nähergekommen. Nein, entschieden nein, weil sie eine "Vermittlung", wie sie der Schematismus der Einbildungskraft leistete, zwischen der Vernunft und dem "Empirischen" auf keinen Fall zuwege gebracht hat. Durch die Typik und ihre Verstandesvorstellung eines intelligiblen Reiches der Zwecke, die nicht von dieser Welt sind, wurde vielleicht das sittliche Gesetz sogar in eine noch weitere, kaum nochvollziehbare Ferne gerückt. Denn: Wie kann ich mir eine 'intelligible Natur' vorstellen? Auch dafür bedürfte es wohl einer weiteren Typik." Grondin 2000, p. 394.
114 Grondin 2000, p. 394.

d) Type₂ as a "fiction"

In the early twentieth century, the renowned and controversial Kant scholar Hans Vaihinger devoted a substantial part of his *Philosophie des Als-Ob* to adducing ostensible textual evidence that the philosophy of the great Kant was rife with *fictions*, i.e., ideas that we treat *as if* they were true or real even though we know – or *ought* to know, hence the urgency of Vaihinger's message – that they are actually false or impossible. Naturally, Vaihinger pounced on the occurrences of the expression "as if" in and around the Typic chapter, triumphantly declaring that Kant's doctrine that the sensible world serves as the type of intelligible nature proves the latter to be a *fiction*.[115] Famously, Vaihinger's appropriation of Kant so outraged his fellow scholar Erich Adickes that the latter devoted an entire book to decrying and redressing Vaihinger's "fictionalist violation [*fiktionalistische Vergewaltigung*]" of the critical philosophy.[116] Significantly, of the countless passages tendentiously intepreted by Vaihinger, Adickes regarded the Typic as one of the most egregious examples.[117] As Adickes never tired of pointing out throughout his extensive critique, not every occurrence of the expression "as if" in the Kantian corpus denotes a *fiction* in the peculiar sense of Vaihinger's 'as-if' philosophy.[118] And Adickes denounced this philological "sleight of hand [*Kunstgriff*]" in Vaihinger's gloss of the Typic chapter: Kant of course never said – and never would have said – that we are "*only* members of the sensible world" and that we therefore merely fool ourselves into regarding ourselves only "as if" we belonged to a higher order; on the contrary, Kant asserts in many places that the intelligible world *exists*, that we *are* indeed mem-

---

[115] "… die "übersinnliche Natur" besteht eben dann rein nur aus den tatsächlich vorhandenen Willenssubjekten, welche, nach jenem Prinzip der Allgemeinheit zu handeln, entschlossen sind und sich als konstituierende Bürger einer Geisterwelt "betrachten", "ansehen", d.h. so tun, handeln, denken und fühlen, *als ob* sie Glieder einer übersinnlichen Ordnung wären. In diesem Sinne sind wir "gesetzgebende Glieder eines durch Freiheit möglichen, durch praktische Vernunft uns zur Achtung vorgestellten Reiches der Sitten", in diesem Sinne und nur in diesem Sinne "widerfährt uns durch eine reine praktische Vernunft vermittelst des moralischen Gesetzes die Eröffnung einer intelligiblen Welt durch Realisierung des sonst transzendenten Begriffs der Freiheit", d.h. wir handeln, *als ob* wir frei wären, und indem wir durch diese *Idee der Freiheit* unseren Willen bestimmen, fühlen wir uns, als ob wir, trotzdem wir nur Glieder der sinnlichen Welt sind, Glieder einer höheren Ordnung der Dinge wären. In diesem Sinne "betrachtet sich die handelnde Person als Noumenon." Vaihinger 1922, p. 655.
[116] Adickes 1927, p. 169.
[117] "An der wichtigsten von [den von Vaihinger verfiktionalisierten – A.W.] Stellen ist die Interpretation eine so ungeheurliche, daß sie auch nicht einmal den schwächsten Schein eines Rechts für sich in Anspruch nehmen kann. Sie steht in dem Abschnitt "Von der Typik der reinen praktischen Urteilskraft." Adickes 1927, p. 193.
[118] Adickes 1927, p. 17 f.

bers of it and that we can even positively *cognize* its fundamental law. In short, we can agree with Adickes that Vaihinger's construal of intelligible nature as a mere fiction is a theory-driven distortion of Kant's text.

In summary, the difficulties of the above-mentioned interpretations lead to the conclusion that Type$_2$ should not be characterized as a sensible image, a symbol, a teleological hierarchy, the intelligible world per se, or a fiction. Instead, Type$_2$ should be conceived as the abstract form shared by *natura archetypa* and *natura ectypa*, namely the understanding's purely conceptual representation of nature's universal lawfulness (*natura formaliter spectata*). Type$_2$ mediates between reason's Idea of a supersensible 'nature' under the law of freedom and the sensible nature in which we live and act, thereby providing a regulative horizon for our moral vocation that heeds the strictures of Kant's critical rationalism. More generally, I will suggest in the Conclusion that the Typic marks a decisive stage in the evolution of Kant's conception of nature and morality as two distinct realms, mediated by the concepts of law and lawfulness (*Gesetzmässigkeit*).

4.2 Accomplishing the task

4.2.1 The typic-procedure

Remarkably, after the abstract discussions of objects of pure practical reason, intellectual synthesis, the form of lawfulness, etc., the resulting procedure that Kant proposes for moral appraisal presents itself as relatively straightforward:

> The rule of the power of judgment under laws of pure practical reason is this: Ask yourself whether, if the action you propose were to take place by a law of the nature of which you were yourself a part, you could indeed regard it as possible through your will. Everyone does, in fact, appraise actions as morally good or evil by this rule. Thus one says: if everyone permitted himself to deceive when he believed it to be to his advantage, or considered himself authorized to shorten his life as soon as he was thoroughly weary of it, or looked with complete indifference on the needs of others, and if you belonged to such an order of things, would you be in it with the assent of your will? (*KpV* 5: 69)[119]

---

119 [*Die Regel der Urtheilskraft unter Gesetzen der reinen praktischen Vernunft ist diese: Frage dich selbst, ob die Handlung, die du vorhast, wenn sie nach einem Gesetze der Natur, von der du selbst ein Theil wärest, geschehen sollte, sie du wohl als durch deinen Willen möglich ansehen könntest. Nach dieser Regel beurtheilt in der That jedermann Handlungen, ob sie sittlich gut oder böse sind. So sagt man: Wie, wenn ein jeder, wo er seinen Vortheil zu schaffen glaubt, sich erlaubte, zu betrügen, oder befugt hielte, sich das Leben abzukürzen, so bald ihn ein völliger Überdruß desselben befällt, oder anderer Noth mit völliger Gleichgültigkeit ansähe, und du gehörtest*

But of course, the devil is in the details; properly understanding this 'typic-procedure', as I shall call it, requires extensive commentary. First, I will explain how the typic-procedure is supposed to enable the task of moral appraisal to be performed. My account will include a step-by-step reconstruction of the typic-procedure together with its underlying principles and assumptions. Second, I will bring out the specificity of the typic-procedure in Kant's ethics. Third, I will present a number of interpretations of the typic-procedure in the secondary literature – by the consequentialist, teleological, logical and 'rational agency' approaches – and assess their exegetical adequacy.

4.2.1.1 The canon of moral appraisal: universalizability as a law of nature

I want to suggest that the typic-procedure enables the task of moral appraisal to be performed by operationalizing the "canon" for moral appraisal that Kant had introduced in the *Groundwork*. Kant defines a *canon* in general as "the sum of the *a priori* principles of the correct use of certain cognitive faculties in general" (*KrV* A796/B824). Accordingly, the canon for the power of pure practical judgment consists of one or more *a priori* principles for subsuming actions under the concepts of good and evil. And as we know, the concepts of good and evil, in turn, derive from the moral law, which commands that actions be willed through maxims that are fit to be universal laws.[120]

In the *Groundwork*, Kant at first formulates the *a priori* principle of moral appraisal in the most general terms: "We must *be able to will* that a maxim of our action become a universal law: this is the canon of moral appraisal of maxims in general" (*G* 4: 424). This canon is meant to provide a clear, unambiguous rule that extends *a priori* to all possible cases: *an action is good if and only if its maxim can be rationally willed as a universal law, evil if and only if its maxim cannot be rationally willed as a universal law.* (Note that here, for the purposes of judgment, the emphasis shifts from the *action* to the *maxim* according to which it is willed.) One might think that nothing more would be needed for us to go out into the world with this canon in hand and start classifying actions as good or evil by judging their maxims. Kant seems to suggest as much in one passage in the *Groundwork*, where he recommends basing moral appraisal on the Universal Law Formula (FUL) alone: "But one does better always to proceed in moral *appraisal* by the strict method [*nach der Strengen Methode*] and put at

---

mit zu einer solchen Ordnung der Dinge, würdest du darin wohl mit Einstimmung deines Willens sein?]
120 See above, section 1.1.

its basis the universal formula of the Categorical Imperative: *act in accordance with a maxim that can at the same time make itself a universal law*" (G 4: 436– 437). Nevertheless, he manifestly came to see the matter differently, recognizing that the human power of judgment required a more 'user-friendly' procedure for moral appraisal.[121]

Already in the *Groundwork*, Kant goes a step beyond the "strict method" by spelling out two ways in which a maxim can fail to meet the criterion expressed by the general principle:

> Some actions are so constituted that their maxim cannot even be thought without contradiction as a universal law of nature, far less could one will that it should become such. In the case of others that inner impossibility is indeed not to be found, but it is still impossible to will that their maxim be raised to the universality of a law of nature because such a will would contradict itself (G 4: 424).

Notice that here, Kant does not invoke a "universal law" *simpliciter*, i.e, a normative principle for how rational agents *ought* to or are *permitted* to act (*sollen, dürfen*), but the universal law *of nature*, i.e., a law governing how people *must* or *can* act (*müssen, können*).[122] In addition, Kant introduces two elements that are not explicitly mentioned in the strictest formulation of the canon, namely two distinct ways in which a maxim can fail to be universalized as a law of nature: the *contradiction in conception* and the *contradiction in volition* (or *contradiction in the will*), as these have come to be called.[123] Thus the canon of moral appraisal, in the extended form that Kant gives it in the *Groundwork*, states that *an action shall be judged as good or evil by determining whether or not the corresponding maxim is so constituted that it can be rationally conceived and willed without contradiction as a universal law of nature*. These additional specifications assist the power of judgment by giving rise to a pair of *universalization tests* for assessing the constitution of maxims and appraising them accordingly. Thus we can ask (1) 'Is the maxim so constituted that it can be *conceived* without contradiction as a universal law of nature?' and (2) 'Is the maxim so constituted that it can be *willed* without contradiction as a universal law of nature?'[124] The purpose of the typic-procedure, I will argue, is to operationalize these tests.

---

121 Cf. Wood 1999, p. 79; Rawls 2000, p. 212n.
122 See Wood 1999, p. 79f.
123 Nell (O'Neill) 1975; O'Neill 1989; Korsgaard 1996. Compare the analogous distinction between "primary" and "secondary" universalizability criteria in Dietrichson 1969, p. 184ff.
124 Kant specifies that the maxims which lead to a contradiction in conception when universalized are those that strict, or perfect, duty enjoins us to avoid, while those which can be con-

Precisely characterizing Kant's criterion of universalizability poses a notoriously difficult and controversial problem for Kant scholarship. I will discuss the main interpretive approaches in section 4.2.3. For now, I simply aim to work out the criterion that provides what I view as the most plausible interpretation of the typic-procedure based on the Typic chapter and closely related texts. For a helpful indication of what the universalizability of a maxim implies, I propose to begin with the *Groundwork* passage where Kant explains what a *violation* of the canon of moral appraisal consists in:

> If we now attend to ourselves in any transgression of a duty, we find that we do not really will that our maxim should become a universal law, since that is impossible for us, but that the opposite of our maxim should instead remain a universal law, only we take the liberty of making an *exception* to it for ourselves (or just this once) to the advantage of our inclination. Consequently, if we weighed all cases from one and the same point of view, namely that of reason, we would find a contradiction in our own will, namely that a certain principle be objectively necessary as a universal law and yet subjectively not hold universally but allow exceptions. Since, however, we at one time regard our action from the point of view of a will affected by inclination, there is really no contradiction here but instead a resistance of inclination to the precept of reason (*antagonismus*), through which the universality of the principle (*universalitas*) is changed into mere generality (*generalitas*) and the practical rational principle is to meet the maxim halfway. Now, even though this cannot be justified in our own impartially rendered judgment, it still shows that we really acknowledge the validity of the Categorical Imperative and permit ourselves (with all respect for it) only a few exceptions that, as it seems to us, are inconsiderable and wrung from us (*G* 4: 424).

This passage suggests that a bad maxim is an *exceptionalist* maxim, one which consists in giving myself special treatment, or more precisely, in adopting a private rule of conduct by which I *authorize myself* to make an exception to a public rule that I expect everyone else to follow (cf. *VE Mrongovius* 29: 629). In the Typic chapter Kant calls attention to this feature when he enumerates examples of maxims that cannot be universalized because they *licence exceptions* to a general rule that is normally followed: "if everyone *permitted himself* [*sich erlaubte*] to deceive when he believed it to be to his advantage, or *considered himself authorized* [*sich befugt hielte*] to shorten his life as soon as he was thoroughly weary of it ..." (*KpV* 5: 69). In the *Groundwork* passage Kant also mentions that these private exceptions to the moral law must be *hidden*, and the maxims that license them, *kept* secret – a point he repeated in other places:

---

ceived but not willed without contradiction conflict with wide, or imperfect, duties (*G* 4: 424; *MS* 6: 389).

> "Everyone sees the moral law as something he can openly profess. But everyone sees his maxims as something that must be kept hidden, because they are contrary to morality, and cannot serve as a universal rule" (*VE Collins* 27: 1427).
>
> "We must *conceal* those of our maxims that cannot be universalized from others, and even from ourselves" (*R* 6: 38).

Kant adduces a variety of reasons for why people must conceal their exceptionalist maxims. On the one hand, he affirms that even when our inclinations push us to make exceptions for ourselves, we nevertheless do so *reluctantly* because of our feeling of respect for the moral law: "The universality of the rule is holy to everyone, but we all want to retain for ourselves the right of being able, at times, to make exceptions to it ..." (*VE Mrongovius* 29: 629). On the other hand, Kant fully recognized that rationalist *pudeur* is not the only, or even the main factor leading us to cover up our trespasses. In addition, instrumental cleverness (*Klugheit*) incites us to actively deceive others in order to achieve our selfish aims. Indeed, we selfishly count on the *generality* of the very law whose *universality* we have ourselves violated: like Hume's 'sensible knave', we will only venture an exception if we can take advantage of the fact that *most* people, in *most* situations, will continue to act as they ought to.[125] Conversely, if our decent fellows ever caught wind of our selfish exceptionalism, then they would be up in arms:

> For a maxim that I cannot *divulge* without thereby defeating my own purpose, one that absolutely must *be kept secret* if it is to succeed and that I cannot *publicly acknowledge* without unavoidably arousing everyone's opposition to my project, can derive this necessary and universal, hence *a priori* foreseeable, resistance of everyone to me only from the injustice with which it threatens everyone (*EF* 8: 381).

For all of these reasons – pure respect for the law, instrumental shrewdness in achieving our selfish aims, and the inherent unfairness of making exceptions for ourselves – we must *conceal* those of our maxims that cannot be universalized. By contrast, a morally legitimate maxim must, in principle, be fit for being publicly communicated and justified.

Indeed, this discussion of exceptions shows that while universalizability does have an abstract, formal dimension, that does not make it an *empty* moral principle. Rather, as we have just seen, Kant stresses that the way in which we frame our maxims has concrete practical implications for how we relate, in words and deeds, to ourselves and others: honestly and fairly in the case

---

125 Hume 1957, p. 102f.

of good maxims; deceitfully and unjustly in the case of bad ones. Thus moral law's formal requirement that maxims be universalizable translates into a substantive ethical demand to make fairness, honesty and good faith prevail over selfishness, deceit and hypocrisy, as O'Neill explains:

> The intuitive idea behind the thought that a universality test can provide a criterion of moral acceptability may be expressed quite simply as the thought that if we are to act as morally worthy beings, we should not single ourselves out for special consideration or treatment. Hence whatever we propose for ourselves should be possible (note: not 'desired' or 'wanted' – but at least *possible*) for all others.[126]

Conversely, the "true or strict universality [*wahre oder strenge Allgemeinheit*]" of a law consists in its applying to all cases *without exception* – as opposed to mere "generality," which applies to most cases while allowing some exceptions (*KrV* B3–4). Consequently, a maxim can be deemed suitable for adopting the universal form of a law as such if and only if it can be followed as a rule of conduct *without exception*; i.e., by all agents, in all situations of the specified type, at all times (cf. *G* 4: 421).[127] Thus, if my maxim (insofar as it is be to submitted to moral appraisal) takes the form 'I am to do X in circumstances C (without exception)', then the universalized version of this maxim – namely, 'Everyone is to do X in circumstances C (without exception)' – must be capable of becoming a practical law, i.e., an objective principle of action valid for all rational beings (*G* 4: 421).[128] I will refer to this most basic criterion with respect to maxims' formal constitution as "strict universalizability." This criterion is clearly meant to follow from Kant's key thesis that once we have deprived the will of all material incentives, the only thing left to serve as a determining ground of the will is conformity with the universality of a law in general (*G* 4: 4: 401–402, 420–421; *KpV* 5: 29,

---

126 O'Neill 1989, p. 94.
127 Jens Timmermann elaborates on this point in his commentary on the *Groundwork*: "A law lacks universality if it fails to apply in all relevantly similar circumstances, not just at present but also in the past and in the future. (A truly universal law cannot change.) That is why, at IV 424.19 below, Kant says that some actions violate the commands of duty because the agent takes the liberty of making an exception from a generally valid law in favour of inclination 'for just this once'." In a footnote to this remark, Timmermann adds: "There are indications of this throughout Kant's work. According to the formulation of the moral principle in the lectures, our actions must cohere (*übereinstimmen*) with a rule that is valid 'at all times and for everyone' (Mrongovius, XXVII 1427.1–4). (The passage is missing in Collins.) See also *Critique of Practical Reason*, V 36.15." Timmermann 2007, p. 80–81.
128 Cf. Rawls 2000, p. 168.

33).¹²⁹ Furthermore, since the concepts of good and evil derive from this supreme principle, the "appraisal of what is "good and evil in itself" comes down to ascertaining whether the "the mere lawful form of the maxim" determined the willing of a particular action under consideration (*KrV* 5: 62) – and Kant reiterates this very point at the beginning of the Typic chapter (*KpV* 5: 67–68). In short, strict universalizability serves as the *conditio sine qua non* for assessing the formal constitution of maxims and hence for appraising the moral status of actions (*KpV* 5: 41).

While *strict* universalizability concerns the aptitude of a maxim to be a universal law *simpliciter*, the requirement that a maxim be able to assume the form of a *law of nature* imposes some additional constraints. First of all, the law of natural causality determines how people *actually* act – i.e., not merely how everyone *ought* to act or *may* act – and therefore a maxim can stand the test of a law of nature if and only if everyone could *actually* perform (or attempt to perform) the action prescribed by the law in *every* relevant situation without fail, as Wood explains: "In practice, to suppose that one's maxim is a universal law of nature is apparently to suppose that every rational being without exception adopts the maxim and acts on it unfailingly whenever it applies."¹³⁰ Secondly, as we will see in more detail below, the typic-procedure imposes the additional constraint (not mentioned explicitly in the *Groundwork* canon) that the person judging a maxim must consider herself *as situated within* the context of nature. In sum, a maxim can be considered universalizable as a law of nature if and only if the judging agent can consistently conceive and will for everyone within a nature to which she herself belongs to really act according to it with the regularity of a law of nature.

4.2.1.2 The typic-procedure: a blueprint for constructing moral thought experiments

The basic idea behind the typic-procedure is that we can use the law of nature as a standard against which to test maxims' universalizability because it is the best "type," or analogue, we have, within the world in which we act, of the moral law's prescription of strict universality (cf. *G* 4: 421). We all understand that every event in nature, *without exception*, must have a preceding cause; and this gives us a standard for how a truly universal maxim should be constituted:

---

129 I say 'meant to follow' because the validity of this deduction has been challenged on philosophical grounds – see Wood 1999, 81 f.
130 Wood 1999, p. 79 f.

it should be capable of being a law admitting of *no exceptions*.[131] Accordingly, the typic-procedure instructs one to undertake a *moral thought experiment* whereby one mentally constructs a counterfactual world in order to determine whether one's maxim could conceivably be a truly universal law of nature. Here again is Kant's description of this procedure:

> The rule of the power of judgment under laws of pure practical reason is this: Ask yourself whether, if the action you propose were to take place by a law of the nature of which you were yourself a part, you could indeed regard it as possible through your will. Everyone does, in fact, appraise actions as morally good or evil by this rule. Thus one says: if everyone permitted himself to deceive when he believed it to be to his advantage, or considered himself authorized to shorten his life as soon as he was thoroughly weary of it, or looked with complete indifference on the needs of others, and if you belonged to such an order of things, would you be in it with the assent of your will? (*KpV* 5: 69)[132]

Thus, just as in the actual world there is a law of nature such that water will always boil when heated to 100 degrees Celsius, so in the counterfactual nature would there be a law such that one's contemplated action would always occur in a certain type of situation. The universality of the law of nature implies that in such a world, not only would *I* necessarily perform the action I am considering in *the situation at hand*, but also in *every situation* of the *same kind*, and *everyone else* would also invariably act in the same way in *all situations of that kind*, as if they were compelled to do so by a law of nature. Kant hastens to add the important point that one knows full well that the resulting scenario is not actual, or even probable:

> "Now everyone knows very well that if he permits himself to deceive secretly it does not follow that everyone else does so, or that if, unobserved, he is hard-hearted everyone would not straightaway be so toward him; accordingly, this comparison of the maxim of

---

131 See below, section 5.1.2.
132 [*Die Regel der Urtheilskraft unter Gesetzen der reinen praktischen Vernunft ist diese: Frage dich selbst, ob die Handlung, die du vorhast, wenn sie nach einem Gesetze der Natur, von der du selbst ein Theil wärest, geschehen sollte, sie du wohl als durch deinen Willen möglich ansehen könntest. Nach dieser Regel beurtheilt in der That jedermann Handlungen, ob sie sittlich gut oder böse sind. So sagt man: Wie, wenn ein jeder, / wo er seinen Vortheil zu schaffen glaubt, sich erlaubte, zu betrügen, oder befugt hielte, sich das Leben abzukürzen, so bald ihn ein völliger Überdruß desselben befällt, oder anderer Noth mit völliger Gleichgültigkeit ansähe, und du gehörtest mit zu einer solchen Ordnung der Dinge, würdest du darin wohl mit Einstimmung deines Willens sein?*]

his actions with a universal law of nature is also not the determining ground of his will" (*KpV* 5: 69).[133]

In other words, one remains cognizant, when employing the typic-procedure, that one is constructing a *counterfactual, 'as-if' scenario under stipulated conditions* rather than prognosticating about how the world would likely turn out if a certain way of acting were universally practiced. The point of the exercise is to ask oneself 1) whether one could conceive of this counterfactual nature as a coherent system and 2) whether one could rationally will to belong to it as a member. Moreover, while the typic is often referred to as a thought experiment *tout court*,[134] it may be more accurately described as a general *procedure* for constructing individual moral thought experiments according to a certain "blueprint" or "template [*Muster*]" (5: 43).[135] This construal seems to correspond best to the passage above, where Kant first articulates a general "rule of the power of judgment" and subsequently provides individual examples of its implementation, sketching how one would run a *first* thought experiment for evaluating fraud, a *second* for suicide, and a *third* for indifference – all according to the same single template prescribed by the typic-procedure. The typic-procedure does not instantly provide a definitive answer to all moral queries through a single infallible operation; rather, the procedure must be applied *à la pièce* to each particular action (or kind of action) being considered in order to determine its moral status.

A few other preliminary remarks are in order. It must be kept in mind that the textual basis is slim: the passage that articulates the typic-procedure – "The rule ... morally impossible" (*KpV* 5: 69–70) – is very brief: at 215 words it fills only half a page in the *Akademie* edition and accounts for less than than a fifth of the Typic chapter. This condensed form is common for philosophical thought experiments; philosophers tend to address the 'participant' directly, while suppressing the implicit assumptions and mechanisms underlying the exercise.

Also, there seems to be a discordance, at first sight, between the extended canon in the *Groundwork* (*G* 4: 424) and the typic-procedure in the second *Cri*-

---

133 [*Nun weiß ein jeder wohl: daß, wenn er sich ingeheim Betrug erlaubt, darum eben nicht jedermann es auch thue, oder, wenn er unbemerkt lieblos ist, nicht sofort jedermann auch gegen ihn es sein würde; daher ist diese Vergleichung der Maxime seiner Handlungen mit einem allgemeinen Naturgesetze auch nicht der Bestimmungsgrund seines Willens.*]
134 Horn 2007, p. 226; Paton 1947, p. 146; Pieper 2009, p. 114ff.; Pieper 2011, p. 194ff.; Silber 1974, p. 211f.; Timmermann 2007, p. 78; Vaihinger 1918, p. 655.
135 See the "Four-Step CI-Procedure" in Rawls 2000, p. 167–170; cf. Pogge 1998, p. 206.

tique (*KpV* 5: 69): the former invites one to consider whether one's *maxim* can be thought and willed as a law of nature, whereas the initial formulation of the typic-procedure makes no mention of maxims, but only of one's *action:* "Ask yourself whether, if *the action* you propose were to take place by a law of the nature of which you were yourself a part, you could indeed regard it as possible through your will" (*KpV* 5: 69). Nonetheless, the discrepancy is only apparent: the instruction to 'represent your *action* as if were *the effect* of a law of nature' should be read as a shorthand for 'represent the *maxim* of your act as if it were *itself* a law of nature'. Just a few sentences further, Kant characterizes the typic-procedure as a "comparison of *the maxim* of one's actions with a universal law of nature [*Vergleichung der Maxime seiner Handlungen mit einem allgemeinen Naturgesetze*]" (*KpV* 5: 69, my emphasis). And as Beck has explained, it only makes sense for the typic-procedure to test the universalizability of maxims, rather than actions per se, for otherwise the thought experiment would lead to absurd results: "In the *Critique*, however, [Kant – A.W.] speaks also of actions as universalizable ... This is an inaccuracy in the *Critique*. If lying were universal, we would be able to get along far better than in this world, where it is only frequent; we should simply interpret affirmative sentences negatively and negative ones affirmatively."[136]

Let us also recall that Kant conceives of a maxim as a subjective principle of action (*G* 4: 421n.). As familiar as this characterization may be, a number of points must be kept in mind for what follows. First, maxims do not merely specify the execution of a *particular* action in a *particular* situation, but rather express a more encompassing rule according to which the agent vows to perform a certain *type* of action in a certain *type* of situation.[137] Second, maxims are firm, substantive *Lebensregeln* that express an agent's long-term, or even-life-long, resolution *always* to act in a certain way; correspondingly, an agent's maxims are relatively few in number and are to be judged with due care and seriousness.[138] Third, moral appraisal involves a special consideration of maxims' form. When it is a matter of *planning* or *executing* actions, the maxim includes a reference to the *end* that the agent aims to achieve: 'When in situations of type S, I will do an action of type A in order to achieve an end of type E.'[139]

---

[136] Beck 1960, p. 159n. Cf. O'Neill 1989, p. 83. Incidentally, this consideration speaks against Gerhard Luf's characterization of the typic-procedure as "a universalization of concrete sensible contents" – see Luf 1975, p. 60.
[137] Cf. Schwartz 2006, p. 121.
[138] Manfred Kuehn has emphasized this point in connection with Kant's conception of moral character (cf. *APH* 7: 294–295) – see Kuehn 2002, p. 146f. See also Höffe 2012, p. 122.
[139] Rawls 2000, p. 168.

When it comes to *morally appraising* maxims, however, the agent must *abstract from the end and attend only to the rule* connecting a certain type of action with a certain type of situation: 'When in situations of type *S*, I will do an action of type *A*.' And since the typic-procedure subserves moral appraisal, any maxims that come into play there will assume this pared-down form.

How is the 'comparison' of one's maxim with a law of nature meant to bear on the appraisal of the moral status of actions? The answer, in a nutshell, is that this operation serves as a *test* of the formal constitution of the maxim with respect to its universalizability as a putative law of a counterfactual nature within which the deliberating agent imagines herself: if the maxim *passes* the test (i.e., proves to be suitable for assuming the universal form of a law of nature), then, according to the extended canon of moral appraisal, it must be deemed morally possible, and hence the corresponding action must be appraised as good (i.e., subsumed under the concept of *das sittlich Gute*); if the maxim *fails* the test (i.e., proves to be unsuitable for assuming the universal form of a law of nature), then, according to the extended canon of moral appraisal, it must be deemed morally impossible, and hence the action must be judged as evil (i.e., subsumed under the concept of *das sittlich Böse*). Kant encapsulates the way in which the law of nature serves as "a *type* for the appraisal of maxims in accordance with moral principles" in a condensed and elliptical sentence: "If the maxim of the action is not so constituted that it can stand the test as to the form of a law of nature in general, then it is morally impossible [*Wenn die Maxime der Handlung nicht so beschaffen ist, daß sie an der Form eines Naturgesetzes überhaupt die Probe hält, so ist sie sittlich unmöglich*]" (*KpV* 5: 69–70).

What follows is a step-by-step reconstruction of typic-procedure.

Step 1. Formulation of the maxim
First of all, one must formulate the maxim of the action to be appraised. To illustrate, let us take Kant's false promise example. If I am short of money at a particular time and consider taking out a loan from someone by making a false promise of repayment, I would first formulate the corresponding maxim in terms of a more general 'behaviour policy', as follows: "Whenever I am in financial need, I will borrow money with a false promise to repay it in order to get out of my financial difficulties." Here – where it is a matter of formulating the principle on which I plan to *execute* the action – the maxim does not include the specifics of my particular situation, but instead takes the form of a *rule* prescribing the same kind of action in all situations of the same kind in order to achieve a certain kind of end (i.e., a particular hypothetical imperative): "I am do to *X* in

circumstances *C* in order to bring about *Y*."¹⁴⁰ However, insofar as this maxim is to be *appraised morally* – i.e., with respect to the unconditional moral law – we must *abstract from its matter* (i.e., the end to be achieved by the action – in this case, to get out of financial difficulties), and *retain only its form*, which is a simple conditional *rule* prescribing the same kind of action in all situations of the same kind: *Whenever I am in financial need, I will borrow money with a false promise to repay it.* And it is *this* form of the maxim that will be put to the test as a putative law of nature.

Step 2. Conversion of the maxim into a law of nature

As originally formulated, the typic-procedure instructs me to mentally construct a counterfactual world in which the action occurs *as if* by a universal law of nature. Accordingly, I mentally construct a world in which a law of nature would cause me to make a false promise every time I need money, and so too everyone else whenever they find themselves in similar circumstances. The law of nature compelling all of the inhabitants of this world always to act in this deceitful manner is, *qua* law, a universal and necessary rule. And if one were to formulate the rule corresponding to this example, it would surely read as follows: 'For all agents in nature, when an agent finds herself in a situation where she needs money, then that agent will knowingly make a false promise to acquire some.' Clearly, this formulation expresses *the maxim as if it were converted into a counterfactual law of nature* – a law that causes everyone with in its ambit to act in a certain way whenever they find themselves in a certain kind of situation (*KpV* 5: 69). The newly minted, 'as if' law of nature can be referred to as the "universalized typified counterpart" of the maxim,¹⁴¹ or more simply as the "typified maxim."

Step 3. Testing for contradictions

Although Kant's universalization tests have elicited several different interpretations and a great deal of controversy among scholars,¹⁴² Kant himself seems to have thought that the identification of contradictions in conception and contradictions in volition was a fairly straightforward matter. In the Typic chapter, he simply lists off three examples of how the typic-procedure is applied, without

---

140 Cf. Rawls 2000, p. 168.
141 Nell (O'Neill) 1975, p. 62.
142 See the discussion below, in section 4.2.3.

any analysis at all: "Thus one says: if *everyone* permitted himself to deceive when he believed it to be to his advantage, or considered himself authorized to shorten his life as soon as he was thoroughly weary of it, or looked with complete indifference on the needs of others, and if you belonged to such an order of things, would you be in it with the assent of your will?" (*KpV* 5: 69). In the Deduction, he provides slightly more indications as to how a morally unacceptable maxim, when tested by the typic-procedure, will immediately and unmistakably give rise to a *contradiction in conception:*

> "When the maxim on which I intend to give testimony is tested by practical reason, I always consider what it would be if it were to hold as a universal law of nature. It is obvious that in this way everyone would be necessitated to truthfulness. For it cannot hold with the universality of a law of nature that statements should be allowed as proof and yet be intentionally untrue" (*KpV* 5: 44).

The maxim tested here is presumably 'When I believe it to be to my advantage, I will give false testimony'. Once the maxim has been converted into a counterfactual law of nature, it compels *everyone* to act in the same way *whenever* they find themselves in analogous circumstances. But this maxim clearly fails the "test [*Probe*]" as a putative law of nature (*KpV* 5 : 70), because a world in which *everyone* gave false testimony whenever they believed it to be to their advantage would fatally undermine the practice, or institution, of giving testimony. No one, in such a world, would believe what was testified, and hence a world in which the maxim of deceitful testimony enjoyed the same universality as a law of nature is *inconceivable*. (Not so, conversely, for the maxim of truthful testimony.) Ultimately, this glaring contradiction betrays the fact that the real, secret intention of the agent entertaining this maxim is to permit herself a *exception* to a rule that she expects *everyone else* to follow.[143]

In the Typic chapter, Kant also briefly mentions an example of a maxim that would elicit a *contradiction in volition:* the maxim of indifference, i.e., 'When I am not so inclined, I shall refrain from aiding others, even if it may be in my power to give them the help they need.' The typic-procedure enjoins the agent to consider a scenario in which that maxim were a law of nature compelling everyone in similar circumstances to act in the same manner: "if *everyone* ... looked with complete indifference on the needs of others, and if you belonged to such an order of things, would you be in it with the assent of your will?" (*KpV* 5: 69). Unlike the false testimony example, this scenario does not straightaway evoke a

---

[143] This interpretation is modelled on Timmermann's gloss of the false promise example in the *Groundwork* (*G* 4: 422): Timmermann 2007, p. 82 f.

contradiction in conception; nevertheless, it does create a contradiction in the agent's will. As Kant explains in his discussion of the same example in the *Groundwork*, "although it is possible that a universal law of nature could very well subsist in accordance with such a maxim, it is still not possible to *will* that such a principle hold everywhere as a law of nature" (*G* 4: 423). Because if I chose to "belong to such an order of things" – i.e., if I were a member of a world in which *everyone* (not just myself) "looked with complete indifference on the needs of others" – then I would be voluntarily depriving myself of the very possibility of aid that I might someday require, namely assistance in meeting my "true human needs"[144] as well as in furthering my general interests as a finite rational being (*G* 4: 423).[145] If the maxim of indifference were universalized as a law of nature, then my will would contradict itself – and therefore the maxim is morally unacceptable. Once again, the typic-procedure reveals that the unacceptable maxim involves permitting oneself a private *exception* to the rule that one expects everyone else to follow: here, I can only will the maxim of indifference if I can simultaneously count on the fact that everyone else would continue to follow the opposite rule of benevolence if *I* were to fall on hard times.

Step 4. Subsumption
Ultimately, the typic-procedure must culminate in the *definitive moral appraisal* of a particular action as morally good or morally evil. And there are indeed a series of logical steps leading from the thought experiment to the conclusion that a particular action must be subsumed either under the concept of morally evil (*das sittlich Böse*) or the concept of the morally good (*das sittlich Gute*):
a) As we just saw, the typic-procedure is so constructed that the attempt to mentally universalize a flawed (i.e., exceptionalist, non-universalizable) maxim as a counterfactual law of nature will elicit either a contradiction in conception or a contradiction in volition; conversely, a well-formed maxim could become a universal law of nature without any contradiction.
b) This "test [*Probe*]" of the maxim's form operationalizes the canon of moral appraisal in the *Groundwork*, which states that if a maxim *cannot* be conceived and willed as a law of nature without contradiction, then it is morally

---
144 I.e., basic needs common to all human beings (*MS* 6 : 393, 432f. 453ff.), including elementary physical necessities like nutrition and shelter, and arguably things like "security" (*MS* 46ff.). See Rawls 2000, p. 173ff.; Korsgaard 1996, p. 99.
145 Cf. Nell (O'Neill) 1975, p. 88, 90–91.

impossible, and if a maxim *can* be both conceived and willed without contradiction, then it is morally possible (*G* 4: 424).
c) Therefore, if the thought-experiment reveals that "the maxim of the action is not so constituted that it can stand the test as to the form of a law of nature in general, then it is morally impossible" (*KpV* 5: 69–70); if the maxim does pass this test, then it is morally possible.
d) An action whose corresponding maxim is morally impossible may not be willed as an "object of pure practical reason"; an action whose corresponding maxim is morally possible may be willed as an "object of pure practical reason" (*KpV* 5: 57–62).
e) If an action may not be willed as an object of pure practical reason, then it is morally evil;[146] if an action may be willed as an object of pure practical reason, then it is morally good (*KpV* 5: 57–62).
f) Therefore, "the rule of the power of judgment" (*KpV* 5: 69) when using the typic-procedure amounts to this: if the maxim through which a particular action is willed does not pass the test as to the form of a law of nature, then the pure practical power of judgment must subsume the action under the concept of the morally evil (*das sittlich Böse*); if the maxim through which the action is willed does pass the test, then the pure practical power of judgment must subsume the action under the concept of the morally good (*das sittlich Gute*) (*KpV* 5: 67–8).

Thus, the typic-procedure allows one to pass a *definitive judgment* on whether a particular action is good or evil – and thereby accomplishes, in principle, the task of moral appraisal.[147]

4.2.2 The typic-procedure's place in Kant's ethics

I will now bring out the specificity of the typic-procedure by contrasting it with some other elements of Kant's ethics with which it can easily be confused.

---

146 As I mentioned above, "good" should be taken in a broad sense here, i.e., including merely permissible actions; see section 1.1.
147 In my view, the contention that the typic-procedure serves "to supply the moral law with a non-constitutive, purely heuristic, illustrative mediation-principle" is therefore too weak; compare Dietrichson 1969, p. 176.

4.2.2.1 The typic-procedure and the Natural Law Formula

The typic-procedure, whereby one asks oneself, for a particular action, whether one could will to be part of a world in which everyone always acted in the same way in similar circumstances *as if* they were compelled to do so by a natural law, readily recalls the Natural Law Formula (FLN) of the Categorical Imperative from the *Groundwork:*

> ... act as if the maxim of your action were to become by your will a *universal law of nature* [handle so, als ob die Maxime deiner Handlung durch deinen Willen zum allgemeinen Naturgesetze werden sollte] (G 4: 421).

> ... maxims must be chosen as if they were to hold as universal laws of nature [... *daß die Maximen so müssen gewählt werden, als ob sie wie allgemeine Naturgesetze gelten sollten*] (G 4: 436).

> act in accordance with maxims that can at the same time have as their object themselves as universal laws of nature [*Handle nach Maximen, die sich selbst zugleich als allgemeine Naturgesetze zum Gegenstande haben können*] (G 4: 437).

This raises the question of the typic-procedure's relation to FLN. Is the typic-procedure "just Kant's new name" for FLN?[148] Or is there a "radical difference in function" between the two?[149] The answer, I think, is somewhere in between. In the Typic chapter, Kant takes the basic idea behind FLN – the analogy between the moral law and the law of nature – and adapts it to the specific problem of moral appraisal. The main function of FLN, as a formula of the Categorical Imperative, was not moral judgment per se; rather, it was the systematic *derivation of duties*. By contrast, the typic-procedure is explicitly introduced as a tool for "the pure practical power of judgment" (*KpV* 5: 67). Indeed, Kant did not even consider FLN to be suitable, much less indispensable, for the purpose of *moral judgment per se*; rather, he first proposed the FLN variant only "tentatively, cautiously," as Timmermann has observed,[150] privileging instead the "strict method" based on FUL for moral appraisal (compare G 4: 421 with G 4: 422). But in the Typic chapter, Kant decidedly affirms that we are "entitled and even required to use nature ... as the *type* of judgment" (G 5: 70), and he spells out a new, more detailed *procedure* for constructing thought experiments.[151]

---

[148] Guyer 2010, p. 824.
[149] Grandjean 2004, p. 44. While I find his conclusion somewhat overstated, I take up a number of Grandjean's comparisons in this paragraph.
[150] Timmermann 2007, p. 78.
[151] Höffe 2012, p. 108. Nell (O'Neill) 1975, p. 62, also notes that the typic-procedure supplies more detailed instructions than either FUL or FLN.

Moreover, in the *Groundwork*, Kant only accords FLN the secondary role of making the austere Categorical Imperative more subjectively "accessible" by bringing it "closer to intuition and thereby to feeling" (*G* 4: 436), whereas in the second *Critique* he relegates this auxiliary matter of making the moral law psychologically vivid to the Doctrine of Method. On the other hand, *only* in the Typic chapter does Kant explicitly thematize the deeper problem of '*schematizing*' the supersensible moral law (in the broad sense) and propose a technical solution to it (i.e., typification).[152] In sum, the introduction of the typic-procedure in 1788 marked a significant new development in Kant's thinking about moral judgment – one that is certainly related to FLN, but is not identical with it.[153]

4.2.2.2 Not an instrument for determining the will

Although it has been claimed that "the determination of the will by the moral law requires a type,"[154] I would contend that the typic-procedure's special epistemic status as a kind of counterfactual, 'as if' thinking provides a decisive reason for rejecting any construal of it as a means for directly *determining the will*. As I have already mentioned, when one considers an action *as if* it were to universally follow from a law of nature, one of course *knows* besides that not everyone in the world will *actually* start acting in the same way, and therefore the merely counterfactual scenario does not determine one's motivation, as Kant explicitly states:

> Now everyone knows very well that if he permits himself to deceive secretly it does not follow that everyone else does so, or that if, unobserved, he is hard-hearted everyone would not straightaway be so toward him; accordingly, this comparison of the maxim of his actions with a universal law of nature is also *not the determining ground of his will* (*KpV* 5: 69, my emphasis)[155]

---

152 Cf. Renaut's note on this topic in Kant 1994, p. 194n-195n.
153 Conversely, it is not advisable, much less necessary, to read the typic back into FLN or any of the other formulas in the *Groundwork*, as in Marty 1955, p. 64ff. This is not to say that there is an outright incompatibility or contradiction between the *Groundwork* and the Typic, but rather that one must give proper due to the latter's special task – see Höffe 2012, p. 108–110.
154 Marty 1997, p. 249.
155 [Nun weiß ein jeder wohl: daß, wenn er sich ingeheim Betrug erlaubt, darum eben nicht jedermann es auch thue, oder, wenn er unbemerkt lieblos ist, nicht sofort jedermann auch gegen ihn es sein würde; daher ist diese Vergleichung der Maxime seiner Handlungen mit einem allgemeinen Naturgesetze auch nicht der Bestimmungsgrund seines Willens].

Inded, as Beck puts it, "Kant was quite well aware that if I lie, it does not mean that all other men will lie, and therefore the fear of the consequences of my lying does not include the fear of the consequences which would follow from the existence of a world in which everyone lied."[156] Moreover, any interpretation of the typic-procedure as an instrument of *motivation* conflicts with basic tenets of Kant's moral philosophy. Firstly, Kant insists that "(1) The principle of appraisal [*dijudication*] of obligation and (2) the principle of its performance or execution," must be sharply distinguished:

> If the question is, 'what is morally good or not?', that is the principle of appraisal, whereby I judge the goodness or depravity of actions. But if the question is: 'What moves me to live according to this law?', that is the principle of incentive. The approbation [*Billigung*] of the action is the objective ground, but not yet the subjective ground. That which impels me to do the thing, of which understanding tells me that I ought to do it, is the *motiva subjective moventia*. The supreme principle of all moral judgment lies in the understanding; the supreme principle of the moral impulse to do this thing lies in the heart. This incentive is the moral feeling (*VE Collins* 27: 274–5, my emphasis).

Secondly, if the typic-procedure did influence the will, it could only do so by holding up the ulterior *consequences* of one's act before one's eyes – but that would be a fundamental distortion not only of the typic-procedure but also of Kant's moral theory as a whole, according to which any influence of the will by consequences is *heteronomy* (*KpV* 5: 64, 33, 35–7).[157] Thirdly, Kant asserts that the objective and the subjective motivation of the will occur in other ways. As for the *objective* source of motivation, neither the typic-procedure, nor even the *power of judgment* in general determines the will, instead it is *practical reason* that does so; indeed, the whole point of the *Critique of Practical Reason* is to prove that "pure reason *of itself alone* suffices to determine the will [*daß reine Vernunft zur Bestimmung des Willens allein zulange*]" (*KpV* 5: 15, my emphasis; see also *KpV* 5: 30) – and for this objective determination of what the will *ought* to do, practical reason has no need of judgment per se. As for the *subjective* source of motivation for performing good actions and avoiding evil ones, in the chapter immediately following the Typic Kant introduces *moral feeling* (re-

---

156 Beck 1960, p. 158n.
157 "Failure to recognize the difference between the type of moral judgment and the motive of moral action has led some critics to say that the in the categorical imperative Kant has committed himself to a utilitarian or even egoistic doctrine (cf., for example, Mill, *Utilitarianism*, chap. i). But Kant did not fall into this confusion, which he warns against." Beck 1960, p. 158n. See also below, section 4.2.3.1.

spect) to play the role of an incentive (*Triebfeder*) – and again, reason produces this feeling entirely on its own (*KpV* 5: 75–76).

4.2.2.3 Not egocentric deliberation ex ante

The typic-procedure's emphasis on the subject's own conscience, characteristically expressed by the question "Ask yourself whether … [*Frage dich selbst, ob* …]" has induced many interpreters to construe the typic's function *egocentrically*, so to speak – that is, primarily as a means for deliberating about *one's own* actions. Thus Marty[158] frames the typic against the backdrop of what he calls "*le problème de la décision*" – i.e., as a means for answering the question 'What should I do?' – and Guyer sees deliberation *ex ante* on one's own prospective actions as the purpose of the thought experiment, denying that it serves to evaluate actions *ex post facto* at all.[159]

Nevertheless, several considerations speak against the narrow, egocentric construal and in favour of a wider application of the typic-procedure. It seems arbitrary to limit the function of the typic to deliberation *ex ante* by the agent. If that were so, one could only sensibly apply the typic-procedure to one's own *prospective* actions, to be performed at some point in the *future*. But Kant specifies no such time restriction, and it seems entirely plausible that one could use the typic-procedure to reconsider one's *past* actions (e.g., '*Was* that the right thing to do?'; '*Did* I do the right thing?'). It seems equally arbitrary to limit the typic-procedure's field of application to the actions of a particular agent. When in the Typic chapter Kant describes how people commonly *employ* the typic-procedure, he writes that they evaluate actions *tout court*, not specifically *their own* actions: "Everyone does, in fact, appraise actions [*Handlungen*, not '*seine Handlungen*' – A.W.] as morally good or evil by this rule" (*KpV* 5: 69). Indeed, in the Doctrine of Method of the *Critique of Practical Reason*, Kant observes that people commonly enjoy morally judging *the actions of other people* (even historical figures and fictional characters) (*KpV* 5: 153).[160] In sum, while the typic-procedure can undoubtedly aid the agent's deliberation and guide her choices by enabling her to properly appraise the actions she is entertaining – and that may well be its most common application – it remains a method for appraising the maxims of actions *in general*, not merely those that a single agent is considering performing herself in the future.

---

[158] Marty 1997, p. 233 ff.
[159] Guyer 2007, p. 141.
[160] Cf. Nell (O'Neill) 1975, p. 77 f., 126–132; Recki 2001, p. 244.

4.2.2.4 Determining or reflecting judgment?

Finally, several scholars have claimed that the typic-procedure is, in whole or in part, an exercise of *reflecting judgment*,[161] however these claims are unconvincing. To begin with, they are anachronistic: the notion of reflecting judgment did not enter Kant's conceptual repertoire until two years after the second *Critique*.[162] As a consequence, the attempts to read reflecting judgment back into the Typic chapter are inevitably strained and artificial. There simply is no explicit characterization of the typic-procedure as an exercise of reflective judgment in either the Typic chapter or the third *Critique*. Grandjean, for his part, attempts to drum up some textual evidence with the following argument: given that in the Typic Kant used the same *term* for moral appraisal that he would later employ for reflecting judgment, namely "*Beurtheilung/beurtheilen*," this choice must have been in contradistinction to the terms "*Urtheil/urtheilen*" associated with determining judgment.[163] But the claim need only be stated to see how implausible it is. Are we to believe that during the composition of the second *Critique* – and even before (the expression "*moralische Beurtheilung*" occurs as early as the *Groundwork* in 1785, to say nothing of the pre-critical writings) – Kant was strictly following a subtle terminological nuance corresponding to a conceptual distinction that he would introduce years later? In reality, Kant employed the expression "*die moralische Beurtheilung*" because that is just the normal term in German for moral appraisal, although he of course assigned it a specific meaning within his moral philosophy. Moreover, one can just as easily turn Grandjean's weak terminological argument on its head: Kant refers to the capacity for reflecting judgment as a "*Beurtheilungsvermögen*," (*EEKU* 20: 211) whereas the Typic pertains explicitly to the "*Urtheilskraft*" (*KpV* 5: 69).

More fundamentally, such claims are self-defeating, since they conflict with the very definition of reflecting judgment. In the third *Critique* Kant makes it clear that reflecting judgment serves to *generate a new general concept* from the comparison of particular representations:

> [t]he power of judgment can be regarded either as a mere faculty for *reflecting* on a given representation, in accordance with a certain principle, *for the sake of a concept that is thereby made possible* [*zum Behuf eines dadurch möglichen Begriffs*], or as a faculty for *determining* an underlying concept through a given *empirical* representation. In the first case it is the *reflecting*, in the second case, the *determining power of judgment*. To *reflect* (to consider) [reflectiren (überlegen)] however, is to compare and to hold together given representations

---

[161] Dierksmeier 1998, p. 43; Grandjean 2004, p. 48–51; Johnson 1985, p. 272ff.; Longuenesse 2005, p. 236–238; Recki 2001, p. 242–252; Recki 2008, p. 198. See above, section 1.2.
[162] Höffe 2008, p. 292.
[163] Grandjean 2004, p. 51n.

either with others or with one's faculty of cognition, *in relation to a concept thereby made possible [in Beziehung auf einen dadurch möglichen Begriff]* (*EEKU* 20: 211, my emphasis).

But it is obvious that none of the general concepts involved in the typic-procedure depend on reflective comparison to be first "made possible." Quite the opposite: the moral law, the concepts of good and evil, and the law of nature are *all given a priori* – respectively as a fact of reason, as pure practical concepts deduced from the moral law, and as a theoretical category "the concept of which occurs even in the most common use of reason" (*KpV* 5: 70). The whole point of the typic-procedure is to enable the *subsumption of particular cases under these pre-given a priori concepts* according to a definite hierarchy (*KrV* 5: 67), and therefore it clearly and unequivocally pertains to the *determining power of judgment alone:* "If the universal (the rule, the principle, the law) is given, then the power of judgment, which subsumes the particular under it … is *determining*" (*KpV* 5: 179).

On this issue, I side with Beck, Guyer, and Höffe, all of whom have rejected the thesis that the typic belongs to reflecting judgment and have held instead that both moral appraisal and the typic-procedure are exclusively determining.[164] Guyer puts the point clearly:

> 'typification' [i.e., the 'typic-procedure' – A.W.] … fits the model of what Kant subsequently called determinant judgment pretty well. Kant defines determinant judgment as that in which we seek to apply a given universal to a particular, and that is precisely what we are doing when we ask whether the universalization of our maxim would be consistent with the particular consisting in our proposed action on the maxim.[165]

Moreover, Guyer adds that Pieper's suggestion that the typic-procedure represents an entirely novel form of judgment corresponding neither to determining nor reflecting judgment is unconvincing.[166] And I would say the same of Grandjean's oxymoronic thesis that the typic produces "a reflecting judgment whose outcome is determining [*un jugement réfléchissant dont l'issue est déterminante*]."[167] In my view, most of these interpretations of the typic-procedure in terms of reflecting judgment are symptomatic of a compulsion to read the third *Critique* back into the Typic, even to the point of distortion – a tendency that I will critically examine more extensively in Chapter 6.

---

[164] Beck 1960, p. 154n; Guyer 2010; Höffe 2008, p. 292; Torralba 2007, p. 14.
[165] Guyer 2010, p. 824.
[166] Guyer 2010, p. 824; compare Pieper 2009, p. 190ff.; Pieper 2011, p. 110ff.
[167] Grandjean 2004, p. 48–51.

4.2.3 The typic-procedure in the secondary literature

The problem of interpreting Kant's universalization tests has become, to paraphrase the first Preface of the *Critique of Pure Reason*, a battlefield of endless controversies. I will present the four most influential approaches – consequentialist, teleological, logical, and 'rational agency' – and assess how accurately they respectively interpret the typic-procedure. This exegetical analysis will shed additional light on the Typic chapter by clarifying certain points of contention and also bring out its special value for testing these interpretive approaches which, all too often, are selectively applied to a small number of convenient examples.

4.2.3.1 The consequentialist interpretation
a) Presentation

Perhaps the most tempting way to interpret the typic-procedure is along the following lines: "If *everyone* acted as *you* propose to do, then the world would go to hell in a handbasket, and therefore you shouldn't act that way."[168] This familiar and intuitive moral reasoning expresses a consequentialist decision procedure which can be spelled out more abstractly as follows: *an action is good if and only if it causes an increase in happiness (and/or a decrease in suffering); an action is evil if and only if it causes a reduction in happiness (and/or an increase in suffering)*. This formula admits of rational egoist or utilitarian variants depending on whether the happiness under consideration is that of the deliberating agent alone or of "the greatest number" (the utilitarian variant can also be declinated as rule utilitarianism if one considers not just individual actions but rules for acting). J. S. Mill famously argued that the Categorical Imperative can *only* acquire meaning if translated into utilitarian terms:

> When Kant ... propounds as the fundamental principle of morals 'So act, that thy rule of conduct might be adopted as a law by all rational beings', he virtually acknowledges that *the interest of mankind* collectively, or at least of mankind indiscriminately, must be in the mind of the agent when conscientiously deciding on the morality of the act. ... Otherwise he uses words without a meaning: for, that a rule even of utter selfishness could not possibly be adopted by all rational beings – that there is any insuperable obstacle in the nature of things to its adoption – cannot be even plausibly maintained. To give any meaning to Kant's principle, the sense put upon it must be, that we ought to shape our conduct by a rule which all rational beings might adopt *with benefit to their collective interest*.[169]

---

[168] Castillo 2007, p. 31–34; Horn 2007, p. 238.
[169] Mill 1998, p. 13–25.

Mill's allegation that Kant must appeal, *nolens volens*, to consequentialist considerations in order to derive substantive ethical conclusions from the Categorical Imperative has been reiterated by Broad and Singer.[170] On the consequentialist interpretation, the typic-procedure serves for estimating the expected costs and benefits of certain rules of action with respect to the happiness of "the greatest number" of people concerned: an action that would, if universalized, have a net positive (or at least neutral) effect on general happiness is morally acceptable; an action that would, if universalized, have net negative consequences on happiness is morally unacceptable.[171]

b) Assessment

To be sure, such thought-experiments can be quite powerful means for encouraging individuals to assume more responsibility for the consequences of their actions. These days they are often employed in environmental ethics, which concerns situations where the small actions of billions of individuals do in fact add up to large-scale effects on all current and future inhabitants of the planet: "What if *everyone* drove a polluting car, ate meat daily, wasted water, etc.?" From an exegetical point of view, however, Mill's *Umdeutung* of the typic-procedure is untenable. Although both rule-utilitarianism and Kant's universalization test involve envisaging what would happen if everyone acted in a certain way, they must be distinguished, as Timmons has explained: "The rule utilitarian is interested in the values of the consequences of everyone acting in some way or accepting a certain rule, while Kant's tests focus on whether, in willing one's maxim as universal law, one is caught in some sort of inconsistency."[172] That is, the rule utilitarian considers the *net consequences* of everyone's acting according to a certain policy of conduct – hence there is no veritable *contradiction* in the universalization of a bad maxim, but simply a *trade-off* or *difference* (in a quasi-arithmetic sense) between expected outcomes with respect to happiness. But in the typic-procedure one considers whether one could *rationally conceive and will without contradiction* for everyone to universally follow the *principle* of one's action, but one pays no heed to whether the *consequences* would have beneficial or deleterious consequences for happiness as such: "Here, however, we have to do with ... the *determination of the will* (not the action with ref-

---

170 Broad 1965, p. 130; Singer 1961, p. 262 – both cited in O'Neill 1989, p. 82n.
171 Horn et al. 2007, p. 232.
172 Timmons 2006, p. 172 f. Marty and Silber construe the typic-procedure primarily in terms of the consideration of consequences, although neither explictly endorses Mill's utilitarian interpretation outright: Marty 1997, p. 251; Silber, p. 212 f.

erence to its result) through the law alone without any other determining ground ..." (*KpV* 5: 68–9). For instance, it is not because the false promise maxim would *make everyone worse off* if universally followed that acting on it should be deemed morally wrong, according to the typic-procedure, but rather because the conversion of that maxim into a universal law cannot be rationally conceived or willed without *contradiction* – a very different concept from a negative balance of consequences.[173] Indeed, Mill himself drew attention to this distinction in his criticism of Kant: "he fails, almost grotesquely, to show that there would be any contradiction, any logical (not to say physical) impossibility, in the adoption by all rational beings of the most outrageously immoral rules of conduct. All he shows is that the consequences of their universal adoption would be such as no one would choose to incur."[174] On the other hand, Kant could retort to Mill's allegation of unintelligibility that the difference between these two ways of appraising an action could not be clearer: "So distinctly and sharply drawn are the boundaries of morality and self-love that even the most common eye cannot fail to distinguish whether something belongs to the one or the other" (*KrV* 5: 36; cf. *TP* 8: 286–7). Furthermore, the consequentialist mode of deliberation only makes sense if one considers the most *realistic* or *probable* outcomes of action. By contrast, the typic-procedure involves imagining a counterfactual and highly unrealistic scenario with no expectation that the envisaged consequences will actually, or even probably, occur: "Now everyone knows very well that if he permits himself to deceive secretly it does not follow that everyone else will do so ..." (*KrV* 5: 69). Finally, Kant could not possibly endorse a consequentialist version of the typic-procedure, since on his view all consequentialist universalization tests are unavoidably *heteronomous*.[175] In sum, Kant clearly did not intend for the typic-procedure to be employed as an exercise in utilitarian deliberation *à la* Mill, nor as a tool for calculating one's personal advantage. Indeed, when we

---

[173] Höffe 2010.
[174] Mill 1998, p. 26–34.
[175] "Since universality tests of these sorts all make moral acceptability in some way contingent upon what is wanted (or, more circumspectly expressed, upon what is preferred or found acceptable or promises the maximal utility), they all form part of moral theories that are heteronomous, in Kant's sense of the term. Such theories construe moral acceptability as contingent upon the natural phenomena of desire and inclination, rather than upon any intrinsic or formal features of agents and intentions. If we rely on any of these proposed criteria of moral acceptability, there will be no types of act that would not be rendered morally acceptable by some change or changes in human desires." By contrast, in the typic-procedure Kant invites us "to consider what we can will or intend, what it is possible or consistent for us to 'will as a universal law' (not what we would will or would find acceptable or would want as a universal law." O'Neill 1989, p. 81.

examine Kant's discussion of what he calls the "empiricism of practical reason" (*KpV* 5: 70–1), we will see that one of the typic's critical functions consists in *guarding against* the employment of the principle of happiness as a criterion for moral appraisal. From an exegetical point of view, therefore, the consequentialist interpretation of the typic-procedure must be rejected.

4.2.3.2 The teleological interpretation
a) Presentation

H. J. Paton advanced the strongest version of the teleological interpretation in his classic study, *The Categorical Imperative* (1947), where he argued that the typic-procedure must be understood as entirely – and exclusively – teleological:

> Kant is not concerned with causal laws nor with finding breaches in them: his arguments, if interpreted in this way, are completely broken-backed. In every case he appeals to teleological considerations; and there is no possibility of even beginning to understand his doctrine, unless we realise that the laws of nature he has in mind are not causal, but teleological.[176]

In other words, the "law of nature" referred to in the typic cannot be the law of natural causality produced by the understanding: that law is too poor and indeterminate for appraising actions, because "action as such is essentially purposive" and hence goes beyond merely efficient causation.[177] In addition, we ought to consider the universalization of actions with respect to human nature, which is also intrinsically purposive; relatedly, the reference to "the order of nature" in the Typic chapter must be understood as a systematic teleological whole into which human purposes are inextricably woven (a widely held view of the cosmos in the eighteenth century).[178] Only against the backdrop of these teleological assumptions can we even make sense of Kant's text, Paton avers, as "all of this was so much taken for granted by Kant that he fails to state it explicitly, and so tends to mislead his readers."[179] Accordingly, Paton suggests the following way of construing the typic-procedure: "When we ask whether we can *will* a proposed maxim as if it were to become thereby a law of nature, we are asking whether a will which aimed at a systematic harmony of purposes in human nature could consistently will this particular maxim as a law of

---

[176] Paton 1947, p. 149 ff.
[177] Paton 1947, p. 151, 155.
[178] Paton 1947, p. 151, 162 f.
[179] Paton 1947, p. 151.

human nature."¹⁸⁰ On this model, in order to determine whether it is morally possible to make a false promise, commit suicide, let one's talents rust, and so on, we must consider whether universalizing those actions would somehow undermine the attainment of the *ends* respectively aimed for by those actions and thereby enter into contradiction with the purposiveness of human nature and of the cosmos as a whole. Otherwise, Paton alleges, Kant's universalization tests remain not only ineffectual, but also meaningless: "Kant's doctrine becomes intelligible only when his law of nature is interpreted teleologically as concerned with the harmony of human purposes."¹⁸¹ More recently, Konhardt has elaborated on Paton's interpretation,¹⁸² and Aune has also argued for an overtly teleological construal of the typic.¹⁸³

Beck, for his part, proposed an attenuated version of the teleological interpretation. In the section of his *Commentary* devoted to the Typic, he largely endorses Paton's "definitive and exemplary exposition" while watering down the strong claim that the typic-procedure refers *exclusively* to a teleological conception of nature.¹⁸⁴ Beck points out that Kant entertained, alongside his teleological conception of the order of nature, a "concept of causal uniformity" and suggests, as a friendly amendment, that the latter "does have ... at least a minor role."¹⁸⁵ Accordingly, Beck suggests that the typic-procedure involves testing the universalizability of the maxim as an efficient-causal law; nevertheless he agrees with Paton that the decisive consideration must be teleological, namely whether the maxim-become-law could in turn fit into a harmonious teleological cosmos:

> *I do not merely ask* myself whether a realm of nature consisting of rational beings acting uniformly in the way I propose to act would be possible, i.e., if the maxim could be a universal law and accomplish the ends I have and express in the maxim; *I ask, further,* whether I, as a creator of the world in which every part should have its natural place and function, would will that certain maxims should have the force of law. Would it be a world in which the natural ends of things would be systematically thwarted? If so, though such a world is possible as a territory of uniform event-sequences, it would not be a realm which would be rationally desired by a being who consistently traced out the implications of his desires. That is, when I will an immoral action, one that would sow discord among rational beings,

---

180 Paton 1947, p. 155.
181 Paton 1947, p. 155.
182 Konhardt 1979, p. 295 ff.
183 Aune 1979, p. 58 ff.
184 Beck 1960, p. 154–163.
185 Beck 1960, p. 159n.

I will according to the maxim of the act and also will (tacitly) that my maxim *not* be universal. And such a maxim is not then analogous to a law of nature.[186]

More recently, Beck's interpretation of the typic-procedure has been endorsed by Bielefeldt, who finds this construal "more persuasive" than Paton's exclusively teleological model.[187]

b) Assessment

The most one can say in favour of the teleological interpretation of Kant's universalization test is that he does seem to appeal to teleological considerations in some of his *examples* of moral judgment. However, one must be careful when interpreting Kant's discussions of particular examples to distinguish between his rhetoric, which may use teleological language, and his philosophical justification, which does not necessarily invoke teleological principles. For instance, even in his infamous condemnation of masturbation in the *Metaphysics of Morals* (*MS* 6: 424–6), where he openly reviles the "unnaturalness" of the act, Kant nevertheless admits that its "contrapurposiveness" does not *by itself* constitute a legitimate "rational proof" that the action is also contrary to duty (*MS* 6: 425).

More generally, the teleological interpretation of Kant's universalization tests has been roundly criticized on textual and systematic grounds, to the point that "most interpreters now reject that approach."[188] I will not reiterate the standard criticisms here, except to confirm that the teleological interpretation fails to offer a satisfactory account of the typic-procedure in particular. To begin with, Kant does not employ any teleological language in the Typic chapter,[189] yet Paton and the other defenders of the teleological interpretation offer no plausible explanation as to why Kant should have altogether suppressed such language here but did not in other, related contexts. The most plausible explanation for this absence is, quite simply, that neither moral appraisal nor typification depends on teleological concepts or principles. Indeed, Kant denies a decisive

---

186 Beck 1960, p. 161.
187 Bielefeldt 2003, p. 53.
188 Guyer 1998, p. xxxiii. See also Horn et al. 2007, p. 238 ff.; Korsgaard 1996, p. 87 ff.; Nell (O'Neill) 1975, p. 64 f.
189 The only expression with a whiff of teleology is the "invisible Kingdom of God [*unsichtbares Reich Gottes*]" (*KpV* 5: 71); however, the context makes it clear that this expression, far from being a reference to the Kingdom of Ends, is a semi-quotation that Kant critically attributes to the mystics.

role to ends in moral appraisal. While the defenders of the teleological interpretation are correct to note that Kant conceives of rational action as end-directed, they neglect that Kant clearly and repeatedly states that when it comes to the *moral status* of actions – which is just what moral appraisal is concerned with – we must *abstract from all consideration of ends* and attend to the strict formal universalizability of maxims, independently of any ends to be achieved: "For without some end there can be no *will*, although, if it is a question only of lawful necessitation of actions, one must abstract from any end and the law alone constitutes its determining ground" (*TP* 8: 279n). Morally obligatory actions, for instance, "are necessary without any end, and for whose existence no intention or purpose provides the motive" (*VE Vigilantius* 27: 487). Indeed, it would be absurd for an obligatory action to be indexed to an arbitrary end, since its obligatory status as such must be as *unconditional* as the principle from which it derives in the first place, namely the Categorical Imperative – which, as a purely formal principle, abstracts from material ends altogether: "the Categorical Imperative carries with it an unconditioned moral necessitation, which is founded not at all on the end or purpose of the action; so all that is left is the *form of lawfulness*, which is the determining ground of free action..." (*VE Vigilantius* 27: 495).[190] Correspondingly, the moral *worth* of an action commanded by duty derives from the principle of volition rather than from the end to be achieved: "an action from duty has its moral worth *not in the purpose* to be attained by it but in the maxim in accordance with which it is decided upon ... without regard for any object of the faculty of desire" (*G* 4: 399–400). Accordingly, when morally appraising the moral status of an action we must attend exclusively to the formal universalizability of the corresponding maxim:

> In all moral judgments we frame the thought: What becomes of the action if it is taken universally? ... In no sense does [the understanding] contain the end of the action; the morality of the action consists, rather, in the universal form of the understanding (which is purely intellectual), assuming, that is, that the action is taken universally, so that it can exist as a rule (*VE Collins* 27: 1428).

Correspondingly, in the typic-procedure, where we are concerned with evaluating the *moral status* of actions, we abstract from their ends. And as we have already

---

190 Kant apparently stressed this point especially heavily in the lectures on ethics recorded by Vigilantius: "This is inherent in the nature of the unconditioned necessitation of the law, which enjoins fulfillment of duty without end or purpose, and regardless of advantage or disadvantage" (*VE Vigilantius* 27: 496); "In and for itself alone, the rule of my will must at the same time be the sufficient reason for determining it; the act must rest solely on this unconditioned imperative, without being coupled to any end ..." (*VE Vigilantius* 27: 487).

seen, both Type₁ (the law of natural causality) and Type₂ (*natura formaliter spectata*) are *formal* representations produced by the understanding – the "faculty of rules" – and therefore contain no matter, i.e., neither ends nor teleological hierarchies.[191] Indeed, only on this condition can they serve as types for morality, since the moral law determines the will "through *the mere form* of giving universal law" rather than through its matter (*KpV* 5: 27, my emphasis; *G* 4: 400).

4.2.3.3 The logical interpretation
a) Presentation

The most distinctive element of the logical interpretation, defended most prominently by Otfried Höffe, is its way of framing *contradictions in conception*. (To be clear, these only arise in cases where perfect, narrow duties are violated, whereas violations of imperfect, wide duties give rise instead to contradictions in volition.)[192] The core thesis is that a maxim incompatible with a strict duty will inevitably 'destroy itself' when universalized because it will give rise to a *logical contradiction*, which can be formal (the maxim asserts or implies both A and not-A) or conceptual (e.g., an insincere promise is as absurd as a round square).[193] Höffe's most recent analysis of Kant's deposit example (*KpV* 5: 27; *TP* 8: 286–7) represents a paradigmatic application of the logical interpretation:

> Dort, wo ein Depositum via Ableugnen das zum Begriff unverzichtbare, sogar entscheidende Moment der "fremden" Sache verliert, wird es in seinem "Wesen" *fremdes* Eigentum zu sein, zerstört, und in diesem begrifflichen […] Sinn vernichtet. […] Weil ein Verwahrungsvertrag seinem Begriff nach – etwas Fremdes verwahren – die Verpflichtung zur Rückgabe begrifflich einschließt, bedeutet eine Ableugnung des Verwahrten, daß man eine fremde Sache verwahrt und die Sache doch nicht als eine fremde ansieht. Einem Depositum, das man im Wissen und der Absicht annimmt, es zu behalten, liegt also tatsächlich die "in sich widersprüchliche" Maxime zugrunde, etwas als fremde Sache anzuerkennen und es zugleich als fremd zu leugnen. Diese Widersprüchlichkeit wird im Einzelfall praktiziert und erweist sich damit als denkmöglich und darüber hinaus als problemlos praktizierbar, erst die zu einem Naturgesetz gewordene Verallgemeinerbarkeit ist nicht denkmöglich. Denn ein strenges Gesetz erlaubt den Widerspruch nicht, daß etwas eine fremde Sache und doch keine fremde Sache ist.[194]

---

191 See above, section 4.1.2., esp. 4.1.2.4.
192 Höffe 2011, p. 118.
193 See Höffe 1977; Höffe 2010; Höffe 2011; Höffe 2012. For general descriptions of the logical interpretation as compared with other interpretive approaches, see Horn et al. 2007, p. 233 ff.; Korsgaard 1996, p. 81 ff.
194 Höffe 2012, p. 119 f.

Höffe specifies that his analysis of Kant's universalization tests applies not only to the treatments of FUL and FLN in the *Groundwork*, but also to the Typic chapter.[195] On this view, the purpose of the typic-procedure, when applied to strict duties, consists in testing for such logical or conceptual contradictions in the corresponding maxims. Moreover, since the proponents of the logical interpretation regard the criterion of logical-conceptual universalizability as both necessary and sufficient for the moral appraisal of strict duties, they tend to accuse the teleological, consequentialist, and rational agency interpretations of introducing irrelevant criteria.[196]

b) Assessment

On the one hand, the logical interpretation has several virtues: it offers a sophisticated analysis of what a 'contradiction in conception' might consist in; it can claim textual support from those passages where Kant writes that morally unjustifiable maxims "destroy themselves [*sich selbst zerstören*]" or "annihilate themselves [*sich selbst vernichten*]" upon being universalized (*G* 4: 403; *KpV* 5: 27; *VE Collins* 27: 1428–9); it has the merit of having shown up the flaws in Hegel's (characteristically uncharitable) criticisms of Kant's universalization tests;[197] and it avoids the main pitfalls of the teleological and consequentialist interpretations by denying ends or consequences decisive weight in moral appraisal.

Of course, like all the major interpretive approaches, the logical interpretation faces a number of objections that are still being debated in the literature.[198] Rather than enter into these general debates, I would like to highlight one particular element of the logical interpretation of the typic-procedure that I find problematic. Specifically, it seems to me that the logical interpretation misconstrues the criterion of strict universalizability by equating it with 'contradictionlessness' (*Widerspruchslosigkeit*), whereas Kant in fact equates strict universality with 'exceptionlessness' (*Ausnahmslosigkeit*). This comes out clearly in Höffe's explanation of why the maxim authorizing oneself to appropriate deposits at will cannot be universalized as a law: "For a strict law does not permit *the contradiction* that something should be both somebody else's property and yet not

---

[195] Höffe 2012, p. 120, 108–112. The same goes for the logical interpretation of the typic-procedure in Dietrichson 1969.
[196] Höffe 2012, p. 119 f.
[197] See Korsgaard 1996, p. 86 f.; Höffe 2011, p. 61–65. Compare Hegel, 1970, p. 462 f.; Hegel 1970, p. 322 f.
[198] An influential assessment of the strengths and weaknesses of the logical interpretation is Korsgaard 1996.

somebody else's property [*Denn ein strenges Gesetz erlaubt den Widerspruch nicht, daß etwas eine fremde Sache und doch keine fremde Sache ist*]" (my translation and emphasis). Höffe's statement is not false in and of itself, yet it implies that what the law's strict universality proscribes, in the first instance, are *contradictions*. But that is simply not how Kant defines strict universality per se in either his theoretical or practical works; rather, he holds in both contexts that "universality is set against particularity (*exception*)" (*Refl* 4490, 17: 570). In the Introduction to the second edition of the *Critique of Pure Reason* (written immediately before or even concurrently with the *Critique of Practical Reason*), he states that "a judgment is thought in strict universality" just in case it is thought "in a such way that *no exception at all* is allowed to be possible [*wird also ein Urteil in strenger Allgemeinheit gedacht, d. i. so, daß* gar keine Ausnahme *als möglich gestattet wird*]" – and, tellingly, he gives as an example the synthetic *a priori* judgment corresponding to *the law of nature*, i.e., "the proposition that every alteration must have a cause" (*KrV* B4, my emphasis, cf. *KrV* A542/B570). And we find the exact same definition of strict universality in Kant's moral philosophy. In the *Groundwork*'s "canon of moral appraisal in general," he makes it very clear that a *maxim* that one can will as a strictly universal law must, in the first instance, exclude *exceptions* (*G* 4: 424). That is why I argued above that what the typic-procedure tests for, in the first instance, is whether maxims can be thought such that *no exception* at all is possible.[199] To be sure, the typic-procedure does elicit 'contradictions' (in conception and in volition); however, these contradictions pertain not to the logical form of the maxim per se but rather to *the agent's rational reactions to the exceptions highlighted by the thought experiment*.[200]

4.2.3.4 The rational agency interpretation
a) Presentation
The rational agency interpretation, advanced most prominently by John Rawls, is based on a rich concept of an ideal "reasonable and rational agent."[201] On this view, the thought-experiment tests maxims according to whether or not they could be adopted by such agents, as Rawls explains: "In assessing the maxims implicit in their actions, I suppose that ideal reasonable and rational agents, who are also lucid and sincere, use [moral – A.W.] principles intuitively in

---

199 See above, section 4.2.1.
200 See below, section 5.1.3.
201 Rawls 2000; Rawls 1989; Green 1982; Herman 1993; Korsgaard 1996; Nell (O'Neill) 1975; O'Neill 1989; Pogge 1998.

their moral thought and judgment."[202] Accordingly, a good deal of the justification of this interpretation depends on spelling out what rational agency consists in and what constraints it is subject to, particularly when it comes to moral judgment. I will not be evaluating these accounts of rational agency per se, as they draw on many theoretical resources, such as contemporary action theory, that transcend the historical and systematic bounds of Kant's moral philosophy. Instead, I propose to focus on the reconstruction of the typic-procedure that Rawls proposes in his influential analysis of the application of the Categorical Imperative, which he calls "the CI-procedure."[203] While his analysis concerns the Categorical Imperative in general, he specifies that it includes the Typic as well, to which he refers at key junctures.

Rawls' interpretation is highly condensed and succinct, and so I will present it mostly in his own words. The CI-procedure has four main steps. In the first step, the agent formulates her maxim as a hypothetical imperative of the following standard form:

> 1. "'I am to do X in circumstances C in order to bring about Y unless Z.' (Here, X is an action and Y is an end, a state of affairs.)"[204]

Rawls stresses that the maxim specifies an end, since all rational action is end-directed. From the outset, he also proposes two assumptions regarding the maxim. First, the maxim is assumed to be rational from the agent's point of view: "the maxim is rational given the agent's situation and the available alternatives, together with the agent's desires, abilities and beliefs (taken to be rational in the circumstances)."[205] Second, "the maxim is also assumed to be sincere: that is, it reflects the agent's actual reasons for the intended action as the agent, presumed to be lucid, would truthfully describe them."[206] In the second step, the maxim is generalized into what Rawls calls a "universal precept" that applies to *all* rational agents:

> 2. "Everyone is to do X in circumstances C in order to bring about Y unless Z."[207]

---

[202] Rawls 2000, p. 165.
[203] Rawls 2000, p. 167–170; for a more condensed version, see also Rawls 1989.
[204] Rawls 2000, p. 168.
[205] Rawls 2000, p. 167.
[206] Rawls 2000, p. 167 f.
[207] Rawls 2000, p. 168.

4.2 Accomplishing the task — 107

In the third step, we convert the universal precept from step 2 into a law of nature:

> 3. "Everyone always does X in circumstances C in order to bring about Y, as if by a law of nature (as if such a law was implanted in us by natural instinct) [G 4: 422–423]."[208]

Rawls formulates the fourth and final step as follows:

> 4. The intuitive idea is this: We are to adjoin the as-if law of nature at step (3) to the existing laws of nature (as these are understood by us) and then think through as best we can what the order of nature would be once the effects of the newly adjoined law of nature have had sufficient time to work themselves out.[209]

This step is by far the most complicated, as Rawls proposes a number of assumptions that he argues are necessary for making the thought experiment work as a procedure for moral appraisal.

The first assumption, which could be called the *equilibrium assumption*, pertains to the counterfactual natural order generated at this stage of the thought experiment:

> It is assumed that a new order of nature results from the addition of the law at step (3) to the other laws of nature, and that this new order of nature has a settled equilibrium state the relevant features of which we are able to figure out.[210]

Given that the as-if laws that we contemplate in the typic-procedure hypothetically govern social behaviour, Rawls terms the resulting order or equilibrium state of nature the "adjusted social world" (e.g., a society where everyone 'looks with indifference on the needs of others', etc.).[211]

The second is the *perpetuity assumption:*

> [W]e are to think of the adjusted social world as if it has long since reached its conjectured equilibrium state. It is as if it has always existed, exists now, and always will exist. ... There is no lapse of time.[212]

The idea that we must 'fast-forward' time in the thought-experiment is meant to close a potential loophole. It should not be possible for an agent to take advant-

---

208 Rawls 2000, p. 168.
209 Rawls 2000, p. 169.
210 Rawls 2000, p. 169.
211 Rawls 2000, p. 169.
212 Rawls 2000, p. 171 f.

age of the lapse of time between the private adoption of a selfish maxim (e.g. false promising) and the moment when everyone else catches on (cf. *TP* 8: 286–7). As Rawls explains, "[i]t is not as if the agent working through the CI-procedure says, 'I will that my maxim be a law of nature from now on.' This would allow time for the equilibrium state to be reached, in which interval the agent might gain a considerable fortune by deceit."[213] Moreover, this formulation of the perpetuity assumption ("It is as if it has always existed, exists now, and always will exist") corresponds nicely to the strict universalizability criterion, whereby a truly universal law must hold *at all times*.[214]

The third is the *publicity assumption*, which Rawls illustrates with the false promising example:

> Now, plainly Kant assumes [in *G* 4: 422 – A.W.] ... that people learn from experience and remember the past; hence once it becomes, as it were, a law of nature that everyone tries to make a false promise (in certain circumstances), the existence of the law becomes public knowledge. Everyone knows of it, and knows that others know of it, and so on. ... We make this explicit by saying that in the equilibrium state of the adjusted social world, the as-it-were laws of nature ... are publicly recognized as laws of nature, and we are to apply the CI-procedure accordingly.[215]

This assumption does not figure explicitly in the text, but Rawls supposes that if *everyone* always acted according to a law as ubiquitous as, say, the law of universal gravitation, then they would all have some knowledge of it.

The fourth can be called the *ignorance assumption*. Unlike the previous three assumptions, however, it does not concern the representation generated within the thought experiment, but rather the agent conducting the thought experiment. Rawls proposes that the typic-procedure implicitly imposes two limits on information:

> The first limit is that we are to ignore the more particular features of persons, including ourselves, as well as the specific content of their and our final ends and desires.
> The second limit is that when we ask ourselves whether we can will the adjusted social world associated with our maxim, we are to reason as if we do not know what place we may have in that world.[216]

These limits on information are meant to safeguard the fairness of the CI-procedure by preventing egoistic interests or individual variations from biasing moral

---

[213] Rawls 2000, p. 168.
[214] See above, section 4.2.1.1.
[215] Rawls 2000, p. 171.
[216] Rawls 2000, p. 175.

appraisal. Otherwise, there would be nothing to prevent a billionaire, for example, from rationally adopting the maxim of refraining from helping others (cf. *G* 4: 423): he could just shrug at the prospect of a world in which indifference were a universal law of nature, since he could safely predict in advance that, given his vast wealth, he would surely be able to take care of himself regardless. But such a case would undermine the thought experiment by allowing egoistic prudential calculations to trump the properly moral appraisal of what is good and evil 'in itself'. Significantly, Rawls specifically refers to the text of the Typic chapter in justifying this assumption, arguing that its wording and inherent logic imply that the agent's eventual place within the counterfactual natural order is indeterminate.[217]

In sum, the CI-procedure determines the moral status of actions by *testing idealized rational agents*, subject to the assumptions stated above, with respect to two conditions:

> "First, we must be able to intend, as sincere, reasonable, and rational agents, to act from that maxim when we regard ourselves as a member of the adjusted social world associated with it, and thus as acting within that world and subject to its conditions;
> Second, we must be able to will this adjusted social world itself and affirm it should we belong to it".[218]

Correspondingly, the CI-procedure identifies morally unacceptable actions by giving rise to *contradictions in conception* (when the first condition is violated) or *contradictions in volition* (when the second condition is violated). On Rawls' reading, a *contradiction in conception* results when a rational agent entertains a maxim that, if universalized as a law of nature in the adjusted social world, would defeat her original purpose, since a rational agent as such cannot intend, on pain of self-contradiction, to do something that she knows in advance will be futile.[219] For example, once the maxim of deceitful promising becomes a law of nature in the equilibrium state, it becomes publicly known (as per the publicity assumption). In the adjusted social world, consequently, everyone knows – and

---

[217] "I find it hard to read, say, Kant's discussion of the Typic [*KpV* 5: 69 f.] without feeling that some such idea is implicit. He says: "Ask yourself whether …" Here what suggests some limit on our knowledge of our place in the adjusted social world is Kant's speaking of our being "a part" of that system of nature, and the suggestion at the end of the passage that we are to consider whether we would "assent of [our] own will," that is, freely assent, to being a member of such a world. That surely depends on what we know about our place in that world." Rawls 2000, p. 176.
[218] Rawls 2000, p. 169.
[219] Rawls 2000, p. 170f.; O'Neill 1989, p. 89–98.

everyone knows that everyone knows – that every member of that world will necessarily attempt to make a deceitful promise when they are in financial need. As a result, no agent can rationally intend to deceive in this context, for she knows in advance that she will fail to achieve her aim.[220] A *contradiction in volition* results when an agent entertains a maxim that, when universalized, would create an adjusted social world of which she could not rationally want to be a member – or, better, some member or other. For example, a rational agent as such *cannot will* to be a member of an adjusted social world in which the maxim of indifference were a universal law, for it would not be rational to *voluntarily* rob herself of the very possibility of receiving assistance that – as per the ignorance assumption – she cannot know in advance that she would not eventually need.[221]

b) Assessment

Although Rawls presents his model of the CI-procedure as a way to express "Kant's characteristic and deeper ideas,"[222] his interpretation has a predominantly Rawlsian flavour. For instance, the two limits on information immediately bring to mind his famous notion of the "veil of ignorance." And sure enough, in the chapter on the original position in *A Theory of Justice* Rawls explicitly refers to Kant's typic.[223] Incidentally, this close connection raises the interesting question of whether Rawls read his own conception of the veil of ignorance into Kant or if he derived it from Kant in the first place, or yet again if this convergence represents a case of independent invention. Rawls himself seems to suggest the third possibility when he remarks that "[t]he veil of ignorance is so natural a condition that something like it must have occurred to many."[224] In any event, the exegetical adequacy of this interpretation vis-à-vis *Kant's* thought is another matter.

Some of the assumptions that Rawls proposes can be justified to a certain extent on properly Kantian terms. For instance, the idea of imposing limits on the specific information available to the agent engaged in moral appraisal in order to minimize self-serving biases harmonizes well with Kant's repeated emphasis on the need to sharply distinguish the appraisal of what is good and evil "in itself" from the *egoistic assessment* of what is good for *me*, i.e. for *my partic-*

---

[220] Rawls 2000, p. 170–172; Green 1982, p. 22–25.
[221] Rawls 2000, p. 172–175.
[222] Rawls 2000, p. 163–164.
[223] Rawls 1999, p. 118n.
[224] Rawls 1999, p. 118n.

ular state of well-being (*KpV* 5: 57 ff., 70 – 71).[225] In addition, the 'anonymity' of the thought experiment accords well with the *universality of autonomy*, which is intrinsically impersonal, as Adorno has also underlined: "the law I give myself is not concerned simply with my own personal needs or inclinations or the chance nature of my individuality."[226]

But generally speaking, most proponents of the rational agency interpretation explicitly prioritize *Kantian ethics* over *Kant's ethics*; that is, they aim primarily for philosophical or 'systematic' plausibility rather than for exegetical fidelity. Thus, Rawls' additions to Kant's thought experiment no doubt stem from a guiding principle of his *Lectures on the History of Moral Philosophy*, namely to present each author's thought in the most philosophically plausible form.[227] However charitable and however valuable these amendments may be, I feel it is important to point out that some of Rawls' assumptions and interpolations seem to conflict with Kant's text.

First, Rawls and other proponents of the rational agency interpretation include the *end* in the formulation of the typified maxim, and correspondingly interpret the contradictions in conception and in volition in terms of "thwarted purposes."[228] But as I argued against the teleological interpretation, the typified maxim, *qua* law of nature, cannot include a material end; rather, it must be a formal if-then rule between a situation-type and an action.

Second, by universalizing and depersonalizing the thought-experiment through the ignorance and publicity assumptions, Rawls shifts the typic-procedure away from ethical concerns and towards matters of justice and politics: "the CI-procedure force[s] us to view ourselves as *proposing public moral practice for an ongoing social world*."[229] One telling indication of this shift towards the political sphere is that Rawls' model of the typic-procedure is not significantly different from the publicity test that Kant would later propose for *States*.[230]

---

225 See Kant's treatment of moral "empiricism" (*KpV* 5: 70 – 71), discussed below in section 5.2.1; see also 5.1.3.
226 Adorno 2000, p. 118.
227 Rawls 2000, p. xvi-xviii.
228 Korsgaard 1996, p. 96 ff.
229 Rawls 2000, p. 176 (my emphasis).
230 In *Perpetual Peace*, based on the principle that "justice can be thought only as publicly known," Kant proposes testing the 'publicizability' of any given claim to a right in an "experiment of pure reason": "Every claim to a right must have this capacity for publicity, and since one can very easily appraise whether it is present in a case at hand – that is, whether or not publicity is consistent with an agent's principles – it can yield a criterion to be found *a priori* in reason that is very easy to use; in case they are inconsistent we can cognize at once, as if by an experi-

Third, the rational agency interpretation assumes – and assumes that *Kant* assumes – that the typic-procedure is performed by *idealized rational agents*. But as we will see in the next chapter, Kant actually claims to be presenting a model of how "everyone, in fact, judges actions" including the "the most common understanding" (*KpV* 5: 69–70).[231]

Fourth, the rational agency interpretation faces the awkward task of reconciling two seemingly incompatible epistemic viewpoints during the thought experiment. How is the agent using the typic-procedure supposed to consider herself as rational, sincere, lucid, etc. *and at the same time* as a kind of automaton blindly following a new law of nature "as if ... by natural instinct"?[232] Conversely, how can that same automaton within the 'adjusted social world' determine what she could conceive or will without contradiction as an ideal rational agent? Note that this mental juggling act is not called for by the other main interpretations of the typic-procedure. On the logical interpretation, for instance, all one has to determine is whether the *maxim* contradicts itself logically or conceptually when universalized, not whether the *agent* contradicts herself *in situ*, so to speak.

Fifth, while Rawls' suggestion that the typic-procedure is primarily designed for maxims that reasonable people might plausibly adopt is a welcome contrast to the widespread preoccupation in the secondary literature with highly contrived maxims (e.g., "I will get money on a false promise whenever it is March 8 and I can get it from someone name Igor Cycz in order to buy a metal detector"),[233] his assumption, if taken at face value, raises the opposite worry: How can a maxim that is assumed in advance to be fully "sincere and rational" turn out to be immoral at all?

Lastly, there is one feature of the rational agency interpretation that merits special examination, namely the claim that the typic-procedure tests whether maxims are possible *in our current world*, and that it therefore requires general empirical knowledge of what nature is actually like. I want to show that although this suggestion may sound uncontroversial, it is, strictly speaking, inaccurate from an exegetical point of view – but it is all the more illuminating, because it reveals a tension in Kant's conception of the typic-procedure. The assumption is that the Categorical Imperative can only be applied to our situation if it is "adapted to our circumstances in the order of nature ... [and] takes into account

---

ment of pure reason, the falsity (illegitimacy) of the claim in question (*praetensio iuris*)" (*EF* 8: 381).

231 See below, section 5.1.
232 Cf. Rawls 2000, p. 168.
233 Timmons 2012, p. 310 ff.

the normal conditions of human life."²³⁴ That is why Rawls states that, at step four of the CI-Procedure, "we are to *adjoin* the as-if law of nature at step (3) *to the existing laws of nature* (as these are understood by us)" (my emphasis). Thomas Pogge has formulated the upshot of this interpretation as follows:

> So I take Kant's considered view to be that moral philosophy – though entirely based upon its pure part – is not entirely pure. We don't need any empirical knowledge to see that the permissibility of our maxims hinges on their meeting the test of the Categorical Imperative. But we may need some general knowledge in order to see whether some given maxim does meet this test. *Kant's question is not whether I can will my maxim to be universally available in any context, but whether I can will this in our world, against the backdrop of the actual laws of nature.*²³⁵

It certainly seems as if Kant's thought experiment presupposes some general empirical knowledge about the world in which we live. For instance, how could an agent properly appraise the false-promising maxim without the basic psychological knowledge that human beings have the capacity to remember the past?²³⁶

However, these supplementary specifications of the typic-procedure raise the problem of false negatives. A false negative, in this context, is a maxim that should be good or permissible according to our considered moral views, but turns out to be impermissible according to the typic-procedure because it cannot be universalized as a law of nature. This problem, currently much discussed in the secondary literature, was actually first pointed out by Jacob Sigismund Beck in a letter to Kant on May 31ˢᵗ, 1792:

> The procedure of the *Critique of Practical Reason* seems extraordinarily illuminating and excellent. ... But I confess that, although the transition from synthetic principles of the transcendental faculty of judgment to objects of the sense world (by means of the schemata) is quite clear to me, the transition from the moral law by means of its type is not clear. I would feel myself freed from a burden if you would kindly show me the emptiness of this question: Can't one imagine the moral law commanding something that might contradict its type? In other words, couldn't there be actions that would be inconsistent with a natural order but that are nevertheless prescribed by the moral law? It is a merely problematical thought, but it has this truth at its basis: the strict necessity of the Categorical Imperative is in no way dependent on the possibility of the existence of a natural order. Yet it would be a mistake to account for the agreement of the two as accidental (11: 340, trans. mod.).²³⁷

---

234 Rawls 2000, p. 168.
235 Pogge 1998, p. 195 (my emphasis).
236 Cf. Rawls 2000, p. 170–172.
237 [[M]ir [ist] *das Verfahren der Critick der practischen Vernunft ausserordentlich einleuchtend und fürtreflich. ... Aber ich gestehe, daß so einleuchtend wie der Uebergang der synthetischen Grundsätze der transc. Urtheilskraft zu Gegenständen der Sinnenwelt, die ihnen unterworfen*

Beck's worry – that the typic-procedure might be too specific and constricting vis-à-vis the unconditioned moral law – poses a problem not just for Kant, but for the rational agency interpretation as well, insofar as this difficulty would surely be exacerbated on the latter's requirement that a maxim become a law of nature "in our world, against the backdrop of the actual laws of nature."

Kant replied to Beck a few months later. His letter must be given significant weight, as it constitutes the only text in the entire corpus, besides the Typic chapter itself, where Kant discusses the typic. Kant's strategy for avoiding the problem of false negatives hinges on the theoretical distinction, made in the *Critique of Pure Reason* and *Prolegomena*, between the purely formal, *a priori* notion of "a natural order in general [*eine Naturordnung überhaupt*]" governed by universal laws of nature, on the one hand, and, on the other, the notion of a "particular nature [*eine bestimmte Naturordnung*]," as a particular constellation of nature at a particular time, governed by particular empirical laws which must discovered *a posteriori* (P 4: 320; *KrV* A216/B263, A126–8, B165):

> As for the question, Can there not be actions incompatible with the existence of a natural order but which are yet prescribed by the moral law? I answer, Certainly! If you mean, a *particular order of nature*, for example, that of the present world. For example, a courtier, must recognize it as a duty always to be truthful, although he would not remain a courtier for long if he did. *But that type only contains the form of a natural order in general*, that is, the agreement of actions as events with moral laws just as with natural laws, *but only as regards their universality, for this in no way concerns the particular laws of any one nature or other* (11: 348, trans. mod., my emphasis).[238]

---

sind vermittelst der Schemate, mir vorkömmt, mir der des Sittengesetzes vermittelst des Typus desselben, nicht erscheint, und ich würde wie von einer Last befreyet seyn, wenn Sie freundschaftlich, die Nichtigkeit folgender Frage mir zeigen wollten. Ich frage nehmlich, kann man sich nicht denken, daß das Sittengesetz etwas geböte, das seinem Typus zuwider wäre, mit andern Worten: kann es nicht Handlungen geben, bey denen eine Naturordnung nicht bestehen kann, und die doch das Sittengesetz vorschreibt? Es ist ein bloß problematischer Gedanke, aber ihm liegt doch das Wahre zum Grunde, daß die strenge Nothwendigkeit des categorischen Imperativs, keinesweges von der Möglichkeit des Bestehens einer Naturordnung herzuleiten ist; aber darin werde ich irren, wenn ich die Uebereinstimmung beyder für zufällig erkläre.]

238 [*Was die Frage betrifft: Kan es nicht Handlungen geben, bey denen eine Naturordnung nicht bestehen kan und die doch das Sittengesetz vorschreibt, so antworte ich, allerdings! namlich eine bestimmte Naturordnung z. B. die der Gegenwärtigen Welt z. B. ein Hofmann muß es als Pflicht erkennen jederzeit warhaft zu seyn, ob er gleich alsdann nicht lange Hofmann bleiben wird. Aber es ist in jenem Typus nur die Form einer Naturordnung überhaupt d.i. der Zusammenhang der Handlungen als Begebenheiten nach sittlichen Gesetzen gleich als Naturgesetzen blos ihrer Allgemeinheit nach; denn dieses geht die besondere Gesetze irgend einer Natur garnicht an.*] Letter to Jacob Sigismund Beck, July 3, 1792 (11: 348).

To be sure, Kant's reply is somewhat perplexing, as the courtier example seems to appeal to particular *social* facts and conventions in a given historical period rather than, as one would have expected, overtly *natural* facts and laws. Kant seems to be employing the expression "a particular order of nature" to denote the present constellation of our world as a whole, including its natural and social organization – that is, precisely the richly textured "present world" that, according to Rawls and Pogge, must always serve as a backdrop when we carry out the universalization test. But here we find Kant flatly contradicting that suggestion. He emphasizes to Beck, to the contrary, that the typic-procedure judges maxims not in the context of the "present world," which is just some contingent "nature or other," but instead against the more abstract standard of "the form of a natural order in general" constituted by universal laws – wording which exactly matches the language of the Typic chapter, where Kant speaks of "merely the *form of lawfulness* in general" (*KpV* 5: 70). On strictly textual grounds, then, this suggestion by the rational agency interpretation seems untenable.

Kant seems to think that this abstract, universal construal of the typic-procedure allows him to dodge the problem of false negatives raised by Beck: a maxim will not be unduly disqualified if, when universalized, it conflicts in some way with the merely contingent parameters of the world in its current, particular state. Returning to the example, the maxim of truthfulness, if consistently followed by the courtier, would doubtless ruin his career and, if universalized, damage the institution of the court itself, which is predicated on flattery and deceit. However, those consequences within the contingent configuration of "the present world" should not detract from the proper conclusion of the typic-procedure in this case, namely that the maxim of truthfulness can nonetheless be conceived as fitting into a system of universal practical laws (governing all actions without exception) that is formally analogous, qua universally lawful, to a natural order in general (governing all events without exception).[239] On this reading, Kant's letter dovetails with his injunction in the Deduction to judge the imperfect, "ectypal" world in which we live and act in light of the ideal moral world, which is in turn conceived on the model of the thoroughgoing lawfulness of nature (Type$_2$) as a "*natura archetypa*" (*KpV* 5: 43).[240]

On the other hand, Kant's strategy here may invite the opposite problem of false positives: Does the concept of formal universalizability in a natural order in general provide a sufficiently determinate criterion for excluding all the maxims

---

[239] See Part 2, Ch. 7, section 4.2. Conversely, the maxim of untruthfulness could never be conceived as a universal law in an enduring order of nature (*KpV* 5: 44).
[240] See above, section 4.1.2.

that we would reasonably consider to be morally impermissible? The worry is all the more pressing, as Kant's account does not make it clear how to run the thought-experiment in such an abstract way. How can one mentally construct a world where the maxim of (un)truthfulness were universalized as a law of nature *without* assuming the backdrop of the laws and facts of biology (the functioning of the vocal tract, auditory system, etc.), physics (the propagation of sound waves), and psychology (memory, theory of mind, etc.)? Ironically, by trying to make Kant's thought-experiment as plausible as possible, the rational agency interpretation seems to have uncovered a philosophical problem, or at least a tension, in the typic-procedure – one that calls for additional examination by scholars, as it directly concerns the applicability of the Categorical Imperative.

Chapter 5.
The outcome and effectiveness

5.1 The Typic's heuristic effectiveness for the 'common understanding'

The typic is not some subtle trick or sophisticated mechanism reserved for clever moral philosophers, Kant avers, but rather a way of thinking that *everyone* actually employs: "Everyone does, in fact, appraise actions as morally good or evil by this rule [*Nach dieser Regel beurtheilt in der That jedermann Handlungen, ob sie sittlich gut oder böse sind*]" (*KpV* 5: 69). He stresses that conducting thought experiments using the typic-procedure requires no special instruction, as even the untutored human mind already possesses the necessary representations and cognitive capacities:

> This is how even the most common understanding judges; for the law of nature always lies at the basis of its most ordinary judgments, even those of experience. Thus it has the law of nature always at hand, only that in cases where causality from freedom is to be appraised it makes that *law of nature* merely the type of a *law of freedom* ... (*KpV* 5: 70).[241]

In other words, Kant claims that the typic is so user-friendly that "even the commonest understanding" can – and does "in fact" – carry out such thought-experiments with ease, as if by second nature.[242] The purpose of the present chapter is to explain this claim from an exegetical point of view.

5.1.1 The common understanding's moral discernment

Kant's comments about the common understanding's use of the typic must be read in light of his numerous remarks throughout the corpus attesting the common understanding's competence, and even acuity, in all aspects of moral judgment.[243] Beck sums up Kant's attitude as follows:

---

[241] [*So urtheilt selbst der gemeinste Verstand; denn das Naturgesetz liegt allen seinen gewöhnlichsten, selbst den Erfahrungsurtheilen immer zum Grunde. Er hat es also jederzeit bei Hand, nur daß er in Fällen, wo die Causalität aus Freiheit beurtheilt werden soll, jenes Naturgesetz blos zum Typus eines Gesetzes der Freiheit macht ...*]
[242] Cf. Dietrichson 1969, p. 170f., 180ff.
[243] (*KrV* A831/B859; *KpV* 5: 36–7, 44, 92; *G* 4:402–405; *TP* 8: 286–7; *VE Collins* 27: 1426–9; *VE Mrongovius* 29: 628–9, 632).

Kant, more than any philosopher of his age, respected the "ordinary moral consciousness" of the ordinary man; under the influence of his early Pietism and of Rousseau, he came to regard the unshakable moral convictions of the simple and humble as the proper starting point for philosophical analysis; and philosophy, so far from being the moral teacher of mankind, is given the task of defending it from its outward enemies – the philosophers of heteronomous ethics – and its internal dangers – moral fanaticism and mysticism.[244]

Kant's praise of the common understanding's moral discernment was no platitude; other philosophers, such as Schopenhauer, have openly shown disdain for it.[245] But on what basis does Kant regard the common understanding's capacity for moral judgment so highly? In addition to the well-known historical influences mentioned by Beck, two general reasons can be adduced.

The first reason is an *a priori* argument based on the principle that 'ought implies can'. The moral law requires that *everyone* reliably determine what particular actions comply with its commands, and therefore *everyone* – "even the commonest understanding" – is in principle capable of making accurate moral judgments: "… the commonest human understanding can easily discern whether a thing be right or wrong, for it merely has to ask itself whether that thing could be a universal law. A principle of morality must at the same time be comprehensible to the commonest understanding, because every man must possess it, and such is the case here" (*VE Mrongovius* 29: 628, trans. mod).[246] *A fortiori*, Kant surely held that the common understanding *must* be capable of employing the typic-procedure, since it is the *only* possible method for moral appraisal.[247]

The second reason is *a posteriori*. Throughout his life, Kant keenly observed how ordinary people engaged in moral appraisal, in particular during spirited conversations in which groups of friends and acquaintances debated the

---

244 Beck 1960, p. 235. See also (*BB* 20: 44) and Kuehn 2002, p. 144–187. Below, in section 5.1., I discuss why and how Kant defends the common understanding from these two "dangers."
245 "Bei den Meisten Menschen ist die Urteilskraft bloß nominell vorhanden: es ist eine Art Ironie, daß man sie den normalen Geisteskräften beizählt, statt sie allein den monstris per excessum zuzuschreiben. Die gewöhnlichen Köpfe zeigen selbst in den kleinsten Angelegenheiten Mangel an Zutrauen zu ihrem eigenen Urtheil; eben weil sie aus Erfahrung wissen, daß es keines verdient. Seine Stelle nimmt bei ihnen Vorurteil und Nachurteil ein; wodurch sie in einem Zustand fortdauernder Unmündigkeit erhalten werden, aus welcher unter vielen Hunderten kaum Einer losgesprochen wird." Schopenhauer 2008, p. 108.
246 See also (*KrV* 807/B835, A831/B859; *G* 4: 404; *KpV* 5: 36–7; *Refl* 3345, 16: 789–790). Of course, other philosophers have doubted whether moral judgment is really as self-evident as Kant claims here, e.g., Adorno 2000, p. 116.
247 See Allison 2011, p. 178.

moral worth of other peoples' actions. In the *Critique of Practical Reason* Kant provides a telling description of such conversations:

> If one attends to the course of conversation in mixed companies consisting not merely of scholars and subtle reasoners but also of business people or women, one notices that their entertainment includes, besides story-telling and jesting, arguing [*Räsonieren*] ... Now, of all arguments there are none that more excite the participation of persons who are otherwise soon bored with subtle reasoning and that bring a certain liveliness into the company than arguments about the *moral worth* of this or that action by which the character of some person is to be made out. Those for whom anything subtle and refined in theoretical questions is dry and irksome soon join in when it is a question of how to make out the moral import of a good or evil action that has been related, and to an extent one does not otherwise expect of them on any object of speculation they are precise, refined, and subtle in thinking out everything that could lessen or even just make suspect the purity of purpose and consequently the virtue in it (*KpV* 5: 153–4).

If we take these empirical observations at face value, we can understand Kant's claim that ordinary people can – and do in fact – readily employ the typic-procedure.[248]

5.1.2 An 'example in a case of experience'

Nevertheless, Kant's insistence that the common understanding is adept at employing the typic-procedure remains puzzling from an epistemological point of view. On the one hand, Kant defines the common understanding as "the faculty of cognition and of the use of rules *in concreto*, as distinguished from the *speculative understanding*, which is a faculty of rules *in abstracto*. ... The common understanding, therefore, has a use no further than the extent to which it can see its rules confirmed in experience (although these rules are actually present in it *a priori*) ..." (*P* 4: 369–370, trans. mod.; cf. *JL* 9: 27). On the other hand, the typic-procedure operates with extremely abstract representations of formal lawfulness. Thus there seems to be mismatch between the *concreteness* needed by the common understanding and the *abstractness* required by the typic. Nonetheless, I will argue that this gap can be bridged if one appreciates that the *example* provided by the typic serves as a concrete, easily recognizable cue that triggers the common understanding's *a priori* representation of the law of natural causal-

---

[248] Incidentally, passages such as this one also conflict with Longuenesse's contention that, according to Kant, the common understanding can infallibly *derive duties* yet struggles with *moral appraisal*. Cf. Longuenesse 2005, 238 f.

ity, which can then be employed, by means of (largely unconscious) analogies, as a type for moral appraisal.

Let us begin by taking a closer look at the relevant passage:

> If the maxim of the action is not so constituted that it can stand the test as to the form of a law of nature in general, then it is morally impossible. This is how even the most common understanding judges; for the law of nature always lies at the basis of its most ordinary judgments, even those of experience. Thus it has the law of nature always at hand, only that in cases where causality from freedom is to be appraised it makes that *law of nature* merely the type of a *law of freedom*, because without having at hand something which it could make an example in a case of experience, it could not provide use in application for the law of a pure practical reason (5: 69–70).[249]

In other words, the common understanding, uncomfortable with abstraction, is ill-suited to employ what was described in the *Groundwork* as "the strict method [*die strenge Methode*]" of moral appraisal based solely on FUL: "*act only in accordance with a maxim that can at the same time make itself a universal law*" (G 4: 436). This abstract and austere injunction, on its own, would draw a blank stare. However, this resistance is not a sign of obtuseness; on the contrary, the demand that abstractions be elucidated by means of concrete examples is entirely legitimate.[250] Whence the difficulty that makes the typic necessary: no sensible intuition – and hence no example – can be given of the moral law or of the morally good, because they are supersensible Ideas (*KpV* 5: 69).[251]

A similar difficulty arises in the theoretical sphere, where there is a mismatch between the concretely-minded common understanding and the law of natural causality, which is an abstract, pure law of the understanding (*Verstandesgesetz*): "The common understanding will, then, hardly be able to understand the rule: that everything which happens is determined by its cause, and it will never be able to have insight into it in such a general way. It therefore demands

---

249 [*Wenn die Maxime der Handlung nicht so beschaffen ist, daß sie an der Form eines Naturgesetzes überhaupt die Probe hält, so ist sie sittlich unmöglich. So urtheilt selbst der gemeinste Verstand; denn das Naturgesetz liegt allen seinen gewöhnlichsten, selbst den Erfahrungsurtheilen immer zum Grunde. Er hat es also jederzeit bei Hand, nur daß er in Fällen, wo die Causalität aus Freiheit beurtheilt werden soll, jenes Naturgesetz blos zum Typus eines Gesetzes der Freiheit macht, weil er, ohne etwas, was er zum Beispiele im Erfahrungsfalle machen könnte, bei Hand zu haben, dem Gesetze einer reinen praktischen Vernunft nicht den Gebrauch in der Anwendung verschaffen könnte.*]
250 (*KrV* Axvii-xviii, Bxliv; *JL* 9: 62–3; *VL* Dohna-Wundlacken 24: 729–30; *VL* Wiener 24: 834–6, 848–9). I stress the importance of this "intuitive," or "aesthetic," clarity in A. Westra 2009, p. 1–14.
251 See above, section 2.2.

an example from experience …" (*P* 4: 369). Here, though, the common understanding's demand for an example can be met – indeed, nothing could be easier, as *all events in nature* necessarily comply with the law of natural causality. The law *of nature* is a representation that possesses "aesthetic universality," i.e., it can be illustrated by a virtually infinite number of examples, any one of which cues the rule under which it falls as concrete instance (*JL* 9: 39). Thus, when the common understanding "hears that this rule means nothing other than what it had always thought when a windowpane was broken or a household article had disappeared, it then understands the principle and grants it" (*P* 4: 369). In other words, when presented with a broken windowpane, the common understanding will never assume that it simply shattered out of the blue; rather, it will judge that *something* (e.g., a thrown rock), *must have caused the window to break*. Likewise, when it notices that a household article has gone missing, it will not assume that the object spontaneously vanished, but that *someone must have removed it*. Note that these judgments are neither inductive generalizations ("Windowpanes are often broken by stones") nor inferences to the best explanation ("This windowpane was most likely broken by those kids playing catch next door"). Rather, as Kant declares in the B Introduction of the first *Critique*, such judgments attest that "we are in possession of certain *a priori* cognitions, and even the common understanding is never without them" (*KrV* B3–6) That is, these judgments, as applications of the (implicit) synthetic *a priori* proposition that "every alteration must have a cause," are thought "in strict universality, i.e., in such a way that no exception at all is allowed to be possible" (*KrV* B4). Thus the common understanding is capable of applying the universal principle, despite its inability to spell it out in abstract terms, as long as it has at hand a concrete example, i.e., an *instance* of that very law (*casus datae legis*).

Kant's ingenious strategy in the Typic chapter is to show how this solution in the theoretical sphere can provide the basis for solving the particular difficulty of giving the common understanding a concrete handle on the supersensible moral law for the purpose of moral appraisal. Although no example can be given of the Ideas themselves, he recalls that "in the most ordinary judgments" the common understanding duly represents every single "case of experience" as necessarily conforming to the law of natural causality. And, as we have just seen, such judgments are thought "in strict universality, i.e., in such a way that no exception at all is allowed to be possible" (*KrV* B4). Thus, any event in experience, no matter how banal, can serve as a concrete instance – and thus as an example (*Beispiel*) in the proper sense – that points towards the strict universality of the law of natural causality to which all "objects of sensible intuition as such are subject" (*KpV* 5: 69). Indeed, an "example [*Beispiel*]" is defined as a *direct presentation* of a concept, i.e., "a particular (*concretum*), represented in accordance with concepts as contained under a universal (*abstractum*)" (*MS* 6: 479n). In other words, any "case of experience" can be an example of the law of nature because every case of experience is an instance of that law. And once a concrete event has triggered the representation of *universal physical law* of which it is an example, the common understanding can then employ this representation (which it already possesses *a priori*) as "the type of the law of freedom" in virtue of an *analogy* between the two laws *qua* universal and hence 'exceptionless'. Just as the law of natural causality necessarily applies to each and every "case of experience" *without exception* (*KrV* A542/B570), so must the moral law govern each and every action *without exception* (*G* 4: 421, 424). This analogy, in turn, guides the common understanding's *moral appraisal:* just as "in the most ordinary judgments of ... experience" one must reject – i.e, *disbelieve* – each and every purported *exception* to the law of nature as superstition (*KU* 5: 294; *JL* 9: 11; *VA Friedländer* 25: 549), so "in cases where causality from freedom is to be appraised" (*KpV* 5: 70) must one reject – i.e., *condemn* – each and every purported *exception* to the moral law as morally unacceptable (*G* 4: 424). Thus, the common understanding "has the law of nature always at hand" – i.e., *in every instance* – for use as the type of the moral law (*KpV* 5: 70; cf. *P* 4: 369–370; *KrV* B4).

To be sure, Kant never states that the common understanding works through these abstract analogies *consciously,* but it seems reasonable to infer that some of the principles and cognitive processes underlying the typic can operate largely *unconsciously.* This suggestion is not as unorthodox as it might sound. Kant does in fact state that the complex mechanics of human cognition operate mostly unconsciously and are only retrospectively spelled out by conscious examination: "The exercise of our powers also takes place according to certain rules that we follow, *unconscious* of them at first, until we gradually arrive at cognition of them through experiments and lengthy use of our powers, indeed, until we finally become so familiar with them that it costs us much effort to think them *in abstracto*" (*JL* 9: 11). For instance, in the *Critique of Pure Reason* Kant famously describes the schematism as "a hidden art in depths of the human soul whose true operations we can divine from nature and lay unveiled before our eyes only with difficulty" (*KrV* A141/B181), and he also hints that the understanding's transcendental "combination" operates partly unconsciously (*KrV* B129–130). And in a section of the *Anthropology* entitled "On the representations that we have without being conscious of them," he ventures that "the field of *obscure* representations [dunkle *Vorstellungen*] is the largest in the human being" (*APH* 7: 136; cf. *VA Friedländer* 25: 179). Kant cites the ubiquitous example of *language:* human beings deftly apply the abstract rules of grammar in an unconscious manner and without special instruction.²⁵² Tellingly, he specifically states that *the common understanding* makes universally valid judgments according to unconscious rational principles: "One must not regard what is universally judged through sound understanding to be absurd because it has no principle [*Grund*], but the principle exists in reason, for otherwise human beings could not judge universally. The principle however still exists in obscurity …" (*VA Friedländer* 25: 480, trans. mod.). Regarding the typic, then, it seems reasonable to propose that just as the common understanding can perfectly well make ordinary experiential judgments of cause and effect without consciously calling to mind its a *priori* representations of the law of nature or of *natura formaliter spectata* in their abstract forms, so can it make a habitual, unconscious use of these same representations for the purpose of moral appraisal without being consciously aware of *how* it's doing what it's doing.

One last point to note in this connection is that, to the extent that Kant's philosophical account of the typic makes its underlying processes and principles explicit, it may deviate from the way in which flesh-and-blood human beings ordinarily *experience* moral judgment first-hand (just as a linguist's scientific reconstruction of the grammar of a given language differs from a native speaker's internal representation of it). Yet Kant was well aware of the difference between the philosopher's abstract, theoretical point of view and the common understanding's own concrete, immediate cognition. In the *Prolegomena* Kant distinguishes clearly between the two viewpoints with respect to the principles of theoretical cognition: "to have insight into these rules *a priori* and independently of experience falls to the speculative understanding, and lies completely beyond the horizon of the common understanding" (*P* 4: 370, trans. mod.). And in the first section of the *Groundwork* he famously effects a marked "transition from common rational to philosophical moral cognition" (*G* 4: 493ff.), declaring that with the identification of the principle of duty "we have arrived, within the moral cognition of common human reason, at its principle, which it admittedly does not think so abstractly in a universal form, but which it always actual-

---

252 "Thus universal grammar is the form of a language in general, for example. One speaks even without being acquainted with grammar, however; and he who speaks without being acquainted with it does actually have a grammar and speaks according to rules, but ones of which he is not himself conscious" (*JL* 9: 11). This remarkable passage, which appears to anticipate certain themes of Noam Chomsky's revolution of linguistics, raises an intriguing possibility that is currently being explored in cognitive science: Could linguistic cognition provide an analogical model for how the human mind engages in moral cognition, *viz.* by unconsciously computing abstract rules that together constitute a largely innate 'moral grammar'? See Mikhail 2011.

ly ... uses as the norm of its appraisals [*welches sie sich zwar freilich nicht so in einer allgemeinen Form abgesondert denkt, aber doch jederzeit wirklich ... zum Richtmaße ihrer Beurteilung braucht*]" (G 4: 403–404). This leaves the philosopher with the theoretical task of as it were retrospectively spelling out, systematizing and justifying the implicit principles of moral appraisal that the common understanding already effectively employs in virtue of an "obscurely conceived" metaphysics.[253] Now, the Typic chapter, situated at the heart of *Critique of Practical Reason*, clearly belongs to the moral philosopher's task thus characterized. Consequently, Kant's *primary objective* in the Typic chapter was surely to provide a technical and systematic account of how the 'practical heterogeneity problem' is overcome rather than a phenomenological description of ordinary moral cognition from a first-person perspective.

5.1.3 Isolation and amplification

Although the conceptual mechanics underlying *typification* may operate largely unconsciously, the *typic-procedure* does have some heuristic functions that facilitate the common understanding's moral reflection. For Kant avers that the typic-procedure does more than just make moral appraisal *possible:* it also makes it *easier, more reliable and more accurate.* The typic-procedure accomplishes this feat by means of two heuristics which I will call *isolation* and *amplification:* by isolating and amplifying the conscience of the person doing the appraising, the typic-procedure helps to counteract our egoistic bias with respect to our own behaviour, especially our tendency to make exceptions for ourselves. These two heuristics have been aptly explained by Pogge in his account of the application of the Categorical Imperative:

> ... its ingenuity consists in that it facilitates a decision by transforming it from one concerning oneself in a concrete situation (where it may be quite difficult to avoid bad faith and dishonesty) to one concerning the world at large. Such a thought experiment shows whether I, as a rational agent in a world of human beings, can really will the maxims I am about to adopt. In this way, the [typic-procedure – A.W.] *amplifies* my conscience by transforming the decision from one of marginal significance into one concerning the world at large, and also *isolates* my conscience by screening out any personal considerations that might affect my choice of maxims but are irrelevant.[254]

---

253 Cf. Piché 2003, p. 128.
254 Pogge 1998, p. 206.

Thus, the typic-procedure promotes the reliability of moral judgment by affording us a point of view from which we can judge actions with greater seriousness, responsibility and openness. We must regard our maxims as *fully* our own, but not as *merely* our own. From framing private decisions that ostensibly only concern ourselves (and can perhaps be treated as insignificant or secret exceptions), we envision ourselves as *legislators* whose judgment affects everyone. This simulation can act as a powerful psychological counterweight to our egoistic duplicity towards others and even ourselves. Together, isolation and amplification make moral appraisal easy, even *obvious:*

> When the maxim on which I intend to give testimony is tested by practical reason, I always consider what it would be if it were to hold as a universal law of nature. *It is obvious* that [*Es ist offenbar, daß* ...] in this way everyone would be necessitated to truthfulness. For it cannot hold with the universality of a law of nature that statements should be allowed as proof and yet be intentionally untrue. Similarly, the maxim that I adopt with respect to disposing freely of my life is *at once determined* [*sofort bestimmt*] when I ask myself what it would have to be in order that a nature should maintain itself in accordance with such a law. *It is obvious* that [*Offenbar* ...] in such a nature no one could end his life *at will*, for such an arrangement would not be an enduring natural order. *And so in all other cases (KpV* 5: 44, my emphasis).

In other words, the typic-procedure's heuristic functions make contradictions in conception and contradictions in volition leap out at the moral agent in such a way that she cannot miss or ignore them.[255]

5.2 The typic's protective functions

Kant closes the Typic chapter with a relatively long concluding remark (a quarter of the chapter's total length), which, he says, "will serve to prevent reckoning among concepts themselves that which belongs merely to the *typic* of concepts" (*KpV* 5: 70).[256] Significantly, he maintains that the Typic is so "important and advisable" because it "guards against" or "protects from [*bewahrt von*]" from two dangers threatening morality: empiricism and mysticism.

---

[255] See section 4.2.1. above.
[256] [... *so dient die gegenwärtige Anmerkung dazu, um zu verhüten, daß, was blos zur Typik der Begriffe gehört, nicht zu den Begriffen selbst gezählt werde.*]

5.2.1 Guarding against empiricism

In the Typic chapter Kant offers the following definition of the philosophical doctrine that he calls the "empiricism of practical reason" (hereinafter: "moral empiricism"): it "places the practical concepts of good and evil merely in experiential consequences (so-called happiness)" (*KpV* 5: 70). In other words, moral empiricism holds that the supreme principle of morality is the *principle of happiness*, whereby "a rational being's consciousness of the agreeableness of life uninterruptedly accompanying his whole existence" ought to be "the supreme determining ground of his choice" (*KpV* 5: 22). This doctrine is *empirical* in two respects. Firstly, its principle designates an empirical state: *happiness* is a maximum feeling of pleasure or well-being in the human being *qua* sensible organism. Secondly, it entails an empirical consideration of the "experiential consequences [*Erfahrungsfolgen*]" (*KpV* 5: 70) of actions, i.e., their effects – in accordance with *natural causality* – on happiness. As is well known, Kant developed a wide-ranging and fundamental critique of this form of consequentialism throughout his critical works on moral philosophy. In the present context, I will limit myself to two issues of direct relevance to the Typic: firstly, moral empiricism falsifies moral appraisal; secondly, it "degrades humanity" by corrupting our moral dispositions.

Moral empiricism proposes a consequentialist criterion for moral appraisal: *an action is good if and only if it causes an increase in happiness and/or a decrease in suffering; an action is evil if and only if it causes a reduction in happiness and/or an increase in suffering*. However, by equating the concepts of good and evil with happiness and suffering, respectively, moral empiricism conflates Kant's fundamental distinction between, on the one hand, the properly moral concepts of good (*das sittlich Gute*) and evil (*das sittlich Böse*) and, on the other, the empirical concepts of well-being (*das Wohl*) and ill-being (*das Übel*) or woe (*das Weh*). Kant lays out the difference in the chapter immediately preceding the Typic, "On the concept of an object of pure practical reason":

> *Well–being* or *ill-being* always signifies only a reference to our state of *agreeableness* or *disagreeableness*, of gratification or pain, and if we desire or avoid an object on this account we do so only insofar as it is referred to our sensibility and to the feeling of pleasure or displeasure it causes. But *good* [*gut*] or *evil* [*böse*] always signifies a reference to the *will* insofar as it is determined by the *law of reason* to make something its object; for, it is never determined directly by the object and the representation of it, but is instead a faculty of making a rule of reason the motive of an action (by which an object can become real) (*KpV* 5: 59–60).

As a result, moral empiricism misconstrues the nature of moral appraisal altogether, for it neglects the fact that there are correspondingly "two very different appraisals of an action depending upon whether we take into consideration the *good* and *evil* of it or our *well-being* and *woe* (ill-being)" (*KpV* 5: 59–60). Only the former kind of appraisal is properly moral, in Kant's view, whereas the latter remains an empirical matter pertaining to theoretical judgment. But moral empiricism collapses this distinction by reducing the appraisal of actions to an empirical problem of figuring out the most reliable technique for producing the most frequent, intense and durable feelings of pleasure in our bodies.[257] By contrast, the typic guards against any such reduction by emphasizing the distinction between theoretical and pure practical judgment: "Subsumption of an action possible to me in the sensible world under a *pure practical law* does not concern the possibility of the *action* as an event in the sensible world; for it belongs to the theoretical use of reason to appraise that possibility in accordance with the law of causality" (*KpV* 5: 68).[258]

Furthermore, empirical moral judgments cannot yield the *universality* that is required for all pronouncements of the pure practical faculty of judgment. Kant has no shortage of arguments to this effect. To begin with, all empirical propositions about happiness are contingent and *a posteriori*; hence, they can at best attain mere "generality" (i.e., validity for *most* cases), but never "true universality" (*KrV* B4), i.e., *a priori* validity for *all* possible objects to which they refer – a point that Kant reiterates in the second *Critique:* "It is an outright contradiction to want to extract necessity from an empirical proposition (*ex pumice aquam*) and to give a judgment, along with necessity, true universality ..." (*KpV* 5: 12, cf. *G* 4: 424). In addition, as a true moral rationalist, Kant insists that we must in principle be able to reach a universal and definitive *consensus* on which actions to will or avoid: "[w]hat we are to call good or evil must be an object of the faculty of desire *in the judgment of every reasonable human being*, and evil an object of aversion *in the eyes of everyone*; hence for this appraisal reason is needed, in addition to sense" (*KpV* 5: 61, my emphasis). By contrast, the utilitarian principle that those actions which cause people to suffer should be condemned while those which foster human well-being should be lauded may seem straightforward, yet it turns out to be difficult to apply. Ironically, it is an empirical fact that the sources of pleasure and happiness vary so wildly from one individual to another that not even a general consensus could ever

---

[257] For a contemporary – and unabashed – defense of this conception of ethics that would doubtless horrify Kant, see Harris 2010.
[258] See above, section 3.1.2.2.

be arrived at. Indeed, even a single person who set out to maximize only his own happiness would be hard pressed to arrive at a coherent and definitive strategy, as Kant explains in a famous *Groundwork* passage reminiscent of Ecclesiastes: "If he wills riches, how much anxiety, envy and intrigue might he not bring upon himself in this way! If he wills a great deal of knowledge and insight, that might become only an eye all the more acute to show him, as all the more dreadful, ills that are now concealed from him and that cannot be avoided, or to burden his desires, which already give him enough to do, with still more needs. ..." (*G* 4: 418). In the *Critique of Practical Reason*, Kant restates this point in more abstract terms. The empirically conditioned principle of happiness cannot generate rules susceptible of being *universalized as laws* for the will, in the absence of which individual judgments will inevitably diverge:

> "The principle of happiness can indeed furnish maxims, but never such as would fit for laws of the will ... For, because cognition of this rests on sheer data of experience, each judgment about it depending very much upon the opinion of each which is itself very changeable, it can indeed give *general* rules but never *universal* rules, that is, it can give rules that on the average are most often correct but not rules that must hold always and necessarily; hence no practical laws can be based on it ... and then the variety of judgment must be endless (*KpV* 5: 36, trans. mod.).

Relatedly, Kant maintains that the process of conscious calculation involved in making appraisals based on considerations of happiness is far too complex, uncertain and inconclusive to be reliably executed by the common understanding: "what brings true lasting advantage, if this is to extend to the whole of one's existence, is always veiled in impenetrable obscurity, and much prudence is required to adapt the practical rule in accordance with it to the ends of life even tolerably, by making the appropriate exceptions" (*KpV* 5: 36–7). Once again showing his rationalist colours, Kant holds that only the pure rational criterion of universalizability can explain the simplicity, reliability, and naturalness of common moral judgments: "The concept of duty in its complete purity is ... incomparably simpler, clearer and, for practical use, more readily grasped and more natural to everyone than any motive derived from happiness, or mixed with it and with regard for it (which always requires much art and reflection)" (*TP* 8: 287–287).

In sum, happiness fails as a criterion for moral appraisal, as it prevents us from arriving at universally applicable judgments about which particular actions should or should not be performed. By contrast, the typic-procedure *guards against* all of this confusion, uncertainty and dissensus by operationalizing a truly *universal* criterion for moral appraisal that *abstracts* from individuals' private ends and opinions.

The second major danger that Kant sees in moral empiricism is that it corrupts the morality of dispositions and thereby *degrades humanity:*

> However, it is much more important and advisable to guard against *empiricism* of practical reason, since *mysticism* is ... not natural and not in keeping with the common way of thinking ... so that the danger from this side is not so general; empiricism, on the contrary, destroys at its root the morality of dispositions (in which, and not merely in actions, consists the high worth that humanity can and ought to procure for itself through morality), and substitutes for it something quite different, namely in place of duty an empirical interest, with which the inclinations generally are secretly leagued; and empiricism, moreover, being on this account allied with the inclinations, which (no matter what fashion they put on) degrade humanity when they are raised to the dignity of a supreme practical principle and which are, nevertheless, so favorable to everyone's way of feeling, is for that reason much more dangerous than any enthusiasm, which can never constitute a lasting condition of any great number of people (*KpV* 5: 71).

Empiricism poses a greater danger than mysticism for two reasons. Firstly, it threatens a greater number of people: the principle 'if it feels good, then it can't be wrong' immediately appeals to everyone's "way of feeling" – rather than to their principled "way of *thinking*" or *Denkungsart* (*APH* 7: 294 ff.) – easily finding support from our sensible inclinations, egoism and complacency. Secondly, empiricism does greater damage than mystical *Schwärmerei*. By substituting the empirically conditioned principle of self-love for that of duty, empiricism prevents us from exercising our will in a morally pure way (*G* 4: 426). Worse still, it is positively shameful, Kant believes, to privilege self-interest or even combine it with considerations of duty. Thus, regarding the example of a person faced with the possibility of appropriating a deposit (*Depositum*) entrusted to him, Kant writes: "He even feels, if the concept of duty counts for something with him, a *revulsion* merely at calculating the advantages he could gain by transgressing it" (*TP* 8: 286–7). By deriving the concept of the good from the feeling of pleasure, which is in turn determined by natural causes acting on our bodies, moral empiricism posits a *heteronomous* principle of morality (cf. *KpV* 5: 64, 33, 35–7) and thereby degrades our conduct to "mere animality," i.e. the instinctive, merely mechanical pursuit of pleasure and avoidance of pain. By contrast, the true *worth* and *dignity* that humanity "can and ought to procure for itself" rests on the exercise of autonomy and on the employment of pure practical reason to determine what is good and evil "in itself" (*KpV* 5: 61–2) – and that is precisely what the typic promotes through its *a priori* criterion for moral appraisal. Lastly, we have seen that the typic's heuristics of isolation and amplification counteract our selfish impulses, fostering instead a fair, responsible, and dignified *Denkungsart*.[259]

5.2.2 Type$_3$

Immediately after explaining how the typic guards against empiricism, Kant adds a surprising qualification:

> This, then, as the typic of judgment, guards against *empiricism* of practical reason, which places the practical concepts of good and evil merely in experiential consequences (so-called happiness), although happiness and the endless useful consequences of a will determined by self-love, if this will at the same time made itself into a universal law of nature, can certainly serve as a quite suitable type for the morally good but is still not identical with it (*KpV* 5: 70).[260]

In light of Kant's insistence that empiricism be excluded from moral philosophy, his passing suggestion that *happiness* could serve as a *quite suitable type* for the morally good is puzzling. How is this third formulation of the type (henceforth "Type$_3$") supposed to work?

The answer is not immediately clear. We must first of all try to understand what it means for "a will determined by self-love" to "ma[k]e itself into a universal law of nature." One interpretation could be that the principle of self-love can easily be universalized to all finite beings, all of whom *eo ipso* feel the "empirical interest [*empirisches Interesse*]" (*KpV* 5: 70) in happiness. That is, the pursuit of happiness appeals to "*everyone's* way of feeling [*der Sinnesart* aller]" (*KpV* 5: 71) and therefore expresses a form of universality that is easy to understand. One complication, however, is that any *determinate content* given to the concept of happiness will impugn its universality. As we have seen, "happiness is not an ideal of reason but of imagination" – i.e., a protean ideal that changes shape depending who is pursuing it (*G* 4: 418). In the same vein, Kant warned earlier in the *Critique* that universalizing the maxim of *one's own happiness* as a law of nature would have catastrophic consequences (*KpV* 5: 28) – which in turn seems to

---

259 Cf. Renaut 1997, p. 313.
260 [*Diese also als Typik der Urtheilskraft bewahrt vor dem Empirism der praktischen Vernunft, der die praktischen Begriffe des Guten und Bösen blos in Erfahrungsfolgen (der sogenannten Glückseligkeit) setzt, obzwar diese und die unendlichen nützlichen Folgen eines durch Selbstliebe bestimmten Willens, wenn dieser sich selbst zugleich zum allgemeinen Naturgesetze machte, allerdings zum ganz angemessenen Typus für das sittlich Gute dienen kann, aber mit diesem doch nicht einerlei ist.*]

directly contradict the very premise of Type₃. On the other hand, the contradiction can perhaps be lifted: although the principle of happiness cannot be universalized with respect to its *content*, it may nevertheless be universalizable with respect to its *form*. This proposition can indeed be maintained, as Beck and other commentators have explained, on the assumption that the "will determined by self-love" also *harmonize* with all the other wills that are simultaneously pursuing their own happiness (cf. *KpV*, 5: 34–35; *KrV*, A809/B837).²⁶¹ The universal adoption of this magnanimous principle, in turn, would conceivably produce universal happiness and "endless useful consequences" (*KpV* 5: 70), or "infinite utility" (*KpV* 5: 162), as Kant variously puts it. Finally, this *mathematically infinite* happiness in the sensible world may, in turn, typify the *metaphysically infinite* happiness enjoyed by rational beings in the intelligible realm where the Idea of the morally good would be realized, i.e., where freedom would be united under universal laws and virtue would be universally practiced.²⁶² For my part, I would venture that Type₃ can be viewed as an audacious attempt on Kant's part to appropriate the very touchstone of moral empiricism: he effects what could be called a rationalist 'sublimation' of happiness by transforming it from the concrete goal of physical pleasure into a merely formal type of the purely rational Idea of the morally good.

5.2.3 Guarding against mysticism

The second danger from which the typic protects the pure practical power of judgment is what Kant calls the "mysticism of practical reason":

> The same typic also guards against *mysticism* of practical reason, which makes what served only as a *symbol* into a *schema*, that is, puts under the application of moral concepts real but not sensible intuitions (of an invisible kingdom of God) and strays into the transcendent (*KpV* 5: 70–71).²⁶³

---

261 Beck 1960; Marty 1955; Sala 2004; compare Reath 2010, p. 36f.
262 Kant seems to have played with this idea in a number of *Reflektionen* (*Refl* 1187, 15: 524–525; *Refl* 5445, 18: 184; *Refl* 7196, 19: 270; *Refl* 7211, 19: 286; *Refl* 7260, 19: 296–7). On the special significance of the relation between the mathematical and the metaphysical conceptions of the infinite in Kant, see Moore 1988.
263 [Eben dieselbe Typik bewahrt auch vor dem Mysticism der praktischen Vernunft, welcher das, was nur zum Symbol diente, zum Schema macht, d.i. wirkliche und doch nicht sinnliche Anschauungen (eines unsichtbaren Reichs Gottes) der Anwendung der moralischen Begriffe unterlegt und ins Überschwengliche hinausschweift.]

We can best understand what the "mysticism of practical reason" amounts to with an example. While Kant does not name anyone in particular here, the mystic *par excellence* in Kant's cultural horizon was Emanuel Swedenborg (1688–1772).[264] After a fruitful career as a scientist and inventor, in 1744 Swedenborg suddenly entered a spiritual phase which would last for the following three decades. During this time, he experienced mystical visions which he described in eighteen published theological works. In *Heaven and its Wonders and Hell From Things Heard and Seen*[265] and the eight-volume *Heavenly Mysteries*,[266] Swedenborg gave elaborate accounts of his visions of the 'spiritual world' and its inhabitants, including details about how spiritual beings eat, sleep, talk, read, play, marry, and even procreate. In effect, Swedenborg claimed to enjoy special insights thanks to his divinely imparted spiritual vision – and he also drew substantive theological, metaphysical, and moral conclusions from these revelations. As is well known, Kant took an initial interest in Swedenborg's claims about the *mundus intelligibilis* but quickly became disenchanted, ultimately lambasting and ridiculing the Swedish mystic in his *Dreams of a Spirit-Seer* (*Träume eines Geistessehers*) of 1766. Kant continued to combat mysticism in his subsequent writings: in the Typic chapter, he flags mysticism as a "danger" in the moral sphere; later on, he frequently reiterated his warning that mystical "madness" will lead to "the moral death of reason" (*SF* 7: 86; *R* 6: 101, 174–5) unless philosophy tirelessly "censures" the excesses of *Schwärmerei* (*R* 6: 601, 683; *VpR* 28: 1109; *SF* 7: 46).

In the Typic chapter, Kant specifically criticizes mysticism for denaturing the representation of the moral law: insofar as it "puts under the application of moral concepts real but not sensible intuitions," mysticism "makes what served only as a *symbol* into a *schema*" (*KpV* 5: 70).[267] Kant's formulation here lends itself to confusion, because in fact he countenances no such thing as "real but not sensible intuitions" (at least for human beings), nor does he allow that the mystical mode of representation amounts to a genuine "schema" as characterized in the *Critique of Pure Reason*. Rather, as Kant repeatedly stresses in the second *Critique*, human beings do not possess a faculty of intellectual intuition (*KpV* 5: 31, 42, 45, 46), and therefore the mystics' ostensibly supersensible illuminations are

---

[264] Other contemporaries whom Kant considered mystics were Friedrich Heinrich Jacobi (1743–1819), Johann Georg Schlosser (1739–1799), and Johann Kaspar Lavater (1741–1801).
[265] *De Caelo et Ejus Mirabilibus et de inferno, ex Auditis et Visis* (1758).
[266] *Arcana Cœlestia, quae in Scriptura Sacra seu Verbo Domini sunt, detecta* (1749–1756).
[267] Part Two provides an extensive analysis of the significance of this statement regarding the typic's place in Kant's theory of symbolism.

merely delusional *"pseudo-intuitions* of an invisible Kingdom of God"²⁶⁸ engendered by their own overheated – even sick – imaginations: "the *enthusiast (visionary, fanatic)* ... is genuinely deranged from an alleged immediate revelation and from a great familiarity with the powers of heaven. Human nature knows no more dangerous deception" (*KK* 2: 267). Consequently, Kant dismisses all attempts to attach such pseudo-intuitions to the moral Ideas as "a magic lantern of chimeras [*Zauberlaterne von Hirngespenstern*]" (*KpV* 5: 141). Critical moral philosophy must therefore "ward off *fanaticism,* which promises such an extension by means of supersensible intuitions or feelings" (*KpV* 5: 135 – 6).

Although he definitely considers mysticism a danger, Kant adopts a relatively lenient tone in the Typic chapter:

> However, it is much more important and advisable to guard against *empiricism* of practical reason, since *mysticism* is still compatible with the purity and sublimity of the moral law and, besides, it is not natural and not in keeping with the common way of thinking to strain one's imagination to supersensible intuitions, so that the danger from this side is not so general ... [E]nthusiasm [*Schwärmerei*] ... can never constitute a lasting condition of any great number of people (*KpV* 5: 70).

In other words, Kant concedes that the very *effort* involved in dreaming up these otherworldly visions testifies to the sublimity of the moral law, infinitely elevated above sensibility.²⁶⁹ Indeed, there are signs that, despite his deep philosophical misgivings, Kant continued to admire Swedenborg's visions as "quite sublime" from an aesthetic point of view.²⁷⁰ Moreover, he notes that whereas empiricism appeals directly to everyone's way of feeling, mysticism will likely only appeal to a small number of individuals. Despite these concessions, some commentators find that Kant is still too hard on mysticism in the Typic. For instance, Bulnes bemoans the strict limitations that the typic places on mystical experience, notably its preclusion of directly intuiting or feeling God's will, which leads her to charge that Kant's conception of intelligible nature "shows a great psychological and ethical poverty."²⁷¹ She then pleads for *replacing* the cold, rationalist typic with the "profoundly Christian experience" of opening one's heart to a direct influx of God's love.²⁷² In a similar vein, Grondin claims that the remote and overly intellectualized typic fails to mediate the moral law and so must give way to the feelings of "admiration and awe [*Bewunderung und Ehrfurcht*]" (*KpV* 5: 161), in-

---

268 Adickes 1927, p. 194.
269 See also Ch. 6, 3.2.1.
270 Johnson 2002, p. xv.
271 Bulnes 1989, p. 137.
272 Bulnes 1989, p. 141.

spired by what he calls "the miracle of moral elevation above and beyond the sensible world [*das Wunder der sittlichen Erhebung über das Sinnliche hinaus*]."[273]

However, it is crucial to recognize that Kant had strong philosophical reasons for excluding mysticism from morality. Firstly, Kant argues that we should not accord mystical experiences a constitutive role in morality because they cannot be publicly validated through open communication and debate. While truly "numinous" experiences can perhaps be intimated through works of art (such as Bernini's *Ecstasy of Saint Teresa*), they cannot be communicated through ordinary language or concepts.[274] And if everyone based their judgments of right and wrong on their own private, ineffable visions and feelings, then confusion and conflict would inevitably ensue, as there would be no possibility for reasoned debate, much less consensus: "For unless the supersensible … is anchored to determinate concepts of reason, such as those of morality, fantasy inevitably gets lost in the transcendent … and leads to an illuminism in which everyone has his private, inner revelations, and there is no longer any public touchstone of truth" (*SF* 7: 46; cf. *TG* 2: 342).[275] Indeed, in *Was ist Aufklärung?* Kant famously exhorted his fellow citizens to rely instead on their own reason to arrive at moral principles that could be openly communicated and debated. Accordingly, Kant also fiercely opposed those "adepts of the philosopher's stone" who promised "visionary treasures" through their ostensible "*leaps of genius*," i.e., pompous philosophers who claimed to have gained access to hidden truths about morality and humanity's place in the universe through mystical intuition, insight, or feeling (*KpV* 5: 163; *MS* 6: 377). For instance, Kant directed his 1796 essay, *On a Recently Prominent Tone of Superiority in Philosophy*, against Johann Georg Schlösser, who preached an esoteric form of Christianized Neo-Platonism. Allison has aptly explained the philosophical significance of Kant's critique: "*Tone* is an attack on philosophical esotericism, that is, any view which sees philosophy as containing secret doctrines expressed in a mysterious language that are accessible only to a few adepts by means of some special power of intuition. Not only is

---

[273] Grondin 2000, p. 394.
[274] See Otto 2004.
[275] Tellingly, even Freud recognized the priority of public rationality over private 'illumination' in *Die Zukunft einer Illusion* (1927) for this precise reason: "Es gibt keine Instanz über der Vernunft. Wenn die Wahrheit der religiösen Lehren abhängig ist von einem inneren Erlebnis, das diese Wahrheit bezeugt, was macht man mit den vielen Menschen, die solch ein seltenes Erlebnis nicht haben? Man kann von allen Menschen verlangen, daß sie die Gabe der Vernunft anwenden, die sie besitzen, aber man kann nicht eine für alle giltige Verpflichtung auf ein Motiv aufbauen, das nur bein ganz wenigen existiert. Wenn der eine aus einem ihn tief ergreifenden ekstatischen Zustand die unerschütterliche Überzeugung von der realen Wahrheit der religiösen Lehren gewonnen hat, was bedeutet das dem anderen?" Freud 2007, p. 131.

any such view ... completely antithetical to the very idea of a critique of pure reason, it is also anathema to Kant's political republicanism."[276] Relatedly, Kant criticized the sects and secret societies to which so many of his contemporary intellectuals belonged, notably Freemasonry, for proceeding *per initiationem* – jealously guarding esoteric truths.[277]

As Cassirer has pointed out, Kant also holds that mysticism can corrupt moral motivation by colluding, as it were, with the principle of happiness. This happens when ecstatic visions of "Mohammed's paradise or the fusional union with the Godhead of the theosophists and mystics, according to the taste of each" (*KpV* 5: 120) entice mere mortals into committing 'holy' atrocities here on Earth in order to receive a promised reward in the afterlife; conversely, the vivid threat of gruesome tortures in Hell (fire and brimstone, gnashing of teeth, etc.) as punishments for evil deeds replaces genuine respect for duty with fear and trembling.[278] Consequently, Kant avers that if the mystics' desire for insight into the noumenal world were granted, moral motivation would inevitably be corrupted: "if God and eternity with their awful majesty stood unceasingly before our eyes ... most actions conforming to the law would be done from fear, only a few from hope, and none at all from duty" (*KpV* 5: 147). And this perversion, in turn, would debase moral personality and degrade autonomy into heteronomy: "the moral worth of actions, on which alone ... the worth of the person and even that of the world depends, would not exist at all. ... [H]uman conduct would thus be changed into mere mechanism in which, as in a puppet show, everything would *gesticulate* well but there would be no *life* in the figures" (*KpV* 5: 147). In a word, the mystics should be more careful about what they wish for.

The typic, by contrast, protects morality from these dangers of mysticism by instituting the "rationalism of judgment [*der Rationalism der Urtheilskraft*]":

> Only *rationalism* of judgment is suitable for the use of moral concepts, since it takes from sensible nature nothing more than what pure reason can also think for itself, that is, conformity with law, and transfers into the supersensible nothing but what can, conversely, be really exhibited by actions in the sensible world in accordance with a formal rule of a law of nature in general.[279]

---

276 Allison, 2002, p. 23; see also Piché 1990, p. 632–635.
277 See Piché 2013.
278 Cassirer 1987, p. 260; Cassirer 2001, p. 250.
279 [*Dem Gebrauche der moralischen Begriffe ist blos der Rationalism der Urtheilskraft angemessen, der von der sinnlichen Natur nichts weiter nimmt, als was auch reine Vernunft für sich denken kann, d.i. die Gesetzmäßigkeit, und in die übersinnliche nichts hinein trägt, als was umgekehrt sich*

By analogically transposing the pure form of nature's lawfulness (*natura formaliter spectate* – Type$_2$) into the intelligible sphere, we can as it were trace a conceptual blueprint of the architecture of an intelligible moral order (*natura archetypa*) using representations which "can, conversely, be really exhibited" in the sensible world in which we live and act (*natura ectypa*).[280] In this way, sober minds can employ the typic to *think* about the intelligible world without transgressing the boundaries set by critical rationalism: "By *thinking* itself into a world of understanding practical reason does not at all overstep its boundaries, but it would certainly do so if it wanted to intuit or feel itself into it [*sich hineinschauen, hineinempfinden*]" (G 4: 458). And for the purposes of exercising pure practical judgment we have no need of more: the typic-procedure is sufficient for "even the most common understanding" (*KpV* 5: 70, 44).[281] Thus, the rationalist typic, based on a concept of lawfulness "which occurs even in the most common use of reason" (*KpV* 5: 70), is in no way reserved for a dubious *élite* of visionaries ostensibly endowed with extraordinary faculties (cf. *TG* 2: 339–340). In sum, the typic dovetails with Kant's long-running campaign against *Schwärmerei* in the name of rationalism as well as, more generally, with the protective function of Kant's critical moral philosophy as a whole (cf. *KpV* 5: 135–136, 162–163).[282]

---

durch Handlungen in der Sinnenwelt nach der formalen Regel eines Naturgesetzes überhaupt wirklich darstellen läßt.]
280 See above, section 4.1.2.3.
281 See above, section 5.1., and Ch. 7, 4.5.
282 See Conclusion, 3.1., and Cassirer 1987, p. 260 ff.; Cassirer 2001, p. 250 ff.

The Typic's Place in Kant's Theory of Symbolic Representation

Kant's statement that the typic functions not as a schema, but "served only as a symbol" (*KpV* 5: 70) is a valuable clue, suggesting that the typic should be understood as a particular mode of symbolic representation. The business of Part Two is to situate the typic in Kant's theory of symbolic representation. This is easier said than done, however; aside from the sentence fragment just quoted, Kant never mentions the typic in connection with symbolic representation. In fact, Kant never elaborated a unified, comprehensive and detailed *theory* of symbolic representation in general, acknowledging that "this business has as yet been little discussed, much as it deserves a deeper investigation" (*KU* 5: 352).[283] Rather, he seems to have developed several different forms of symbolism over the course of his philosophical development, inventing new tools piecemeal in order to deal with problems as they arose. I will situate the typic vis-à-vis these different forms of symbolic representation by means of a *comparative analysis*. Part Two is divided into two Chapters. In Chapter 6, I compare the typic with *symbolic hypotyposis* as described in the *Critique of the Power of Judgment*, mostly stressing the differences. In Chapter 7, I compare the typic with *symbolic anthropomorphism* as described in the *Prolegomena*, mostly stressing the similarities. This analysis will show in more detail how Kant's theory of symbolic representation changed over time, and the general Conclusion contains a section (3.1) on the typic's distinctive place in this evolution.

---

[283] See Bielefeldt 2003, p. 5 f., 180.

Chapter 6.
The typic and symbolic hypotyposis

> "Thou shalt not make unto thyself any graven image, nor any likeness either of that which is in heaven, or on the earth, or yet under the earth" (*Exodus* 20:4).

Many scholars have argued that the typic should be identified with "symbolic hypotyposis" as defined in the famous § 59 of the *Critique of the Power of Judgment* entitled "On Beauty as a Symbol of Morality." Essentially, symbolic hypotyposis is a procedure for providing abstract concepts, notably supersensible Ideas of reason, with an indirect presentation in the form of an intuitive symbol. Likewise, it is suggested, the typic is a procedure for concretely symbolizing the moral law. The purpose of the present chapter is to present this interpretation in detail, and to subject it to a critical examination. Yet as I mentioned in the general Introduction, the secondary literature on the Typic is so disparate and disconnected that even commentators who defend the same thesis, as here, generally seem unaware of each other's studies. Consequently, the first task is to weave the existing studies together into a complete, unified interpretation. In section 1, I present this "symbolist interpretation" within the same global framework as the Commentary (task, particular difficulties, resources, etc.) so as to facilitate direct comparisons between the two accounts. In section 2, I then critically examine the symbolist interpretation, arguing that it is anachronistic, inaccurate, and arbitrary. The type is not a "symbol" in the sense of *KU*, § 59, I contend, nor does typification function in the same manner as symbolic hypotyposis. In section 3, I further charge that the tendency of the 'symbolists' to assimilate the typic with symbolic hypotyposis is not only mistaken, but misguided. Many such attempts are motivated by a desire to *aestheticize* the typic – and with it, Kant's moral philosophy as a whole. But even from a properly aesthetic point of view, this enterprise is ill-advised, since the *sublime* and the *aesthetic idea* respectively provide far more powerful aesthetic expressions of the moral Ideas than symbolic hypotyposis could ever muster.

6.1 The symbolist interpretation of the Typic chapter

6.1.1 The task

The way in which one frames the task that the typic is meant to accomplish decisively influences how one characterizes its corresponding function. The proponents of the symbolist interpretation agree that the typic is meant to enable moral appraisal, but their construal of this task is far *more general* than what I proposed in the Commentary. On this view, moral appraisal involves more than merely subsuming actions under the *a priori* concepts of good and evil: it belongs to the broader problematic of the application of the moral law and other moral Ideas to concrete experience, all the way down to the "actual situations encountered in our daily experience" and the "messy and intricate circumstances of our lives."[284] Furthermore, the proponents of the symbolist interpretation tie the concrete application of the moral law to a more profound human need for meaning and orientation when faced with the question: "How shall I represent to myself what I ought to do, what my duty commands me to realize in the world?"[285] Unless the abstract formula of the Categorical Imperative can be made more comprehensible to the common human understanding, they argue, it will remain empty of significance and otiose for moral praxis.[286] As finite, "image-dependent" (*bilderbedürftig*) beings (*KU* 5: 408), we inevitably feel "the analogue of a need for schematization" with respect to the abstract moral Ideas.[287] In order to make these supersensible representations comprehensible and meaningful, a way must be found to connect them with "the intuitive, sensible dimension of moral experience."[288] Correspondingly, the symbolists will argue that moral appraisal should be regarded as an essentially "imaginative process of deliberating on specific cases" rather than as a dry, discursive method, [289] and that only by enlisting the "moral imagination" can moral appraisal consummate the human need for a vivid sensible presentation of moral Ideas.[290] On this interpretation, the ultimate goal of moral appraisal – and hence of the typic – will be to make the moral law comprehensible and efficacious *in concreto* by galvanizing our sensibility and feelings.[291] Thus, from the outset, the advocates of the symbolist interpretation ascribe the typic a primarily *subjective* and *aesthetic* function. Let me also mention that in this chapter I will be taking the term "aesthetic" in a broad sense, encompassing not only the

---

[284] Johnson 1985, p. 265f. See also Dietrichson 1969, p. 164f.; Grandjean, 2004, p. 43ff.; Schwartländer 1981; Schwartländer 1968.
[285] Castillo 2007, p. 29; cf. Silber 1974, p. 219.
[286] Schwartländer 1968, p. 154f.; Dietrichson 1969, p. 167ff.
[287] Castillo 2007, p. 30f.
[288] Silber 1966, p. 267.
[289] Johnson 1985, p. 265.
[290] Especially Johnson 1985.
[291] Castillo 2007, p. 30f.

third *Critique's* notions of the beautiful, art, judgments of taste, etc., but also feelings and emotions in general.[292]

6.1.2 The 'particular difficulties'

By contrast, the symbolists tend to frame the 'particular difficulties' of the power of judgment in objective, ontological terms. Grandjean defends the most overtly ontological interpretation, going so far as to reject any construal of the problem as "a merely subjective heterogeneity" between two kinds of representations, attributing instead the particular difficulties of practical judgment to an "objective heterogeneity with respect to the represented *object*."[293] In support of this interpretation, Grandjean highlights the passage where Kant specifies that "the morally good *as an object* is something supersensible [*dem Objekte nach*] (*KpV* 5: 68, Grandjean's italics)" – and then infers that the particular difficulties arise because no object in the sensible world can furnish an ontologically adequate counterpart to the intelligible objects we invoke in moral appraisal.[294] Paton, for his part, does characterize the moral law as an Idea – hence as a supersensible *representation* rather than an as intelligible *object* – nevertheless, he traces the particular difficulties of moral appraisal to the ontological deficiency of actions *qua* objects in the sensible world to instantiate this Idea:

> The difficulty about our concept of the unconditioned and absolute law of morality is that it is an Idea of reason and therefore *ex hypothesi* it can have *no corresponding object* in sensuous experience. The actions which we wish to bring under the moral law are – from one point of view – mere *events* subject to the law of nature and not to the law of freedom. They cannot be adequate to the Idea of an unconditioned law, and we have no schema, transcendental or otherwise, whereby we can exhibit an *object* for such an Idea of reason (my emphasis).[295]

Similarly, Dietrichson locates the source of the particular difficulties in an 'existential' mismatch: "So the important problem [is] how we are to go about applying the purely formal, abstract, existentially indeterminate moral law as a crite-

---

[292] Cf. Dumouchel 2000, p. 109.
[293] In section 2.2.3. of the Commentary, I argued that the "particular difficulties" of the pure practical power of judgment consist in a *subjective* mismatch between two kinds of *representations* involved in moral appraisal: supersensible Ideas on the one hand and sensible intuitions on the other.
[294] Grandjean 2004, p. 46.
[295] Paton 1947, p. 159.

6.1.3 The resources

The symbolists then argue that we need some way of bringing the moral law down to earth: "There is obviously a need for some principle of *mediation*, whereby the purely abstract moral law can be made concretely applicable as a standard for determining whether such-and-such a material maxim of voluntary actions is morally legitimate."[297] While noting a certain analogy between the problematics of mediation in the first and second *Critiques*,[298] the symbolists duly recognize that the schematism of theoretical judgment cannot solve the difficulties of pure practical judgment. Tellingly, though, virtually none of them raise the problem – heavily stressed in the Commentary[299] – that the schematism, as a procedure of the imagination, produces *sensible* intuitions that would contaminate the *supersensible* Ideas of morality; instead, they bring up a number of unrelated factors, such as purely epistemological considerations.[300] As for Kant's explicit rejection of the sensible imagination as a faculty for producing the type (*KpV* 5: 69), the symbolists pass it over completely, mention it only in passing, or openly contest it.[301] For instance, Johnson states outright "I want to argue that, in spite of his repeated insistence on the purely rational nature of moral judgment, Kant recognized the need for imagination in order to apply moral rules to specific cases."[302] But whatever the specific reasons given, the upshot is framed in the same way: if we cannot schematize the supersensible moral Ideas *directly*, then we must schematize them *indirectly*.

Framing the rejection of schematic presentation only *qua* direct is crucial to the symbolist interpretation, because it leads to a different characterization of the nature and function of the typic than on the interpretation proposed in the Commentary. On the latter view, Kant rejects the schematism as a means

---

296 Dietrichson 1969, p. 167f., cf. 170, 173f. See also Johnson 1985, p. 259, 270.
297 Dietrichson 1969, p. 168.
298 Grandjean 2004, p. 45.
299 See section 3.2.1.1.
300 Dietrichson 1969 p. 173, 176; cf. Grandjean 2004, p. 46.
301 Grandjean 2004, p. 46. Alquié wavers: on the one hand, he denies that there is or even can be a "moral imagination," but on the other hand he characterizes the type as an "image" – Alquié 2005, p. 232f.
302 Johnson 1985, p. 265f.

of presentation *qua* sensible and therefore turned to the pure understanding to provide representations devoid of sensible contamination (the form of the law of nature and *natura formaliter spectata*).[303] On the other hand, by contending that Kant rejects the schematism as a means of presentation only *qua* direct, the symbolists can argue that while we cannot schematize the moral Ideas *directly*, we are nevertheless permitted, even compelled, to find a way to "schematize" these Ideas – i.e., exhibit them in sensible intuition – *indirectly:* "Kant's solution is that, while there can be no direct presentation or schematism of the moral law, there can be an *indirect* or symbolical presentation."[304] Correspondingly, the function they assign to the typic is to serve as a *"figurative substitute* for a schematization of the moral law"[305] designed to furnish an *"indirect* sensible presentation of the supersensible, which is a *symbolic* presentation of the supersensible."[306]

6.1.4 The solution

6.1.4.1 Overcoming the 'particular difficulties'

We have now come to the crux of the symbolist interpretation: the problem of the remoteness of the moral law can only be solved by means of *symbolization*, which consists in expressing the abstract representation of the moral law in the form of a concrete *symbol* in sensible intuition that human beings can readily comprehend and apply. Dietrichson explains the rationale for this solution using an analogy with dramaturgy:

> The problem of expressing the principle of the abstract moral law in terms of a *Typus* is analogous to that of a playwright who wants to portray a certain moral virtue in a morality play. A purely formal idea of a certain moral virtue has no concreteness as an idea for dramatic presentation in a play. The playwright therefore devises an artistic construct in the form of a fictional character (a *dramatis persona*) which in a symbolically concrete manner *typifies* the abstract principle of the virtue he wants to portray. In other words, he develops a heuristic dramatic construct which serves as its *type* … The *dramatis persona* is simply a practical device for symbolizing concretely the abstract idea of the virtue in question. I have to proceed in a similar manner if I am to succeed in concretizing the abstract principle of the moral law.[307]

---

[303] See section 4.1. of the Commentary.
[304] Johnson 1985, p. 270; cf. Castillo 2007, p. 35; Paton 1947, p. 160f.; Silber 1966, p. 267.
[305] Dietrichson 1969, p. 176f.
[306] Castillo 2007, p. 35.
[307] Dietrichson 1969, p. 177.

In the typic, accordingly, *the law of nature personifies the moral law*, imparting the latter with a vivid, "symbolically concrete form."[308] While the symbolists do not explicitly distinguish between Type$_1$ and Type$_2$ (or even mention Type$_3$),[309] they suggest that the law of nature, as the *analogue* of the moral law *qua* law, can serve as the latter's "intuitive counterpart,"[310] just as sensible nature as a whole can concretely symbolize the analogous lawfulness (*Gesetzmäßigkeit*) of the intelligible world.[311] In this respect, the typic works in the same way as the Natural Law Formula in the *Groundwork*, which brings the moral law "closer to intuition and to feeling" by means of an analogy.[312] Johnson suggests, along these lines, that "the typification of the Categorical Imperative is essentially a *metaphorical* process," where we intuitively and imaginatively grasp morality by means of the metaphor "MORAL LAWS ARE NATURAL LAWS."[313] Nature, employed as a symbolic image or metaphor, promises to satisfy our deep human need for some form of mediation between the sublime Ideas of morality and our lived, sensible reality: "Kant meets this need; what he calls the '*type*' (*Typus*) of the moral law is precisely a concretizing of the moral law, namely a restatement of the abstract moral law in a symbolically concrete form."[314]

Furthermore, it is claimed that this symbolic function of the typic gives the key to the elusive meaning of the term "*Typus*," as Paton maintains:

> The word 'type' is commonly used in theology in more or less the same way as Kant uses the word 'symbol': it is that by which something is symbolised or figured. Thus the people of Israel are said to be a type of God's people, and the Paschal lamb is said to be a type of Christ. Kant's application of the word to the law of nature is a natural extension of this usage.[315]

Thus, when Kant says that the law of nature serves as the "*type*" of the moral law, he just means that the former serves as the *symbol* of the latter, which is

---

308 Dietrichson 1969, p. 168.
309 Cf. Commentary, sections 4.1.1, 4.1.2, and 5.2.2.
310 Grandjean 2004, p. 46f.
311 Alquié 2005, p. 232; Castillo 2007, p. 34f. According to Paton, it is nature as a harmonious teleological whole, or 'kingdom of nature', that serves as a symbol for the analogously constituted kingdom of ends in the intelligible world – Paton 1947, p. 160–162.
312 Paton 1947, p. 147, 158f. Grandjean, for his part, emphasizes the differences between FLN and the Typic – Grandjean 2004, p. 44.
313 Johnson 1985, p. 271f. Here Johnson is doubtless alluding to the highly influential Conceptual Metaphor Theory developed in Lakoff and Johnson 2003 (first edition published in 1980).
314 Dietrichson 1969, p. 168.
315 Paton 1947, p. 160.

in turn an indirect sensible rendering (*Versinnlichung*) of an abstract moral Idea. But the symbolist interpretation is not content to characterize the typic as a symbol only in this general sense; several commentators aim to situate it precisely within Kant's own theory of symbolism. And so they turn to the well-known theory of "symbolic hypotyposis" described in § 59 of the *Critique of the Power of Judgment:*

> All *hypotyposis* (presentation, *subjecto ad aspectum*), as making something sensible [*Versinnlichung*], is of one of two kinds: either *schematic*, where to a concept grasped by the understanding the corresponding intuition is given *a priori*; or *symbolic*, where to a concept which only reason can think, and to which no sensible intuition can be adequate, an intuition is attributed with which the power of judgment proceeds in a way merely analogous to that which it observes in schematization, i.e., it is merely the rule of this procedure, not the intuition itself, and thus merely the form of the reflection, not the content, which corresponds to the concept. ... All intuitions that are ascribed to concepts *a priori* are thus either *schemata* or *symbols*, the first of which contain direct, the second indirect presentations of the concept. The first do this demonstratively, the second by means of an analogy (for which empirical intuitions are also employed), in which the power of judgment performs a double task, first applying the concept to the object of a sensible intuition, and then, second, applying the mere rule of reflection on that intuition to an entirely different object, of which the first is only the symbol. Thus a monarchical state is represented by a body with a soul if it is ruled in accordance with laws internal to the people, but by a mere machine (like a handmill) if it is ruled by a single absolute will, but in both cases it is represented only *symbolically*. For between a despotic state and a handmill there is, of course, no similarity, but there is one between the rule for reflecting on both and their causality (*KU* 5: 351).[316]

It's a perfect fit, the symbolists claim: § 59 spells out the precise sense in which the type is a "symbol [*Symbol*] (*KpV* 5: 70); correspondingly, typification is an instance of symbolic hypotyposis, i.e., an indirect presentation of a supersensible Idea in sensible intuition by means of an analogy.[317] Castillo claims that *only* by situating the typic in Kant's critical theory of symbolic hypotyposis can one explain why Kant holds that the power of judgment is "entitled and even required" to employ it (*KpV* 5: 70).[318]

---

[316] See the related discussion of symbolic hypotyposis in the 1804 *Preisschrift* (*FM* 20: 279–80). The mechanics of symbolic hypotyposis are discussed in more detail in Ch. 7, section 3.
[317] All of the following commentators explicitly identify the type with symbolic hypotyposis: Alquié 2005, p. 232; H. Cassirer 1938, p. 76; Dierksmeier 1998, p. 42, 47; Grandjean 2004, p. 47; Johnson 1985, p. 270–272; Krüger 1931, p. 84–86; Mumbrú Mora 2009, p. 131 f.; Paton 1947, p. 159–162, esp. 159n; Schwartländer 1968, p. 83–86; Silber 1966, p. 267.
[318] Castillo 2007, p. 35–38; Irrlitz 2010, p. 331 f.

6.1.4.2 Accomplishing the task

Pursuant to this interpretation of typification as a symbolic *Versinnlichung* of the moral law, the symbolists propose that the typic-procedure is a primarily *imaginative* process that projects a scene before the mind's eye.[319] This makes the moral law more intuitive, as Paton affirms: "the best, if not the only, way to make such a law vivid in our imagination is to picture to ourselves a world in which everybody in fact acted in accordance with it."[320] Similarly, Dietrichson claims that imagining the scene that would result if a corresponding maxim were to become a law of nature improves moral appraisal: "*by projecting in imagination* the sort of world that would come into existence were the maxims of our act to become a universal law of nature … the moral agent gains *a clearer intuitive sense* of the consistency and universality of his volition" (my emphasis).[321] Finally, the proponents of the symbolist interpretation emphasize that the imagination "render[s] the moral law efficacious *in concreto*" and thereby provides it with "subjective access" – i.e., an influence on the subject's *feeling*.[322] Accordingly, many of the commentators who endorse the symbolist interpretation maintain that the typic's primary function is *aesthetic*.

6.1.5 The outcome and effectiveness

Finally, as we will see in more detail below, the symbolists interpret Kant's remarks on the common understanding (*KpV* 5: 69–70) to mean that the typic effectively meets the latter's need for concreteness by means of a *symbol* that renders the moral law comprehensible, vivid, and applicable to our daily lives: "Once the typification of the Categorical Imperative is accomplished, we no longer have the abstract notion of universal law. Instead, we have the notion of 'universal law of nature', which gives us, symbolically, some direction in applying the moral law."[323] And some go on to claim that Kant thereby provides a psychologically realistic picture of moral reasoning: "Moreover, the typified imperative is not merely a philosopher's answer to philosophers' metaphysical concerns

---

[319] Johnson issues the disclaimer that by calling the thought experiment an "imaginative" procedure he does not mean that it only yields *images* – Johnson 1985, p. 276. In the rest of his work, however, Johnson champions a conception of the imagination that is deeply rooted in embodied sensibility: see Johnson 2007, reviewed by A. Westra 2008.
[320] Paton 1947, p. 146.
[321] Silber 1974, p. 212f; cf. Alquié 2005, p. 232.
[322] Castillo 2007, p. 30f.
[323] Johnson 1985, p. 272; cf. Louden 2009, p. 70–72.

about bridging the gap between the realms of freedom and nature – it is also an adequate reconstruction of an actual reasoning process that all of us recognize in our moral deliberations from time to time."[324]

6.2 Critical assessment of the symbolist interpretation

What follows is a critical assessment the symbolist interpretation of the Typic chapter. I will argue that retrojecting the theory of symbolic hypotyposis from the third *Critique* into the second is anachronistic, inaccurate, and arbitrary.

6.2.1 The task

Firstly, the symbolist interpretation of the Typic chapter begins with a very broad conception of moral judgment: interpreting complex and nuanced situations from a moral point of view, making moral concepts personally meaningful, and applying universal moral principles to the particular circumstances of our individual lives. To be sure, all of these activities involve moral judgment in a general sense, and one would have to give them due attention if one aimed to give a comprehensive account of moral life in its real richness and complexity. However, if one sets oneself the more pointed interpretive aim of *understanding the typic in its specificity*, then one must *identify the specific task that Kant intends it to solve* – and from this point of view, the symbolists' characterization of moral judgment is far too broad. Indeed, by throwing together different exercises of the power of judgment – pure and applied, ethical and aesthetic, determining and reflecting – the symbolist interpretation obscures the typic's proper task. In fact, as Kant indicates in the title of the chapter, the typic belongs to the "*pure* practical power of judgment" [*der reinen praktischen Urtheilskraft*] (*KpV* 5: 67, my emphasis), whose proper business consists in subsuming particular actions under the two "concepts of an object of *pure* practical reason," namely the morally good and evil (*das sittlich Gute und Böse*), which are in turn derived *a priori* from the moral law.[325] Contrary to the symbolist interpretation, then, Kant designed the typic to enable a strictly *a priori*, determining exercise of the pure practical power of judgment – no more and no less. And because the

---

[324] Johnson 1985, p. 272. For other positive assessments of the typic's symbolic efficacy, see: Castillo 2007; Schwartländer 1968; Silber 1974.
[325] As explained in the chapter immediately preceding the Typic, "On the concept of an object of pure practical reason" (*KpV* 5: 57–67). See Ch. 1 of the Commentary.

symbolist interpretation construes the typic's task so broadly, it mischaracterizes the typic by ascribing it functions that Kant never designed it to perform. Of course, Kant's own conception of what it takes to be a competent moral judge in the real world involves far more than this narrowly defined task – yet he treats of the fine-tuned, concrete application of moral judgment *in other contexts and with other resources*. As a deeply moral person, Kant was acutely aware of the complexity of real-life moral situations "that call upon judgment to decide how a maxim is to be applied in particular cases" (*MS* 6: 411), and as a philosopher he consequently introduced supplementary resources for meeting this challenge (including casuistry, a moral catechism, examples, and moral didactics) in the "Doctrine of the method of pure practical reason" in the *Critique of Practical Reason* (*KpV* 5: 151–163), the "Doctrine of the methods of ethics" in the *Metaphysics of Morals* (*MS* 6: 411, 477–484), and in his *Lectures on Pedagogy* (*VP* 9: 488–493).[326]

Secondly, the symbolist interpretation lays great weight on the premise that we finite human beings have a deep-seated *need* (*Bedürfnis*) for supersensible representations to be presented in sensible intuition in order for them to be comprehensible to us (*KU* 5: 408). Kant elaborates on this special need in a pair of passages in *Religion within the Boundaries of Mere Reason*:

> It is plainly a limitation of human reason, one which is ever inseparable from it, that ... we always need a certain analogy with natural being in order to make supersensible characteristics comprehensible to us (*R* 6: 61n).[327]

> Yet for the human being the invisible needs to be represented through something visible (sensible), indeed what is more, it must be accompanied by the visible for the sake of praxis and, though intellectual, made as it were an object of intuition (according to a certain analogy) (*R* 6: 192, trans. mod.).[328]

And since this need calls for a "schematism of analogy [*Schematismus der Analogie*]" (*R* 6: 192) – which is just another name for symbolic hypotyposis[329] – the symbolists argue that the function of the typic is likewise to furnish a sym-

---

326 See Bacin 2010; Louden 2009; Louden 2000; Torralba 2007.
327 [*Es ist freilich eine Beschränktheit der menschlichen Vernunft, die doch einmal von ihr nicht zu trennen ist, daß ... wir bedürfen, um uns übersinnliche Beschaffenheiten faßlich zu machen, immer einer gewissen Analogie mit Naturwesen.*]
328 [*Allein das Unsichtbare bedarf doch beim Menschen durch etwas Sichtbares (Sinnliches) repräsentiert, ja, was noch mehr ist, durch dieses zum Behuf des Praktischen begleitet, und, obzwar es intellektuell ist, gleichsam (nach einer gewissen Analogie) anschaulich gemacht zu werden.*]
329 Chignell 2011, p. 114f.; Maly 2012, p. 312ff.

bolic presentation of the supersensible Ideas of the moral law and the morally good.³³⁰

These passages appear to speak strongly in favour of the symbolist interpretation, but on closer inspection their relevance to the Typic becomes tenuous. Kant wrote his *Religionsschrift* five years after the *Critique of Practical Reason*; consequently, it is *prima facie* anachronistic to assume that the two texts deal with the very same problems and concepts. In fact, both *Religion* passages concern religion's proper contribution to moral *praxis*.³³¹ The first passage explains how the figure of Christ in Scripture serves "*as an example to be emulated*" (R 6: 64) insofar as he represents an "archetype [*Urbild*]" (R 6: 61, trans. mod.)³³² – *not* "type" – of a perfect moral disposition. The second passage deals with the question of how churches can best cultivate the "the true (moral) service of God" (R 6: 192) by their members without encouraging dogmatic anthropomorphism or superstition. By contrast, the typic does *not* primarily concern fostering virtuous action, much less religion's moralizing function, but rather the prior, abstract problem of how to represent the supersensible moral law in such as way as to subsume actions under it in the first place. Moreover, the focus of the *Religion* passages is *internal:* the goal is to provide a lively and inspiring presentation of the *characteristics* or *qualities inherent in people's moral disposition* that are necessary for promoting virtue, e. g., the Devil's temptation of Christ as a parable of moral fortitude (R 6: 61).³³³ By contrast, the typic's focus is *external:* it is a matter of disinterestedly, even impersonally, evaluating maxims' conformity to the form of universal law. In light of these differences, it is problematic to take the 'need for symbolism' as formulated here and read it back into the Typic chapter.

Thirdly, a closer look at how Kant articulates the semantic relationship between aesthetic and moral judgments in § 59 belies the claim that moral Ideas are completely empty of significance unless they are given an aesthetic presentation. On the contrary, Kant states that when "we call buildings or trees majestic

---

330 The argument from these *Religion* passages to the identification of the typic with symbolic hypotyposis is especially direct in Dierksmeier 1998, p. 40 ff.
331 Maly 2012, p. 326.
332 Showler 2008, p. 49 f.
333 Maly has stressed this point with respect to the second passage quoted above (R 6: 192): "Was hier also durch Sinnliches repräsentiert oder anschaulich gemacht werden soll, ist der wahre moralische Dienst Gottes bzw. *die Gesinnung, in der dieser ‚Dienst im Herzen' besteht*. Es geht also nicht um eine Eigenschaft des höchsten Wesens, sondern vielmehr um *eine moralische Eigenschaft oder Disposition des Menschen, die anschaulich gemacht werden soll*, wobei diese moralische Disposition des Menschen in einem religiösen Kontext reflektiert wird." Maly 2012, p. 326 (my emphasis). On this theme, see also Chignell 2011.

and magnificent, or fields smiling and joyful [or] colors innocent, modest and tender," we are effectively transferring moral attributes *that we already grasp* onto beautiful objects in nature, and this, only because the latter "arouse sensations that contain something analogical to the consciousness *of a mental state produced by moral judgments*" (*KU* 5: 354, my emphasis). In other words, we try to make sense of the feeling of experiencing a natural object as beautiful by analogy with the feeling of judging an action to be good – not the other way around: "we often designate beautiful objects of nature or of art with names that seem to be *grounded in a moral judging*" (*KU* 5: 354, my emphasis). Put in the terminology of today's theory of analogy, morality functions here as the *source domain* and aesthetics as the *target domain*. This suggests, contrary to the symbolist interpretation, that we do not require a *prior* sensible presentation of moral notions in order to analogically grasp their meaning; instead, we predicate moral epithets that we *already* employ in moral judgment onto the objects that we judge to be beautiful – without confusing the original moral meaning with the derivative, "symbolic" meaning.[334]

6.2.2 The 'particular difficulties'

In the Commentary I have already raised a number of objections to the ontological construal of the "particular difficulties" faced by pure practical judgment.[335] Here I wish to draw attention to an inconsistency within the symbolist interpretation itself: while its proponents frame the task of moral appraisal in terms of the particular needs and capacities of the *subject*, they characterize the problem in terms of an incompatibility between different kinds of *objects*. Why the shift? Because if the symbolists located the "particular difficulties" *within the subject*, then they would have to admit that Kant in fact emphasizes the *inadequacy* of the finite subject's sensible imagination vis-à-vis the Ideas of reason; and since the symbolist interpretation will go on to appeal to this very faculty, the problem must first be *displaced outside of the subjet* so as not to disbar the subjective prerequisites for symbolic hypotyposis.

---

334 This view differs most sharply from Johnson 1985, p. 271 ff.
335 See section 2.1.1. of the Commentary. This is perhaps the closest Kant comes to Aquinas' analogy of attribution. See Ch. 7, section 2.

6.2.3 The resources

Given that the imagination cannot present the moral law *directly* (through *schematic hypotyposis*), the symbolists infer that it must therefore present the moral law *indirectly* (through *symbolic hypotyposis*). The inference does not follow, however, as it stems from a false alternative (based on § 59 of the third *Critique*). By assuming that the only substitute for 'direct' presentation through the schematism must be 'indirect' presentation through symbolic hypotyposis, the symbolists overlook the possibility that the typic may provide its own, specific form of indirect presentation – typification – that corresponds neither to the schematism nor to symbolic hypotyposis. As I argued in the Commentary, the tool that Kant selects for overcoming the particular difficulties of pure practical judgment, the *Typus*, is neither a *schema* in the strict sense of the first *Critique*, nor a *symbol* in the special sense of the third, but instead a "schema of a law itself," i.e., (1) a sensibly uncontaminated representation of (2) the form of universal law that (3) can mediate the subsumption of particular actions under the law of freedom and (4) provide a procedure for moral appraisal according to a rational standard (namely *Gesetzmässigkeit* – conformity to a universal law admitting of no exception).[336]

6.2.4 The solution

6.2.4.1 Overcoming the 'particular difficulties'

Retrojecting the theory of symbolic hypotyposis from the third *Critique* into the Typic chapter is anachronistic, inaccurate, and arbitrary. To begin with, Kant never refers to the typic as a "symbolic hypotyposis [*symbolische Hypotypose*]," nor as a "schematism of analogy" [*Schematismus der Analogie*]." And while the symbolists jump on the single occurrence of the word "symbol [*Symbol*]" in the Typic chapter, they are too quick to assume that it refers to symbolic hypotyposis. A search of the electronic edition of Kant's complete writings (Kant 2007a) for the terms "*Symbol*" and "*symbolisch*" prior to 1788 turns up six main types of occurrences in about as many texts. Examining these occurrences individually will make it clear that the notion of symbolic hypotyposis was not in fact present in the corpus until after the publication of the *Critique of Practical Reason*.
1. **Mystical symbolism.** The earliest references to symbolism in Kant's writings appear in his 1766 treatise, *Dreams of a Spirit-Seer, Elucidated by Dreams of*

---

336 See section 4.1.1. of the Commentary.

Metaphysics (*Träume eines Geistessehers, erläutert durch Träume der Metaphysik*), a scathing critique of the self-proclaimed visionary Immanuel Swedenborg (and, by association, of dogmatic metaphysics). The text presents two conceptions of symbolism.

In the "historical" part of *Dreams*, Kant explains that a central concept in Swedenborg's mysticism was the symbolic relation between the material and the spiritual worlds. Swedenborg held that cognition of material things had a "double significance": first, an "external sense," of minor importance, that concerns only physical things as such; second, a far more important "internal sense," insofar as material things, recognized as effects, point towards forces in the spiritual realm, as their causes. From the second point of view, the material world could thus be regarded as a *symbol* of the spiritual world – although Swedenborg claimed that only a visionary with his special gifts was capable of recognizing the *symbolic significance* of the material world and of communicating it to the rest of humanity, as Kant explains: "This inner sense is unknown to man, and it is this inner sense which Schwedenberg [sic], whose inmost being was opened up, wished to make known to man. ... the important thing in this symbolic connection of corporeal things, as images, with the inner spirit-state [*in dieser symbolischen Verknüpfung körperlichen Dinge als Bilder mit dem innern geistigen Zustande*] is the fact that all spirits at all times present themselves to each other under the semblance of extended forms, and the influences which these spirit-beings exercise upon each other, also arouse within them the appearance of yet other extended beings, as, as it were, the appearance of a material world, the images of which are, indeed, merely symbols [*Symbole*] of their inner state" (TG 2: 364). For instance, as Swedenborg would expound upon at length in the eight-volume *Heavenly Mysteries*[337] and other works, the positions of spirits in space (e. g., on different planets in the Solar System) symbolize their spiritual positions relative to one another within the spiritual world. Conveniently, this doctrine of symbolism allowed Swedenborg to explain why his visions were genuinely spiritual even though they invariably assumed a material form: the concrete images he recounts in such detail (e. g., the spirits he describes have bodies, eat, speak, and even have children) were thus symbolic manifestations of spiritual truths hidden from ordinary consciousness, which takes the material world only in its "external sense." Clearly, Swedenborg's conception of symbolism can correspond neither to the typic nor to symbolic hypotyposis. From a Kantian point of view, insofar

---

[337] *Arcana Cœlestia, quae in Scriptura Sacra seu Verbo Domini sunt, detecta* (1749–1756).

as Swedenborg ontologically hypostasizes the symbol as a material, visible *thing*, he flagrantly "makes what served only as a *symbol* into a *schema*" of the "invisible kingdom of God" (*KpV* 5: 70) and *a fortiori* violates the careful critical restrictions on reflective judgment spelled out in the third *Critique*.[338]

In the "dogmatic" part of *Dreams*, however, Kant elaborates another version of symbolism that purports to be more philosophically respectable: "This heterogeneity between spirit-representations and those which belong to the bodily life of man need not, however, be regarded as an impediment serious enough to prevent all possibility of our becoming aware, from time to time, even during this present life, of the influences which emanate from the spirit-world. *For these influences can enter the personal consciousness of man, not, it is true, directly, but, nonetheless, in such a fashion that they, in accordance with the law of association of ideas, excite those images which are related to them, and awaken analogous representations of our senses. They are not, it is true, the spirit-concept itself, but they are symbols of it*" (*TG* 2: 338–339, trans. mod., my emphasis).[339] How does this second view compare with Swedenborg's? On the one hand, Kant, like Swedenborg, grants the symbol the general role of expressing an intelligible or spiritual meaning in a more concrete form. On the other hand, Kant demotes the ontological status of the symbol from a *thing* in the material world to a mere *image* produced by the imagination (*Bild der Phantasie*). What is more, after arguing that these symbolic images are evoked by mere psychological association rather than by direct spiritual causation, Kant ironically reverses Swedenborg's claim to special insight by insinuating that the latter's susceptibility to experience visions was abnormal, even pathological: "Phenomena of this type cannot, however, be something common and usual; they can only occur with persons whose organs are endowed with an exceptionally high degree of sensitivity for intensifying the images of the imagination, according to the inner state of the soul … and do so to a greater degree than usually happens, *or, indeed, ought to happen with people of sound constitution* (*TG* 2: 339–340, my emphasis).[340] Thus the theory of symbolism that Kant proposes here serves the *negative* function of deflating Swedenborg's

---

[338] Müller 2001, p. 601.
[339] [Denn sie können in das persönliche Bewußtsein des Menschen zwar nicht unmittelbar, aber doch so übergehen, daß sie nach dem Gesetz der vergesellschaften Begriffe machen, die mit ihnen verwandt sind und analogische Vorstellungen unserer Sinne unserer Sinne erwecken, die wohl nicht der geistige Begriff selber, aber doch deren Symbolen sind.]
[340] Müller 2001, p. 600f.

hyperbolic claims.

Yet within the treatise itself, Kant ironically disavows this conception of symbolism as a *positive* account of the relations between the intelligible and sensible world. In other words, he does not, contrary to first appearances, fully endorse it as a legitimate philosophical theory. Kant goes on to intimate that, in truth, this "fragment of occult philosophy" (*TG* 2: 329) represents merely a parody, a "fairy tale from the cloud-cuckoo-land of metaphysics" (*TG* 2: 356) serving to highlight that dogmatic metaphysical theories, while apparently more sophisticated than Swedenborg's ravings, can be just as preposterous – or, as he puts it in the title to his work, that "the dreams of a spirit-seer" can be "illustrated by dreams of metaphysics." Indeed, the pervasively sardonic tone of Kant's treatise struck its most influential reviewer, Moses Mendelssohn, who remarked, "The joking pensiveness with which this little work is written leaves the reader sometimes in doubt as to whether Herr Kant intends to make metaphysics laughable or spirit-seeing credible."[341] By the same token, this thoroughly polemical and ironic character of the conception of symbolism that Kant advances in *Dreams* makes untenable any full identification with his later theory of symbolic hypotyposis, which, by contrast, is both 'official' as well as properly critical. Needless to say, in *KU* § 59 Kant does not characterize symbols as fantastical images evoked through the feverish associations of an idiosyncratic imagination. Moreover, the treatment of symbolism in the pre-critical *Dreams* lacks numerous critical distinctions that characterize Kant's mature theory in the third *Critique:* we find no distinction between determining and reflecting judgment; no distinction between schematic and symbolic hypotyposis; no distinction between genius-like inspiration and intersubjective aesthetic validity; no distinction between imagination (*Phantasie*) and the faculty of imagination (*Einbildungskraft*); and no distinction between association and analogy.[342]

2. **Esoteric symbols.** Related occurrences of the word "symbol" in Kant's writings appear in a pair of letters to Hamann on the 6th and 8th of April, 1774. Here is a representative passage from the first letter: "This figure ⊗, the mystical number 7, the days of the week, etc., constituting the universal monument to the first instruction which God himself gave to human beings, have thus been clothed in different symbols [*in allerley* symbola *eingehüllt worden*] by different nations, each according to its taste" (10: 155, trans.

---

[341] Moses Mendelssohn, Review of Kant's *Dreams of a Spirit-Seer, Allgemeine deutsche Bibliothek*, vol. 4, no. 2 (Berlin, 1767), in Johnson 2002, p. 123.
[342] Cf. Müller 2001, p. 601.

mod.). Here, Kant is indulging his friend's fervent interest in esoteric symbols that supposedly shroud mystical truths. But are these numbers, allegories, letters, notes, etc. *symbolic hypotyposes*? Perhaps, but I believe that a better case can be made that these representations should instead be classified as *aesthetic ideas* insofar as they vehicle no determinate concept of reflection, but instead serve to evoke mystical notions like "the sublimity and majesty of creation" by "animating the mind" through "affinity," that is, furnishing it with suggestive images and impressions that "open up for it the prospect of an immeasurable field of related representations," thereby intimating a mystical harmony resonating throughout the universe (cf. *KU* 5: 315–6). In any case, it would be very surprising if Kant had had this sense in mind when calling the type a "symbol," given that he derided the dependence on esoteric symbolism to express rational concepts as "mere child's play," unsuitable for philosophical discourse (*JL* 9: 28).

3. **Creed.** The noun "*Symbol*" occurs four times in the 1784 essay, "What is Enlightenment?", as in the following passage: "So too, a clergyman is bound to deliver his discourse to the pupils in his catechism class and to his congregation in accordance with the creed [*Symbol*] of the church he serves, for he was employed by it on that condition" (*WA* 8: 38). Reading Gregor's English translation in the Cambridge Edition, one would not even notice the term *Symbol*, as she quite rightly renders it as "creed." In this context, Kant was using the term in the technical sense that it had acquired in Christian theology since the sixteenth century, namely a formal statement of Christians' beliefs, more precisely the Gospels.[343] Obviously, this sense is not germane to the Typic.

4. **Symbolic representation in the plastic arts.** The 1785 essay, "On the Wrongfulness of Unauthorized Publication of Books," Kant contrasts symbolic representation with the proper function of a book: "A book is the instrument for delivering a *speech* to the public, not merely a thought, as is, for example, a picture, a *symbolic representation* [*symbolische Vorstellung*] of some idea or event." (*UB* 8: 81n). At first sight, this "symbolic representation" of an "idea" in the form of a "picture" might seem like an early instance of symbolic hypotyposis. However, such an identification quickly dissipates on closer inspection. First of all, by the term "idea" (*Idee*), Kant is far from

---

[343] This sense is listed in the Grimm dictionary: "*Symbol*. Seit dem 16. Jarhundert für das chritlische Glaubensbekenntnis, namentlich das Apostolikum; in der theologischen Fachsprache seit dem 16. Jh. auch 'Bekenntnisschrift', von Bekenntnissen und Lehrzeugnissen des evangelischen Glaubens und später von den Lehrschriften der christlichen 'Erkennungszeichen'." See "Symbol" 1984, p. 1377.

referring to the Idea of reason, but is just talking in a more general way of "some idea or other" (*irgend einer Idee*). Secondly, Gregor's translation here obscures the fact that Kant's example of a such a symbolic representation is not a generic "picture" – which could in turn be associated with an *image* or an *intuition* – but more specifically a painting (*Gemälde*). This suggests that Kant was making a passing reference to the notion, already well known in his time thanks to authors such as Lessing, that *the plastic arts* portrayed ideas and events "symbolically" – a notion so common, indeed, that Kant manifestly felt the need to *distinguish* it from the mode of representation proper to the book, his main subject in the essay.[344]

5. **Algebra.** The expression "symbolic construction" turns up once in the *Critique of Pure Reason* in the context of a discussion of mathematical method: "But mathematics does not merely construct magnitudes (*quanta*), as in geometry, but also mere magnitude (*quantitatem*), as in algebra, where it entirely abstracts from the constitution of the object that is to be thought in accordance with such a concept of magnitude. In this case it chooses a certain notation for all construction of magnitudes in general (numbers), as well as addition, subtraction, extraction of roots, etc., and, after it has also designated the general concept of quantities in accordance with their different relations, it then exhibits all the procedures through which magnitude is generated and altered in accordance with certain rules in intuition; where one magnitude is to be divided by another, it places their symbols together in accordance with the form of notation for division, and thereby achieves by a *symbolic construction* [*einer symbolischen Construction*] equally well what geometry does by an ostensive or geometrical construction (of the objects themselves), which discursive cognition could never achieve by means of mere concepts (*KrV* A717/B745)." As Lisa Shabel and Daniel Sutherland have insightfully explained,[345] "symbolic construction" is a technical designation of the method used in *algebra* for representing ratios of "mere magnitudes" with arbitrary signs, such as 'A', 'B' and ':'. Now, it goes without saying that the Typic has nothing to do with algebra. But neither can there be any question of symbolic hypotyposis here, as in § 59 of the third *Critique* Kant will explicitly distinguish the latter, *qua* form of presentation in intuition, from algebraic "symbols," which fall into a more general class of signs serving as visual memory-aids, that is, as "mere *characteriza-*

---

344 As a common meaning of *Symbol/symbolisch* in the eighteenth century, the Grimm dictionary lists, citing Lessing and Herder, "*eine anschauliche, sinnbildliche Erscheinung von bestimmter Bedeutung ... namentlich in der Darstellung bildender Kunst.*" See "Symbol" 1984, p. 1378f.
345 Shabel 1998; Shabel 2003; Sutherland 2006; Sutherland 2004.

tions [*bloße Charakterismen*], i.e., designations of the concepts by means of accompanying sensible signs [*sinnliche Zeichen*], which contain nothing at all belonging to the intuition of the object, but only serve them, in accordance with the laws of association of the imagination, and hence in a subjective regard, as a means of reproduction; such things are either words, or visible (algebraic, even mimetic) signs, as mere *expressions* [*bloße Ausdrücke*] for concepts" (*KU* 5: 352). This sense of "symbol" is therefore not specific to Kant, but rather corresponds to yet another sense of the word in the scholarly literature of his time.[346]

6. **Symbolic anthropomorphism.** The remaining occurrence of the term "symbolic" appears in the context of Kant's discussion of "symbolic anthropomorphism" in §§ 57–9 of the *Prolegomena* (1783). I propose to treat this occurrence separately, in Chapter 7, where I will analyse it in detail and argue that it directly informs the "symbolic" dimension of the typic while also differing in important ways from the conception of symbolic hypotyposis in the third *Critique*.

In sum, this brief survey of the corpus up to the *Critique of Practical Reason* shows that although Kant was acquainted with several contemporary meanings of the terms "*Symbol/symbolisch*" and incorporated them directly into his philosophical writing, not one of these usages corresponds to his later concept of symbolic hypotyposis.

Indeed, Kant almost certainly did not have this special meaning in mind when writing the second *Critique* for the simple reason that *he hadn't invented the concept of symbolic hypotyposis yet*. According to Zammito, Kant did not elaborate the notion of symbolic hypotyposis until the fall of 1789, a time when Kant's attitude towards the symbolic and artistic expression of rational Ideas underwent a marked shift.[347] This innovation therefore did not occur until *over two years after* Kant had completed the manuscript of the *Critique of Practical Reason*, in June 1787.[348] Conversely, the symbolists never mention, much less explain, the fact that Kant *never once mentions the typic in any of his later treatments of symbolic hypotyposis*. But if the typic really did represent a groundbreaking introduction of symbolism into the heart of his moral philosophy, as they claim, then why doesn't Kant ever refer back to it? Weil has pointed out the conspicuous ab-

---

[346] "*Symbol*. Bildliches Merkzeichen, Erkennungsmarke ... so von künstlichen Hilfszeichen und Hilfsmitteln rationaler Verständigung." See "Symbol" 1984, p. 1378, 1380.
[347] Zammito 1992, p. 269, 285.
[348] See Kant's letter to C. G. Shütz, editor of the *Jenaische Allgemeine Literaturzeitung*, on 25 June 1787 (10: 490).

sence of any mention of typic in § 59 of the *Critique of the Power of Judgment*, the *locus classicus* of symbolic hypotyposis:

> It should be noted that Kant does not speak here of the *typic of practical reason* [sic] as one would have expected given its analogous function to that of the schema and of the symbol in the two other *Critiques*; the reason is that this typic, stemming as it does from reflections on the form of the law of nature, is essentially conceptual, not intuitive and immediate.[349]

As Weil aptly remarks, Kant does not mention the typic in connection with symbolic hypotyposis because *he never conceived of the type as an intuitive symbol at all*. Indeed, a symbol in the sense of § 59 is a *sensible intuition* produced by the imagination: "the symbolic is merely a species of the intuitive" (*KU* 5: 351), and every sensible intuition, in turn, is a "representation of the imagination" (*KU* 5: 314). Elsewhere Kant also refers to the symbol as a "sensible image [*Sinnbild*]" or "*analogon* from sensibility" (*VA Friedländer* 25: 356; *VA Mrongovius* 25: 1294). The purpose of the symbol is to provide a lively sensible rendering (*Versinnlichung*) of an abstract concept (*KU* 5: 361).[350] In contrast, the representations that Kant actually selects to serve as *types* could not be further removed from lively, intuitive "sensible images": Type$_1$ – "the form of a law of nature in general [*die Form eines Naturgesetzes überhaupt*]" (*KpV* 5: 70) – and Type$_2$ – "the understanding's pure form of nature [*die Natur (der reinen Verstandesform derselben nach)*]" – are both *pure, formal and abstract concepts* produced by the understanding's intellectual synthesis.[351] Indeed, in the Typic chapter Kant never calls the type a "symbol" *tout court*; what he actually writes is that the type "*serves only* as a symbol [nur *als Symbol* dient]" (*KpV* 5: 70, my emphasis). In Chapter 7 (esp. section 4), we will see the full significance of this contrastive restriction: *functioning merely symbolically* means something quite different, I will argue, from *being a symbol* in the sense that the term would later acquire in the third *Critique* – something much closer, in fact, to the conception of symbolic anthropomorphism that Kant had previously introduced in the *Prolegomena*.

Furthermore, typification works differently from symbolic hypotyposis. Strictly speaking, the expression "symbolic hypotyposis" refers not to the symbol

---

349 Weil 1970, p. 93n.
350 Sebastian Maly, to whose painstakingly thorough treatment of symbolic hypotyposis I am indebted, defines a symbol as follows: "Ein Symbol ist eine Anschauung, die auf der Grundlage einer Analogie durch das doppelte Geschäft der Urteilskraft einem Begriff unterlegt wird, wobei die unterlegte Anschauung dem Begriff nicht korrespondiert bzw. ihm nich angemessen ist. [...] Die Aufgabe von Symbolen besteht darin, Begriffe indirekt darzustellen und dadurch Begriffe auf eine anschauliche, lebendige Weise vorzustellen." Maly 2012, p. 178, 290.
351 See section 3.3. of the Commentary.

per se, but rather to the *process that produces the symbol,* which Kant famously characterizes in § 59 as the "double task [*doppeltes Geschäft*]" (*DG*) of the power of judgment (*KU* 5: 352–353). The two stages, as applied to Kant's own example of the handmill as the symbol of the despotic state, can be summarized as follows:

> DG_1: The imagination produces an image in sensible intuition of a handmill, and the power of judgment ascribes to it the specific causality elaborated by reflection from its corresponding empirical concept (i.e., mechanical causality).
> DG_2: The power of judgment analogically transfers the rule of reflection on the specific causality of the handmill given in intuition onto the concept of the despotic state; in this way, the handmill becomes a *symbol* that indirectly presents the concept of the despotic state, particularly its specific causality (i.e., the mechanism of the handmill, whereby the crank moves the 'passive' gears through an external force, *symbolizes* the mechanism of a despotic state, where the despot's absolute will compels his passive subjects through an external force).[352]

Several differences can now be adduced between symbolic hypotyposis and typification as described in section 4.1. of the Commentary:

1. **Purpose.** The purpose of symbolic hypotyposis is quite general, namely the sensible rendering (*Versinnlichung*) of abstract concepts in general, including, but not limited to, moral Ideas.[353] Typification serves the more specific, technical purpose of overcoming the heterogeneity between the supersensible Ideas of the moral law and the morally good on the one hand and particular actions given in sensible intuition on the other, and this in order to enable a precise procedure for moral appraisal.[354]
2. **Procedure.** In symbolic hypotyposis, one begins by producing an image of an empirical concept in sensible intuition; following that, one establishes an analogy between the schematized concept and an Idea (or other abstract

---

[352] Cf. Maly 2012, p. 146, 198.
[353] For instance, Kant also mentions symbols of pure concepts of the understanding and of certain logical notions: "Our language is full of such indirect presentations, in accordance with an analogy, where the expression does not contain the actual schema for the concept but only a symbol for reflection. Examples are the words *ground* (support, basis) [*Grund (Stütze, Basis)*], *depend* (be held from above) [*abhängen (von oben gehalten werden)*], from which *flow* (instead of follow) [*fließen (statt folgen)*], *substance* (as Locke expresses it: the bearer of accidents [*Substanz ... der Träger der Akzidenten*]), and innumerable other nonschematic but symbolic hypotyposes and expressions for concepts ..." (*KU* 5: 352). Based on this passage and others, it can be argued that concepts of all kinds (empirical concepts, pure concepts of the understanding, Ideas of reason) can, in principle, be symbolized – see Maly 2012, p. 178–181.
[354] See section 3.2. of the Commentary.

concept). In typification, one begins by establishing an abstract analogy between the Idea and its type, and only afterwards does one schematize the type.[355]

3. **Specific vs. generic causality.** Symbolic hypotyposis highlights the *specific* causality of the symbol (e. g., the *mechanical* causality of the handmill).[356] By contrast, typification operates with the most abstract and generic representation of natural causality, taking only its mere form while stripping it of all intuitive trappings and abstracting from its specific "determining grounds" (*KpV* 5: 70).

4. **Reflecting vs. determining judgment.** In symbolic hypotyposis, reflecting judgment is needed to elaborate the specific causality from an empirical concept presented in intuition.[357] In typification, only determining judgment is needed, since on the one hand the concept of the causality of the law of freedom is given *a priori* as a fact of reason, and on the other hand the concept of natural causality is given *a priori* as a category of the understanding under which events can be directly subsumed.[358]

Clearly, the symbolists' identification of typification with symbolic hypotyposis is inaccurate.

Finally, the various proponents of the symbolist interpretation (most of whom do not cite each other) give inconsistent, seemingly arbitrary accounts of what symbolizes what. In general, they do not differentiate between Type$_1$ and Type$_2$, and as a result they do not clearly distinguish between 1) the law of nature as the 'symbol' of the moral law, and 2) the nature of the sensible world as the 'symbol' of intelligible nature. And depending on how each commentator construes the analogy underlying each symbol, he or she will come up with different – often inconsistent – combinations of symbolizing and symbolized entities.[359] For example, Paton suggests that, through the typic, events in nature come to symbolize moral actions, which are in turn symbols of the

---

[355] This is explained in more detail in Ch. 7, 4.2.
[356] See section 3 of Ch. 7; Maly 2012, p. 123.
[357] "Es kann sich in DG$_1$ nicht *nur* um ein bestimmendes Urteil handeln. Denn die bestimmende Urteilskraft vermag lediglich, Gegenstände unter allgemeine Naturgesetze bzw. unter die Kategorie der Kausalität überhaupt zu subsumieren. …. [E]ntscheidend für den Vorgang der Symbolisierung [ist] das Auffinden der Regel und des empirischen Begriffs der spezifischen Kausalität der betroffenen Gegenstände. Und dazu ist die reflektierende Urteilskraft nötig." Maly 2012, p. 124 f.
[358] See section 4.2.2.4. of the Commentary.
[359] See Ch. 7, section 4.2.

moral law[360] – implausible suggestions, given that Kant says that we cannot help representing actions as spatio-temporal events, which is what gives rise to the very problem that the typic was designed to solve in the first place. Krüger, for his part, maintains that "the empirical human being or the empirical whole of mutually interacting human beings" symbolize the morally good.[361] Irrlitz adduces a symbolic relation between individual maxims and the moral law, and in the same breath adds that "empirical behaviour" is a symbol of ... something unspecified.[362] Furthermore, some symbolist interpretations can themselves become symbolic or metaphorical. For example, Shell turns the etymology of the word *Typus* into a metaphor for moral obligation: "Like the *túpos* or stamp, which translates force into image, the typic translates the moral law, which 'forces itself' on our consciousness, into a figure we can 'see' or 'imagine' (*einbilden*)."[363] And Schwartländer's fanciful interpretation of the "symbolic function" of the understanding reads like a Kantian morality play: "Although it is the spontaneous faculty, the understanding represents the unconditional claim of the moral being by adopting this claim obediently and translating it into a part of human consciousness."[364]

6.2.4.2 Accomplishing the task

The symbolists' suggestion that the typic-procedure turns moral appraisal into a kind of mental theatre highlights both the appeal of the symbolist interpretation as a reflection on moral psychology and aesthetics as well as its inadequacy – for better or worse – as an interpretation of Kant. On the one hand, the symbolists' proposal that the thought experiment functions by projecting in imagination the world that would result if one's maxim were universalized does have a certain appeal, notably the suggestion that one could gain "a clearer intuitive sense" of the inconsistency of one's maxim if one could visualize it writ large in nature. Surprisingly, though, while the symbolists mention Medieval morality plays and theological symbols, they neglect far more compelling expressions of this insight in literature and myth, where the symbolic amplification of an evil action in the form of a disrupted, unbalanced and distorted nature has long

---

[360] Paton 1947, p. 161, 163.
[361] Krüger 1931, p. 186
[362] Irrlitz 2010, p. 331 f.
[363] Shell, 1980, p. 82.
[364] Quoted (in English translation) in Bielefeldt 2003, p. 48; cf. Schwartländer 1968, p. 148.

been employed as a powerful trope.³⁶⁵ For example, the following scene from *Macbeth* could be taken as a vivid typification, in the form of a disrupted and distorted natural order, of the maxim "If I believe it to be to my advantage, I will betray someone to whom I have sworn loyalty in order to supplant him":

OLD MAN:
Threescore and ten I can remember well,
Within the volume of which time I have seen
Hours dreadful and things strange, but this sore night
Hath trifled former knowings.
ROSS:
Ha, good father,
Thou seest, the heavens, as troubled with man's act,
Threaten his bloody stage: by th' clock, 'tis day,
And yet dark night strangles the traveling lamp:
Is't night's predominance, or the day's shame,
That darkness does the face of earth entomb,
When living light should kiss it?
OLD MAN:
'Tis unnatural,
Even like the deed that's done. On Tuesday last,
A falcon, tow'ring in her pride of place,
Was by a mousing owl hawk'd at and kill'd.
ROSS
And Duncan's horses—a thing most strange and certain—
Beauteous and swift, the minions of their race,
Turned wild in nature, broke their stalls, flung out,
Contending 'gainst obedience, as they would
Make war with mankind.
OLD MAN
'Tis said they eat each other.
ROSS
They did so, to th'amazement of mine eyes
That looked upon't.³⁶⁶

This horrifying vision of a nature out of joint, where even the celestial bodies and animals obey the new "unnatural" law, symbolizes the evil of "the deed that's done," namely Macbeth's treacherous murder of Duncan, his king. Scenes

---

365 For example, the opening of scene of Sophocles' *Oedipus Rex*, or Luke's depiction of the crucifixion (Luke 23:33–46). For a more general study of such moral symbolism, see Ricoeur 1967.
366 Shakespeare 1993, Act 2, Scene 4.

such as this one certainly testify that the imagination has the power to render moral concepts intuitively vivid and emotionally moving.

But from a Kantian point of view, we could claim no *rational validity* for our moral judgments if, like Ross and the Old Man, we were to let our *emotions* of horror of disgust sway our moral appraisal of a deed like Macbeth's instead of measuring it against the universal principles of practical reason. For Kant, individuals' feelings provide no philosophically legitimate basis for appraising the morality of actions (*KpV* 5: 58f.), since "in fact no moral principle is based, as people sometimes suppose, on any *feeling* whatsoever" (*MS* 6: 376–377). Rather, he holds that one ought to exclude biasing emotional factors and instead exercise one's "judicial office" with "well-meant strictness [*wohlgemeinte Strenge*] in determining genuine moral import in accordance with an uncompromising law" (*KpV* 5: 154). Wood explains Kant's thinking as follows:

> the way of thinking (closer to "intuition") that does best at animating human hearts and actions on behalf of morality is not the same as the way of thinking that does best when it comes time to pass critical judgment either on the actions we have performed or on the maxims we are proposing to adopt. For this latter task, a more austere and abstract principle is better because, corrupt human nature being what it is, the same feelings and intuitions that make us enthusiastic friends of virtue also make us susceptible to self-deception and more likely to pass off corrupt actions and maxims to ourselves as morally commendable ones.[367]

Indeed, even in his pre-critical period Kant insisted on making all moral judgments "with moral strictness [*nach moralischer Strenge*]" even in situations where our emotional strings are being pulled (*B* 2: 234; cf *TP* 8: 286–7). Kant hereby subscribes to a wider current of modern philosophy that regards feeling as something "suffered" by the subject and hence as a "pathological" phenomenon of subjectivity; on this view, feeling acts as a perturbing element, or factor of instability, in moral judgment.[368] This position may seem austere, but Kant has his own philosophical and psychological arguments for it.[369] Yoking moral ap-

---

[367] Wood 1999, p. 82.
[368] Dumouchel, 2001, p. 172.
[369] Indeed, the roots of this position can be traced back to Kant's reservations about the theory of 'moral feeling' in the 1760s: "Ainsi, dès les *Remarques sur le sentiment du beau et du sublime* (1765–1767), Kant signalait la variabilité du sentiment moral selon le sexe, l'âge, l'éducation, le mode de gouvernement, les races et les climats [20: 49–50]. Cela signifie qu'une morale édifiée sur des bases aussi fragiles ne peut parvenir à établir un standard fixe, à moins d'en faire une propriété innée de l'humanité. Le sentiment moral fournit donc des raisons purement 'contingentes', qui ne peuvent au mieux prétendre qu'à une 'validité privée' [*VE Collins*, 27: 254, 276; *VE Powalski*, 27: 119]. Seul un critère rationnel est en mesure, par-delà toute considération

praisal to feelings elicited by the so-called 'moral imagination' would prevent any one person's moral judgments from becoming *public* in the *Aufklärung* sense of *communicable* between interchangeable perspectives.³⁷⁰ It is no coincidence that Kant stresses this very point in the chapter immediately preceding the Typic: "... good and evil [must] always be appraised by reason and hence through concepts, which can be universally communicated, not through mere feeling, which is restricted to individual subjects and their receptivity ..." (*KpV* 5: 58). And even in the Doctrine of Method in the *Critique of Practical Reason*, devoted to making the principles of morality more subjectively accessible, Kant warns that the basic principles of action must be based not on passing feelings, but on firm concepts and principles: "On any other foundation only passing moods can be achieved which give the person no moral worth and not even confidence in himself, without which the consciousness of his moral disposition and character, the highest good in man, cannot arise" (*KpV* 5: 157).

By contrast, the symbolists' mental theatre, by its very design, would trigger violent and confusing affective reactions that would inevitably throw moral judgment into disarray. Indeed, Kant's very definition of affect opposes it to deliberate rational reflection: "affect ... quickly grows to a degree of feeling that makes reflection impossible (it is thoughtless)" (*APH* 7: 251–2, 254; *KU* 5: 272; *M* 15: 940). Worse still, if moral appraisal were practiced as the symbolists advocate, it would degrade *moral motivation* into a delusional exercise of pushing our own emotional buttons with fictions. The moral theatre, by as it were pre-empting the pure moral incentive of respect by a fictional mechanism that plays on our aversion to negative feelings and our attraction to pleasant ones, reinstates on a psychological level the egoistic "empiricism" that the typic is designed to guard against (*KpV* 5: 71). Thus, the more psychologically powerful the mental theatre would be, the more it would corrupt one's moral disposition. Indeed, one can gain a sense of how sharply Kant would criticize the symbolists' mental theatre when one considers how harshly he condemned the moralistic literature and theatre of his own time: "Novels, sentimental plays, shallow moral precepts, which make play with (falsely) so-called noble dispositions, ... in fact enervate the heart, and make it unreceptive to the rigorous precept of duty and incapable of all respect for the dignity of humanity in our own person and the right of

---

anthropologique, de procurer à la théorie morale un principe invariable et universel, c'est-à-dire accessible dès le départ à tout être rationnel." Piché 2003, p. 136.

370 Cf. (*WA* 8: 37–38; *O* 8: 144–7; *KU* 5: 294ff; *EF* 8: 381–6); see also section 5.2.3. of the Commentary and section 3.1. of the Conclusion.

human beings ... and in general incapable of all firm principles ..." (*KU* 5: 273; cf. *VA Mrongovius*, 25: 1213).[371]

More fundamentally, Kant would categorically reject as *heteronomous* the principle that our motivation to perform or refrain from certain acts should be influenced, let alone determined, by what we *feel* while spectating a mental play (cf. *KpV* 5: 64f.). And as he explains in the chapter immediately following the Typic, the *only* genuine source of moral motivation is "moral feeling [*das moralische Gefühl*]," i.e., "respect [*Achtung*]" for the moral law.[372] This singular feeling is evoked by pure practical reason and comes into play not *before* or *during* moral appraisal but only *following* it, as reason's distinctive *effect* on sensibility:

> It is here that we have to bring in the already-mentioned distinction between the objective principle of the appraisal of the action, and subjective principle of its performance. Of the former we have just been speaking, but the subjective principle, the motive, is the moral feeling. ... *The moral feeling is a capacity for being affected by a moral judgment*. When I judge by understanding that the action is morally good, I am still very far from doing this action of which I have so judged. But if this judgment moves me to do the action, that is the moral feeling (*VE Collins*, 27: 1428, my emphasis).

> Certainly, the will must have *motives*; but these are not certain objects proposed as ends related to *natural feeling*, but nothing other than the unconditional *law* itself; and the will's receptivity to finding itself subject to the law as unconditional necessitation is called *moral feeling, which is therefore not the cause but the effect of the determination of the will*, and we would not have the least perception of it within ourselves if that necessitation were not already present within us" (*TP* 8: 283, emphasis added).

> "There is a moral feeling; however this is not the basis of judgment, but of inclination [*Es giebt ein moralishes Gefühl; dieses ist aber nicht ein Grund des Urtheils, sondern der Neigung*]" (*Refl* 6696, 19: 135, my translation)

Kant goes so far as to affirm that we have a positive duty to cultivate *moral apathy* – which is not an absence of all feeling, but rather an active ability to prevent sensibly conditioned affects from overpowering the genuinely moral feeling of respect produced by reason: "Since virtue is based on inner freedom it contains a positive command to a human being, namely to bring all his capacities and in-

---

[371] See also Cassirer 1987, p. 269. In this respect, Kant belongs to a long line of moralists who have been suspicious of the very idea that theatre could serve a moralizing function. For Saint Augustine's rejection of mere aesthetic pleasure derived from literature, see H. Westra 2007; for Pierre Nicole's denunciation of the theater, see A. Westra 2008.

[372] See the chapter immediately following the Typic, "On the incentives of pure practical reason" (*KpV* 5: 71–89).

clinations under his (reason's) control and so to rule over himself, which goes beyond forbidding him to let himself be governed by his feelings and inclinations (the duty of *apathy*); for unless reason holds the reins of government in its own hands, his feelings and inclinations play the master over him" (*MS* 6: 408; cf. *KU* 5: 272; *APH* 7: 252). This rational control over one's own emotions is indispensable for moral appraisal, of course, where we must calmly and deliberately reflect on the principles of actions.[373]

Furthermore, Kant's own descriptions of how "everyone, in fact, judges actions as good or evil" (*KpV* 5: 69) belie the symbolists' assumption that the applicability of the moral law depends on a kind of mental theatre. In fact, Kant sees no need to league moral appraisal with the so-called "moral imagination" or the emotions evoked thereby in order to make moral principles accessible, since the criterion that reason puts forward is unmistakably clear: if I cannot condone the principle on which I act as a law *for everyone*, then I cannot condone it *for myself*. And Kant affirms again and again that this criterion of universalizability is in fact easy to apply and suffices to produce fair, accurate, even subtle moral judgments in practice:

> The principle of morality is thus the Idea of a will, insofar as it is a law unto itself. The will, whose maxims can hold good as universal laws, is a law unto itself, for what it wills is always a universal law, and that is the good will. *In this way the commonest human understanding can easily discern whether a thing be right or wrong, for it merely has to ask itself whether that thing could be a universal law.* The agreement of an action with the principle of my will, as a universal legislator, is thus the principle of morality. If we cannot consider our will to be universally legislative, we reject the action. *A principle of morality must at the same time be comprehensible to the commonest understanding, because every man must possess it, and such is the case here* (*VE Mrongovius* 29: 628, trans. mod., my emphasis).[374]

As far as moral appraisal goes, therefore, there is no specific need to symbolically personify the moral law like a virtue in a morality play – besides, what kind of character would the law of nature be, anyway? As we have seen in the Commentary, the typic employs the law of nature not as an *image*, but rather as a *formal standard* with which the common understanding carries out a "comparison [*Vergleichung*]" (*KpV* 5: 69) of maxims' form. When measured against this standard, the partiality of a self-serving maxim becomes glaringly "obvious [*offenbar*]," be-

---

[373] I am indebted to the insightful and nuanced treatment of the role of affects and passions in Kant's ethics in Wehofsits forthcoming.
[374] See also (*KpV* 5: 44; *G* 4:402–5, 422–4; *VE Collins* 27: 1426–9; *TP* 8: 286–7; *EF* 8: 381–6) and section 5.1. of the Commentary.

cause it clearly cannot have the *universality* that the common understanding expects of a law of nature (*KpV* 5: 44).

Finally, Kant believes that we genuinely *care* about the aptitude of our maxims to become a universal law – and this rational care, while it may be difficult to spell out, is nevertheless the *bona fide* source of moral motivation:

> The understanding pays regard to everything that eliminates the possibility of rules; it accepts everything that accords with the use of its rule, and opposes itself to everything that is contrary to that rule. Now since immoral actions are contrary to rules, in that they cannot be made into a universal law, the understanding is resistant to them, because they run counter to the use of its rule. Hence, in virtue of its nature there resides in the understanding a moving force (*VE Collins* 27: 1428 – 9; cf. *G* 4: 460).

What could be further from the visceral disgust and horror in the Macbeth scene? On Kant's view, moral appraisal does give rise to an emotional response, yet it does so not by triggering our emotions through the imagination, but instead by eliciting our *sui generis* rational attitudes via the understanding. All this being said, one can of course *disagree* with Kant's account of moral judgment on independent philosophical or empirical grounds, but if one purports to provide an exegesis of his text one should not attribute views to him that he would vigorously reject.

6.2.5 The outcome and effectiveness

The symbolists take Kant's observation that "without having at hand something which it could make an example in a case of experience, [the common understanding – A.W.] could not provide use in application for the law of a pure practical reason" (*KpV* 5: 70) as a confirmation of their claim that the ultimate function of the typic is to meet the common understanding's need for concrete images by means of an intuitive symbol in sensible experience.[375] However, the "example" mentioned in the Typic chapter should not be construed as a *symbol* in the sense of *KU* § 59. Indeed, in the latter text Kant makes a clear distinction between the example (*Beispiel*) and the symbol (*Symbol*) (*KU* 5: 351). As we know, a symbol is defined as an *indirect* presentation of a concept attributed by means of the "double task" of the reflecting power of judgment. But an "example [*Beispiel*]," by contrast, is defined as a *direct* presentation of a concept, i.e., "a particular (*concretum*), represented in accordance with concepts as contained

---

[375] Dierksmeier 1998, p. 42.

under a universal (*abstractum*)" (*MS* 6: 479n). The example is subsumed directly under the rule by the *determining* power of judgment (*KrV* A133/B172). Unlike a symbol, which should have lively, distinctive features that spur reflection, the example is merely *some concrete instance or other* serving to cue the universal rule under which it falls: it can – and should – be ordinary, generic, and self-effacing, pointing beyond itself to the rule of which it is a mere case (*casus datae legis*). And that is precisely what occurs in the Typic chapter. The purpose of the "example" mentioned there is not to furnish an image that indirectly symbolizes something ineffable, but instead to trigger an abstract representation of the law of nature *qua* universal rule that applies directly to every single "case of experience," no matter how banal.[376] And it is in turn the *universal rule*, the law "as such" – not the example per se – that corresponds to the moral law as its formal type (*KpV* 5: 70). Therefore, the symbolists' talk of a "symbolic relation of type to instance" is incorrect, if not incoherent.[377]

More fundamentally, the symbolists' emphasis on *visualization* conflicts with a fundamental tenet of Kant's quintessentially rationalist ethics. Kant held that the true and original standards or "archetypes" of moral appraisal, the moral law and the morally good, are both Ideas of reason that one *cannot see:* "when moral worth is at issue, what counts is not actions, which one sees [*die man sieht*], but those inner principles of actions that one does not see [*die man nicht sieht*]" (*G* 4: 408). Kant even borrows a famous dictum of Jesus' to express the sacrosanctity of this very notion: "Why do you call me (whom you see) [*den ihr sehet*] good? None is good (the archetype of the good) [*das Urbild des Guten*] but God only (whom you do not see) [*den ihr nicht sehet*]" (*G* 4: 409, based on *Mark* 10:18). Kant's recourse to a pure, internal model of morality testifies to the enduring influence of Rousseau,[378] who extolled virtue as "this divine model which I carry within me and which serves both as the object of my desires as well as the rule of my actions [*ce divin modèle que je porte au dedans de moi, et qui servoit à la fois d'objet à mes désirs et de règle à mes actions*]."[379] Even the common understanding possesses this "obscurely thought *metaphysics*," for it is "inherent in every human being because of his rational predisposition" (*MS* 6: 376–377).[380] Ultimately, both philosophers hark back to Plato, according to whom, as Kant puts it in the first *Critique*, every person always already possesses "in his own head [*in seinem eigenen Kopfe*]" the "true original [*das*

---

[376] See section 5.1.2. of the Commentary.
[377] Freydberg 2013, p. 115.
[378] Piché 1990.
[379] Rousseau 1964, p. 223f., 255, 358.
[380] Cf. Rousseau 1964, p. 358.

wahre Original]" of the "model of virtue [*Muster der Tugend*]" – an Idea to which no sensible example can ever be adequate (*KrV* A315/B372).³⁸¹ But while Rousseau and Plato both postulated an *intuitive* access to the Ideas – through *sentiment* and *anamnesis*, respectively – Kant emphasized the non-intuitive, purely conceptual – i.e., invisible – nature of the Ideas.³⁸² Moreover, if the typic functioned primarily as a top-down symbolic *Versinnlichung* of the supersensible, as the symbolists claim, then it would actually do the common understanding a disservice by reinforcing its counterproductive tendency, much bemoaned by Kant, to turn the intelligible into an image: "… the most common understanding … is very much inclined to expect behind the objects of the senses something else invisible and active of itself – but it spoils this again by quickly making this invisible something sensible in turn, that is, wanting to make it an object of intuition, so that it does not thereby become any the wiser" (*G* 4: 451–452). Therefore, the challenge of enabling moral appraisal in the Typic chapter is not a matter of *making the invisible visible*, as the symbolists aver, but rather of *measuring the visible against an invisible standard*. Particular actions present themselves to us as spatio-temporal events given in sensible intuition – *we can already see them*. But for the purposes of moral appraisal we are not interested in the actions *qua* visible, but only with respect to an abstract, 'invisible' standard, namely the suitability of the corresponding maxims to be universalized as laws. What the typic does is assist the common understanding in making the transition from the concrete level at which it *perceives* actions to the abstract level where it *judges* their corresponding maxims in a principled manner.³⁸³ And as we will see next, the very non-visualizability of the moral Ideas opens the door to the most powerful way to experience them aesthetically – the sublime.

6.3 Against aestheticizing the Typic

6.3.1 Two agendas

Having presented and critically examined the symbolist interpretation in detail, we must now address the question of interpretive intent. What do the commentators who advocate the symbolist interpretation of the Typic intend to achieve? Two tendencies can be distinguished.

---

381 Cf. Rousseau 1964, p. 223.
382 Piché 1990, p. 630 f.
383 See section 5.1.2. of the Commentary.

On the one hand, some commentators seek to provide an accurate exegesis of the Typic, and they propose the notion of symbolic hypotyposis in good faith as a means for illuminating this obscure chapter. For instance, while Dietrichson's attempt to analogize the typic to the symbolic operation of morality plays undoubtedly has problems, his stated aim remains to furnish a satisfactory explanation of how the typic serves to enable moral appraisal, and he devotes the greater part of his article to a valuable analysis of the universalizability criterion.[384] I view this interpretation as a legitimate, if mistaken, exegetical hypothesis.

On the other hand, certain commentators seem to be wilfully pursuing a different agenda: to *aestheticize* the typic. Johnson, for example, uses Dietrichson's treatment as springboard to the position that the most important role of the typic is not merely to enable moral appraisal according to the criterion of universalizability, but rather to open up a new dimension of moral life saturated with symbolic, metaphorical meaning.[385] On this interpretation, the typic functions as an imaginative metaphorical procedure that not only enriches but also personalizes moral reflection: symbolizing moral concepts in and through nature "has its own special appeal, suggests its own perspective on the moral law, and calls up its own peculiar cluster of experiences, concepts, feelings, images, etc., which guides us in seeing how the law applies in particular cases."[386] Castillo echoes this point – the symbolic typic connects us with a more sensitive, hermeneutical, and existentially authentic dimension of experience:

> The analogical and poetic dimensions of the symbol situate this representation in the field of interpretation ... Besides its capacity to aestheticize our relation to the sensible, the symbol serves as the foundation for a particularly fruitful hermeneutic in the domain of belief ... In this way, the critical symbol opens the path towards a genuine symbolic disalienation.[387]

In a word, the aesthetic reading aims to transform the typic into a *poetic* device. But that's not all. The proponents of the aesthetic interpretation of the typic extend their reading to other fundamental components of Kant's ethics. As for moral praxis, Silber proclaims that "Kant did think of the embodiment of the highest good in terms of symbolic schematism"[388] and that we are called upon to symbolically "incarnate" the Idea of the highest good through a "moral

---

[384] Dietrichson 1969, p. 168.
[385] Johnson 1985, 271 ff.
[386] Johnson 1985, 275.
[387] In the same vein, see Bahr 2004; Schwartländer 1968, p. 83 f.
[388] Silber 1974, p. 210.

schematism."³⁸⁹ And in line with the conception of the typic as a kind of mental theatre, Freydberg claims that the concepts of good and evil are ultimately produced not by pure practical reason but by the "imagination's synthesizing."³⁹⁰ Indeed, Freydberg insists so adamantly that the typic is an activity of the imagination that he must allege that Kant didn't know what he was talking about when he distinguished the typic from the schematism: "The difference between the two *Critiques* that Kant attempts to sharpen in the Typic does not amount to very much once the internal workings of imagination are discerned."³⁹¹ In a similar vein, Johnson argues that "rational" moral deliberation should be recharacterized as an "imaginative metaphorical process" that "requires a form of reflective creative judgment."³⁹² For Johnson, it is only fitting that moral appraisal should be metaphorical, for *all* of Kant's moral principles flow from an interrelated set of core metaphors, notably "MORALITY IS A STRICT FATHER."³⁹³ From here, it is just a short step to the extreme thesis that all philosophical discourse is primarily or even entirely metaphorical: Johnson declares that "in a very strong sense, philosophy *is* metaphor";³⁹⁴ and de Man notoriously endeavoured to collapse all forms of judgment into symbolic hypotyposis in order to show that all philosophical discourse is intrinsically metaphorical, eschewing determinate concepts altogether.³⁹⁵ And if judging, conceptualizing, and reasoning are essentially metaphorical, then we must fundamentally reconceive the Kantian architectonic as well, Johnson argues: "the presence of such imaginative acts calls into question any strict interpretation of the dichotomy between imagination and reason and that between imagination and understanding ... On the contrary, genuine understanding is permeated by imaginative reflection."³⁹⁶ In the final

---

389 Silber 1966, p. 270.
390 Freydberg 2005, p. 80.
391 Freydberg 2005, p. 82. More recently, Freydberg seems to have partially retracted this construal of the typic, although he still maintains that the moral law, maxims, and moral actions all have an "ultimate relation to imagination" – see Freydberg 2013, p. 112–117, 120.
392 Johnson 1985, p. 277.
393 Lakoff and Johnson 1999, p. 415–439.
394 Johnson 2008, p. 44. Although Johnson concedes that his construal of the typic as a metaphorical procedure is "unorthodox," it seems to me that he understates just how much this interpretation conflicts with Kant's principles. Later on, he will directly attack Kant – and the entire Western philosophical tradition, no less – in a self-proclaimed revolution on the basis of his theory of metaphor and embodied cognition. Compare the rhetoric in Johnson 1985 with Lakoff and Johnson 1999 or with Lakoff and Johnson 2008.
395 See de Man 1979 – cited and (critically) discussed in Pillow 2000, p. 276f.
396 Johnson 1985, p. 266, 280. Let me state from the outset that I find it unhelpful, to say the least, to slide from the general, vague claim that "understanding" (*das Verstehen*) in a generic sense can in some circumstances be "imaginative" to the Kant-specific claim that *the faculty of*

analysis, these commentators use their symbolist interpretation of the Typic as the thin end of the wedge in order to aestheticize Kant's philosophy as a whole. In the current section I explain why I regard this interpretation as not just mistaken but also misguided.

6.3.2 Betting on the wrong horse

Instead of producing a litany of general arguments against aestheticizing Kant's ethics and *a fortiori* his philosophy as a whole, I will conduct a more focused, immanent critique of the aesthetic interpretation of the Typic. I will argue that the contention that the moral law's aesthetic and emotional resonance depends on *symbolic hypotyposis* betrays a misappreciation of the resources offered by Kant's aesthetics: the *sublime* and the *aesthetic idea* each provides, in its own way, far richer aesthetic expressions of moral Ideas than symbolic hypotyposis could ever muster. In other words, the commentators so keen on aestheticizing the typic are not even going about it in an effective way.

6.3.2.1 The sublime: a more *powerful* expression of moral Ideas

The sublime expresses the most essential characteristic of the Ideas, namely that they infinitely surpass sensibility. The apprehension of an object judged as sublime "stretches the imagination to its limit" (*KU* 5: 268), whereby the "objective inadequacy of the imagination in its greatest extension" to attain the Ideas of reason is judged as "subjectively purposive," as Kant puts it, insofar as it makes palpable our *supersensible* vocation (*KU* 5: 269). Thus the experience of the sublime, while negative and painful, exerts for this very reason an extraordinary aesthetic power:

> There need be no anxiety that the feeling of the sublime will lose anything through such an abstract presentation, which becomes entirely negative in regard to the sensible; for the imagination, although it certainly finds nothing beyond the sensible to which it can attach itself, nevertheless feels itself to be unbounded precisely because of this elimination of the limits of sensibility; and that separation is thus a presentation of the infinite, which for that very reason can never be anything other than a merely negative presentation, which nevertheless expands the soul (*KU* 5: 274).

---

understanding (*der Verstand*) must therefore stand in a new relation to *the faculty of imagination* (*die Einbildungskraft*).

When it comes to the aesthetic and emotional force of the moral law, therefore, the symbolists' contention that the law would remain empty and cold without some sort of *symbolic image* could not be further removed from Kant's own aesthetics. On the contrary, he believes that the moral law attains its greatest aesthetic and emotional power precisely when presented in its purest, most sublime form, as he emphatically states in the very same passage:

> Perhaps there is no more sublime passage in the Jewish Book of the Law than the commandment: Thou shalt not make unto thyself any graven image, nor any likeness either of that which is in heaven, or on the earth, or yet under the earth, etc. [...]. *The very same thing also holds of the representation of the moral law and predisposition to morality in us. It is utterly mistaken to worry that if it were deprived of everything that the senses can recommend it would bring then with it nothing but cold, lifeless approval and no moving force or emotion. It is exactly the reverse:* for where the senses no longer see anything before them, yet the unmistakable and inextinguishable idea of morality remains, there it would be more necessary to moderate the momentum of an unbounded imagination so as not to let it reach the point of enthusiasm, rather than, from fear of the powerlessness of these ideas, to look for assistance for them in images and childish devices (*KU* 5: 274, my emphasis).

As Cassirer aptly observes, "in words like these we are in touch with Kant whole and entire."[397] And tellingly, we find Kant advancing the very same view in the Typic chapter, asserting almost word for word that the "purity and sublimity [*Reinheit und Erhabenheit*]" of the moral law produce emotions so powerful that they can even excite people into mystical *Schwärmerei* (*KpV* 5: 71).[398] Thus, while the symbolists hope to bring out the typic's full aesthetic potential, from Kant's point of view they are in fact debasing it into a "childish device" on a par with stilted morality plays and tired theological symbols, thereby robbing the moral law of its true aesthetic power. Indeed, the sublime also outdoes symbolic hypotyposis as an aesthetic vehicle for the Idea of the morally good. The sublime produces a more profound emotional impact than the beautiful, as it better intimates the purely *intellectual* nature of the good and thereby fosters a more genuine moral interest – which leads Kant to declare that "the intellectual, intrinsically purposive (moral) good, judged aesthetically, *must not be represented so much by the beautiful but rather as sublime*" (*KU* 5: 271, my emphasis).

---

[397] Cassirer 1987, p. 260f.; Cassirer 2001, p. 251.
[398] That being said, the experience of the sublime, insofar as it is taken as a purely negative presentation, is not *itself* a form of *Schwärmerei* (*KU* 5: 265).

6.3.2.2 Aesthetic ideas: a more *poetic* expression of moral Ideas

While some of the symbolists are eager to ascribe the typic a poetic function, the privileged vehicle in Kantian aesthetics for the *poetic* expression of Ideas of reason is not in fact the *symbol*, but the *aesthetic idea*. Tellingly, despite their grand claims about the power of moral symbolism, the symbolists offer no additional examples from the Kantian corpus. It turns out that images symbolically representing moral Ideas are few and far between, and tend to be brought up occasionally as illustrations during lectures. Here is a typical selection:

> That man, moreover, should act in accordance or adequacy with moral laws, can occur only insofar as he has repressed and conquered, through the moral law, the inclination he harbours to deviate or do the opposite. The struggle of inclination with the moral law, and the constant disposition (*intentio constans*) to carry out his duties, therefore constitutes what we call *virtue*. The very Latin word *virtus* originally signifies nothing else but courage, strength and constancy, and the symbol for it indicates the same: a Hercules, with lionskin and club, striking down the hydra, which is the symbol of all vice. (*VE Vigilantius* 27: 491; cf. *MS* 6: 376)

> Now it is impossible to explain the phenomenon that at this parting of the ways (where the beautiful fable places Hercules between virtue and sensual pleasure) the human being shows more propensity to listen to his inclinations than to the law (*MS* 6: 380n).

> The tutelary god of morals does not yield to Jupiter (the god of power); for Jupiter is still subject to fate, that is, reason is not sufficiently enlightened to survey the series of predetermining causes that would allow it to predict confidently the happy or unhappy results of human actions in accordance with the mechanism of nature (though it is sufficiently enlightened to hope they will be in conformity with its wish). But it throws enough light everywhere for us to see what we have to do in order to remain on the path of duty (in accordance with rules of wisdom), and thereby do toward the final end (*EF* 8: 370).

One does not need to be a literary critic to appreciate that these lacklustre conventional symbols drawn from Greek and Roman mythology fall short of creative, inexhaustibly meaningful metaphors.[399] Moreover, not even the example *par excellence* of moral symbolism – the beautiful as the symbol of the morally good – can give the symbolists what they yearn for. As so many readers of the famous § 59 discover to their disappointment, Kant's tantalizing assertion that beauty is the symbol of the morally good does not open up a boundless new field of interpretation, but is instead constrained by a strict – some might say pedantic – analogy between two *judgments* with respect to four abstract features: immediacy, disinterestedness, freedom, and universality (*KU* 5:

---

399 Johnson's identification of symbolic hypotyposis with his own conception of metaphor has been convincingly challenged. See Pillow 2000, p. 247–284; Pillow 2001.

353–4).⁴⁰⁰ Moreover, *taste* in the beautiful in nature does not open a path towards a deeply personal "symbolic disalienation"; rather, it accustoms us to value things *in a disinterested, impersonal manner* (*KU* 5: 354). In short, moral symbolism in Kant is a far cry from poetic.

The privileged vehicle of the poetic in Kant's aesthetic theory is instead the *aesthetic idea*. In § 49 of the *Critique of the Power of Judgment*, Kant defines the "aesthetic idea [*die ästhetische Idee*]" as an intuitive representation, produced by the imagination, that evokes an unlimited chain of associations around a rational Idea. Just as no individual intuition can be adequate to the infinity evoked by the Idea of reason, so no determinate concept can be adequate to the infinite manifold of representations evoked by the imagination's aesthetic idea:

> by an aesthetic idea, however, I mean that representation of the imagination that occasions much thinking without it being possible for any determinate thought, i.e., *concept*, to be adequate to it, which, consequently, no language fully attains or can make intelligible. – One readily sees that it is the counterpart (pendant) of an *idea of reason*, which is, conversely, a concept to which no *intuition* (representation of the imagination) can be adequate" (*KU* 5: 314, cf. 342).

Aesthetic ideas "strive toward something lying beyond the bounds of experience, and thus seek to approximate a presentation of concepts of reason (of intellectual ideas)" (*KU* 5: 314). They also have a strong affective force insofar as they "animate the mind by opening up for it the prospect of an immeasurable field of representations" (*KU* 5: 315) where the imagination has free rein:

> In a word, the aesthetic idea is a representation of the imagination, associated with a given concept, which is combined with such a manifold of partial representations in the free use of the imagination that no expression designating a determinate concept can be found for it, which therefore allows the addition to a concept of much that is unnameable, the feeling of which animates the cognitive faculties and combines spirit with the mere letter of language (*KU* 5: 316).

Finally, as inimitable expressions of the ineffable, aesthetic ideas are quintessential products of artistic genius (*KU* 5: 313–9).

While some commentators have identified aesthetic ideas with symbols or ascribed them a symbolic function, the two kinds of representation must be distinguished.⁴⁰¹ The key difference, as Pillow has explained, is that the mean-

---

400 Cf. Pillow 2000, p. 83 f., quoted below.
401 Coleman 1974, p. 161; Makkreel 1990, p. 122–128; Nuyen 1989, p. 101–103 – cited and critically discussed in Pillow 2000, p. 80 ff. Gadamer mischaracterizes the symbol in terms more

ing of a symbol is *constrained* by the underlying analogy from which it derives, whereas the meaning of an aesthetic idea is *inexhaustible:*

> Now the problem with construing aesthetic ideas as symbols is that the analogical rule-content of a Kantian symbol is too determinately specifiable. ... The meaning of a Kantian symbol can be determined by specifying the rule governing the analogy, and this determination of meaning is entirely at odds with the *inexhaustibility* of meaning Kant attributes to aesthetic ideas. The meaning of an aesthetic idea cannot be determined by *any* rule, certainly not by an analogical one, and so aesthetic ideas cannot have a *symbolic* function in Kant's sense of the term. Aesthetic ideas are not structured as analogies, and hence they do not exhibit rational ideas (or anything else) symbolically. They do not *exhibit* concepts or ideas at all, in fact; instead, they *express* an indeterminate and expansive range of meaning that no rule, concept or rational idea can encompass. The relationship between aesthetic and rational ideas is one of indeterminate expression, rather than symbolic exhibition ...[402]

Thus Kant's "symbol" and his "aesthetic idea" function in different ways and should not be confused. Correspondingly, the imagination plays a different role in producing each kind of representation. In symbolic hypotyposis, the imagination merely produces the image specified by the underlying analogy; this process *restricts* the imagination – and perhaps even dulls aesthetic sensibility itself, as Nietzsche would later argue.[403] By contrast, when the imagination produces aesthetic ideas, it strives for an *unbounded* aesthetic expression.

---

appropriate to the aesthetic idea in Gadamer 2002, p. 74 f.; Gadamer 1990, p. 81. See also section 3.1. of the Conclusion.

402 Pillow 2000, p. 83 f. Compare: "Derjenige, der ein Symbol verstehen will, kann selbstständig ausgehend von der unterlegten Anschauung die zugrundeliegende Analogie rekonstruieren. Symbole ... bringen zum Ausdruck, was durch eine Analogie von einem Gegenstand gedacht werden kann." Maly 2012, p. 202.

403 See section 3 of Chapter 7 and section 3.1. of the Conclusion. Nietzsche warned that overly intellectual symbolism can "desensualize" art and aesthetic experience: "§217. *Die Entsinnlichung der höheren Kunst.* – Unsere Ohren sind, vermöge der ausserordentlichen Uebung des Intellects durch die Kunstentwicklung der neuen Musik, immer intellektualer geworden. Deshalb ertragen wir jetzt viel grössere Tonstärke, viel mehr "Lärm", weil wir viel besser eingeübt sind, auf die *Vernunft in ihm* hinzuhorchen, als unsere Vorfahren. Thatsächlich sind nun alle unsere Sinne eben dadurch, dass sie sogleich nach der Vernunft, also nach dem "es bedeutet" und nicht mehr nach dem "es ist" fragen, etwas abgestumpft worden ... Was ist von alledem die Consequenz? Je gedankenfähiger Auge und Ohr werden, um so mehr kommen sie an die Gränze, wo sie unsinnlich werden: die Freude wird in's Gehirn verlegt, die Sinnesorgane selbst werdern stumpf und schwach, das Symbolische tritt immer mehr an Stelle des Seienden, – und so gelangen wir auf diesem Wege so sicher zur Barbarei, wie auf irgend einem anderen." Nietzsche 1999, p. 177 f.

And so it is actually surprising that those commentators keen on attributing the typic a *poetic* function should not have had recourse instead to the aesthetic idea, which, according to Kant, is both a product and source of the *poetic imagination* and finds its greatest expression in *poetry:*

> *The poet* ventures to make sensible rational ideas of invisible beings, the kingdom of the blessed, the kingdom of hell, eternity, creation, etc., as well as to make that of which there are examples in experience, e.g., death, envy, and all sorts of vices, as well as love, fame, etc., sensible beyond the limits of experience, with a completeness that goes beyond anything of which there is an example in nature, by means of an imagination that emulates the precedent of reason in attaining to a maximum; *and it is really the art of poetry in which the faculty of aesthetic ideas can reveal itself in its full measure* (KU 5: 314, my emphasis).

In contrast to the stilted symbolism of morality plays and allegories, where each one-dimensional character personifies a particular vice or virtue, the aesthetic idea provides a genuinely *poetic* expression of moral Ideas and thereby fulfills the *desiderata* of the aesthetic interpretation far better than symbolic hypotyposis. Firstly, the aesthetic idea functions as "the spur to an open-ended exploration of meaning or significance" insofar as it is an aesthetic representation of the imagination that elicits much thinking without it being possible for any determinate concept to be adequate to it.[404] Secondly, the aesthetic idea is deeply personal: it can only come into existence through the genius of an individual poet; and since it functions through association, it could quite conceivably "call up its own peculiar cluster of experiences, concepts, feelings, images, etc.," in each individual person who contemplates it. And thirdly, the aesthetic idea gives meaning to moral Ideas with a uniquely powerful imaginative and affective force, "animating the mind" with a flow of emotionally charged images.

This brief excursus through Kant's aesthetics suggests that even if one wanted to aestheticize the typic, identifying it with symbolic hypotyposis would not be the best way to go about it. More generally, I submit that it is both more faithful as well as more fruitful simply to acknowledge that the typic has a pure function, which later gets *supplemented* by the second, "impure" part of Kant's ethics, which gives due attention to aesthetics and moral anthropology.[405] Aesthetics may play a *complementary* role to the typic, but not a *constitutive* one. This thesis does justice to the distinctive philosophical contribution of Kant's ethics to his own historical period, as Cassirer has emphasized: "Thus it was precisely the formalistic nature of Kantian ethics that proved historically

---

[404] Pillow 2000, p. 86.
[405] See Louden 2000.

to be the peculiarly fruitful and effective moment; by the very fact that it conceived the moral law in its maximum purity and abstraction, Kantian ethics immediately and tangibly invaded the life of Kant's nation and age, imparting to them a new direction."[406] And the symbolists would do well to note that it was *the great poets and playwrights* of Kant's time who most clearly recognized this achievement: "Not only Schiller, who explicitly lamented in a letter to Kant that he had momentarily taken on the 'aspect of an opponent,' but Wilhelm von Humboldt, Goethe and Hölderlin also concur in this judgment."[407]

6.4 Conclusion

The upshot of the analysis conducted in this chapter (summarized in section 2.1. of the Conclusion) is that the symbolist interpretation of the Typic chapter is unsatisfactory. From the outset, the attempt to read the third *Critique* back into the second was anachronistic and textually unsupported. The concepts that the symbolists purport to assimilate – typification and the type on the one hand, symbolic hypotyposis and the symbol on the other – show significant and, one is tempted to say, obvious differences. Furthermore, the many variants of the symbolist interpretation, when examined in detail, turn out to be arbitrary and mutually inconsistent. Finally, the wilful attempt to aestheticize the Typic chapter not only distorts Kant's text, but also fails to achieve its own purpose, due to a false assessment of the resources offered by Kant's aesthetic theory. In the final analysis, the symbolists read the Typic chapter backwards – not only historically, but also philosophically: the challenge of enabling moral appraisal is not a matter of making the invisible visible, as they assume, but rather of judging the already visible against an invisible, formal standard, namely maxims' capacity to be universalized as laws. The next question is how to characterize *this* function in terms of a mode of symbolic representation that is distinct from symbolic hypotyposis.

---

406 Cassirer 1987, p. 270.
407 Letter from Schiller to Kant, 13 June, 1794 (11: 487), cited in Cassirer 1987, p. 270.

Chapter 7.
The typic and symbolic anthropomorphism

> "The human mind comes equipped with an ability to penetrate the cladding of sensory appearance and discern the abstract construction underneath – not always on demand, and not infallibly, but often enough and insightfully enough to shape the human condition. Our powers of analogy allow us to apply ancient neural structures to newfound subject matter, to discover hidden laws and systems of nature, and not least, to amplify the expressive power of language itself." – Steven Pinker[408]

To recall, the aim of this second part of the present study is to situate the typic within Kant's theory of symbolic representation. Kant provided a valuable clue when he indicated that the typic functioned not as a schema, but rather "served only as a symbol [*nur als Symbol diente*]" (*KpV* 5: 70). But as I argued in Chapter 6, most commentators spoil any insight to be gained from this remark by hastily identifying the typic with the notion of "symbolic hypotyposis" that Kant developed two years later in § 59 of the *Critique of Judgment* (1790). This is a misreading that distorts the typic's nature and function, and it even threatens to denature Kant's ethics as a whole. Instead of anachronistically reading the third *Critique* into the second, therefore, it would surely be more responsible and promising to investigate whether the typic may have been informed by an *earlier* conception of symbolic representation. In section 2.4. of the previous chapter, I examined the occurrences of the terms "symbol" (*Symbol*) and "symbolic" (*symbolisch*) prior to the publication of the *Critique of Practical Reason* in 1788, suggesting that the most plausible source appears five years earlier: the discussion of "symbolic anthropomorphism" in §§ 57–59 of the *Prolegomena*. Surprisingly – almost inexplicably – this connection has not been explored by commentators of the Typic chapter (the most one finds is a passing reference to the *Prolegomena*). In the present chapter, I remedy this oversight by conducting a full, detailed comparison of the two texts, which shows that the typic in fact has significant continuities, both historical and conceptual, with symbolic anthropomorphism. Section 1 analyzes Kant's conception of symbolic anthropomorphism in terms of six characteristic features, presenting it as a (1) non-absolute, (2) analogical, and (3) non-sensible mode of representation which is (4) permitted, required and (5) sufficient for reason's purposes and which (6) performs a number of critical, protective functions. Section 2 provides some historical background to Kant's theory of symbolic anthropomorphism by comparing it

---

[408] Pinker 2007, p. 276.

with St. Thomas Aquinas' influential doctrine of analogical predication. Section 3 compares symbolic anthropomorphism with the notion of symbolic hypotyposis as described in the *Critique of the Power of Judgment*, noting the differences between these two forms of symbolic representation. Section 4 systematically compares symbolic anthropomorphism with the typic, stressing the significant continuities between the two notions while identifying the latter's specific differences and innovations.

7.1 'Symbolic anthropomorphism' in the *Prolegomena*

The discussion of symbolic anthropomorphism figures in the Conclusion to the *Prolegomena*, entitled "On Determining the Boundary of Pure Reason" (§§ 57–59; *P* 4: 350–365), where Kant deals with the delicate problem of reconciling two apparently conflicting epistemological demands. On the one hand, the *Critique of Pure Reason* had already delimited the legitimate extension of synthetic *a priori* principles to the sphere of possible experience, circumscribed by the concept of the noumenon in the negative sense. Accordingly, the main negative result of the first *Critique* was the prohibition against transgressing the sphere of possible experience in attempts to acquire determinate cognition of noumenal beings. On the other hand, the central theme of the first *Critique* was that reason does not find satisfaction within the sphere of empirical knowledge, but is "pushed by its own need" (*KrV* B21) ever higher towards the unconditioned, which necessarily transcends possible experience. Consequently, reason forms Ideas of the intelligible objects that would ground every conditional nexus, and demands that the latter be pursued until reaching the former, namely "an immaterial being, an intelligible world, and a highest of all beings (all noumena)" (*P* 4: 355).

Nevertheless, Kant maintains that since these two requirements are equally valid, it must be possible to satisfy both of them, and in so doing, determine and cognize "the boundary [*Grenze*] of all permitted use of reason ..." (*P* 4: 356). Kant employs a spatial metaphor to illustrate the nature of his proposed solution: unlike limits, "which are merely negative," he explains, "in all boundaries there is something positive," i.e., a space wedged between two other spaces; accordingly, rather than stopping short of the boundary or transgressing beyond the boundary, there is a third possibility, namely remaining directly "on" it (*P* 4: 354). Analogously, the boundary between phenomena and noumena constitutes an epistemic space which reason can occupy by positively cognizing the *connection* between noumenal beings and the sensible world (*P* 4: 355, 361). In the *Prolegomena* Kant discusses this form of cognition with respect to God: How should reason conceive the supreme cause of the world? The answer that Kant gives corresponds neither to strict deism nor to theism. We are to conceive of God by means of a "symbolic anthropomorphism":

> But we hold ourselves to this boundary [of all permitted use of reason – A.W.] if we limit our judgment merely to the relation that the world may have to a being whose concept itself lies outside all cognition that we can attain within the world. For we then do not attribute to the supreme being any of the properties *in themselves* by which we think the objects of experience, and we thereby avoid *dogmatic* anthropomorphism; but we attribute those properties, nonetheless, to the relation of this being to the world, and allow ourselves a *symbolic* anthropomorphism, which in fact concerns only language and not the object itself (*P* 4: 357).

In the rest of this section, I will analyze Kant's conception of "symbolic anthropomorphism" in §§ 57–59 of the *Prolegomena* in terms of six characteristic features. To be sure, this part of the *Prolegomena* is related to Kant's treatment of the regulative use of the Ideas in the *Critique of Pure Reason* (*KrV* A642–68/B670–96); nevertheless, for the sake of concision and consistency I will focus my analysis on the *Prolegomena*, and refer to the *Critique* only to supplement certain points. Moreover, the *Prolegomena* contains elements not elaborated upon in the same way in the *Critique*, notably its relatively detailed treatment of analogy.

7.1.1 Merely symbolic, as opposed to absolute

On the one hand, in accordance with reason's demand to ascend to the Ideas, symbolic anthropomorphism targets "intelligible beings [*Verstandeswesen*]" beyond the horizon of possible experience, notably God, yet Kant repeats several times that this mode of representation does not allow us to cognize intellectual beings or their intrinsic properties "absolutely [*schlechthin, absolut*]" (*P* 4: 358, 358n) or "in themselves [*an sich, selbst, an sich selbst*]" (*P* 4: 355, 357, 358, 359, 360, 360n, 361).

Kant situates his conception of symbolic anthropomorphism vis-à-vis two traditional modes of cognizing God: theism and deism. Kant condemns theism – i.e., taking properties from our own natures, limited as they are to the conditions of sensibility, such as a physical body, a will, etc. and ascribing them directly to the divine being – as "*dogmatic* anthropomorphism" (*P* 4: 355, 4: 357). On the other hand, reason's need to employ the Ideas must still be satisfied, but deism – i.e., the representation of God through pure, unschematized categories alone – remains too empty and indeterminate (*P* 4: 355–356). Indeed, the only conceivable way in which one could attain absolute knowledge of God would be to cognize him as he cognizes himself, that is, through intellectual in-

7.1 'Symbolic anthropomorphism' in the *Prolegomena* — 183

tuition – but of course human beings have no such faculty (*KrV* B307, B159). Consequently, we must forswear all dogmatic attempts to determine intelligible beings as they are in themselves and instead admit modestly that – to us – they must remain "absolutely unknown [*absolut unbekannt*]" (*P* 4: 358n). This admission of ignorance is the starting-point of *symbolic* anthropomorphism – which, contrary to what some commentators have maintained, is thoroughly *anti-metaphysical*.[409]

Kant explains that reason's epistemic need can be met in an appropriate way if, and only if, reason restricts itself, "as befits knowledge of a boundary, ... *solely to the relation* [bloß auf das Verhältnis] of what lies outside the boundary to what is contained within (*P* 4: 361, trans. mod., my emphasis). Kant maintains that if we "restrict our judgment merely to the relation [*wir unser Urtheil bloß auf das Verhältnis einschränken*]" that intelligible entities have to the sensible world (*P* 4: 357, 359, 361, 361–2), we can determine intelligible beings' relation "with respect to the world and hence with respect to us [*respektiv auf die Welt und mithin auf uns*]" (*P* 4: 358) in a manner consonant with our epistemic finitude.[410] And we determine the relation between an intelligible being and the sensible world by assimilating it with a known relation between two things within the sensible world. In this way we represent God's relation to the sensible world according to a merely *symbolic anthropomorphism*, which Kant illustrates as follows:

> If I say that we are compelled to look upon the world *as if* it were the work of a supreme understanding and will, I actually say nothing more than: in the same way that a watch, a ship and a regiment are related to an artisan, a builder, and a commander, the sensible world (or everything that makes up the basis of this sum total of appearances) is related to the unknown – which I do not thereby cognize according to what it is in itself, but only according to what it is for me, that is, with respect to the world of which I am a part (*P* 4: 357).

The first point to note concerning this key passage is that symbolic anthropomorphism proceeds, as Kant puts it repeatedly, "merely by analogy [*nur/bloß nach der Analogie*]" (*P* 4: 359, 361). As we will see in more detail below, symbolic anthropomorphism is a form of analogical thinking insofar as it involves asserting a similarity between two relations. The point to appreciate here is that symbolic cognition is "only [*nur*]" or "merely [*bloß*]" analogical insofar as it yields no determinate cognition of the "missing" term (i.e., the term of the analogy corre-

---

[409] Guérin 1974; Marty 1997. Contrast with Pieper 1996, p. 112.
[410] Kühn doubts this claim, however I do not share his epistemological worry: see Kühn 2012, p. 241 f.

sponding to the intelligible being), but *only of the relation* of that being to the sensible world, insofar as that relation is construed as *analogous* to a certain relation *within* the sensible world. As Kant puts it in the first *Critique:* "And now we are thinking of a Something about which we have no concept at all of how it is in itself, but about which we think a relation to the sum total of appearances, which is analogous to the relation that appearances have to one another" (*KrV* A674/B702; cf. *KrV* A698/B726). For example, when one represents God's relation to his creation by analogy with a human artisan and his artifact, one does not thereby transfer properties onto the Creator himself, but only on his causal relation to the world:

> reason is not thereby transposed as a property onto the first being in itself, but *only onto the relation of that being to the sensible world*, and therefore anthropomorphism is completely avoided. For here only the cause of the rational form found everywhere in the world is considered, and the supreme being, insofar as it contains the basis of this rational form of the world, is indeed ascribed reason, *but only by analogy* [nur nach der Analogie], *i.e., insofar as this expression signifies only the relation* [nur das Verhältnis] *that the highest cause (which is unknown to us) has to the world*, in order to determine everything in it with the highest degree of conformity to reason (*P* 4: 359; my italics).

Consequently, the mode of representation described here is "anthropomorphic" only in an *epistemological* sense. Intelligible beings are not represented as they are in themselves, but only according to their *relation* to human beings and to the human world: for instance, God is represented "not according to what it is in itself, but still with respect to me and world of which I'm a part [*zwar nicht nach dem, was es an sich selbst ist, aber doch nach dem, was es für mich ist, nämlich in Ansehung der Welt, wovon ich ein Teil bin*]" (*P* 4: 357). In addition, this mode of representation is executed by means of human conceptual capacities, for the sake of human needs and goals. But as we will see in more detail, symbolic anthropomorphism does *not* produce a symbol, or image, of intelligible entities in the shape of a human being.

Furthermore, symbolic anthropomorphism is accompanied by a *semantic limitation* on the *language* used to talk about intelligible beings. In the case of symbolic anthropomorphism, we are only authorized to speak of God "as if [*als ob*]" he were an artisan, and the world, his artifact. This characteristically Kantian expression signals that such a claim about God "in fact concerns only language and not the object itself [*in der Tat nur die Sprache und nicht das Objekt selbst angeht*]" (*P* 4: 357); it is just a *façon de parler* that should not be interpreted in any strict, literal, or absolute sense (*per eminentiam*). The expression "*als ob*" also figures prominently in the *Critique*'s discussion of "the regulative use of the Ideas of pure reason" to indicate the same kind of restriction (*KrV* A672–68/

B700–96, A699/B727).[411] In a word, such anthropomorphic, 'as-if' language is *only symbolic*. Kant's employment of the word "*symbolisch*" to signal a semantic restriction can therefore be seen as an epistemological adaptation of a more common eighteenth-century usage listed in the Grimm dictionary: "*in ausgesprochener oder unausgesprochener Einschränkung, soviel wie 'uneigentlich, übertragen, nicht im wirklichen, wörtlichen Sinne.*"[412] This is not to say that merely symbolic, 'as-if' language is hollow or empty, however; as we will see next, the proper meaning of an as-if statement can be reconstructed as an analogy.

In sum, when Kant speaks of symbolic anthropomorphism in §§ 57–59 of the *Prolegomena*, the term is associated with definite restrictions. Indeed, in this short text, Kant uses the restricting words "mere [*bloß*]" and "only [*nur*]" eighteen and fourteen times, respectively, to emphasize that this mode of representation is not absolute, but *merely* symbolic insofar as it determines intelligible beings not as they are in themselves, but *merely* in their relation to "the world of which I am part," and this *merely* by analogy, and with *merely* symbolic language.

7.1.2 Analogical

We have just seen that Kant repeatedly characterizes symbolic anthropomorphism as cognition "*merely* by analogy [*bloß nach der Analogie*]." At first sight, this characterization may strike one as doubly disappointing: we do not cognize intelligible beings as they are in themselves; worse still, the ersatz is epistemologically second-rate, a 'mere analogy.' Indeed, in the philosophical tradition analogy has commonly been looked down upon as a sketchy resemblance, a shaky inference, or an insidious source of semantic ambiguity. However, in the *Prolegomena* Kant explicitly disavows such negative views, defending instead his own positive conception of analogy as a precise and reliable instrument for representing conceptual *relations*.

Kant begins his discussion of analogy in the *Prolegomena* by quickly forestalling any confusion between the widespread notion of analogy as a rough, superficial similarity and his own, properly *philosophical*, form of analogy that underlies symbolic anthropomorphism: "This type of cognition is cognition according to analogy, which surely does not signify, as the word is usually

---

[411] This is not the place to discuss the epistemological significance of '*als ob*' thinking to Kant's philosophy in general. For the classic debate on this topic, see Adickes 1927; Vaihinger 1922; Vaihinger 2009.
[412] "Symbolisch" 1984, p. 1389.

taken, an imperfect similarity between two things, but rather a perfect similarity between two relations in wholly dissimilar things" (*P* 4: 357). The common conception of analogy as an approximate similarity does not do justice to the focus, degree, and depth of similarity involved in Kant's "philosophical analogy" (*KrV* A179–180/B222–223).

Firstly, Kant's analogy does not concern the similarity between *individual things*, but rather the similarity between *relations*. Accordingly, Kant's philosophical analogy must be sharply distinguished from inductive analogies based on *the similarity between two things*; indeed, the distinction is all the more pressing, since inductive analogies are sometimes employed in philosophical contexts. One kind of inductive analogy allows one to make an *a posteriori* inference of the following form: if entity *A*, with the properties *P1*, *P2*, *P3*, and *P4* is known to share the properties *P1*, *P2*, and *P3* with entity *B*, then one can infer, on the basis of the known similarity between entities *A* and *B*, that entity *B* probably also possesses the property *P4*. Kant discusses this form of analogical inference in his lectures on logic, yet it is distinct from his own model of philosophical analogy.[413] Another form of inductive analogy licences an *a posteriori* inference from the similarity between two *effects* to the similarity between their respective *causes*. This form of analogy is obliquely alluded to in the *Prolegomena*, when Kant notes that Hume had rightly criticized it as an inadequate basis for proving the existence of a divine Creator from the alleged similarity between the universe and an artifact (*P* 4: 356). Here is how Hume analyzed that analogy:

> If we see a house, … we conclude, with the greatest certainty, that it had an architect and builder; because this is precisely that species of effect, which we have experienced to proceed from that species of cause. But surely you will not affirm, that the universe bears such a resemblance to a house, that we can with the same certainty infer a similar cause, or that the analogy is here entire and perfect. The dissimilitude is so striking, that the utmost you can here pretend to is a guess, a conjecture, a presumption concerning a similar cause.[414]

Obviously, this is not the model of analogy that Kant endorses for his own purposes.

Secondly, the degree of relational similarity posited by a philosophical analogy is not imperfect or approximate, but rather a "perfect similarity [*eine vollkommene Ähnlichkeit*]," "sameness [*Gleichheit*]" (*KrV* A179/B222) or even "identity [*Identität*]" (*KU* 5: 464n) between relations. Indeed, the similarity should be deep enough that the analogous relations can correspond to each other "in spite of

---

[413] Callanan 2008, p. 749ff.
[414] Hume 1935, p. 178.

[*ungeachtet*]" the superficial dissimilarity of the elements between which they respectively obtain. In the *Prolegomena*, Kant illustrates this important point with the following example:

> Such is an analogy between the legal relation of human actions and the mechanical relation of moving forces: I can never do anything to another without giving him a right to do the same to me under the same conditions; just as a body cannot act on another body with its motive force without thereby causing the other body to react just as much on it. *Right and motive force are here completely dissimilar things, but in their relation is nonetheless complete similarity* [Hier sind Recht und bewegende Kraft ganz unähnliche Dinge, aber in ihrem Verhältnisse ist doch völlige Ähnlichkeit] (*P* 4: 357n, my emphasis).

Kant's definition of analogy in the third *Critique* also highlights this point: "An analogy (in a qualitative sense) is the identity of the relation [*die Identität des Verhältnisses*] between grounds and consequences (causes and effects), insofar as that identity obtains in spite of the specific difference between the things ... [*sofern sie ungeachtet der spezifischen Verschiedenheit der Dinge ... stattfindet*]" (*KU* 5: 464n).

We can further characterize Kant's conception of analogy by referring to the "Analogies of Experience" in the first *Critique*, where, as above, Kant distinguishes his technical conception of analogy from another form with which it could easily be confused – not the common view, this time, but the technical *mathematical* sense:

> In philosophy analogies signify something very different from what they represent in mathematics. In the latter they are formulas that assert the identity of two relations of magnitude, and are always *constitutive*, so that if two members of the proportion are given, the third is also thereby given, i.e., can be constructed. In philosophy, however, analogy is not the sameness of two *quantitative* but of two *qualitative* relations [*nicht die Gleichheit zweener quantitativen, sondern qualitativen Verhältnisse*], where from three given members I can cognize and give *a priori* only the relation to a fourth member but not *this* fourth member itself ... [*nicht aber dieses vierte* Glied *selbst*] (*KrV* A179 – 180/B222 – 223).

Kant's description of the form and function of mathematical analogies calls for a brief digression, as it has lent itself to confusion. As for the *form*, readers of the *Critique of Pure Reason* had long been puzzled by the fact that mathematical analogies are described as having only *three* members, rather than four; accordingly, many editors and translators, notably Mellin, emended the text to read "... wenn drei *Glieder gegeben sind, auch das* vierte *dadurch gegeben wird* ..." – whereas others, such as Guyer and Wood, in the passage quoted above, revert to the original three-term formulation. It turns out that this debate cannot be settled on philological grounds alone, but depends on an understanding of the proper *function* of the mathematical analogy. Most scholars who favour the four-term formulation apparently think that the mathematical analogy is an algebraic formula that functions something like the well-known "Rule of Three" in elementary arithmetic:

> For an equation of the form $a/b = c/x$ where the variable to be evaluated is in the right-hand denominator, the Rule of Three states that: $x = bc/a$.

This seems to correspond perfectly to the four-term model of mathematical analogy: if three members of the proportion are given (a, b, c), the fourth (x) is thereby also given; e.g. If $a = 3$; $b = 4$; $c = 75$, then we can calculate that $x = 100$. On this interpretation, then, a "mathematical analogy" designates a four-term formula of elementary algebra symbolizing numbers (whole integers) and basic arithmetic operations (here, multiplication and division), which allow one to determine the missing fourth term by calculating it from the given three terms. Plausible as it may seem, this interpretation rests on an anachronistic assumption, as Shabel has shown. The mathematical analogy is indeed an "algebraic" formula, she suggests, but Kant's notion of algebra differed significantly from the modern, arithmetical notion – and we must adjust our interpretation of the analogy accordingly: "in a Kantian context 'algebra' cannot be taken simply to denote the arithmetic of indeterminate or variable numeric quantities, but must be recognized as a method applied to the solution of arithmetic *and* geometrical problems, *resulting in a geometrical construction* of 'magnitude in general': a line segment expressing either a number, or the determinate size of a magnitude (*quantum*)."[415] In other words, the mathematical analogy symbolically expresses determinate *ratios* that can be used to determine "which and how great" the missing term is by means of a geometrical construction. This account makes mathematical analogy a special case of "symbolic construction," and it also explains why Kant specifies, in the above-quoted passage, not that the missing member is given by a process of calculation, but rather by being "constructed" (*konstruiert*): the geometrical procedure for constructing the three-term formula (a : b :: b : c – determining the third proportional), is described in Proposition VI.11 of Euclid's *Elements*, while the procedure for constructing the four-term formula (a : b :: c : d – determining the fourth proportional) is descri-

---

[415] Shabel 1998, p. 617 (my emphasis). Callanan addresses the controversy over the interpretation of the mathematical analogy in Callanan 2008, p. 759–764. For accounts of the relation of Kant's philosophy of mathematics to the Greek mathematical tradition, in particular the Eudoxean theory of proportions, see Sutherland 2006, p. 533–558; Sutherland 2004, p. 161–164; Carson 1999.

bed in Proposition VI.12. Since Proposition VI.11 is a special case of Proposition VI.12, it turns out that a mathematical analogy can have four distinct terms a : b :: c : x or only three a : b :: b : c. Accordingly, both readings of the passage cited above (*KrV* A179–180/B222–223) are technically possible, depending on whether one counts the number of terms in the analogy as such (four) or the number of *distinct* terms (three or four). But the upshot is that the mathematical analogy determines the missing term by *constructing* it according to the same *mathematical ratio* that holds between the "given" terms.

In any case, the mathematical analogy operates on *quantitative* relations, whereas Kant's *philosophical* analogy deals with *qualitative* relations (notably causal relations, cf. *KU* 5: 464n). Consequently, the philosophical analogy does not *construct* the missing term; rather, the philosophical analogy allows us to perfectly determine the second *relation*, insofar as it posits the second relation's perfect "sameness" (*Gleichheit*) to the first, known relation. Accordingly, the proper form of a philosophical analogy in Kant's sense is **a : b :: c : x**.[416] Returning to symbolic anthropomorphism, conceiving of God as if he were an artisan allows us to determine his causal relation to the sensible world by positing that this relation is *perfectly similar* to the causal relation between an artisan and the artifact he produces, according to the analogy *God : sensible world :: artisan : artifact*. Correspondingly, *speaking* about God as the 'artisan' of the world should be interpreted as no more than a condensed linguistic expression of this very analogy; in general, the *legitimate interpretation* of any symbolic statement must be determined by reconstructing its underlying analogy.[417]

In summary, symbolic anthropomorphism employs "philosophical analogy" as a conceptual instrument for determinately representing the *relation* between an intelligible being and the sensible world. The analogy functions by construing that unknown relation as *perfectly similar* to a known relation between certain things in the sensible world – and this, regardless of the dissimilarity of the individual terms of the analogy, and without cognizing the fourth term as it is in itself.

7.1.3 Non-sensible

The third feature of symbolic anthropomorphism is, like the first, a restriction: *it yields no sensible intuition (i.e., no image) of the intelligible object that it "symbol-*

---

[416] Callanan 2008, p. 761.
[417] Maly 2012, p. 288f.

ically" represents, nor does it 'sensibilize' the noumemon's relation to the world. Indeed, an intelligible being (*Verstandeswesen*) would be denatured if one were to attribute sensible properties to it, as in theism: "… if we think [an intelligible being – A.W.] through properties borrowed from the sensible world, it is no longer an intelligible being: it is thought as one of the phenomena and belongs to the sensible world" (*P* 4: 355). Accordingly, Kant castigates *dogmatic* (i.e., non-critical) anthropomorphism because it "transfers [*überträgt*] predicates from the sensible world onto a being wholly distinct from the [sensible] world" (*P* 4: 358). In so doing, dogmatic anthropomorphism denatures the deistic representation of God – a "wholly pure concept of reason" (*P* 4: 355) – by contaminating it with sensible intuitions. In *symbolic* anthropomorphism, by contrast, the analogy functions in a non-sensible, purely conceptual way. For example, in the *Prolegomena* Kant construes God's love for humanity in terms of "the *mere* category [*die* bloße *Kategorie*]" of causality; i.e., the *pure* concept of the understanding, devoid of any sensible qualities: "*But here the relational concept is a mere category, namely the concept of cause, which has nothing to do with sensibility* [Der Verhältnisbegriff aber ist hier eine bloße Kategorie, nämlich der Begriff der Ursache, der nichts mit der Sinnlichkeit zu tun hat]" (*P* 4: 357n; trans. mod., my emphasis).[418] Relatedly, in his contemporaneous *Lectures on the Philosophical Doctrine of Religion*, Kant recommended "the noble way of analogy" because it enables us "to remove from our cognition of God everything sensible inhering in our concepts" (cf. *VpR* 28: 1023, 1046–1048).[419]

In short, the properly "symbolic" use of analogy enables us to form a determinate representation of a purely conceptual relation with which we are not acquainted by assimilating it to a second, purely conceptual relation with which we are familiar– yet no sensible properties are thereby attributed to either of the relations, nor onto the entities between which they obtain. Thus, the use of analogy that Kant condones as properly "symbolic" in contrast to "dogmatic" is *not figurative*; rather, it respects the critical interdiction against exhibiting supersensible representations as sensible images.[420] Despite the name, then, "symbolic anthropomorphism" does not in fact produce a *symbol in the image of a human being.*

---

[418] See section 3 below.
[419] Ludwig Pölitz published the *Vorlesungen über die philosophische Religionslehre* in 1817 (second edition, 1830); however, Kant delivered the lectures on which this text is based sometime between 1783 and 1786 – roughly contemporaneously with the *Prolegomena* and just prior to the composition of the *Critique of Practical Reason*.
[420] *Pace* Caruth 1988.

7.1.4 Permitted and required

Kant makes it quite clear in the *Prolegomena* that the use of analogy in symbolic anthropomorphism is justified and legitimate within critical philosophy. As we have seen, Kant motivated the *prima facie* feasibility of symbolic anthropomorphism as a way of squaring a "proscription" (*Verbot*) with an equally legitimate "prescription" (*Gebot*), both announced in the *Critique of Pure Reason:* while we cannot even cognize intelligible beings as they are in themselves, we may nonetheless expect to determine "at least their relation to the sensible world and bring it to clarity" (*P* 3: 354). Indeed, reason positively bids us to do so, for, driven by its speculative and architectonic interests (*KrV* A467/B495, A474–5/B502–3), it refuses to stop short of the bounds of experience, demanding a standpoint from which to view experience as a whole – which is just what 'knowledge on the boundary' promises to provide. And since Kant considers symbolic cognition by means of analogy to be the *only* possible way to sufficiently determine this relation without falling into the errors of dogmatism, we "can allow ourselves [*wir erlauben uns*]" (*P* 4: 357) to employ it – and indeed "we are compelled [*wir sind genöthigt*]" (*P* 4: 357) to do so.[421] In the *Prolegomena*, thus, Kant is reiterating the gist of the "transcendental deduction" he provided in the related discussion of the analogical, 'as if' employment of the Ideas in the *Critique*, where he declared that we are "not only warranted but even compelled [*nicht allein befugt, sondern auch genötigt*]" to posit God's relation to the world by analogy (cf. *KrV* A677–8/B705–6, cf. A671/B99).

7.1.5 Sufficient

Kant goes on to assure us that while our permitted use of symbolic anthropomorphism may be subject to certain restrictions, it is nevertheless *sufficient* for us and we have reason to be *satisfied* with it. Thus when I regard the world *as if* it were an artifact produced by an artisan-God, for instance, I must accept that I do not gain any absolute knowledge of God as he may be constituted in himself, yet I nevertheless grasp this notion "according to what it is for me, that is, with respect to the world of which I am a part" (*P* 4: 357). In other words, symbolic anthropomorphism may be relative to the human perspective, but that makes it all the more relevant to us. Indeed, Kant insists that this anal-

---

[421] Compare the "transcendental deduction" of the regulative, 'as if', use of Ideas in the *Critique* (A671/B699 and following).

ogy yields a concept of God's relation to the sensible world that is *sufficiently* determinate for our theoretical needs:

> By means of this analogy there still remains a concept of the supreme being *sufficiently determinate for us*, though we have omitted everything that could have *determined* this concept unconditionally and *in itself*; for we determine the concept only with respect to the world and hence with respect to us, *and we have no need of more* (P 4: 358, emphasis added; cf. *VpR* 28: 1023).

We do not actually need more than this "cognition by analogy," Kant insists, because reason's true vocation is not to determine God's intrinsic properties *a priori* – an enterprise that the first *Critique* proved to be a futile attempt to transcend the boundaries of possible experience – but instead to provide *regulative principles* for the systematic use of the understanding *within* possible experience. And reason *can* give the understanding its greatest systematic extension by instructing it to investigate nature *as if* it were an artifact designed and constructed by a supreme intelligence; indeed, "such a principle must be thoroughly advantageous to reason and can nowhere harm it in its use in nature" (P 4: 359).[422] Kant concludes that "this is, however, all of the benefit that can reasonably even be wished for here, and *there is cause to be satisfied with it*" (P 4: 361–2, my emphasis). Symbolic anthropomorphism therefore forms part and parcel of Kant's epistemological bargain in the first *Critique*, i.e., the demand to renounce the excesses of dogmatic metaphysics in exchange for the assurance that heed-

---

[422] The history of science has repeatedly confirmed Kant's insight that a well-chosen analogy can serve as a powerful tool for unifying diverse phenomena in an overarching theory. A spectacularly successful example is Darwin's theory of evolution by natural selection, in which 'Nature' is conceived by analogy with a breeder who carefully selects and passes on the heritable traits of his fittest animals – whereby no intelligent agency is *literally* attributed to 'Nature' itself. Also worth noting in connection with the first feature discussed above are Darwin's remarks to the effect that the anthropomorphic language based on this analogy is merely symbolic: "In the literal sense of the word, no doubt, natural selection is a false term; but who ever objected to chemists speaking of the elective affinities of the various elements? – and yet an acid cannot strictly be said to elect the base with which it in preference combines. It has been said that I speak of natural selection as an active power or Deity; but who objects to an author speaking of the attraction of gravity as ruling the movements of the planets? Every one knows what is meant and is implied by such metaphorical expressions; and they are almost necessary for brevity. So again it is difficult to avoid personifying the word Nature; but I mean by nature, only the aggregate action and product of many natural laws, and by laws the sequence of events as ascertained by us." Darwin 2011, ch. 4. For more treatments of the role of analogies in science, see Bailer-Jones 2002; Black 1962; Hesse 1966; "Models" 1998; "Models and Analogies in Science" 1967.

ing the strictures of critique is the surest and indeed the only way "to bring human reason to full satisfaction" (*KrV* A856/B884).

7.1.6 Protective

The final feature of symbolic anthropomorphism is its critical, protective function, which flows from the previous two features: as the only possible way to accomplish the difficult feat of satisfying reason's demands while still heeding the strictures of critique, symbolic anthropomorphism serves to discredit and ward off several rival epistemological approaches: *dogmatism, scepticism, empiricism,* and *mysticism.*

Kant frames symbolic anthropomorphism as "the true middle way ... determined precisely and according to principles" between the opposite dangers of dogmatism and scepticism (*P* 4: 360). As we have seen repeatedly, Kant takes great care to avoid dogmatic anthropomorphism: symbolic anthropomorphism is merely analogical, "and we are thereby prevented [*verhütet*]" from making spurious claims to absolute knowledge of God's inner properties or transferring any sensible properties onto the Supreme Being (*P* 4: 359). In contrast, if one refuses to give up the "fantastical concepts" of dogmatism, Kant warns, one exposes oneself to the sceptical attacks that brought theism to its knees (*P* 4: 356). Indeed, Kant pleaded for this shift to merely symbolic anthropomorphism during his contemporaneous *Lectures on the Philosophical Doctrine of Religion*, in which he exhorted his audience to renounce both the arrogance of dogmatism as well as the despair of scepticism and adopt instead the reasonable and modest 'way of analogy':

> It would be easiest to deal successfully with all the consequences of anthropomorphism if only our reason voluntarily relinquished its claim to have cognition of the nature of God and his attributes, as to how they themselves are constituted internally, and if, mindful of its weakness, it never tried to exceed its bounds but were content to cognize only so much of him, who must always remain the object of an eternal quest, as it has need of. This interest of humanity is best attained *per viam analogicam.* ... [If] we understand analogy to be the perfect similarity of relationships ... then we will be satisfied at once; we can then form a concept of God and of his predicates which will be so sufficient that we will never need anything more (*VpR* 28: 1048, 1023).

When it comes to cognition of God, less is more.

While dogmatism and scepticism certainly represent the two main dangers Kant warns against in the *Prolegomena*, a close reading of the text reveals that he alludes, albeit subtly, to two additional dangers. They appear in the following passage, in connection with Kant's metaphor of the *boundary* of experience:

> But *setting the boundary* to the field of experience through something that is otherwise unknown to it is indeed a cognition that is still left to reason from this standpoint, whereby reason is *neither locked inside the sensible world nor raving outside it* [*nicht innerhalb der Sinnenwelt beschlossen, auch nicht außer derselben schwärmend*], but, as befits knowledge of a boundary, restricts itself solely to the relation of what lies outside the boundary to what is contained within (*P* 4: 361, trans. mod., my italics).

As I read this passage, Kant is presenting symbolic anthropomorphism, as cognition "on the boundary," as a suitable way of avoiding two opposing dangers that threaten reason with respect to the delimitation of its use: on the one hand, *empiricism* stultifies reason by confining it to a merely imminent use; on the other hand, *mysticism* deludes reason by inciting it to stray into the transcendent.

Symbolic anthropomorphism wards off empiricism insofar as it offers reason a more satisfying and legitimate alternative. Indeed, the strictly imminent use prescribed by empiricism does not meet reason's needs. Reason, by its very nature, demands completeness in the regression from conditions to their unconditioned ground – and given this drive for metaphysical knowledge, "experience never fully satisfies reason; it directs us ever further back in answering questions and leaves us unsatisfied as regards their full elucidation ..." (*P* 4: 352, cf. *KrV* A314/B370–1). Consequently, Kant castigates the facile complacency of those "naturalists of pure reason" who smugly declare – without bothering to first undertake a critical investigation – that "with all our reason we can never hope to get beyond the field of experiences" (*P* 4: 314). What is more, empiricism cannot even satisfy reason within the realm of experience, as it limits scientific investigation to a piecemeal approach, whereas reason aims to direct natural science, in accordance with an all-encompassing *a priori* principle, towards systematicity and maximal expansion (*P* 4: 359; cf. *KrV* A651/B679, A675/B703).

Moreover, Kant subtly yet unmistakably alludes to the danger of mystical "enthusiasm" (*Schwärmerei*), as evidenced by the tell-tale word "*schwärmend*" used to characterize the tempting but illusory prospect of a direct, inner, and immediate cognition of the intelligible realm through supersensible intuitions. More generally, Kant's discussion of symbolic anthropomorphism can also be read as a critical warning against the delusion of transcending the boundary of the only world that can possibly make sense to us. The best cognition of the intelligible sphere that epistemically finite human beings can hope for is merely symbolic, i.e., according to analogy – and that, Kant assures us, is "all of the benefit that can *reasonably* even be wished for here" (*P* 4: 361–2, my emphasis).

7.2 Symbolic anthropomorphism and Aquinas' doctrine of analogical predication

Before proceeding any further, we should inquire into the relevance of St. Thomas Aquinas' influential doctrine of analogical predication to Kant's conception of symbolic cognition. Indeed, it has been suggested that in the *Prolegomena* "Kant actually speaks in a manner that could be mistaken as coming directly from Aquinas' own pen."[423] Aquinas invoked analogy to deal with the problem of predication with respect to God: How can we legitimately use language to make true, affirmative statements about the Supreme Being? The trouble arises due to the ontological incommensurability between the Creator, who is infinite, and his creatures, who are finite. For instance, take the statement "God has knowledge." If we mean to say that God has knowledge in the *same sense* that we ordinarily attribute knowledge to a human being – *univocity* – then we lapse into anthropomorphism insofar as we thereby attribute the limitations of human knowledge to God, whereas his knowledge is supposedly perfect and unlimited. On the other hand, if we conclude that the word "knowledge," when applied to human beings, has an *entirely different sense* from what we mean by God's "knowledge" – *equivocity* – then we must consequently give up making any fitting affirmation about God using that word and remain agnostic about his attributes. As a way between the opposing pitfalls of anthropomorphism and agnosticism, Aquinas suggests predication according to analogy. In fact, Aquinas successively entertained several different conceptions of analogy, of which I will present two and compare them with Kant's model: the *analogy of proportionality* and the *analogy of attribution*.[424]

a) The analogy of proportionality
In *Disputed Questions on Truth* (*Quaestiones Disputatae de Veritate*, 1256–1259), Aquinas proposes the *analogy of proportionality* for speaking about God's properties. An analogy of proportionality is "a likeness of two proportions to each

---

[423] Gill 1984, p. 22.
[424] This paragraph and the following one are based on the helpful exposition by Danby-Smith 1969, p. 15–17.

other, as six with four because six is two times three, just as four is two times two."⁴²⁵ While this particular example is arithmetical, Aquinas extends the analogy to non-mathematical proportions as well. The analogy of proportionality licences a particular form of non-univocal, non-equivocal predication by transferring vocabulary between corresponding terms of the two proportions. Assuming the analogy *seeing : eye :: understanding : intellect*, for example, one can say that understanding is an intellectual form of "seeing." In the same way, Aquinas suggested, one could affirm – neither univocally nor equivocally, but *analogically* – that what we call "knowledge" plays the same role in God's mental life as knowledge plays in human mental life.⁴²⁶

The form of Aquinas' analogy of proportionality – two perfectly similar relations holding between two pairs of terms – clearly corresponds to the model of analogy that Kant presents in the *Prolegomena*. So it is certainly possible that Kant was influenced by Aquinas on this point. Then again, Aquinas puts the analogy of proportionality to a different epistemological use than Kant, namely to determine God's *properties*, whereas Kant insists that the analogy cannot be employed to determine God's properties in themselves, but only his *relation* to the world. Moreover, Aquinas borrowed this model of analogy from Aristotle, and Kant may well have done the same – without the middleman, so to speak – in which case the common source would explain the similarity.⁴²⁷ Indeed, as Callanan remarks in his article on Kant's theory of analogy, "much of Kant's logic was inherited from the Aristotelian corpus without modification," and so we should not be surprised to find Aristotelian models of analogy directly reproduced in Kant.⁴²⁸

b) The analogy of attribution

In any case, Aquinas later abandoned the analogy of proportionality, realizing that any putative proportional analogy such as *knowledge : God :: knowledge : human beings* was bound to be "deeply flawed ... given that the problem of divine names arises precisely because the relationship of God to his divine properties is so *radically disproportionate* to our relation to our human properties."⁴²⁹ Consequently, in later texts, notably the *Summa Theologiae* (1265–1273), Aquinas

---

425 St. Thomas Aquinas, *De veritate*, q. 2, a. 11, in Klubertanz 1960, p. 89f.
426 Danby-Smith 1969, p. 18–21.
427 Cf. Aristotle 1984: *Poetics* 21, 1457b7–34; *Rhetoric* III, 10–11; *Nicomachean Ethics* V, 3; 6/7, 1131a9; *Eudemian Ethics* VII, 9, 1241b33–38; 10, 1242b2–21.
428 Callanan 2008, p. 750.
429 Ashworth 2013.

7.2 Symbolic anthropomorphism and Aquinas' doctrine of analogical predication — 197

turned to a model of analogy that came to be called the *analogy of attribution*. Unlike the Aristotelian analogy of proportionality, the analogy of attribution has one primary analogue and one or more secondary analogues; each secondary analogue stands in a derivative, or 'epigonic', relation to the primary analogue.[430] Correspondingly, the same word can be predicated in its essential significance, or "focal meaning," when applied to the primary analogue and in a secondary, derivative sense when applied to a secondary analogue.[431] A paradigmatic example is the word "healthy," which is attributed primarily to the physical state of a man and derivatively to medicine or diet (*qua* causes of the man's health) and to urine (*qua* indicator of the man's health). In order to solve the problem of divine names, Aquinas then conjugated this model of analogical predication with his metaphysics of Creation, according to which God had actively transmitted properties resembling his own to his creatures, as when he made humanity "in his own image" (Genesis 1: 27). On this conception, "God is an analogical cause, and this is the reality that underlies our use of analogical language."[432] Accordingly, when we say Adam possessed "knowledge," for example, we mean this word in a weak sense commensurate with his derivative ontological status *qua* creature; yet we can also attribute the same word in a superlative sense to his Creator, as befits the latter's absolute ontological priority. The analogy of attribution thereby provides a solution to the problem of divine predication in the form of an employment of language semantically calibrated to its ontological grounding, as Aquinas explains in the *Summa Theologiae*: "In this way some words are used neither univocally nor purely equivocally of God and creatures, but analogically, for we cannot speak of God at all except in the language we use of creatures and so whatever is said both of God and creatures is said in virtue of the order that creatures have to God is to their source and cause in which all the perfections of things pre-exist transcendentally."[433]

Clearly, Aquinas's analogy of attribution differs in significant respects from Kant's Aristotelian-inspired model in the *Prolegomena*. To begin with, Kant does not adopt all of the metaphysical presuppositions underlying Aquinas's model of analogy. Although Kant leaves room for the metaphysical doctrine of creation

---

430 "Das Verhältnis "von Einem her – auf Eines hin" hat ein schlechthin vorgeordnetes, maßgebliches "erstes" Glied und dem gegenüber beliebig viel "zweite", für die der Bezug auf das "erste" wesentlich ist, während dies wiederum durch den Bezug in keiner Weise betroffen ist. Dieses Verhältnis kann nicht durch die – von Aristoteles allein anerkannte – viergliederige Proportion beschrieben werden." See "Analogie" 1971, p. 217 f.
431 "Analogie" 1996, p. 1242 f.
432 Ashworth 2013.
433 Aquinas 1964, p. 65 (Ia, q. 13, a.5).

(*KpV* 5: 102), he does not endorse the Scholastic axiom that every cause produces an effect *similar* to itself. And while Kant accords analogy an important role in his own theory of causation, the model he proposes in the Analogies of Experience is based on *analogies of proportionality* between abstract relations (*KrV* A179–180/B222).[434] Moreover, Kant's "philosophical analogy" involves two symmetrical relations, while the analogy of attribution is based on a single, asymmetrical relation. And again, the two kinds of analogy serve different epistemological functions: the analogy of attribution serves to ascribe properties to God; Kant's philosophical analogy purports to determine no more than God's *relation to the world*.[435] Incidentally, this analysis also contradicts Gadamer's assertion that there is a deep affinity between the theological *analogia entis*, based on the analogy of attribution, and Kant's conception of *symbolic hypotyposis*, for in fact the latter is also based on Kant's "philosophical analogy," as will be explained in the next section.[436]

7.3 Symbolic anthropomorphism and symbolic hypotyposis

Before exploring the connections between symbolic anthropomorphism and the typic, it will be necessary to compare *symbolic anthropomorphism* as described in the *Prolegomena* with *symbolic hypotyposis* as described in the *Critique of the Power of Judgment*. Not only is this comparison important for the overall argument of the present study, but it is also a pressing exegetical task in its own right. Put more critically, one should not simply *assume* that the expression "symbolic," used (only once) in a text from 1783, means the same as thing as when the corresponding word appears in the midst of a technical discussion in the *Critique of the Power of Judgment*, written seven years later. For instance, Sebastian Maly has criticized Petra Bahr and Heiner Bielefeldt for hastily assim-

---

[434] Renaut 1997, p. 303 f.
[435] Glover 1971 comes to the same conclusion in his study of analogy's role in Kant's epistemology and metaphysics: "Instead of relations between different terms being the same, there is a direct linking of terms [in the analogy of attribution – A.W.]. Thus, man is healthy and the causes of health in a man are considered healthy by analogy. In effect, one property is ascribed to both terms of the analogy. If the use of this concept of analogy were ascribed to Kant in this sense, it would result in grave problems for his epistemological thought since it involves the actual attribution of properties to entities to which nothing can be properly attributed, that is, of which we can have no knowledge. Analogy in the [Aristotelian] sense does not necessarily fall into this difficulty since nothing is ascribed to entities. Instead, the analogy is drawn between relations between entities. In fact, Kant seems to have used the concept … in the Aristotelian sense."
[436] Compare Gadamer 2002, p. 75; Gadamer 1990, p. 81.

ilating the two forms of symbolic representation without having carefully compared the relevant texts.[437] Indeed, I will argue that there are in fact noteworthy differences between symbolic anthropomorphism and symbolic hypotyposis – differences which will, in turn, have an incidence on our understanding of the typic.

To recall, Kant first describes symbolic hypotyposis in the famous § 59 of the *Critique of the Power of Judgment*, entitled "On beauty as the symbol of morality." Here again is the key passage:

> All *hypotyposis* (presentation, *subjecto ad aspectum*), as making something sensible [*Versinnlichung*], is of one of two kinds: either *schematic*, where to a concept grasped by the understanding the corresponding intuition is given *a priori*; or *symbolic*, where to a concept which only reason can think, and to which no sensible intuition can be adequate, an intuition is attributed with which the power of judgment proceeds in a way merely analogous to that which it observes in schematization, i.e., it is merely the rule of this procedure, not the intuition itself, and thus merely the form of the reflection, not the content, which corresponds to the concept. ... All intuitions that are ascribed to concepts *a priori* are thus either *schemata* or *symbols*, the first of which contain direct, the second indirect presentations of the concept. The first do this demonstratively, the second by means of an analogy (for which empirical intuitions are also employed), in which the power of judgment performs a double task, first applying the concept to the object of a sensible intuition, and then, second, applying the mere rule of reflection on that intuition to an entirely different object, of which the first is only the symbol. Thus a monarchical state is represented by a body with a soul if it is ruled in accordance with laws internal to the people, but by a mere machine (like a handmill) if it is ruled by a single absolute will, but in both cases it is represented only *symbolically*. For between a despotic state and a handmill there is, of course, no similarity, but there is one between the rule for reflecting on both and their causality (*KU* 5: 351; cf. *FM* 20: 279–80).

In symbolic hypotyposis, intuitions are put under concepts, although these intuitions are not actually adequate to the concepts but only correspond to them by means of an analogy.[438] In this sense, symbolic hypotyposis can be understood as an "indirect presentation [*indirekte Darstellung*]" of concepts. Correspondingly, the expressions "symbolic hypotyposis" as well as the "indirect presentation of concepts" refer to the *process* of symbolization, while the "symbol" per se, i.e., the intuition that embodies the indirect presentation of a concept, is the *product* of this process.[439] This distinction between the *process*, or *procedure* (*Vorgang*) of symbolization, and the 'symbol', as the former's *product*, or out-

---

437 See Maly 2012, p. 292; Bahr 2004, p. 286–292; Bielefeldt 2003, p. 173f.
438 The account of symbolic hypotyposis given here is largely based on Maly 2012, an excellent study of the topic.
439 Maly 2012, p. 156.

come (*Ergebnis*), is significant. On the one hand, symbolization is an abstract, analogical process that the power of judgment implements by means of a "double task" or "two-step procedure [*doppeltes Geschäft*, abbr. *DG*]." To recall, here are the two steps, as applied to Kant's own example of the handmill symbolizing the despotic state:

> DG_1: The imagination produces an image in sensible intuition of a handmill, and the power of judgment ascribes to it the specific causality elaborated by reflection from its corresponding empirical concept (i.e., mechanical causality).
> DG_2: The power of judgment analogically transfers (*überträgt*) the rule of reflection on the specific causality of the handmill given in intuition onto the concept of the despotic state; in this way, the handmill becomes a *symbol* that indirectly presents the concept of the despotic state, particularly its specific causality (i.e., the mechanism of the handmill, whereby the crank moves the 'passive' gears through an external force, *symbolizes* the mechanism of a despotic state, in which the despot's absolute will compels his passive subjects through an external force).[440]

On the other hand, the *symbol* is the product of this analogical procedure, namely a "sensible image [*Sinnbild*]" or "*analogon* from sensibility" (*VA Friedländer* 25: 356; *VA Mrongovius* 25: 1294). Its main purpose is to provide a lively and easily grasped presentation (*Darstellung*) of a more abstract concept.[441] The key point to note here is that while every symbol necessarily presupposes an analogy, not every analogy necessarily produces a symbol: one *can*, if one wishes, employ an analogy in order to produce a symbol for a given concept, but one does not *have to* actualize the analogy's symbolic potential, so to speak;[442] the analogy can also stand alone or be employed for purposes other than symbolic hypotyposis.

And *symbolic anthropomorphism*, I submit, should be understood as an abstract analogical process that does *not* produce a symbol in sensible intuition, but which serves only to give us a purchase on pure, conceptual relations. The text of the *Prolegomena* already gives a general indication of this. The term "sym-

---

440 Cf. Maly 2012, p. 146, 198.
441 Maly 2012, p. 290.
442 Maly 2012, p. 199f., 167, 290. Significantly, Aristotle makes a similar point about the possibility of producing vivid metaphors by means of analogy: "[The metaphor – A.W.] from analogy is *possible* whenever there are four terms so related that the second is to the first, as the fourth to the third; for *one may then* put the fourth in place of the second, and the second in place of the fourth. ... As old age is to life, so is evening to day. One will accordingly describe evening as the 'old age of the day' ... and old age as the 'evening' or 'sunset of life'" (*Poetics* 1457b15–24, my emphasis). In Aristotle 1984, Vol. 2, p. 2332–2333. This parallel provides additional evidence in favour of the hypothesis that Kant based his theory of analogy directly on Aristotle's.

bolic" appears only once (*P* 4: 357), and when Kant explains what he means by it, he refers only to "cognition according to *analogy*" (*P* 4: 357), never once mentioning "indirect presentation" at all. As I stressed in section 1.1. above, the term "symbolic," in the context of the *Prolegomena*, should be read in conjunction with the ubiquitous restricting modifiers "only [*nur*]" and "mere [*bloß*]," which indicate that this mode of representation operates "merely by analogy [*bloß nach der Analogie*]." In addition, Kant specifies throughout that the analogies must not be used to attach sensible intuitions to supersensible concepts. Indeed, the *Prolegomena*'s emphasis on abstract analogies, rather than on sensible symbols, contrasts markedly with all of Kant's treatments of symbolic hypotyposis, which instead prioritize the problem of symbolic *Versinnlichung*.[443] This is not surprising, considering the different contexts in which symbolic anthropomorphism and symbolic hypotyposis respectively appear: the former pertains to the possibility of *theoretical cognition*; the latter addresses *aesthetic* and *subjectively practical* concerns.

In addition, there is a subtle but important difference between the analogical procedures used in the two modes of symbolic representation. Symbolic anthropomorphism, as we have already seen, produces analogies based on relatively abstract causal relations, notably "causality through reason," i.e., teleological causality (*P* 4: 358). And as Kant explains at length in the Appendix to the Transcendental Dialectic, these analogies assist the *determining* power of judgment in subsuming natural phenomena under higher-order systematic principles (KrV A642ff./B670ff.). By contrast, symbolic hypotyposis operates with analogies based on causal relations which are as *specific* as possible and which are elaborated by the *reflecting* power of judgment *on the basis of sensible intuitions*.

The role of *specific* causal relations in symbolic hypotyposis becomes clear when one examines the two examples that Kant discusses in *KU*, § 59 as possible symbols for a monarchical state: the handmill and the "body with a soul [*beseelter Körper*]" (*KU* 5: 352). Why exactly is the former an apt symbol for a monarchical state "ruled by a single absolute will," and the latter a fitting image for a monarchical state "if it is ruled in accordance with laws internal to the people," but not *vice versa*? Why aren't the two symbols interchangeable? The key difference between the two images, as Maly has explained, lies in the specific kind of causality that each one illustrates:

> In the case of the handmill, there is a mechanical kind of causality; in the case of the body with a soul, by contrast, there is an organic-teleological causality. Both kinds of causality are *specific* insofar as they are only recognizable through *specification in intuition:* whether

---

[443] Maly 2012, p. 317, 292.

an object can be attributed one or the other kind of causality can only be decided on the basis of the intuition of the object.⁴⁴⁴

Accordingly, the handmill is an apt symbol of the despotic state because the mechanical causality that it embodies is a suitable analogue for the causality characteristic of a despotic state: *just as* the internal gears of the handmill are passive vis-à-vis the crank, which makes them turn through an external force, *so* are the subjects of a despotic state passive vis-à-vis the despot's will, which acts as a force external to the people's collective will. Indeed, this analogy corresponds exactly to Kant's definition of despotism in the *Doctrine of Right* as a "*mechanism* [Maschinenwerk] of unifying a nation by coercive laws, that is, when all the members of the nation are *passive* [passiv] and obey one who is over them" (*MS* 6: 339, my emphasis; cf. *WA* 8: 37).⁴⁴⁵ In contrast, just as an animated body is impelled 'from the inside', by its soul, so is a monarchical state governed by a benevolent monarch "ruled in accordance with laws *internal* to the people" (*KU* 5: 352) – and this explains why an animated body is a suitable symbol for a benevolent monarchical state as opposed to a despotic one. Moreover, as Maly aptly notes, the specification of the causal rule in each case is accomplished by the *reflecting* power of judgment, which scrutinizes and compares the *sensible intuitions* of these objects in order to extract and elaborate the appropriate rule (*EEKU* 20: 211). For example, one has to have *seen* a handmill and examined its mechanism before one could possibly use it as a symbol for the 'mechanism' of a despotic state. And the more fine-grained this discrimination, the better: a handmill, with its active, external crank and passive, internal gears, is a far more apt and vivid symbol of a despotic state, than, say, a watch, which, while also an embodiment of mechanical causality, nevertheless gives the appearance of moving itself from the inside, as if it were "autonomous" (*KpV* 5: 96). In short, these examples illustrate that the analogical procedure underlying symbolic hypotyposis operates with specific causal relations reflectively elaborated on the basis of sensible intuitions, in view of producing symbols that are as apt and vivid as possible. But in symbolic anthropomorphism, by contrast, we are not at all concerned with the figurative aptness of individual symbols per se. *It does not matter* whether one says that God is an "artisan," a "builder," or a "commander,"

---

444 Maly 2012, p. 123 (my emphasis).
445 Other scholars have proposed a slightly different – and no less plausible – interpretation of this symbol, whereby the handmill's crushing the grains symbolizes the despot's violent quashing of his hapless subjects – cf. Förster 2011, p. 143; Maly 2012, p. 146, 158f., 198. Note that this interpretation would serve equally well to validate the more general point that the meaning and effectiveness of the symbol depend on its specification in intuition.

because the analogy underlying these very different images is based on a more generic *Verhältnisbegriff* of teleological causality – which is all that reason cares about for its purposes (*P* 4: 357–358; *KrV* A699/B727).

In summary, this analysis suggests that symbolic hypotyposis and symbolic anthropomorphism function in different ways.[446] Symbolic hypotyposis employs an analogical procedure for the purpose of indirectly presenting an abstract concept in the form of an intuitive symbol. By contrast, (merely) symbolic anthropomorphism does not produce a symbol, but consists only of a strictly analogical procedure for representing the causal connection between the sensible and intelligible worlds in such as way as to render the theoretical investigation of nature more systematic. In addition, the analogical procedure underlying symbolic hypotyposis is less abstract, more fine-grained, and more closely tied to intuition than the analogical procedure underlying symbolic anthropomorphism. Last but not least, symbolic hypotyposis depends on reflecting judgment, whereas symbolic anthropomorphism pertains to determining judgment. Given these differences between symbolic anthropomorphism and symbolic hypotyposis, it will be illuminating to investigate, next, whether the *typic* bears greater affinities to the former than to the latter.

7.4 Symbolic anthropomorphism and the typic

7.4.1 Merely symbolic, as opposed to absolute

Just like symbolic anthropomorphism in the *Prolegomena*, the typic establishes a connection to the intelligible sphere (conceived as a 'supersensible nature'), yet it thereby affords *no theoretical cognition* of the intelligible realm, its entities or their properties: "of all the intelligible absolutely nothing [*schlechterdings nichts*] is cognized" (*KpV* 5: 70). To be sure, in the second *Critique* Kant does allow that we can cognize the law of freedom, yet this cognition is afforded us not by the typic per se, but by a special "warrant" of pure practical reason (*KpV* 5 : 50 – 57), which in no way extends our *theoretical* cognition of intelligible entities, as he recalls pointedly in the Typic chapter: "all intelligible objects to which reason might lead us under the guidance of that law have in turn no reality for us except on behalf of that law and of the use of pure practical reason" (*KpV* 5: 70). So even if the typic allows us to conceive of an "intelligible nature" for the sake

---

[446] Tellingly, Caruth 1988 runs these two concepts together in her interpretation of symbolic anthropomorphism as figurative.

of *practical judgment* (*KpV* 5: 71), this "nature" nonetheless remains an empty space for *theoretical reason*. A corresponding epistemological restriction applies to the intellectual *concepts* that designate those intelligible entities: just as in the *Prolegomena* Kant censured the dogmatic use of analogy for transferring "merely" (*bloß*) symbolic properties onto intellectual concepts "themselves" (*selbst*) (e.g., in theism), so his remark in the Typic serves to "prevent reckoning among *concepts themselves* that which belongs *only* to the *typic* of concepts [... *um zu verhüten, daß, was* blos *zur Typik der Begriffe gehört, nicht* zu den Begriffen selbst *gezählt werde*]" (*KpV* 5: 70, my emphasis). As I see it, the first sense in which the typic serves "*only* as a symbol" is that it obeys the same epistemological restriction as *merely* symbolic anthropomorphism: neither of these forms of symbolic representation allow us to cognize the intelligible *as it is in itself*; rather, they afford us a merely symbolic – i.e., analogical – grasp of certain *relations*.

7.4.2 Analogical

We are now led to ask a key question: Is the typic, like symbolic anthropomorphism, an analogical procedure? Although the text of the Typic chapter does not mention analogy explicitly, it contains several clues that analogy may lie just beneath the surface: the statement that "laws as such are the same [*Gesetze als solche sind einerlei*]" (*KpV* 5:70) in spite of their specific differences; the characterization of typification using the verb *übertragen* (to transfer, to transpose) (*KpV* 5: 71) which Kant elsewhere employs to describe how analogies function (e.g. in the second Analogy of Experience, *KrV* A199–200/B245);[447] and the typic-procedure's similarity to FLN, which Kant explicitly characterizes as an analogy (*G* 4: 437). Moreover, from a more general, systematic point of view, analogy performs key functions in Kant's philosophical methodology – especially for presenting abstract concepts – and so we can surmise that it may also intervene in the Typic.[448]

Many interpreters have suggested that analogy plays a role in the Typic chapter. Unfortunately, their various proposals, taken together, compose a bewildering hodgepodge of no less than ten analogies:
1) between a moral order of interacting wills and the order of nature under law;[449]
2) between "the world of sensible data" and "the world of freedoms";[450]

---

[447] See Piché 2000; Renaut 1997, p. 303f.
[448] Renaut 1997, p. 302ff. See also Callanan 2008; Marty 1997, p. 247–266; Pieper 1996, p. 95f., 108f.
[449] Beck 1960, p. 159.
[450] Marty 1997, p. 258.

3) "between the two sets of objects conceived to fall under the two laws, moral wills on the one hand and temporal events on the other";[451]
4) between the "invisible realm of God" and the sensible world;[452]
5) between the "compulsive force" of the moral law and that of natural law;[453]
6) between the understanding and practical reason as "lawgiving authorities";[454]
7) between the relation of maxims to the will and the relation of the law of nature to nature as a whole;[455]
8) between the relation of an appearance to the law of nature and the relation of an action to the moral law;[456]
9) between "the moral world's relation to the will's free causality" and nature's relation to "phenomenal causality";[457] and, last but not least,
10) between the Kingdom of Ends and the Kingdom of Nature.[458]

I will not examine all of these individual proposals in detail, as that would only sow more confusion. What I will point out here is that this striking lack of consensus reflects the regrettable fact that most scholars studying the Typic have apparently not read each other, producing inconsistent interpretations as a result. In the rest of this section, I propose an analysis which I find more compelling and which I will then compare with symbolic anthropomorphism.

It seems to me that the natural place to begin is to ask whether there is an *analogy* between the moral law and its *type*, the law of nature. In the Commentary, I suggested that there is indeed an analogy between the two laws that guides moral appraisal.[459] In the typic-procedure, we employ the universal law of physical causality as "the type of the law of freedom" in virtue of an analogy between the two laws *qua* universal and hence 'exceptionless'. That is, *just as* the law of natural causality governs every "case of experience" without exception (*KrV* A542/B570), *so* does the moral law apply to every action without exception (*G* 4: 421, 424). Conversely, this analogy provides a "model [*Muster*]" for moral appraisal (*KpV* 5: 44): *just as* "in

---

451 Paton 1947, p. 160.
452 Vaihinger 1918, p. 655.
453 Adorno 2000, p. 113; Pieper 2011, p. 115.
454 Pieper 2011, p. 112.
455 Pieper 1996, p. 108.
456 Pieper 1996, p. 109.
457 Grandjean 2004, p. 48.
458 Beck 1960, p. 158–160; Bielefeldt 2003, p. 181f.; Cassirer 1987, p. 259; Cassirer 2001, p. 250; Grondin 2000, p. 394; Rawls 2000, p. 214–216; Shell 1980, p. 88; Paton 1947, p. 149ff. I have already criticized this interpretation in the Commentary; see sections 4.1.2.4. and 4.2.3.2.
459 See section 5.1.2.

the most ordinary judgments of ... experience" one must reject – i.e., disbelieve – all exceptions to the law of nature as superstition (*KU* 5: 294), *so* "in cases where causality from freedom is to be appraised" must one reject – i.e., condemn – all purported exceptions to the moral law as morally evil (*G* 4: 424; *KpV* 5: 44).

While this analogy between the two laws is not explicit in the Typic chapter, it seems to be confirmed – and extended – in three passages where Kant does explicitly refer to an analogy involving the two laws. More precisely, he adduces a more complex analogy between the law of nature's relation to *natura formaliter spectata* and the moral law's relation to supersensible nature. The first passage appears in the *Critique of Practical Reason*, just a few pages before the Typic chapter:

> The moral law is, in fact, a law of causality through freedom and hence a law of the possibility of a supersensible nature, *just as* the metaphysical law of events in the sensible world was a law of the causality of sensible nature ... (*KpV* 5: 47, my emphasis).[460]

Here, the expression "just as [*so wie*]" clearly signals an analogy.[461] The second passage appears in connection with FLN in the *Groundwork*:

> Since the validity of the will as a universal law for possible actions *has an analogy* with the universal connection of the existence of things in accordance with universal laws, which is the formal aspect of nature in general, the Categorical Imperative can also be expressed thus: *act in accordance with maxims that can at the same time have as their object themselves as universal laws of nature* (*G* 4: 437, my emphasis; cf. *G* 4: 421).[462]

The third mention of an analogy between these notions appears in the *Nachlass*:

> The principle of the unity of freedom under laws establishes an *analogon* with that principle that we call nature [...] The unity of the intelligible world according to moral principles, *just like* the unity of the sensible world under physical laws (*Refl* 7260, 19: 296–297, my emphasis).[463]

---

460 [*Das moralische Gesetz ist in der Tat ein Gesetz der Kausalität durch Freiheit, so wie das metaphysische Gesetz der Begebenheiten in der Sinnenwelt ein Gesetz der Kausaliät der sinnlichen Natur war ...*]

461 See Piché 2000, p. 225.

462 [*Weil die Gültigkeit des Willens, als eines allgemeinen Gesetzes für mögliche Handlungen, mit der allgemeinen Verknüpfung des Daseins der Dinge nach allgemeinen Gesetzen, die das Formale der Natur überhaupt ist, Analogie hat, so kann der kategorische Imperativ auch so ausgedrückt werden: Handle nach Maximen, die sich selbst zugleich als allgemeine Naturgesetze zum Gegenstande haben können.*]

463 [*Das Principium der Einheit der freyheit unter Gesetzen stiftet ein analogon mit dem, was wir Natur nennen. ... Die Einheit der intelligibeln Welt nach practischen Principien, so wie der Sinnenwelt nach physischen Gesetzen.*]

7.4 Symbolic anthropomorphism and the typic — 207

These passages all seem to be pointing towards a fundamental analogy between the ways in which the law of nature and the moral law respectively constitute *systems* of natural and moral lawfulness. On one side of the analogy, we have the idea that the law of physical causality functions, in virtue of its universality, as a constitutive "principle of unity" that "makes possible," or constitutes, the formal lawfulness that organizes the sensible world, i.e., 'the formal aspect of nature in general', or *natura formaliter spectata*. Recall that in the first *Critique* Kant characterizes the law "that everything that happens has a cause" as the principle "through which alone appearances can first constitute one *nature [dieses Gesetz, durch welches Erscheinungen allererst eine Natur ausmachen]*" (KrV A542/B570). On the other side of the analogy, we have the idea that the moral law functions, in virtue of its universality, as a constitutive 'principle of unity' that 'makes possible' the formal lawfulness of an intelligible moral order, or 'supersensible nature', as Kant recalls in the second *Critique:* "the moral law ... is therefore the fundamental law of a supersensible nature," whereby "nature" here is meant "in the most general sense [as] the existence of things under laws" (KpV 5: 43). In other words, *just as* the law of physical causality constitutes the unified lawfulness of sensible nature in its formal aspect, *so (mutatis mutandis)* does the law of freedom constitute the unified formal lawfulness of supersensible nature.

What we have here is a Kantian 'philosophical analogy' of the form $a : b :: c : x$, where (**a**) the law of nature *stands in the same relation* to (**b**) nature in the formal sense as does (**c**) the moral law to (**x**) supersensible nature. The analogy can represented schematically:

a <u>constitutes the universal lawfulness of</u> b	
the law of nature	*natura formaliter spectata*
(Type$_1$)	(Type$_2$)
c <u>constitutes the universal lawfulness of</u> x	
the moral law	supersensible nature

The structure of this analogy seems to fit well with the interpretation of the Typic chapter proposed in the Commentary. For the sake of precision, I will refer to the *individual terms* of the analogy as "*analogata*" (sing. *analogaton*) and to the *shared relations* between the terms as "*analoga*" (sing. *analogon*).[464] From a formal perspective, we can note that the *analogaton* of the moral law is none other than Type$_1$, just as the *analogaton* of supersensible nature is Type$_2$, which confirms that a *Typus* in general is the formal *analogaton* of the representation it

---

[464] This is standard terminology. Cf. "Analogie" 1996, p. 1240 ff.

stands in for, which in turn legitimizes the typification of the latter by the former. For instance, we can see that this analogy makes it possible to typify Type$_2$ by taking "the understanding's pure form of nature" (= **b**, *natura formaliter spectata*) and analogically "transferring" it (*übertragen, hineintragen*) into the intelligible realm (= **x**, supersensible nature) (*KpV* 5: 70–71).[465] Conversely, the analogy also suggests (in line with step 3 of the typic-procedure) that a disunited, disjointed, or incoherent representation of nature would be an adequate analogue for inconsistency, capriciousness, and conflict in the moral sphere. More generally, the correspondence between the two *analoga* – i.e., the constitutive relations of universal lawfulness in the natural and moral spheres – speaks to a deep harmony within the Kantian architectonic, as Marty has aptly noted: "we are faced with a properly Kantian analogy as expounded in the *Prolegomena*: the connections are identical – the connections, here, that constitute a universe."[466] Indeed, the idea that nature and freedom should each constitute a universe, world, or *kosmos* governed by law is a characteristic result of Kant's transcendental method, as Cassirer has observed: "The fact that ... the idea of obligation in a general sense crystallizes in the shape of a 'world', has its profound methodological basis."[467]

How does this all compare with symbolic anthropomorphism? On the one hand, the analogical procedure underlying the typic shares certain key characteristics with symbolic anthropomorphism – tellingly, the very characteristics that distinguish them both from symbolic hypotyposis. Just as in symbolic anthropomorphism, the *analoga* underlying the typic are more formal, abstract, and independent of sensibility than the specific causal relations at work in symbolic hypotyposis. In addition, the analogies in the typic are employed to get a conceptual grasp of these relations for use within the sensible world, but not to positively *cognize* – or *symbolize* – the fourth term by transferring sensible intuitions onto it: "Hence it is also permitted to use *the nature of the sensible world* as the *type* of an *intelligible nature*, provided that I do not carry over into the latter intuitions and what depends on them but refer to it merely the *form of lawfulness* in general" (*KpV* 5: 70).[468]

On the other hand, there are also some illuminating differences between the two concepts. While symbolic anthropomorphism generally employs teleological

---

[465] See section 4.1.2.3. of the Commentary and Renaut 1997, p. 309f.; Kant 1994, p. 194n.
[466] Marty 1997, p. 258.
[467] Cassirer 1987, p. 258f.; Cassirer 2001, p. 249. See also section 3.2. of the Conclusion.
[468] [*Es ist also auch erlaubt, die Natur der Sinnenwelt als Typus einer intelligibelen Natur zu brauchen, so lange ich nur nicht die Anschauungen, und was davon abhängig ist, auf diese übertrage, sondern blos die Form der Gesetzmäßigkeit überhaupt.*]

causality as an *analogon*, the typic goes one step further in abstraction, using a transcendental principle of lawfulness in general. Also, while symbolic anthropomorphism analogically maps a relation *within* the sensible world onto the relation *between* the sensible world and the intelligible world, the typic maps a relation *within* the sensible world onto a relation *within* the intelligible world. Finally, the analogy employed in the typic is more abstract, complex and 'higher-order' than those used for symbolic anthropomorphism, since the *analogata* are not individual objects, but rather *laws* or *systems of laws*. (Incidentally, this additional complexity may be another explanation for the lack of consensus among commentators on how to spell out the analogies in detail.) In sum, there does seem to be an analogical procedure at work in the typic – one that shares the key characteristics of symbolic anthropomorphism, but that must be acknowledged as a more abstract, complex, and sophisticated version.

7.4.3 Non-sensible

Just as he did in the *Prolegomena*, Kant stresses in the Typic chapter that these analogies are abstract, formal, purely conceptual correspondences, devoid of sensible content. Just as the deistic concept of God would be inevitably distorted if one were to attribute sensible properties to it, so the "purity and sublimity [*Reinheit und Erhabenheit*]" (*KpV* 5: 71) of the supersensible Ideas of the moral law and the morally good would be contaminated if one were to attach sensible intuitions to them. And just as only a pure concept of the understanding can subtend the analogy to such a being without distorting the latter, so the type of the moral law can only be furnished by the understanding, not the imagination (*KpV* 5: 69). Correspondingly, $Type_1$ is the law of natural causality, a pure concept produced by the understanding's intellectual synthesis, and it functions as a type "only as to its form [*nur seiner Form nach*]" (*KpV* 5: 69). And the nature of the sensible world *qua* sensible cannot serve as $Type_2$; instead we must first extract "the mere form of lawfulness in general [*blos die Form der Gesetzmäßigkeit überhaupt*]" (*KpV* 5: 70) that the understanding thought into nature in the first place. So the underlying analogies in both the *Prolegomena* and the Typic operate with entirely pure, non-sensible representations.

7.4.4 Permitted and required

Another significant correspondence between symbolic anthropomorphism and the typic is that Kant legitimates their 'merely symbolic' employment in almost exactly the same terms. Just as, for theoretical purposes, "we can allow ourselves [*wir erlauben uns*]" (*P* 4: 357) and are even "required" or "compelled [*genöthigt*]" (*P* 4: 357) to employ symbolic anthropomorphism, so, for moral purposes, "reason is entitled and even required [*berechtigt und auch benöthigt*] to use nature ... as the *type* of judgment" (*KpV* 5: 70). The pure practical power of judgment *needs* the typic, because otherwise it could not subsume actions under the concepts of the morally good and evil. Type$_1$ (the law of nature) meets this need by typifying the supersensible Idea of the moral law and by providing a procedure for testing the universalizability of maxims; Type$_2$ (*natura formaliter spectata*) typifies the moral order of the intelligible realm as a whole and harmonizes maxims.

The typic's *permissibility* is tied to three considerations. Firstly, as we just saw, the law of nature and the form of nature in general may be employed since they represent formally adequate analogues of the moral law and of supersensible nature, respectively. Secondly, the typic may be employed for the purposes of moral appraisal because it enables *sufficiently* determinate and reliable moral judgments (to be explained below). Thirdly, Kant states that Type$_2$ is "permitted" insofar as it "serves *only* as a symbol [*nur als Symbol dient*]" (*KpV* 5: 70 – 71, my emphasis), which I interpret to mean that it can be employed by the power of judgment *only* as a non-absolute, non-sensible analogue for the moral realm, and *only* for the sake of moral appraisal:

> Hence it is also permitted [*erlaubt*] to use *the nature of the sensible world* as the *type* of an *intelligible nature*, provided [*so lange*] that I do not carry over into the latter intuitions and what depends on them but refer to it merely the *form of lawfulness* in general [*blos die Form der Gesetzmäßigkeit überhaupt*] (the concept of which occurs even in the most common use of reason), although it cannot be determinately cognized a priori for any purpose other than merely the pure practical use of reason [*blos zum reinen praktischen Gebrauche der Vernunft*]) (*KpV* 5: 70, trans. mod., emphasis added)

The proviso is clear: one must *extract* the formal representation of "nature" that the pure understanding thinks into the sensible world *a priori* – i.e. the "mere [*bloß*]" conceptual form of lawfulness in general, dissociated from all sensible intuition – and analogically transfer (*übertragen*) only that abstract conceptual structure to the intelligible realm. This confirms that the legitimate employment of the typic, just like symbolic anthropomorphism in the *Prolegomena*, rests on a purely conceptual analogy.

7.4.5 Sufficient

Nevertheless, just as Kant held that symbolic anthropomorphism, confined to the boundary of experience, was nevertheless *sufficient* for the purposes of theoretical reason, so, *mutatis mutandis*, does he maintain that the typic is *sufficient* for "the pure practical use of reason" (*KpV* 5:70). Indeed, the thought experiments generated by the typic-procedure ensure that the outcomes of moral appraisal are so clear, even "obvious" (*KpV* 5: 44), that *everyone*, even "the commonest understanding," can employ the law of nature as type for judging a wide range of moral cases with accuracy and ease (*KpV* 5: 69–70, 40; *G* 4: 403–405).[469] In addition, Type$_2$ systematizes and harmonizes all uses of pure practical judgment within the sensible world and thereby provides guidance for our practical vocation as finite rational beings "to furnish the sensible world ... with the form of the world of the understanding," i.e., to remodel "ectypal nature" into the form of "archetypal nature" (*KpV* 5: 43).

7.4.6 Protective

As we saw above, symbolic anthropomorphism serves to prevent a number of dangers in theoretical philosophy, including empiricism, mysticism, dogmatism and scepticism. The typic also performs such preventative, protective functions; indeed, Kant stresses this point even more strongly in the second *Critique*, maintaining that the typic is so "important and advisable [*wichtig und anrathungswürdig*]" in the moral sphere precisely because it "protects from [*bewahrt von*]" empiricism and mysticism (*KpV* 5: 70–71). The typic's protective functions have already been described in section 5.2. of the Commentary; here, the important point to appreciate is that the typic, just like symbolic anthropomorphism, functions as a "safeguard [*Verwahrung*]" in virtue of its *merely symbolic* status (*KpV* 5: 71).

a) Dogmatism and scepticism
Systematically comparing symbolic anthropomorphism with the typic allows us to ascribe two protective functions to the latter that were not mentioned in the Commentary. Symbolic anthropomorphism wards off *dogmatism* and *scepticism* in the theoretical sphere, and we can now see that the typic prevents these two

---

[469] See section 5.1. of the Commentary.

epistemological approaches in the moral sphere as well. Firstly, by countenancing no more than a merely symbolic, 'as-if' correspondence between natural and moral lawfulness, Kant's typic effectively counters those schools of *dogmatic rationalism* that have sought, in various forms – from Stoicism to Natural Law ethics to Wolffian perfectionism – to establish a literal, ontic identity between the natural and moral realms.[470] Secondly, if Kant is correct in asserting that the typic-procedure supplies an effective means for enabling everyone (even the common understanding) to perform moral appraisal, then this would allay the *sceptical* doubt that moral judgments are intrinsically indeterminate and unreliable.[471] Moreover, his caveat that the typic provides no absolute theoretical knowledge of the intelligible realm (*KpV* 5: 70) provides no fodder for sceptical attacks.

b) Empiricism

As we have seen, moral empiricism commits two deep and unforgiveable philosophical errors by taking *literally* that which should function *only symbolically*.[472] Firstly, it distorts moral appraisal by reducing the concepts of good and evil to the "experiential consequences (so-called happiness)" that would actually come about from implementing a given maxim as a rule of human conduct (*KpV* 5: 70 – 1, 57 ff.). Secondly, it corrupts the moral disposition by reducing freedom to the heteronomous, "animal" pursuit of physical pleasure in accordance with natural causality. In the Typic, by contrast, Kant re-construes happiness merely symbolically, i.e., as the merely formal type of the rational Idea of the morally good (Type$_3$).[473] Also, in the typic-procedure, he invites the agent to consider the law of freedom only *as if* it were a law of nature. Only by remaining cognizant of these restrictions can we avoid "reckoning among concepts themselves that which *belongs merely to the typic of concepts* [was blos zur Typik der Begriffe gehört]" (*KpV* 5: 70, my emphasis). There is, however, an instructive difference between the ways in which the *Prolegomena* and the Typic assess the danger of empiricism. In the theoretical sphere, the empirical approach per se is reliable, even commendable, its only limitation being that it does not go far enough to ultimately satisfy reason's highest theoretical needs. It only becomes a *danger* when it categorically denies that those needs can ever be met in prin-

---

[470] Beck 1960, p. 162; Klein 1969, p. 186; Rawls 1989, p. 100f.; Taylor 2007; Timmermann 2007, p. 78f.
[471] See Ware 2010, p. 117ff.; Rawls 1989, p. 101.
[472] See section 5.2.1. of the Commentary.
[473] See section 5.2.2. of the Commentary.

ciple (*P* 4: 351, cf. *KrV* A468–473/B496–501). In the moral sphere, the empiricist way of thinking in and of itself proves to be far more pernicious, as it "destroys at its root the morality of dispositions" and thereby "degrade[s] humanity" (*KpV* 5:71). Moreover, while the scientific mindset characteristic of theoretical empiricism will never become popular (*KrV* A472–473/B500–501), moral empiricism seduces "everyone's way of feeling" by leaguing itself with our sensible inclinations (*KpV* 5: 71). In short, the typic's protection against empiricism in the practical sphere is far more urgent.

c) Mysticism

To my eyes, one of the most significant and telling correspondences between symbolic anthropomorphism and the typic as 'merely symbolic' modes of representation is their common opposition to mysticism. In both cases, we find Kant proposing symbolic anthropomorphism as a way to satisfy the needs of theoretical reason while preventing it from "venturing beyond experience into the incomprehensible and inscrutable [*zu dem Unbegreiflichen und Unerforschlichen*]" (*KrV* A689/B717). In the Typic, Kant extends this strategy to the practical sphere, where mystical *Schwärmerei* threatens to rob the moral Ideas of both their supersensible purity as well as their normative force by turning them into images.[474] But the typic, precisely because it functions not schematically, but only symbolically, effectively counters this pseudo-schematization by providing the power of judgment with a rational alternative that, by contrast, analogically transfers into the supersensible "nothing more than what pure reason can also think for itself" (*KpV* 5: 71), i.e., the form of lawfulness. Thus the similarities between symbolic anthropomorphism and the typic adduced above ultimately crystallize, and perhaps reveal their common root, in Kant's rationalist opposition to mysticism's detrimental tendency to "intuit or feel itself into" the intelligible realm (*G* 4: 458).[475]

7.5 Conclusion

The comparative analysis carried out in this chapter (summarized in section 2.2. of the general Conclusion) appears to have borne out the hypothesis that symbolic anthropomorphism decisively informed the typic. Accordingly, Kant's state-

---

[474] See Cassirer 1987, p. 260; Cassirer 2001, p. 250.
[475] See section 3 of the Conclusion.

ment that the typic "served only as a symbol [*nur als Symbol diente*]" (*KpV* 5: 70) should be read *adverbially*, i.e., as signifying that, like symbolic anthropomorphism, *the typic functions only, or merely, symbolically*, i.e., in a non-absolute, non-sensible, and strictly analogical manner – *unlike symbolic hypotyposis*, the purpose of which is to provide an aesthetically lively, specific symbol in sensible intuition. Indeed, the typic carries the analogical procedure underlying symbolic anthropomorphism to an even higher level of abstraction and complexity. Ultimately, the correspondences between the *Prolegomena* and the Typic chapter have a common historical and philosophical root in Kant's long-running campaign against the tendency – exemplified and exacerbated by mystical *Schwärmerei* – to make the invisible visible, i.e., to degrade supersensible Ideas into images. If symbolic anthropomorphism and the typic can "guard against" this tendency in their respective spheres, it is because these properly *critical and rationalist* modes of symbolic representation provide finite human reason with a necessary, permissible, and sufficient way to apply the supersensible Ideas of reason without thereby denaturing them – a task that is all the more urgent in the practical sphere. In a word, both of these carefully designed forms of symbolic representation foster "the rationalism of the power of judgment [*der Rationalism der Urtheilskraft*]" (*KpV* 5: 71).

Conclusion

1 Summary of Part One

In the Commentary, the Typic chapter was analyzed within a framework which enabled us to work through the text in a systematic and continuous manner. We were able to characterize the *task* at hand, to identify the *'particular difficulties'* impeding its performance, to assess a certain number of *resources* for potentially overcoming this obstacle, to present Kant's *solution* for resolving the difficulties and accomplishing the task, and finally to assess the proposed solution's *outcome* and *effectiveness*.

Chapter 1: The task
In the chapter of the *Critique of Practical Reason* immediately preceding the Typic, Kant defined two "concepts of an object of pure practical reason," namely "the morally good [*das sittlich Gute*]" and "the morally evil [*das sittlich Böse*]," by deriving them *a priori* from the moral law, conceived as a universal rule that commands the will to choose actions according to "the represesentation of a law in general and its form." At the beginning of the Typic chapter, Kant explains how the *application* of these concepts presents the power of judgment with a specific *task*. Kant terms this task "moral appraisal [*moralische Beurtheilung*]," since it consists in appraising actions as good or evil in light of the moral law. Put in the technical language of Kant's theory of judgment, the "pure practical power of judgment [*die reine praktische Urtheilskraft*]" is called upon to *subsume* particular actions, as cases *in concreto*, under a rule *in abstracto*. Moral appraisal is a specific, limited exercise of moral judgment: it is strictly determining, rather than reflecting; it is pure, rather than applied; and it concerns only *finite* rational agents.

Chapter 2: The 'particular difficulties'
However, this task presents the pure practical power of judgment with "particular difficulties" (*KpV* 5: 68). The problem, at the most general level, is that the cases (actions) cannot be subsumed under the rule (the moral law) because of a mismatch between them. This mismatch turns out to be tricky to characterize exactly. While it presupposes a number of fundamental dichotomies in Kant's system (notably natural necessity vs. freedom; 'is' vs. 'ought'), it takes on a more specific and precise form in the Typic. Kant remarks that, in one important

respect, the pure practical power of judgment shares "the very same difficulties" as the theoretical power of judgment in the *Critique of Pure Reason* (*KpV* 5: 68). I interpreted this remark as meaning that in both cases, subsumption is hindered because of the heterogeneity between two species of representations. But unlike the theoretical power of judgment, the pure practical power of judgment does not have to mediate between the pure concepts of the understanding and appearances in sensible intuition for the sake of theoretical cognition, nor can it resort to the schematism. I then argued that moral appraisal creates *particular* difficulties for human beings because it provokes a conflict rooted in our *particular* constitution as finite rational beings. On the one hand, insofar as we are finite, our intuition is limited to sensibility; on the other hand, insofar as we possess reason, we can produce supersensible Ideas that transcend sensibility and can never be directly exhibited within it. In moral appraisal, we become acquainted with actions in the physical world through our sensible intuition, yet we represent the morally good and the moral law as supersensible Ideas of reason. The total mismatch between these two species of representation prevents the subsumption of the cases under the rule; as Kant puts it in the Typic, it is "absurd" to expect the supersensible Idea of the morally good to be presented *in concreto* (*KpV* 5: 68). This particular mismatch – between sensible intuitions and the supersensible Ideas of morality – constitutes the obstacle that will have to be overcome in order to enable moral appraisal.

Chapter 3: The resources

The ensuing problem was to determine whether Kant's conceptual repertoire contained any *resources* suitable for overcoming these particular difficulties and accomplishing the task.

The first resource to assess was the *transcendental schema*, introduced in the *Critique of Pure Reason* as a tool that the *theoretical* power of judgment used to overcome its own difficulties by mediating between the pure concepts of the understanding and sensible intuition. However, the schema turns out to be unsuitable for solving the particular difficulties faced by the *practical* power of judgment, for two reasons. First, as a product of the sensible imagination's figurative synthesis, the schema would inevitably contaminate the supersensible moral Ideas with sensible content. Second, as a tool of the *theoretical* power of judgment, the schematism is unsuitable for moral appraisal: it represents actions as *events* which are entirely necessitated by natural causality, rather than as *deeds* which are freely caused and morally imputable.

On the other hand, this assessment of the transcendental schema opens up a "favourable prospect" (*KpV* 5: 68): we should look for a representation that performs an *analogous function* to that of the schema – i.e., mediation between heterogeneous representations in order to enable the subsumption of cases under a rule – while avoiding the particular characteristics of the transcendental schema that do not fit the "particular difficulties" of the pure practical power of judgment. What is needed, Kant hints, is a "schema of a law itself," whereby "schema" is meant in a broad, functional sense as a mediating representation, and "law" refers to the moral law, in particular its demand that maxims have the form of universal law. Accordingly, I interpreted this peculiar expression as a formula encapsulating four criteria that describe the right tool for overcoming the particular difficulties and accomplishing the task: (1) a sensibly uncontaminated representation (2) of the form of universal lawfulness (3) that can mediate the subsumption of particular actions given in sensible intuition under the supersensible moral law and (4) provide a procedure for moral appraisal.

Lastly, I offered a characterization of two additional resources in Kant's system: the universal law of natural causality (or, simply 'the law of nature') and the representation of nature's form, or *natura formaliter spectata*. Both of these representations are produced by the understanding. The assessment of these resources is promising, as they are both pure, non-sensible representations of formal lawfulness generated by intellectual synthesis.

Chapter 4: The solution
Kant's original *solution* for overcoming the particular difficulties and accomplishing the task is to employ the law of nature as the "type [*Typus*]," or formal analogue, of the moral law. This resource meets the four criteria adduced in Chapter 3. The law of nature meets the first two criteria because, as was just shown, it is a non-sensible representation of the form of universal lawfulness and can therefore be analogically substituted for the supersensible moral law without contaminating it with sensible intuitions (see also Chapter 7, section 4.2.). And as a law *of nature*, its application to all actions in the sensible world is ensured by the schematism. In virtue of these characteristics, the law of nature – or more precisely, its pure form – can meet the third criterion by mediating the subsumption of actions in sensible intuition under the supersensible moral law despite the heterogeneity between the two species of representations – a process I term "typification." The type also meets the fourth criterion insofar as it provides a formal standard that can be used in a thought experiment for testing the universalizability required of all maxims.

Prior to elaborating on this last point, I investigated Kant's remark that "it is also permitted to use the nature of the sensible world as the type of an intelligible nature" (*KpV*, 5: 70). I offered an interpretation of the source, nature, and function of this second, more general formulation of the type ('Type$_2$'). Starting from the etymology of the ancient Greek word "*túpos*," I proposed that Type$_2$ should be conceived as the abstract form shared by *natura archetypa* and *natura ectypa* (in Chapter 7, I characterize this connection as a complex analogy). On this reading, the understanding's purely conceptual representation of nature's universal lawfulness (*natura formaliter spectata*) mediates between, on the one hand, reason's Idea of a supersensible 'nature' in which all rational beings obey the law of freedom, and, on the other, the sensible nature in which we live and act. This provides a regulative horizon for moral appraisal that heeds the restrictions of Kant's critical rationalism. Conversely, I contended against a number of interpretations in the secondary literature that Type$_2$ should *not* be characterized as a sensible image, as a teleological realm, as the intelligible world per se, or as a fiction.

Moral appraisal is executed by means of what I term "the typic-procedure": the agent performs a thought experiment in which she asks herself if she can both conceive and will herself as a part of a counterfactual nature in which the maxim of her action were a universal law. This is a decisive "test [*Probe*]" of the formal universalizability of a maxim and thereby of its moral possibility (*KpV* 5: 69). I offer an interpretation of this thought experiment based on the fundamental principles of Kant's moral philosophy, proposing that the typic-procedure be understood as a new way of operationalizing the "canon of moral appraisal" first introduced in the *Groundwork* (*G* 4: 124).

In addition, I bring out the specificity of the typic-procedure within Kant's moral philosophy. First, the typic is not just a new name for the Law of Nature Formula in the *Groundwork*, since it performs new and important functions that are specific to moral judgment. Second, the typic-procedure does not, by itself, determine the will, but serves only for appraising the moral worth of actions. Third, its employment is not restricted to deliberation *ex ante* about one's own actions: it can also be applied to one's past actions as well as those of other people. Fourth, the typic-procedure should not be construed as an exercise of the reflecting power of judgment, as several commentators have suggested, but rather as strictly determining.

Finally, I evaluate the strengths and weaknesses of the consequentialist, teleological, logical, and 'rational agency' interpretations of the Typic chapter, particularly the typic-procedure. This assessment is carried out from an exegetical point of view: it is a matter of determining how faithful these approaches are to the letter and the spirit of Kant's text.

On the *consequentialist interpretation*, first proposed by Mill, the thought experiment consists in evaluating one's universalized maxim with respect to "the interest of mankind collectively": If everyone acted as I propose to do, would it result in a net increase or decrease of happiness? However, this consequentialist model is inadequate from an exegetical point of view: it conflicts in principle with Kant's rejection of what he calls the "empiricism of practical reason"; it fails to capture the specific kind of *contradiction* operative in Kant's universalization test; and it involves a different process of moral reasoning from Kant's account of moral appraisal.

The *teleological interpretation*, first advanced by Paton and later defended with some modifications by Beck and others, holds that Kant's references in the Typic to nature and its laws should be understood teleologically, i.e., with reference to ends. Thus, one is to ask oneself whether, if one's maxim were universalized as a law, it would harmonize with the cosmos conceived as a hierarchical system in which every part has its natural end. Speaking strongly against the teleological interpretation, however, is the fact that Kant denies a decisive role to ends in moral appraisal; correspondingly, both $Type_1$ (the law of natural causality) and $Type_2$ (*natura formaliter spectata*) are *formal* representations that contain no matter, i.e., neither ends nor teleological hierarchies.

The proponents of the *logical interpretation*, most prominently Höffe, hold that a morally unjustifiable maxim inevitably 'destroys itself' when universalized because it gives rise to a logical or conceptual contradiction. On this view, the purpose of the typic-procedure mainly consists in testing for such contradictions. While the logical interpretation offers a sophisticated analysis of the 'contradiction in conception', it misconstrues the typic-procedure to the extent that it equates the criterion of universality with 'contradictionlessness' (*Widerspruchslosigkeit*), whereas Kant in fact equates it with 'exceptionlessness' (*Ausnahmslosigkeit*).

According to the *rational agency interpretation* championed by Rawls, the thought experiment tests maxims according to whether or not they could be adopted by ideal rational agents. Rawls proposes an elaborate reconstruction of the typic-procedure within the framework of his analysis of the application of the Categorical Imperative, which he calls "the four-step CI-procedure." Although Rawls' model represents an influential attempt to make Kant's thought experiment philosophically plausible, it conflicts with Kant's text in several ways. Finally, Rawls' suggestion that Kant's thought experiment must take place against the backdrop of the *actual* laws of nature is shown to be exegetically inaccurate, but nonetheless illuminating to the extent that it reveals a tension in the typic-procedure between the opposite problems of false negatives and false positives.

Chapter 5: The outcome and effectiveness

The final chapter of the Commentary offers an account of the typic's *outcome* and *effectiveness*. Kant avers that everyone, "even the most common understanding," employs the typic to make accurate, even subtle, moral appraisals with relative ease (*KpV* 5: 70). This claim requires explanation, however, as the typic's abstract and formal mechanism seems to conflict with Kant's conception of the "common understanding" as uncomfortable with abstraction and reliant on concrete examples. First, Kant's statements attesting the common understanding's adept use of the typic-procedure are situated in the context of his more general esteem for the moral discernment of ordinary people – a position for which he had both empirical as well as *a priori* philosophical arguments. Second, Kant's statement that the typic provides the common understanding with "an example in a case of experience" (*KpV* 5: 70) was explained as a mechanism designed to trigger the common understanding's *a priori*, unconscious representation of the law of natural causality, which in turn guides moral appraisal by analogy: just as the law of nature necessarily applies to each and every "case of experience" *without exception*, so must the moral law govern each and every action *without exception*. Thirdly, I show how the typic performs two heuristic functions, *isolation* and *amplification*, that together promote a fair, responsible, and attentive frame of mind in the moral agent while making maxims more salient during moral appraisal.

The typic also performs two *additional, protective functions* insofar as it "guards against" two "dangers" to morality: empiricism and mysticism. The greatest danger stems from the philosophical position that Kant refers to as moral "empiricism," which holds that actions should be judged as good or evil according to their net positive or negative consequences on happiness. This is a grave error, Kant warns, as it turns moral appraisal into a self-interested, contentious, and uncertain estimation of probabilities, and it also corrupts people's moral dispositions by subordinating them to the heteronomous ideal of happiness. In contrast, the typic protects moral appraisal by providing an *a priori* rational standard – the formal universality of the law of nature – that is independent of the messy consideration of empirical consequences. Furthermore, Kant hints at the possibility of transforming the principle of happiness from an empirical and *ipso facto* heteronomous goal-state into a merely formal type ('Type$_3$') of the rational Idea of the morally good.

The second danger to morality is mysticism, the proponents of which claim to *see* or *feel* the supersensible Ideas directly with "real but non-sensible intuitions of a kingdom of God" (*KpV* 5: 71). Mysticism threatens morality in several ways, according to Kant: by contaminating the purity of the moral Ideas through a pseudo-schematization; by reducing moral appraisal to a "private illuminism" that lacks – and even precludes – rational, inter-subjective validity; and by corrupting moral motivation through the enthusiasm and fear evoked by otherworldly visions. The Typic counters these dangers by proposing instead a strictly analogical representation of the moral law by means of the *pure, universal form* of the law of nature – a representation that affords us a conceptual grasp of the supersensible moral Ideas in a way that protects their purity while enabling the objective, communicable and deliberate appraisal of maxims.

In sum, the Commentary paints a picture of the typic as the instrument *par excellence* of "the rationalism of the power of judgment [*der Rationalism der Urtheilskraft*]" in the moral sphere (*KpV* 5: 71).

2 Summary of Part Two

Chapter 6: The typic and symbolic hypotyposis

Many, if not most, of the scholars who have studied the typic have assimilated it to the notion of "symbolic hypotyposis" presented in § 59 of the *Critique of the Power of Judgment*. In Chapter 6, I present this interpretation in systematic manner, subject it to a critical examination, and argue that it is both mistaken and misguided.

Section 1 presents a unified "symbolist interpretation" woven together from the studies of various commentators who have independently identified the typic with symbolic hypotyposis. This exposition adopts the same analytical framework as the Commentary in order to facilitate comparisons between the two accounts.

On the symbolist interpretation, the main *task* to be achieved by the typic is to give meaning to the abstract and formal law of morality by making it visible within our concrete experience and thereby applicable to our daily lives. As "image-dependent [*bilderbedürftig*]" beings (*KU* 5: 408), we need to find some way to connect the supersensible Idea of the moral law with the intuitive, aesthetic dimension of moral experience, for otherwise it will remain devoid of significance and otiose for moral praxis.

The proponents of the symbolist interpretation tend to frame the '*particular difficulties*' of the power of judgment in objective, ontological terms: no object in the sensible world can serve as an adequate counterpart to the Ideas of the moral law and the morally good, for these refer to objects in the intelligible world.

The symbolists then consider what *resources* in Kant's conceptual repertoire might be suitable for mediating the application of the moral law to sensible experience. Noting that Kant rules out a *direct* sensible presentation of the supersensible Idea by means of the schematism, they infer that an *indirect* sensible presentation is both permitted and required. What is needed, then, is a figurative substitute for schematization that can make the law visible in sensible intuition.

The crux of the symbolist interpretation is the thesis that the *solution* must therefore be a process of *symbolization*, which consists in indirectly presenting the abstract representation of the moral law in the form of a concrete *symbol* that human beings can readily see, comprehend, and apply. And it is the law of nature that plays this role: it provides an intuitive analogue, or symbol, of the moral law in sensible experience. On this reading, the *type* of the moral law is like a Biblical 'type' that symbolizes a theological notion, or a *dramatis persona* that symbolizes a virtue in a morality play. More specifically, the symbolists situate the typic in Kant's theory of symbolic representation by claiming that typification, as an indirect, analogically mediated presentation of a supersensible Idea in the form of an intuitive symbol, corresponds to the process of symbolic hypotyposis presented in § 59 of the *Critique of the Power of Judgment*. Furthermore, the symbolists construe the typic-procedure as an *imaginative* procedure that enables moral appraisal by projecting a scene before the mind's eye.

Correspondingly, the symbolists contend that the Typic effectively satisfies the common understanding's need for concreteness by providing it with a symbol that renders the moral law vivid, comprehensible and applicable to everyday life.

Section 2 conducts an extensive critique of the symbolist interpretation, presenting it as anachronistic, inaccurate, and arbitrary.

I argue that the symbolists construe the task set for typic too broadly, as they fail to distinguish moral appraisal, an *a priori* exercise of the *pure* practical power of judgment, from the applied, *a posteriori* exercises of moral judgment that Kant treats in other contexts. The symbolists lay great weight on the notions that we finite human beings have a deep-seated *need* for supersensible representations to be presented in sensible intuition in order for them to be comprehensible to us, and more specifically, that we require an aesthetic presentation of moral Ideas. However, these premises are shown to be less germane to the Typic chapter than the symbolists maintain.

The ontological construal of the 'particular difficulties', already rebutted in the corresponding chapter of the Commentary, is further characterized as an attempt to suppress elements of the Typic that do not fit the symbolist interpretation.

As for the resources, by assuming that the only substitute for 'direct' presentation through the schematism must be 'indirect' presentation through symbolic hypotyposis, the symbolists overlook the possibility that the typic may provide its own, specific form of indirect presentation – typification – that is identical neither with the schematism nor with symbolic hypotyposis.

The identification of the typic with symbolic hypotyposis has major flaws. From a philological point of view, firstly, it is anachronistic and unsupported. A historical study of the corpus shows that Kant did not invent the concept of symbolic hypotyposis until two years after having written the *Critique of Practical Reason*. And contrary to what the symbolist interpretation would lead one to expect, Kant never refers back to the Typic in § 59 of the third *Critique*, nor in any of his subsequent treatments of symbolic hypotyposis. Secondly, I demonstrate through a detailed conceptual analysis that the type is not a symbol in the sense of § 59 and that typification does not function in the same way as symbolic hypotyposis. A *symbol* is a *sensible intuition* produced by the imagination. By contrast, the representations that Kant selects to serve as *types* could not be further removed from "sensible images": Type$_1$ – "the form of a law of nature in general [*die Form eines Naturgesetzes überhaupt*]" (*KpV* 5: 70) – and Type$_2$ – "the understanding's pure form of nature [*die Natur (der reinen Verstandesform derselben nach)*]" – are both *pure, formal and abstract concepts* produced by the understanding's intellectual synthesis. Symbolic hypotyposis, i.e., the process for producing symbols, which Kant characterizes in § 59 as the "double task [*doppeltes Geschäft*]" of the power of judgment (*KU* 5: 352–353), differs from the process of typification in several key respects. Symbolic hypotyposis provides a lively sensible presentation (*Versinnlichung*) of abstract concepts; it begins by producing an image in sensible intuition, followed by establishing an analogy; it highlights the specific causality of the symbol; and it is executed by the reflecting power of judgment. Typification serves not to provide an image per se, but to mediate the application of a formal standard to particular instances; it begins by establishing an abstract analogy between the Idea and its type, and only afterwards does it schematize the type in lieu of the Idea; it operates with the most abstract and generic representation of natural causality, abstracting from its specific determining grounds; and it is executed by the determining power of judgment. Moreover, the many variants of the symbolist interpretation, when examined in detail, turn out to be mutually inconsistent and seemingly arbitrary.

The suggestion that the typic-procedure functions as a kind of mental theatre conflicts with fundamental tenets of Kant's ethics. Kant firmly opposes entrusting moral appraisal to the so-called "moral imagination" and the emotions evoked thereby. On the contrary, moral appraisal must be carried out "with moral strictness [*nach moralischer Strenge*]," i.e., according to purely rational principles (*KpV* 5: 154).

Lastly, Kant's own account of how "everyone, in fact, judges actions as good or evil" (*KpV* 5: 69) belies the symbolists' claim that the ultimate function of the typic is to meet the common understanding's need for concrete images by means of a symbol of the moral law in sensible experience. What Kant actually states is that the typic provides the common understanding with "an example in a case of experience." But this "example [*Beispiel*]," is not a *symbol*; rather it is merely a nondescript concrete instance serving to cue the universal rule under which it falls, namely the law of natural causality. Its purpose is to *trigger an abstract analogy* between the law of nature and the moral law *qua* universal. In the final analysis, the challenge of enabling moral appraisal in the Typic chapter is not a matter of *making the invisible visible*, as the symbolists assume, but rather of *judging the already visible against an invisible* – i.e., formal, abstract and rational – *standard*, namely maxims' universalizability. Correspondingly, the typic assists the common understanding in making the transition from the concrete level at which it *perceives* actions to the abstract level at which it *judges* maxims in a principled manner.

In the third and final section of the chapter, I contend that the tendency to assimilate the typic with symbolic hypotyposis is not only mistaken, but misguided. Many attempts in this direction are motivated by a desire to *aestheticize* the Typic and, with it, Kant's moral philosophy as a whole. But this enterprise is ill-advised even on its own terms, I argue, since the fixation on symbolism stems from a misappreciation of the resources offered by Kant's aesthetic theory. I show that the *sublime* and the *aesthetic idea* respectively provide far more powerful and poetic aesthetic expressions of the moral Ideas than symbolic hypotyposis. In a word, the symbolists are betting on the wrong horse.

Chapter 7: The typic and symbolic anthropomorphism

In the final chapter, I pursue a hitherto unexplored avenue of interpretation, suggesting that the typic was informed by Kant's earlier conception of symbolic anthropomorphism, which figures in the Conclusion to the *Prolegomena* (1783), entitled "On Determining the Boundary of Pure Reason" (*P* 4: 350–365).

The first section of the chapter presents Kant's conception in terms of six characteristic features.

1. When Kant speaks of symbolic anthropomorphism in the *Prolegemena*, the expression carries with it definite restrictions: this mode of representation is not absolute, but "only [*nur*]" or "merely [*bloß*]" symbolic insofar as it determines intelligible beings not as they are in themselves, but *merely* in their relation to the sensible world, and this *merely* by analogy, and with *merely* symbolic, "as if [*als ob*]" language. In this way, *dogmatic* anthropomorphism is avoided.

2. Symbolic anthropomorphism employs *analogy* as a conceptual instrument for determining the relation between an intelligible being and the sensible world (typically, a causal relation). Kant's "philosophical analogy" enables one to construe that unknown relation as *perfectly similar* to a known relation between things within the sensible world, and this regardless of the dissimilarity of the individual terms of the analogy, and without cognizing the fourth term as it is in itself. For example, God's causal relation to the sensible world can be determined by means of the analogy *God : sensible world :: artisan : artifact*, whereby God's causality is represented teleologically. Accordingly, the model of "philosophical analogy" underlying symbolic anthropomorphism must be distinguished from inductive analogies, based on the approximate similarity between individual things, as well as from mathematical analogies, based on quantitative ratios.

3. Despite the name, "symbolic anthropomorphism" does not produce a *symbol in the image of a human being*, nor does it transfer sensible intuitions into the intelligible realm.

4. Symbolic anthropomorphism is both *permitted* and *required* in the critical philosophy: we "can allow ourselves [*wir erlauben uns*]" (P 4: 357) to employ this mode of representation, and indeed "we are compelled [*wir sind genöthigt*]" (P 4: 357) to do so.

5. Although the permitted use of symbolic anthropomorphism may be subject to certain restrictions, it is nonetheless *sufficient* for us and we have reason to be *satisfied* with it. When I regard the world *as if* it were an artifact crafted by an artisan-God, for instance, I must accept the fact that I do not gain any image of God, much less absolute knowledge of God as he may be constituted in himself, yet I nevertheless grasp this notion "according to what it is for me, that is, with respect to the world of which I am a part" (P 4: 357), insofar as I can thereby investigate nature *as if* it had been created in an organized, purposeful manner. And it is only in this epistemological sense that this mode of representation is *anthropomorphic*.

6. Finally, symbolic anthropomorphism fulfills several *protective functions* that flow from the previous two features: as the only possible way to accomplish the difficult feat of satisfying reason's demands while still heeding the strictures of critical rationalism, symbolic anthropomorphism serves to discredit and ward off rival epistemological approaches, including dogmatism, scepticism, empiricism, and mysticism.

Next, Kant's treatment of symbolic anthropomorphism invited a comparison, in Section 2, with St. Thomas Aquinas' influential doctrine of analogical predication. Kant's "philosophical analogy" turns out to have significant continuities with Aquinas' *analogy of proportionality*, but it differs in significant respects from Aquinas' *analogy of attribution*.

Section 3 compares *symbolic anthropomorphism* as described in the *Prolegomena* with *symbolic hypotyposis* as described in the *Critique of the Power of Judgment*. The two modes of symbolic representation are shown to have noteworthy differences. On the one hand, *symbolic hypotyposis* is an "indirect presentation [*indirekte Darstellung*]" of abstract concepts, including Ideas of reason, by means of the "double task [*doppeltes Geschäft*]" of the reflecting power of judgment (*KU* 5: 351ff.). Correspondingly, the expression "symbolic hypotyposis" refers to the *process* of symbolization, while the "symbol" per se, i.e., the intuition that embodies the indirect presentation of a concept, is the *product* of this process. A key consequence of this distinction between process and product is that while every symbol necessarily presupposes an analogy, not every analogy necessarily produces a symbol. I argue that *symbolic anthropomorphism* should be understood as an abstract analogical process that does *not* produce a symbol in sensible intuition, but that instead gives us a grasp of pure, conceptual relations. An additional difference is that the analogical procedure underlying symbolic hypotyposis is more finely grained and closer to sensible intuition than the analogical procedure underlying symbolic anthropomorphism. This reflects the different purposes of these two modes of representation : symbolic hypotyposis aims to produce a vivid and fitting symbol of an abstract concept or Idea of reason; symbolic anthropomorphism serves primarily to establish an analogy between relational concepts. Also, symbolic hypotyposis depends on the reflecting power of judgment, whereas symbolic anthropomorphism belongs only to the determining power of judgment.

Section 4 compares symbolic anthropomorphism with the typic according to the six characteristic features identified in Section 1.

1. The first sense in which the typic serves "*only* as a symbol" (*KpV* 5: 70), I suggest, is that it obeys the same epistemological restriction as *merely* symbolic anthropomorphism: neither of these forms of symbolic representation enables us to cognize the intelligible realm *in an absolute way*; instead, they enable us to grasp only *relations* pertaining to the intelligible world.

2. While not mentioned explicitly, analogy – specifically, Kant's "philosophical" model of analogy – plays important roles in the Typic chapter. The relevance of analogy to the typic has been recognized by commentators; however the secondary literature is plagued by considerable disagreement and confusion. I offer my own detailed analysis of the role of analogy in the Typic chapter. In the Commentary, I suggested that an analogy between the law of nature and the moral law *qua* universal underlies the common understanding's use of the typic-procedure for moral appraisal: *just as* the law of nature necessarily governs

every event without exception, *so* must the moral law govern every action without exception; consequently, *just as* purported exceptions to the law of nature must be rejected as superstition, *so* must purported exceptions to the moral law be rejected as morally evil. I then analyze a number of passages where Kant states that the law of nature's constitutive, unifying relation to the form of nature (*natura formaliter spectata*) is *analogous* to the moral law's constitutive, unifying relation to what Kant calls 'supersensible' or 'archetypal' nature' (i.e., the Idea of the intelligible realm governed by the moral law). This analysis shows that Type$_1$ and Type$_2$ are the *formal analogues* of the moral law and supersensible nature, respectively, and sheds light on several other elements of the Typic chapter. In short, my analysis suggests that the typic-procedure and typification are indeed made possible by an analogical procedure, one which shares key characteristics with the one presented in the *Prolegomena* but which is considerably more abstract and sophisticated.

3. Like the analogies underlying symbolic anthropomorphism, the analogies underlying the typic are abstract, formal, purely conceptual correspondences, devoid of sensible content, and they do not serve to produce a symbol in sensible intuition.

4. As he did for symbolic anthropomorphism, Kant legitimates the merely symbolic employment of the typic as both *permitted* and *required* so long as the strictures of critical rationalism are heeded.

5. Just as Kant averred that symbolic anthropomorphism was *sufficient* for the purposes of theoretical reason, so does he maintain that the typic is *sufficient* for "the pure practical use of reason" (*KpV* 5:70).

6. The comparison with symbolic anthropomorphism highlights that the typic exercises its protective functions against empiricism, mysticism, scepticism, and dogmatism in virtue of its *merely symbolic* – i.e., strictly analogical – status.

In sum, Chapter 7 shows that there are considerable continuities between symbolic anthropomorphism and the typic, suggesting that the latter can be understood as a sophisticated adaptation of the former, employed by Kant in order to solve a complex representational problem that arose at the heart of his moral philosophy.

3 The Typic in the evolution of Kant's thought

The main value in studying the Typic chapter, as Rawls presciently remarked, is "to bring to life and make intelligible Kant's characteristic and deeper ideas."[476] Accordingly, I wish to conclude by highlighting the Typic's distinctive significance to two parallel developments in Kant's thought regarding 1) symbolic representation and 2) the relationship between the domains of nature and morality.

3.1 Symbolic representation

The first general conclusion I would like to draw, especially from Part Two, is that the typic constitutes a pivotal moment in the evolution of Kant's theory of symbolic representation: on the one hand, it was the culmination of Kant's reaction against metaphysical and mystical symbolism; on the other hand, it may thereby have made room within the critical system for a positive, aesthetic conception of symbolism.

As Hans-Georg Gadamer has emphasized, the prevailing conception of symbolism leading up to the modern period had a "metaphysical background" and a "gnostic function," according to which

> [i]t is possible to be led beyond the sensible to the divine. For the world of the senses is not mere nothingness and darkness but the outflowing and reflection of truth. ... [T]he symbol ... presupposes a metaphysical connection between visible and invisible. The inseparability of visible appearance and invisible significance, this "coincidence" of two spheres, underlies all forms of religious worship.[477]

But contrary to what Gadamer claimed in *Truth in Method*, I want to argue that Kant's theory of symbolism should not be construed as a natural extension of this metaphysical conception to the aesthetic sphere,[478] but, on the contrary, as a properly rationalist and critical *Überwindung* of it.

In his youth, Kant was attracted to the idea of a symbolic affinity between the visible heavens and their invisible, spiritual significance. For instance, in the Conclusion to his *Universal Natural History and Theory of the Heavens* (1755), he mused: "the view of the starry sky on a clear night gives one a kind of pleasure that only noble souls feel. In the universal stillness of nature and

---

476 Rawls 2000, p. 163 f.
477 Gadamer 2002, p. 73; Gadamer 1990, p. 79.
478 Gadamer 2002, p. 73 ff.; Gadamer 1990, p. 79 ff.

the calmness of the senses, the immortal spirit's hidden faculty of cognition speaks an ineffable language and provides undeveloped concepts that can certainly be felt but not described" (*ANTH* 1: 366–368). Indeed, that attraction drove him to invest considerable money and time into reading the eight volumes of the *Heavenly Mysteries* by the mystic Emmanuel Swedenborg, who had created, on the basis of his visions, an elaborate system of symbolic correspondences between the visible cosmos and the spirit-world. But in 1766, Kant would decisively reject Swedenborg's symbolism as the nonsensical product of a pathologically overheated imagination (*TG* 2: 339–340).[479] And significantly, it was in his treatise *Dreams of a Spirit-Seer* that Kant developed his first philosophical theory of symbolism as a strategic "recasting [*Umbesetzung*]," as Petra Bahr puts it, of Swedenborg's mystical symbolism with a view to deflating its hyperbolic claims about the intelligible realm.[480] Similarly, Ernst Müller interprets Kant's treatment of symbolism in *Dreams* as the first move towards his "disempowerment [*Depotenzierung*]" of mystical and religious symbolism.[481] Thus, the original impetus for Kant's reflections on symbolic representation came from his *rejection* of the mystical connection between the visible and the invisible realms.

And as the present study has shown, this *anti-mystical* and *anti-metaphysical* impetus continued into the critical period. In 1783, in the *Prolegomena*, Kant renewed his struggle against the exaggerated metaphysical claims of *Schwärmerei* with a more philosophically sophisticated conception of symbolic representation than in *Dreams*. Symbolic anthropomorphism follows the "noble way of analogy" in order to satisfy the needs of theoretical reason by giving it a conceptual purchase on the relations of intelligible beings to the sensible world, while preventing reason from venturing beyond experience into *Schwärmerei*. In 1788, we find Kant employing a strikingly similar strategy for combatting mystical *Schwärmerei*, this time in the practical sphere. In the Typic chapter, Kant counters mysticism's deleterious and delusional tendency to "intuit or feel itself into" the intelligible realm (*G* 4: 458) with yet another strictly rationalist, deflationary form of symbolic representation, based on analogy. Instead of a pseudo-schematism of "the invisible Kingdom of God," *the typic* provides the power of judgment with a merely symbolic, strictly analogical alternative that, by contrast, "takes from sensible nature nothing more than what pure reason can also think for itself, that is, conformity with law, and transfers into the supersensible nothing but what can, conversely, be really exhibited by actions in the sensible world

---

[479] See section 2.4. of Chapter 6.
[480] Bahr 2004, p. 275.
[481] Müller 2001, p. 598; Müller 2004, p. 129–134.

in accordance with a formal rule of a law of nature in general" (*KpV* 5: 71). The typic mediates between supersensible Ideas and sensible intuition not by producing an image, or symbol, but rather by means of an abstract analogy between the *form of lawfulness* common to both the supersensible and sensible spheres. As I have stressed throughout the book, this mediation is *asymmetrical*: it is not a matter of making the invisible visible, but of measuring the already visible against an invisible standard of reason. The typic therefore represents a decisive *Überwindung* of mystical symbolism in the practical sphere by "the rationalism of the power of judgment" (*KpV* 5: 71).

Finally, I would like to suggest – merely as a hypothesis – that the Typic may have contributed to Kant's subsequently granting symbolism a properly *aesthetic* function in the third *Critique*. At the most general level, the Typic chapter prepared the ground for the theory of symbolic hypotyposis in the *Critique of the Power of Judgment* in three ways: (1) it saliently raised the problem of mediating between supersensible Ideas and sensible intuition; (2) it extended and refined the insight, already present in the *Prolegomena*'s theory of symbolic anthropomorphism, that the two could be connected in an indirect, non-schematic way; and (3) it threw a spotlight on the *power of judgment* as the faculty responsible for mediating between supersensible and sensible representations and, more generally, between the domains of theoretical and practical reason. As is well known, all of these themes were taken up and investigated more extensively in the third *Critique*, particularly in § 59. More specifically, the *analogical procedure* deployed in the Typic may have satisfied Kant that symbolic representation as such need not be *schwärmerisch*: analogy provided a means for grounding symbols on *concepts* rather than on wild inspiration or obscure feelings. The discovery that the imagination could thus be tamed may have emboldened Kant to temper his distrust of it and to supplement his originally austere theory of symbolic representation with a positive, aesthetic function. And Kant did go on to develop, in *KU*, § 59, the "double task [*doppeltes Geschäft*]" of the reflecting power of judgment as a way to produce lively symbols which speak to the aesthetic dimension of humanity but which, far from being ineffable or esoteric, have a precise meaning that can be analyzed, spelled out and communicated in terms of the analogies on which they are grounded.[482] It seems as if Kant

---

[482] Tellingly, Gadamer obscures this critical transformation: in his desire to frame Kant's theory of symbolic hypotyposis as the link between the earlier mystical tradition of symbolism and its later aesthetic revival in Romanticism, he characterizes the Kantian symbol as a representation "which can be interpreted inexhaustibly because it is indeterminate" and which spurs "the full freedom of reflection in aesthetic judgment." Gadamer 2002, p. 7 f.; Gadamer 1990, p. 81. But as Kirk Pillow has shown, *that* description applies not to the symbol, but to the *aesthetic idea*, in

first had to push back *mystical* symbolism in order to make room for a form of *aesthetic* symbolism consonant with the principles and strictures of critical rationalism.

3.2 The relation between nature and morality

The Typic chapter also represents a decisive moment in the long evolution of Kant's thought regarding the relation between the realms of nature and morality. Here we can observe a similar transition from an original mystical and metaphysical unity towards a properly critical and rationalist conception of two distinct realms mediated by means of analogy.

In the early phases of Kant's thought, the realms of nature and morality were intertwined. Kant relates that, when he was a child, his mother simultaneously "planted and nourished the seed of the good" and "opened [his] heart to the impressions of nature," thereby instilling in him a deep affective bond between the two.[483] In his first theoretical works as a young scholar, the vision of the grandiose scale and harmony of the natural universe provided by Newtonian cosmology directly inspired moral and metaphysical reflections. For example, he concluded his 1775 *Universal Natural History* with speculations that the stars and planets in other galaxies could eventually provide homes for our immortal souls after the death of the body.[484] As Cassirer observes, "[t]here is no gulf here between the world of the is and the ought, but rather the eye roves directly from one to the other."[485]

---

the production of which the imagination and reflection have free rein (*KU* 5: 316). See Pillow 2000, p. 83 f. On the typic's pertinence to the complex analogy underwriting the symbolization of the morally good by beauty, see Müller 2001, p. 600 f.

483 Reported by Kant's early biographer Jachmann, cited in Beck 1960, p. 282n. See also Kuehn 2002, p. 31 ff.

484 "Should the immortal soul remain forever attached to this point in space, to our Earth for the whole infinity of its future duration, which is not interrupted by the grave itself, but only changed? Should it never obtain a closer view of the remaining wonders of creation? Who knows whether it is not intended to get to know at close quarters those distant spheres of the universe and the excellence of their arrangements that already excite its curiosity from a distance? Perhaps some further spheres of the planetary system will form around them in order to prepare new places for us to reside in other heavens, after the completed passage of time prescribed for our stay here. Who knows, perhaps the satellites orbiting around Jupiter will light our way in the future?" (*ANTH* 1: 366–368).

485 Cassirer 1987, p. 266; cf. Beck 1960, p. 282.

In the Conclusion to the *Critique of Practical Reason*, Kant once again juxtaposes the two realms in those famous words that have come to epitomize Kant's philosophy and, indeed, the man himself: "Two things fill the mind with ever new and increasing admiration and awe, the more often and more steadily we reflect upon them: *the starry heavens above me and the moral law within me*" (*KpV* 5: 161). At first sight, this statement seems of a piece with Kant's earlier speculations, a reaffirmation of an ineffable metaphysical unity between the natural and moral orders. But in reality, as Cassirer and Beck have both emphasized, this passage represents a "decisive advance," or "marked progress," in Kant's philosophical development.[486] For here, unlike in his pre-critical works, Kant clearly separates the two realms and warns against letting them fuse together or even overlap:

> Admiration and respect can indeed excite to inquiry, but they cannot supply the want of it. ... The observation of the world began from the noblest spectacle that was ever placed before the human sense and that our understanding can bear to follow in its vast expanse, and it ended in – astrology. Morals began with the noblest attribute of human nature, the development and cultivation of which promised infinite utility, and it ended in – fanaticism or superstition (*KpV* 5: 162).

Thus, Kant's juxtaposition of nature and morality in the Conclusion consecrates the properly critical *distinction* between the legislative "domains" of theoretical and practical reason (cf. *KU* 5: 175–175). The historical precedents of astrology and fanaticism show that confusing the two legislations works to the detriment of reason. And so, from now on, critical philosophy must serve a protective function by separating them, as Cassirer explains:

> Only the critique of theoretical and practical reason alike can safeguard against both of these false paths, can prevent us from explaining the orbits of the heavenly bodies by spiritual powers and guiding intelligences instead of mathematically and mechanically, and, conversely, keep us from trying to describe in terms of sensuous images the pure laws of obligation and the intelligible order it opens to us. To inculcate this distinction, this "dualism" between Idea and experience, between the is and the ought, and to assert the unity of reason in and through this distinction: this can now be described as the most comprehensive task set by the critical system for itself.[487]

The philosophical separation of the spheres of theoretical and practical reason was accomplished in the first two *Critiques*. The *Critique of Pure Reason* established the thorough-going legislation of the understanding over nature: the sen-

---

[486] Cassirer 1987, p. 268; Beck 1960, p. 283.
[487] Cassirer 1987, p. 268.

sible world is entirely subjected to the universal laws prescribed to it *a priori* by the understanding, under the overarching guidance of theoretical reason. Correspondingly, the first *Critique* forbade admixing human caprice or superstition into the empirical investigation of nature; all "evasions" from the laws of mathematical physics – whether through divine intervention, miracles, or even chance – "must cease" (*KrV* A165/B206, Bxiii-xiv). The *Critique of Practical Reason* proved, through the Idea of freedom, that morality belongs to the domain of practical reason, which prescribes the moral law unconditionally. In addition, the second *Critique* ensured practical reason's *exclusive* purview over morality by condemning as heteronomous both empiricist ethics, which subordinates morality to the principle of happiness, as well as mystical *Schwärmerei*, which makes "God and eternity with their awful majesty stand unceasingly *before our eyes*," thereby turning moral conduct into a "puppet show" of fear and trembling (*KpV* 5: 146–148). Crucially, Kant also took himself to have established that the two legislative domains carved out by the *Critiques* of theoretical and practical reason were *independent* yet still *compatible:* "For just as little as the concept of nature influences legislation through the concept of freedom does the latter disturb the legislation of nature" (*KU* 5: 175). In sum, the Conclusion of the second *Critique* marks the moment when Kant definitively sloughs off his earlier sentimental and speculative *rapprochements* between the nature and morality: "All that is now transcended," as Beck explains, "[t]he stark contrast between the two, not some simple harmony hazarded between them, gives force to their bold contexture" – and from now on, "all that remains of the older conception of the relation of the moral law to the natural is the Typic."[488]

Beck's mention of the Typic at this precise juncture could not be more apt. As we have just seen, in the Typic Kant actively guards against the perversions of the relation between nature and morality by empiricism and mysticism (*KpV* 5: 70–71). Moreover, Beck's mention of the Typic complements Cassirer's analysis by reminding us that the "comprehensive task set by critical philosophy for itself" involves more than these negative functions; it is not enough simply to make the distinction between the natural and moral orders, or even to safeguard it in perpetuity. Kant's "dualism between the is and the ought" can only remain philosophically viable if there is also some sort of bridge spanning the gulf between the two realms; they cannot remain completely separate, without any point of contact. This positive requirement is not merely speculative or architectonic; rather, it confronts us plainly in *moral appraisal*, which raises the clear, pressing need to find some way for ordinary people to apply 'the law of what

---

488 Beck 1960, p. 282.

ought to be' to the actions that we perform in our world, governed by 'the law of what is'. And although the problem of mediating between the domains of theoretical and practical reason would eventually require a third *Critique* to be addressed in its full scope and complexity (*KU* 5: 174–176), it was in the Typic that, for the first time, Kant grappled with the challenge of rejoining the spheres that the *Critiques* of pure and practical reason had cloven asunder, yet without confusing them anew.

Mediation is therefore the main positive function of the typic, and this, in a manner befitting the principles critical rationalism. Mediation, for Kant, cannot lead to a mystical *Verschmelzung* or a dialectical *Aufhebung*, nor can it take the form of a naturalistic theory that reduces morality to a natural phenomenon. Rather, the mediation implemented by the typic clinches the separation of nature and morality even as it forges a connection between them.

This connection, it turns out, is provided by the concepts of *law* (*Gesetz*) and *lawfulness* (*Gesetzmäßigkeit*), as constitutive of an ordered system, or 'nature' in an abstract sense. And it is crucial to appreciate that this concept of law is itself a distinctive product – indeed, a crowning achievement – of the critique of reason. The first *Critique* established that the law of nature is no mere generalization drawn from empirical data, but rather an *a priori*, strictly universal standard that "reason itself puts into nature" (*KrV* B xiii-xiv). The second *Critique* established that the moral law is not a norm handed down from a transcendent source (like the Decalogue),[489] but rather a fundamental, universal, and *a priori* law produced as a *Faktum* by pure practical reason itself (*KpV* 5: 30). The critical philosophy thus reveals that both of these laws share key features: they are pure, universal, formal, and *a priori* products of reason. What is more, each law functions as a principle of unity that constitutes its respective domain as a unified, law-governed system. Consequently, as Kant puts it in a key phrase in the Typic chapter, "laws as such are the same, no matter where they derive their determining grounds from" (*KpV* 5: 70). Correspondingly, the critical philosophy conceives "nature" in an abstract, formal sense that is common to the physical and moral spheres: "*Natural* (*formaliter*) means what follows necessarily according to laws of a certain order of whatever sort, hence under the moral order as well as the physical order" (*ED* 8: 333n, trans. mod.).[490] And because the *Critiques* articulated the concepts of "law" and "nature" in their maximum purity and abstraction, the law of physical nature can then be substituted for the law of supersensible

---

[489] *Pace* Schopenhauer 2007, p. 20.
[490] [Natürlich *(formaliter)* heißt, was nach Gesetzen einer gewißen Ordnung, welche es auch sei, mithin auch der moralischen (also nicht immer bloß der physischen) nothwendig folgt.]

nature, as its *type*, in virtue of a formal analogy between them: *just as* the law of nature transforms the disunited manifold of appearances into a system united under physical laws (*natura formaliter spectata*) by imparting the manifold with the form of universal lawfulness (*Gesetzmäßigkeit*) (*KrV* A542/B570), so does the moral law transform the disunited 'manifold' of actions (cf. *G* 4: 437; *KpV* 5: 65) into a system united under practical laws, which Kant calls a supersensible or archetypal nature, by imparting the manifold with the form of universal lawfulness (*Gesetzmäßigkeit*) (*KpV* 5: 43). Thus the typic mediates between nature and morality in virtue of the quintessential result of the critical method, namely that each of these spheres constitutes a *kosmos*, or 'nature', governed by rational law. And this, finally, is the touchstone of "the rationalism of the power of judgment" instituted and mobilized by the typic, which requires "nothing more than what pure reason can also think for itself, that is, conformity with law [*nichts ... als was auch reine Vernunft für sich denken kann, d.i. die Gesetzmäßigkeit*]" (*KpV* 5: 71).

And although, on a philosophical level, this mediation is extremely abstract, the typic brings the concept of law down to earth and makes it concrete and accessible.[491] For the law *of nature* is a representation that possesses "aesthetic universality," i.e., it can be illustrated by a virtually infinite number of examples, any one of which cues the rule under which it falls as concrete instance (*JL* 9: 39). As a result, anyone, "even the most common understanding," can easily recognize the universal principle of the universal law of physical causality in any "case of experience," since, as the first *Critique* proved, it was the human mind that thought the law of nature into experience *a priori*. Thus, the common understanding "has the law of nature always at hand" (*KpV* 5: 70; cf. *P* 4: 369 – 370; *KrV* B4). And once a concrete "case of experience" has triggered the representation of *universal physical law*, "the concept of which occurs even in the most common use of reason," this representation can then be employed as "the type of the law of freedom" in virtue of an *analogy* between the two laws *qua* universal and hence 'exceptionless'.[492] Just as the law of natural causality necessarily applies to each and every "case of experience" *without exception* (*KrV* A542/B570), so must the moral law govern each and every action *without exception* (*G* 4: 421, 424). This equivalence, in turn, provides an analogy for guiding *moral appraisal:* just as "in the most ordinary judgments of ... experience" one must reject – i.e., *disbelieve* – each and every purported *exception* to the law of nature as superstition, so "in cases where causality from freedom is to

---

491 See sections 5.1.2. and 5.1.3. of the Commentary.
492 See Ch. 7, 4.2.

be appraised" must one reject – i.e., *condemn* – each and every purported *exception* to the moral law as morally unacceptable.

The Typic chapter thus presents a view of nature and morality as distinct realms that can nevertheless be connected in a rational and transparent manner. Disavowed and abandoned is the metaphysical and mystical conception of the relation between nature and morality as an obscure, spiritual connection expressed in a secret, "ineffable language" accessible only to those ostensibly possessed of exceptional insight. Indeed, the Typic represents a decisive moment where Kant's critical philosophy, using its own resources, quashes this elitist obscurantism in the practical sphere and surpasses it with a coherent, self-sufficient model of rationality based on intelligibility and communicability. Accordingly, the Typic should be recognized not only as a decisive moment in Kant's philosophical development, but also as an important, and characteristically Kantian, contribution to the project of *Aufklärung*.

Works Cited

Primary sources

Immanuel Kant's works in German

Complete editions

(1902ff.): *Gesammelte Schriften*. Preussische Akademie der Wissenschaften (Ed.). 29 vols. Berlin: De Gruyter, 1902ff.
(2007a): *Kant im Kontext III. Werke, Briefwechsel, Nachlaß und Vorlesungen auf CD-ROM*. Berlin: Karsten Worm InfoSoftWare, 2007.

Separate editions:

(1992a): *Über den Gemeinspruch: Das mag in der Theorie richtig sein, taugt aber nicht für die Praxis. Zum ewigen Frieden*. Klemme, Heiner F. (Ed.). Philosophische Bibliothek. Hamburg: Meiner.
(1998a): *Kritik der reinen Vernunft*. Timmermann, Jens (Ed.). Philosophische Bibliothek. Hamburg: Meiner.
(1999a): *Was ist Aufklärung? Ausgewählte kleine Schriften*. Brandt, Horst D. (Ed.). Philosophische Bibliothek. Hamburg: Meiner.
(1999b): *Grundlegung zur Metaphysik der Sitten*. Kraft, Bernd/Dieter Schönecker (Eds.). Philosophische Bibliothek. Hamburg: Meiner.
(2000a): *Anthropologie in pragmatischer Hinsicht*. Brandt, Reinhard (Ed.). Philosophische Bibliothek. Hamburg: Meiner.
(2001): *Prolegomena zu einer jeden künftigen Metaphysik, die als Wissenschaft wird auftreten können*. Pollock, Konstantin (Ed.). Philosophische Bibliothek. Hamburg: Meiner.
(2003a): *Kritik der praktischen Vernunft*. Brandt, Horst D./Heiner F. Klemme (Eds.). Philosophische Bibliothek. Hamburg: Meiner.
(2003b): *Die Religion innerhalb der Grenzen der bloßen Vernunft*. Stangneth, Bettina (Ed.). Philosophische Bibliothek. Hamburg: Meiner.
(2005a): *Der Streit der Fakultäten*. Brandt, Horst D./Pietro Giordanetti (Ed.). Philosophische Bibliothek. Hamburg: Meiner.
(2008): *Metaphysische Anfangsgründe der Tugendlehre. Metaphysik der Sitten. Zweiter Teil*. Ludwig, Bernd (Ed.). Second edition. Philosophische Bibliothek. Hamburg: Meiner.
(2009a): *Kritik der Urteilskraft. Beilage: Erste Einleitung in die Kritik der Urteilskraft*. Klemme, Heiner F. (Ed.). Philosophische Bibliothek. Hamburg: Meiner.
(2009b): *Metaphysische Anfangsgründe der Rechtslehre. Metaphysik der Sitten. Erster Teil*. Ludwig, Bernd (Ed.). Philosophische Bibliothek. Hamburg: Meiner.
(2013): *Träume eines Geistessehers. Von dem ersten Grunde des Unterschiedes der Gegenden im Raume*. Reich, Klaus (Ed.). Philosophische Bibliothek. Hamburg: Meiner.
(2014): *Kleinere Schriften zur Geschichtsphilosophie, Ethik und Politik*. Vorländer, Karl (Ed.). Philosophische Bibliothek. Hamburg: Meiner.

Immanuel Kant's works in English translation

(1992b): *Lectures on Logic*. Young, J. Michael (Ed. and Trans.). The Cambridge Edition of the Works of Immanuel Kant. New York: Cambridge University Press.
(1996a): *Practical Philosophy*. Gregor, Mary J. (Ed. and Trans.). The Cambridge Edition of the Works of Immanuel Kant. New York: Cambridge University Press.
(1996b): *Religion and Rational Theology*. Wood, Allen W./George Di Giovanni (Eds. and Trans.). The Cambridge Edition of the Works of Immanuel Kant. New York: Cambridge University Press.
(1997a): *Lectures on Ethics*. Heath, Peter (Trans.). Heath, Peter/J.B. Schneewind (Eds.). The Cambridge Edition of the Works of Immanuel Kant. New York: Cambridge University Press.
(1997b): *Lectures on Metaphysics*. Ameriks, Karl/Steve Naragon (Eds. and Trans.). The Cambridge Edition of the Works of Immanuel Kant. New York: Cambridge University Press.
(1998b): *Critique of Pure Reason*. Guyer, Paul/Allen W. Wood (Eds. and Trans.). The Cambridge Edition of the Works of Immanuel Kant. New York: Cambridge University Press.
(1999): *Correspondence*. Zweig, Arnulf (Ed. and Trans.). The Cambridge Edition of the Works of Immanuel Kant. New York: Cambridge University Press.
(2000b): *Critique of the Power of Judgment*. Guyer, Paul/Eric Matthews (Trans.). Guyer, Paul (Ed.). The Cambridge Edition of the Works of Immanuel Kant. New York: Cambridge University Press.
(2002a): *Theoretical Philosophy after 1781*. Hatfield, Gary/Michael Friedman/Henry E. Allison/Peter Heath (Trans.). Allison, Henry E./Peter Heath (Eds.). The Cambridge Edition of the Works of Immanuel Kant. New York: Cambridge University Press.
(2002b): *Theoretical Philosophy, 1755–1770*. Walford, David (Trans.). Walford, David/Ralf Meerbote (Eds.). The Cambridge Edition of the Works of Immanuel Kant. New York: Cambridge University Press.
(2005b): *Notes and Fragments*. Bowman, Curtis/Paul Guyer/Frederick Rauscher (Trans.). Guyer, Paul (Ed.). The Cambridge Edition of the Works of Immanuel Kant. New York: Cambridge University Press.
(2007b): *Anthropology, History, and Education*. Gregor, Mary/Paul Guyer/Robert B. Louden/Holly Wilson/Allen W. Wood/Günter Zöller/Arnulf Zweig (Trans.). Zöller, Günter/Robert B. Louden (Eds.). The Cambridge Edition of the Works of Immanuel Kant. New York: Cambridge University Press.
(2012a): *Lectures on Anthropology*. Clewis, Robert R./Robert B. Louden/G. Felicitas Munzel/Allen W. Wood (Trans.). Wood, Allen W./Robert B. Louden (Eds.). The Cambridge Edition of the Works of Immanuel Kant. New York: Cambridge University Press.
(2012b): *Natural Science*. Beck, Lewis White/Jeffrey B. Edwards/Olaf Reinhardt/Martin Schönfeld/Eric Watkins (Trans.). Watkins, Eric (Ed.). The Cambridge Edition of the Works of Immanuel Kant. New York: Cambridge University Press.

Secondary sources

Adickes, Erich (1927): *Kant und die Als-Ob-Philosophie*. Stuttgart: Frommann.

Adorno, Theodor W. (2000): *Problems of Moral Philosophy.* Livingstone, Rodney (Trans.). Schröder, Thomas (Ed.). Stanford: Stanford University Press.
Allison, Henry E. (2002): "General Introduction." In: Allison, Henry E. and Peter Heath (Eds.): *Immanuel Kant. Theoretical Philosophy after 1781*, edited by Henry Allison/Peter Heath, 1–28. New York: Cambridge University Press, pp. 1–28.
Allison, Henry E. (2011): *Kant's Groundwork for the Metaphysics of Morals: A Commentary.* New York: Oxford University Press.
Alquié, Ferdinand (2005): *Leçons sur Kant: La morale de Kant.* Paris: La Table Ronde.
Ameriks, Karl (2001): "Text and Context: Hermeneutical Prolegomena to Interpreting a Kant Text." In: Schönecker, Dieter/Thomas Zwenger (Eds.): *Kant verstehen / Understanding Kant: Über die Interpretation philosophischer Texte.* Darmstadt: Wissenschaftliche Buchgesellschaft, pp. 11–31.
"Analogie" (1971): In: *Historisches Wörterbuch der Philosophie.* Basel: Schwabe & Co., pp. 214–230.
"Analogie" (1996): In: *Sprachphilosophie: Ein internationales Handbuch zeitgenössischer Forschung.* Berlin, New York: De Gruyter, pp. 1236–1249.
Aquinas, Saint Thomas (1964): *Summa Theologiae.* McCabe, Herbert (Trans.). New York, London: Blackfriars & McGraw-Hill.
Aristotle (1984). *The Complete Works of Aristotle.* 2 vols. Barnes, Jonathan (Ed.). Princeton (NJ): Princeton University Press.
Ashworth, E. Jennifer (2013): "Medieval Theories of Analogy." In: *The Stanford Encyclopedia of Philosophy.* Winter 2013 Edition. Edward N. Zalta (Ed.). URL = <http://plato.stanford.edu/archives/win2013/entries/analogy-medieval/>. Visited 11 November 2015.
Auerbach, Erich (1984): "Figura." In: *Scenes from the Drama of European Literature.* Minneapolis: University of Minnesota Press, pp. 11–76.
Aune, Bruce (1979): *Kant's Theory of Morals.* Princeton (NJ): Princeton University Press.
Bacin, Stefano (2010): "The meaning of the *Critique of Practical Reason* for moral beings: the Doctrine of Method of Pure Practical Reason." In: Reath, Andrews/Jens Timmermann (Eds.): *Kant's Critique of Practical Reason: A Critical Guide.* Cambridge, New York: Cambridge University Press, pp. 197–215.
Bahr, Petra (2004): *Darstellung des Undarstellbaren. Religionstheoretische Studien zum Darstellungsbegriff bei A. G. Baumgarten und I. Kant.* Tübingen: Mohr Siebeck.
Bailer-Jones, Daniela M. (2002): "Models, Metaphors and Analogies." In: Machamer, Peter K./Michael Silbertein (Eds.): *The Blackwell Guide to the Philosophy of Science.* Malden (MA), Oxford: Blackwell Publishers, pp. 108–128.
Beck, Lewis White (1960): *A Commentary on Kant's Critique of Practical Reason.* Chicago: University of Chicago Press.
Bergfeld, Werner (1933): *Der Begriff des Typus: Eine systematische und problemgeschichtliche Untersuchung.* Bonn: Röhrscheid.
Bielefeldt, Heiner (2001): *Kants Symbolik. Ein Schlüssel zur kritischen Freiheitsphilosophie.* Freiburg & Munich: Aber.
Bielefeldt, Heiner (2003): *Symbolic Representation in Kant's Practical Philosophy.* Cambridge: Cambridge University Press.
Black, Max (1962): "Models and Archetypes." In: *Models and Metaphors: Studies in Language and Philosophy.* Ithaca (NY): Cornell University Press, pp. 219–243.
Broad, C. D. (1965): *Five Types of Ethical Theory.* Totowa (NJ): Littlefield Adams.

Callanan, John J. (2008): "Kant on Analogy." In: *British Journal for the History of Philosophy* 16, pp. 747–772.

Carson, Emily (1999): "Kant on the Method of Mathematics." In: *Journal of the History of Philosophy* 37, pp. 629–652.

Caruth, Cathy (1988): "The Force of Example: Kant's Symbols." In: *Yale French Studies* 74, pp. 17–137.

Cassirer, Ernst (1920): *Zur Einstein'schen Relativitätstheorie: Erkenntnistheoretische Betrachtungen*. Berlin: Bruno Cassirer.

Cassirer, Ernst (1987): *Kant's Life and Thought*. Haden, James (Trans.). New Haven, London: Yale University Press.

Cassirer, Ernst (2001): *Kants Leben und Lehre*. Gesammelte Werke 8. Hamburg: Meiner.

Cassirer, Heinz Walter (1938): *A Commentary on Kant's Critique of Judgment*. New York: Barnes & Noble.

Castillo, Monique (2007): *La Responsabilité des modernes: Essai sur l'universalisme kantien*. Paris: Kimé.

Chen, Zhe (2002): "Analogical Problem Solving: A Hierarchichal Analysis of Procedural Similarity." In: *Journal of Experimental Psychology: Learning, Memory, and Cognition* 28, pp. 81–98.

Chignell, Andrew (2011): "The Devil, the Virgin, and the Envoy: Symbols of Moral Struggle in Religion, Part Two, Section Two." In: Höffe, Otfried (Ed.): *Immanuel Kant. Die Religion innerhalb der Grenzen der bloßen Vernunft*. Klassiker Auslegen 41. Berlin: Akademie Verlag, pp. 111–130.

Cohen, Hermann (1920): *Kants Begründung der Ethik. Nebst ihren Anwendungen auf Recht, Religion und Geschichte*. Second, expanded edition. Berlin: Bruno Cassirer, 1910.

Cohen-Halimi, Michèle (2004): *Entendre raison : Essai sur la philosophie pratique de Kant*, Bibliothèque d'Histoire de la Philosophie. Paris: Vrin.

Coleman, Francis (1974): *The Harmony of Reason: A Study in Kant's Aesthetics*. Pittsburgh: University of Pittsburgh Press.

Danby-Smith, Michael J. (1969): "The Scholastic Doctrine of Analogy." PhD Thesis. McMaster University.

Darwin, Charles (2011): *The Origin of Species*. London: Harper Collins.

de Man, Paul (1979): "The Epistemology of Metaphor." In: Sacks, Sheldon (Ed.): *On Metaphor*. Chicago: University of Chicago Press, pp. 11–28.

Delbos, Victor (1969): *La Philosophie pratique de Kant*. Third edition. Paris: Presses Universitaires de France.

Dierksmeier, Claus (1998): *Das Noumenon Religion. Eine Untersuchung zur Stellung der Religion im System der praktischen Philosophie Kants*. Berlin, New York: De Gruyter.

Dietrichson, Paul (1969): "Kant's criteria of universalizability." In: Wolff, Peter Paul (Ed.): *Foundations of the Metaphysics of Morals with Critical Essays*. Indianapolis: Bobbs-Merrill, pp. 163–207.

Dumouchel, Daniel (2000): "Kant et la 'part subjective' de la moralité." In: Lafrance, Guy/Claude Piché/François Duchesneau (Eds.): *Kant actuel: Hommage à Pierre Laberge*. Montreal, Paris: Bellarmin & Vrin, pp. 109–125.

Dumouchel, Daniel (2001): "La théorie kantienne de la subjectivité et le problème de l'affectivité pratique." In: Gerhardt, Volker/Rolf-Peter Horstmann/Ralph Schumacher (Eds.): *Kant und die Berliner Aufklärung. Akten des IX. Internationalen Kant-Kongresses*. Berlin, New York: De Gruyter, pp. 172–181.

Elton Bulnes, María (1989): "Racionalismo Etico Kantiano y Amor Puro." In: *Anuario Filosófico* 22, pp. 133–145.
Förster, Eckart (2011): *Die 25 Jahre der Philosophie: Eine systematische Rekonstruktion*. Philosophische Abhandlungen 102. Frankfurt a.M.: Klostermann.
Freud, Sigmund (2007): *Massenpsychologie und Ich-Analyse. Die Zukunft einer Illusion*. Frankfurt a.M.: Fischer.
Freydberg, Bernard (2005): *Imagination in Kant's Critique of Practical Reason*. Bloomington, Indianapolis: Indiana University Press.
Freydberg, Bernard (2013): "Imagination in Kant's Critical Philosophy." In: Thompson, Michael L. (Ed.): *Imagination in Kant's Critical Philosophy*. Berlin, Boston: De Gruyter, pp. 105–121.
Gadamer, Hans.-Georg (1990): *Wahrheit und Methode: Grundzüge einer philosophischen Hermeneutik*. Gesammelte Werke 1. Tübingen: Mohr (Siebeck).
Gadamer, Hans.-Georg (2002): *Truth and Method*. Weinsheimer, Joel/Donald G. Marschall (Trans.). Second, revised edition. New York: Continuum.
Gill, Jerry H. (1984): "Kant, Analogy, and Natural Theology." In: *International Journal for Philosophy of Religion* 16, pp. 19–28.
Glover, Douglas H. (1971): "Metaphysical Dualism in Kant's Ethics." PhD Thesis, University of Edinburgh.
Grandjean, Antoine (2004): "Jugement moral en situation et exception chez Kant." In: *Philosophie* 81, pp. 42–57.
Granja, Dulce María (2010): *Lecciones de Kant para hoy*. Autores, Textos y Temas 79. Barcelona, México: Rubí & Anthropos.
Grapote, Sophie (2015): "L'accusation de formalisme et le problème de l'application "morale" : La solution de la 'Typique'". In: Grapotte, Sophie/Margit Ruffing/Ricardo Terra (Eds.): *Kant – la raison pratique. Concepts et héritages*. Paris: Vrin, pp. 93–102.
Green, Michael K. (1982): "Using Nature to Typify Freedom: The Application of the Categorical Imperative." In: *International Studies in Philosophy* 14, pp. 17–26.
Grondin, Jean (2000): "Zur Phänomenologie des moralischen ‚Gesetzes'. Das kontemplative Motiv der Erhebung in Kants praktischer Metaphysik." In: *Kant-Studien* 91, pp. 385–394.
Guérin, Michel (1974): "Kant et l'ontologie analogique: Recherches sur le concept kantien d'analogie." In: *Revue de Metaphysique et de Morale* 79, pp. 516–548.
Guyer, Paul (Ed.) (1998): *Kant's Groundwork of the Metaphysics of Morals: Critical Essays*. New York: Rowman & Littlefield.
Guyer, Paul (2007): *Kant's Groundwork for the Metaphysics of Morals: A Reader's Guide*. London: Continuum.
Guyer, Paul (2010): "*Kant's Moral and Legal Philosophy* by Karl Ameriks and Otfried Höffe, eds." *Ethics* 120, pp. 820–826.
Harris, Sam (2010): *The Moral Landscape: How Science Can Determine Human Values*. New York: Free Press.
Hegel, Georg Wilhelm Friedrich (1970): *Über die wissenschaftlichen Behandlungen des Naturrechts, seine Stelle in der praktischen Philosophie und sein Verhältnis zu den positiven Rechtswissenschaften*. Werke in zwanzig Bänden 2. Frankfurt a.M.: Suhrkamp.
Hegel, Georg Wilhelm Friedrich (1970): *Phänomenologie des Geistes*. Werke in zwanzig Bänden 3. Frankfurt a.M.: Suhrkamp.

Henrich, Dieter (1989): "Kant's Notion of a Deduction and the Methodological Background of the First *Critique*." In: Förster, Eckart (Ed.): *Kant's Transcendental Deductions*. Stanford: Stanford University Press, pp. 29–46.

Herman, Barbara (1993): *The Practice of Moral Judgment*. Cambridge (MA), London: Harvard University Press.

Hesse, Mary (1966): *Models and Analogies in Science*. Notre Dame: Notre Dame University Press.

Höffe, Otfried (1977): "Kants kategorischer Imperativ als Kriterium des Sittlichen." In: *Zeitschrift für philosophische Forschung* 31, pp. 354–384.

Höffe, Otfried (2008): "Urteilskraft und Sittlichkeit. Ein moralischer Rückblick auf die dritte *Kritik*." In: Höffe, Otfried (Ed.): *Immanuel Kant. Kritik der Urteilskraft*. Berlin: Akademie Verlag, pp. 351–366.

Höffe, Otfried (2010): "Kants nichtempirische Verallgemeinerung: zum Rechtsbeispiel des falschen Versprechens." In: Höffe, Otfried (Ed.): *Kants Grundlegung zur Metaphysik der Sitten: Ein kooperativer Kommentar*. Frankfurt a.M.: Klostermann, pp. 206–333.

Höffe, Otfried (2011): "Die Form der Maximen als Bestimmungsgrund (4–6: 27–30)." In: Höffe, Otfried (Ed.): *Immanuel Kant. Kritik der praktischen Vernunft*. Berlin: Akademie Verlag, pp. 55–70.

Höffe, Otfried (2012): *Kants Kritik der praktischen Vernunft: Eine Philosophie der Freiheit*. München: C.H. Beck.

Horn, Christoph/Mieth, Corinna/Scarano, Nico (2007): "Kommentar." In: Horn, Christoph/Corinna Mieth/Nico Scarano (Eds.): *Immanuel Kant: Grundlegung zur Metaphysik der Sitten*. Frankfurt a.M.: Suhrkamp, pp. 105–343.

Hume, David (1935): *Hume's Dialogues Concerning Natural Religion*. Oxford: Clarendon Press.

Hume, David (1957): *An Inquiry Concerning the Principles of Morals*. Hendel, Charles W. (Ed.). Indianapolis, New York: The Liberal Arts Press.

Irrlitz, Gerd (2010): *Kant-Handbuch. Leben und Werk*. Second edition. Stuttgart, Weimar: Metzler.

Johnson, Gregory R. (Ed. and Trans.) (2002): *Kant on Swedenborg: Dreams of a Spirit-Seer and Other Writings*. Swedenborg Studies 15. West Chester (PA): Swedenborg Foundation.

Johnson, Mark (1985): "Imagination in Moral Judgment." In: *Philosophy and Phenomenological Research* 46, pp. 265–280.

Johnson, Mark (2007): *The Meaning of the Body: Aesthetics of Human Understanding*. Chicago: The University of Chicago Press.

Johnson, Mark (2008): "Philosophy's Debt to Metaphor." In: Gibbs, Raymond W., Jr. (Ed.): *The Cambridge Handbook to Metaphor and Thought*. New York: Cambridge University Press, pp. 39–53.

Kant, Emmanuel (1994): *Fondation de la métaphyisque des moeurs*. Renaut, Alain (Ed. and Trans.). Paris: Garnier Flammarion.

Klein, Hans-Dieter (1969): "Formale und materielle Prinzipien in Kants Ethik." In: *Kant-Studien* 60, pp. 183–197.

Kleingeld, Pauline (2010): "Moral consciousness and the 'fact of reason'." In: Reath, Andrews/Timmermann, Jens (Eds.): *Kant's Critique of Practical Reason: A Critical Guide*. Cambridge: Cambridge University Press, pp. 55–73.

Klubertanz, George Peter (1960): *St. Thomas Aquinas on Analogy*. Chicago: Loyola University Press.

Konhardt, Klaus (1979): *Die Einheit der Vernunft: Zum Verhältnis von theoretischer und praktischer Vernunft in der Philosophie Immanuel Kants.* Monographien zur Philosophischen Forschung 178. Regensburg: Forum Academicum.

Korsgaard, Christine M. (1996): "Kant's Formula of Universal Law." In: *Creating the Kingdom of Ends.* Cambridge (MA): Harvard University Press, pp. 77–105.

Krüger, Gerhard (1931): *Philosophie und Moral in der Kantischen Kritik.* Tübingen: Mohr (Siebeck).

Kuehn, Manfred (2002): *Kant: A Biography.* New York: Cambridge University Press.

Kühn, Manfred (2012): "§§ 57–60: Von der Grenzbestimmung der reinen Vernunft." In: Lyre, Holger/Oliver Schliemann (Eds.): *Kants Prolegomena: Ein kooperativer Kommentar.* Frankfurt a.M.: Klostermann, pp. 235–276.

Lakoff, George/Johnson, Mark (1999): *Philosophy in the Flesh: The Embodied Mind and Its Challenge to Western Thought.* New York: Basic Books.

Lakoff, George/Johnson, Mark (2003): *Metaphors We Live By. With a new Afterword.* Chicago, London: The University of Chicago Press.

Longuenesse, Béatrice (2005): "Moral Judgment as a Judgment of Reason." In: *Kant on the Human Standpoint.* New York: Cambridge University Press, pp. 236–264.

Louden, Robert B. (2000): *Kant's Impure Ethics: From Rational Beings to Human Beings.* New York, Oxford: Oxford University Press.

Louden, Robert B. (2009): "Making the law visible: the role of examples in Kant's ethics." In: Timmermann, Jens (Ed.): *Kant's Groundwork of the Metaphysics of Morals: A Critical Guide.* New York: Cambridge University Press, pp. 63–81.

Luf, Gerhard (1975): "Die "Typik der reinen praktischen Urteilskraft" und ihre Anwendung auf Kants Rechtslehre." In: *Wiener Jahrbuch für Philosophie* 8, pp. 54–71.

Makkreel, Rudolph A. (1990): *Imagination and Interpretation in Kant: The Hermeneutical Import of the Critique of Judgment.* Chicago: The University of Chicago Press.

Maly, Sebastian (2012). *Kant über die symbolische Erkenntnis Gottes.* Kantstudien-Ergänzungshefte 165. Berlin, Boston: De Gruyter.

Marty, François (1955): "La Typique du jugement pratique pur: La morale kantienne et son application aux cas particuliers." In: *Archives de Philosophie* 19, pp. 56–87.

Marty, François (1997): *La Naissance de la métaphysique chez Kant: Une étude sur la notion kantienne d'analogie.* Second edition. Paris: Beauchesne.

Mikhail, John (2011): *Elements of Moral Cognition: Rawls' Linguistic Analogy and the Cognitive Science of Moral and Legal Judgment.* New York: Cambridge University Press.

Mill, John Stuart (1998): *Utilitarianism.* Crisp, Roger (Ed.). Oxford Philosophical Texts. Oxford, New York: Oxford University Press.

"Models" (1998): In: *Routledge Encyclopedia of Philosophy.* London, New York: Routledge.

"Models and Analogy in Science" (1967): In: *The Encyclopedia of Philosophy.* New York, London: Collier-Macmillan.

Moore, A.W. (1988): "Aspects of the Infinite in Kant." In: *Mind: A Quarterly Review of Philosophy* 97, pp. 205–223.

Müller, Ernst (2001): "Kants Symbolbegriff in Ästhetik und Religionstheorie. Zum Ursrpung des Begriffs in den Träumen eines Geistesehers." In: Gerhardt, Volker/Rolf-Peter Horstmann/Ralph Schumacher (Eds.): *Kant und die Berliner Aufklärung. Akten des IX. Internationalen Kant-Kongresses.* Berlin, New York: De Gruyter, pp. 596–603.

Müller, Ernst (2004): *Ästhetische Religiosität und Kunstreligion in den Philosophien von der Aufklärung bis zum Ausgang des deutschen Idealismus.* Berlin: Akademie Verlag.

Mumbrú Mora, Alejandro (2009): "Sensibilización y Moralidad en Kant." In: *Eidos* 10, pp. 92–133.
Nell (O'Neill), Onora (1975): *Acting on Principle: An Essay on Kantian Ethics*. New York: Columbia University Press.
Nietzsche, Friedrich (1999): *Menschliches, Allzumenschliches*. Kritische Studienausgabe 2. Berlin, Boston: De Gruyter.
Nuyen, A.T (1989): "The Kantian Theory of Metaphor." In: *Philosophy and Rhetoric* 22, pp. 95–109.
O'Neill, Onora (1989): "Consistency in Action." In: *Constructions of Reason: Explorations of Kant's Practical Philosophy*. Cambridge: Cambridge University Press, pp. 81–104.
Otto, Rudolf (2004): *Das Heilige: Über das Irrationale in der Idee des Göttlichen und sein Verhältnis zum Rationalen*. Beck'sche Reihe. München: Beck.
Paton, H. J. (1947): *The Categorical Imperative: A Study in Kant's Moral Philosophy*. London: Hutchinson's University Library.
Philonenko, Alexis (1981): *L'Œuvre de Kant. La philosophie critique II. Morale et politique*. Second edition. Paris: Vrin.
Piché, Claude (1984): *Das Ideal: Ein Problem der Kantischen Ideenlehre*. Bonn: Bouvier, 1984.
Piché, Claude (1990): "Rousseau et Kant: À propos de la genèse de la théorie kantienne des idées." In: *Revue philosophique* 4, pp. 625–635.
Piché, Claude (2000): "Qu'est-ce qu'une 'analogie' de l'expérience?" In: Lafrance, Guy/Claude Piché/François Duchesneau (Eds.): *Kant actuel: Hommage à Pierre Laberge*. Montreal, Paris: Bellarmin & Vrin, pp. 217–232.
Piché, Claude (2003): "La Phénoménologie de l'expérience morale chez Kant." In: *Kairos* 22, pp. 123–150.
Piché, Claude (2013): "Kant et l'esprit de secte en philosophie." In: Bacin, Stefano/Alfredo Ferrarin/Claudio La Rocca/Margit Ruffing (Eds.): *Kant und die Philosophie in weltbürgerlicher Absicht. Akten des XI. Kant-Kongresses 2010*. Berlin, Boston: De Gruyter, pp. 691–702.
Pieper, Annemarie (1996): "Kant und die Methode der Analogie." In: Schönrich, Gerhard/Yushi Kato (Eds.): *Kant in der Diskussion der Moderne*. Frankfurt a.M.: Suhrkamp, pp. 92–112.
Pieper, Annemarie (2009): "On the Concept of an Object of Pure Practical Reason (Chapter 2 of the Analytic of Practical Reason)." In: Ameriks, Karl/Otfried Höffe (Eds.): *Kant's Moral and Legal Philosophy*. New York: Cambridge University Press, pp. 179–197.
Pieper, Annemarie (2011): "Zweites Hauptstück (57–71)." In: Höffe, Otfried (Ed.): *Immanuel Kant. Kritik der praktischen Vernunft*. Berlin: Akademie Verlag, pp. 101–116.
Pillow, Kirk (2000): *Sublime Understanding: Aesthetic Reflection in Kant and Hegel*. Cambridge (MA), London: MIT Press.
Pillow, Kirk (2001): "Jupiter's Eagle and the Despot's Hand Mill: Two Views on Metaphor in Kant." *Journal of Aesthetics and Art Criticism* 59, pp. 193–209.
Pinker, Steven (2007): *The Stuff of Thought: Language as a Window into Human Nature*. London: Penguin.
Pogge, Thomas (1998): "The Categorical Imperative." In: Guyer, Paul (Ed.): *Kant's Groundwork of the Metaphysics of Morals: Critical Essays*. New York: Rowman & Littlefield, pp. 189–213.
Rawls, John (1989): "Themes in Kant's Moral Philosophy." In: Förster, Eckart (Ed.): *Kant's Transcendental Deductions*. Stanford: Stanford University Press, pp. 81–113.

Rawls, John (1999): *A Theory of Justice*. Revised edition. Cambridge (MA): Harvard University Press.
Rawls, John (2000): *Lectures on the History of Moral Philosophy*. Herman, Barbara (Ed.). Cambridge (MA), London: Harvard University Press.
Reath, Andrews (2010): "Formal principles and the form of a law." In: Reath, Andrews/Jens Timmermann (Eds.): *A Critical Guide to Kant's Critique of Practical Reason*. New York: Cambridge University Press, pp. 31–54.
Recki, Birgit (2001a): *Ästhetik der Sitten. Die Affinität von ästhetischem Gefühl und praktischer Vernunft bei Kant*. Frankfurt a.M.: Klostermann.
Recki, Birgit (2001b): "Die Dialektik der ästhetischen Urteilskraft und die Methodenlehre des Geschmaks (§§ 55–60)." In: Höffe, Otfried (Ed.): *Immanuel Kant. Kritik der Urteilskraft*. Berlin: Akademie Verlag, pp. 189–210.
Renaut, Alain (1997): *Kant aujourd'hui*. Paris: Flammarion.
Ricoeur, Paul (1967): *The Symbolism of Evil*. Buchanan, Emerson (Trans.). Boston: Beacon.
Rousseau, Jean-Jacques (1964): *Julie, ou la nouvelle Héloïse*. Œuvres complètes II. Paris: Gallimard (La Pléiade).
Sala, Giovanni B. (2004): *Kants "Kritik der Praktischen Vernunft": Ein Kommentar*. Darmstadt: Wissenschaftliche Buchgesellschaft.
Schönecker, Dieter (2001): "Textvergessenheit in der Philosophiehistorie." In: Schönecker, Dieter/Thomas Zwenger (Eds.): *Kant verstehen / Understanding Kant: Über die Interpretation philosophischer Texte*. Darmstadt: Wissenschaftliche Buchgesellschaft, pp. 159–181.
Schopenhauer, Arthur (2007): *Über die Grundlage der Moral*. Welsen, Peter (Ed.). Philosophische Bibliothek 579. Hamburg: Meiner.
Schopenhauer, Arthur (2008): *Die Welt als Wille und Vorstellung*. Lütkehaus, Ludger (Ed.). Gesamtausgabe. Fourth edition. München: Deutscher Taschenbuch Verlag.
Schwartländer, Johannes (1968): *Der Mensch ist Person. Kants Lehre vom Menschen*. Stuttgart: Kohlhammer.
Schwartländer, Johannes (1981): "Sittliche Autonomie als Idee der endlichen Freiheit. Bemerkungen zum Prinzip der Autonomie im kritischen Idealismus Kants." In: *Theologische Quartalschrift* 161, pp. 20–33.
Schwartz, Maria (2006): *Der Begriff der Maxime bei Kant: Eine Untersuchung des Maximenbegriffs in Kants praktischen Philosophie*. Berlin: Lit Verlag.
Shabel, Lisa (1998): "Kant on the 'Symbolic Construction' of Mathematical Concepts." In: *Studies in the History and Philosophy of Science* 29, pp. 589–621.
Shabel, Lisa (2003): *Mathematics in Kant's Critical Philosophy: Reflections on Mathematical Practice*, Studies in Philosophy. New York: Routledge.
Shakespeare, William (1993): "The Tragedy of MacBeth." In: Cross, Wilbur L./Tucker Brooke (Eds.): *The Yale Shakespeare*. New York: Barnes & Noble.
Shell, Susan Meld (1980): *The Rights of Reason: A study of Kant's philosophy and politics*. Toronto, Buffalo, London: University of Toronto Press.
Showler, Ryan L. (2008): "Archetypal and Ectypal Ideals in Kant's Practical Philosophy." PhD Thesis, Loyola University.
Silber, John R. (1966): "Der Schematismus der praktischen Vernunft." In: *Kant-Studien* 56, pp. 253–273.
Silber, John R. (1974): "Procedural Formalism in Kant's Ethics." In: *Review of Metaphysics* 28, pp. 197–236.

Singer, Marcus (1961): *Generalization in Ethics*. New York: Alfred Knopf.
Sullivan, Roger J. (1989): *Immanuel Kant's Moral Theory*. New York: Cambridge University Press.
Sutherland, Daniel (2004): "Kant's Philosophy of Mathematics and the Greek Mathematical Tradition." In: *The Philosophical Review* 113, pp. 157–201.
Sutherland, Daniel (2006): "Kant on Arithmetic, Algebra, and the Theory of Proportions." In: *Journal of the History of Philosophy* 44, pp. 533–558.
"Symbol" (1984): In: Grimm, Jacob/Wilhelm Grimm (Eds.): *Deutsches Wörterbuch*. Munich: Deutscher Taschenbuch Verlag.
"Symbolisch" (1984): In: Grimm, Jacob/Wilhelm Grimm (Eds.): *Deutsches Wörterbuch*. Munich: Deutscher Taschenbuch Verlag.
Taylor, Charles (2007): "Modern Social Imaginaries." In: *A Secular Age*. Cambridge (MA), London: Harvard University Press, pp. 159–211.
Tetens, Holm (2006). *Kant's "Kritik der reinen Vernunft": Ein systematischer Kommentar*. Stuttgart: Reclam.
Timmermann, Jens (2007). *Kant's Groundwork of the Metaphysics of Morals: A Commentary*. Cambridge: Cambridge University Press.
Timmons, Mark (2006): "The Categorical Imperative and Universalizability." In: Horn, Christoph/Dieter Schönecker/Corinna Mieth (Eds.): *Groundwork for the Metaphysics of Morals*. Berlin, New York: De Gruyter, pp. 158–199.
Timmons, Mark (2012): *Moral Theory: An Introduction*. Second edition. Lanham (MD): Rowman & Littlefield.
Torralba, José M. (2007): "Facultad del juicio y aplicación de la ley moral en la filosofía de Kant." In: *Methodus. Revista Internacional de Filosofía Moderna / An International Journal for Modern Philosophy* 2, pp. 1–30.
"Typologie" (2009): In: Ueding, Gert (Ed.): *Historisches Wörterbuch der Rhetorik*. Tübingen: Niemeyer, pp. 841–858.
"Typos; Typologie" (1998): In: Ritter, Joachim/Karlfried Gründer (Eds.): *Historisches Wörterbuch der Philosophie*. Darmstadt: Wissenschaftliche Buchgesellschaft, pp. 1587–1607.
"τύπος" (1996): In: Liddel, Henry George/Robert Scott (Eds.): *A Greek-English Lexicon*. Revised and augmented edition. Oxford: Clarendon Press.
Vaihinger, Hans (1918): *Die Philosophie des Als Ob: System der theoretischen, praktischen und religiösen Fiktionen der Menschheit auf Grund eines idealistischen Positivismus; mit einem Anhang über Kant und Nietzsche*. Third edition. Leipzig: Meiner.
Vaihinger, Hans (1922): *Die Philosophie des Als Ob: System der theoretischen, praktischen und religiösen Fiktionen der Menschheit auf Grund eines idealistischen Positivismus; mit einem Anhang über Kant und Nietzsche*. Eighth edition. Leipzig: Meiner.
Vaihinger, Hans (2009): *The Philosophy of 'as if': A System of the Theoretical, Practical and Religious Fictions of Mankind*. C. K. Ogden (Trans.). Mansfield Centre (CT): Martino Publishing.
von Wolff-Metternich, Brigitta-Sophie (2004): "Sobre el papel del juicio práctico en la filosofia moral de Kant." In: *Anuario Filosófico. Doscientos Anos Después. Retornos Y Relecturas De Kant* 37, pp. 733–748.
Ware, Owen (2010): "Kant, Skepticism, and Moral Sensibility." PhD Thesis, University of Toronto.

Wehofsits, Anna (forthcoming): *Anthropologie und Moral: Affekte, Leidenschaften und Mitgefühl in Kants Ethik.* Quelle und Studien zur Philosophie. Berlin, Boston: De Gruyter.
Weil, Eric (1970): *Problèmes kantiens.* Second edition. Paris: Vrin.
Westra, Adam (2008): "Review of 'The Meaning of the Body: Aesthetics of Human Understanding' by Mark Johnson." In: *Ithaque* 2, pp. 163–168.
Westra, Adam (2009a): "Les Yeux grands fermés : une analyse du 'Traité de la Comédie' de Pierre Nicole." In: *Ithaque* 4, pp. 19–34.
Westra, Adam (2009b): "La *Critique de la raison pure*, une oeuvre inachevée." Masters Thesis, Université de Montréal.
Westra, Adam (2015): "*Kritik ist Pflicht:* La dimension éthique de la *Critique de la raison pure.*" In: Grapotte, Sophie/Margit Ruffing/Ricardo Terra (Eds.): *Kant – la raison pratique. Concepts et héritages.* Paris: Vrin, pp. 263–274.
Westra, Haijo (2007): "Augustine and Poetic Exegesis: The Encounter between Classical and Christian Strategies of Interpretation." In: Otten, Willemien/Karla Pollman (Eds.): *Poetry and Exegesis in Premodern Latin Christianity.* Leiden, Boston: Brill, pp. 11–28.
Willaschek, Markus, Jürgen Stolzenburg, Georg Mohr and Stefano Bacin (Eds.) (forthcoming): *Kant-Lexikon.* Berlin, Boston: De Gruyter.
Wood, Allen W. (2001): "What Dead Philosophers Mean." In: Schönecker, Dieter/Thomas Zwenger (Eds.): *Kant verstehen / Understanding Kant: Über die Interpretation philosophischer Texte.* Darmstadt: Wissenschaftliche Buchgesellschaft, pp. 272–301.
Wood, Allen W. (1999): *Kant's Ethical Thought.* Cambridge, New York: Cambridge University Press.
Zammito, John H. (1992): *The Genesis of Kant's Critique of Judgment.* Chicago, London: University of Chicago Press.
Zimmermann, Stefan (2011): *Kants 'Kategorien der Freiheit'.* Kantstudien-Ergänzungshefte 167. Berlin, Boston: De Gruyter.

Appendices

Appendix I : German text of the Typic chapter

Von der Typik der reinen praktischen Urtheilskraft
(*KpV* 5: 69–71; text based on Kant 2007a)

5: 67 Die Begriffe des Guten und Bösen bestimmen dem Willen zuerst ein Object. Sie stehen selbst aber unter einer praktischen Regel der Vernunft, welche, wenn sie reine Vernunft ist, den Willen *a priori* in Ansehung seines Gegenstandes bestimmt. Ob nun eine uns in der Sinnlichkeit mögliche Handlung der Fall sei, der unter der Regel stehe, oder nicht, dazu gehört praktische Urtheilskraft, wodurch dasjenige, was in der Regel allgemein (*in abstracto*) gesagt wurde, auf eine Handlung *in concreto* angewandt wird. Weil aber eine praktische Regel der reinen Vernunft erstlich, als praktisch, die Existenz eines Objects betrifft und zweitens, als praktische Regel der reinen Vernunft, Nothwendigkeit in Ansehung des Daseins der Handlung bei sich führt, mithin praktisches Gesetz ist und zwar |

5: 68 nicht Naturgesetz durch empirische Bestimmungsgründe, sondern ein Gesetz der Freiheit, nach welchem der Wille unabhängig von allem Empirischen (blos durch die Vorstellung eines Gesetzes überhaupt und dessen Form) bestimmbar sein soll, alle vorkommende Fälle zu möglichen Handlungen aber nur empirisch, d.i. zur Erfahrung und Natur gehörig, sein können: so scheint es widersinnisch, in der Sinnenwelt einen Fall antreffen zu wollen, der, da er immer so fern nur unter dem Naturgesetze steht, doch die Anwendung eines Gesetzes der Freiheit auf sich verstatte, und auf welchen die übersinnliche Idee des sittlich Guten, das darin *in concreto* dargestellt werden soll, angewandt werden könne. Also ist die Urtheilskraft der reinen praktischen Vernunft eben denselben Schwierigkeiten unterworfen, als die der reinen theoretischen, welche letztere gleichwohl, aus denselben zu kommen, ein Mittel zur Hand hatte: nämlich da es in Ansehung des theoretischen Gebrauchs auf Anschauungen ankam, darauf reine Verstandesbegriffe angewandt werden könnten, dergleichen Anschauungen (obzwar nur von Gegenständen der Sinne) doch *a priori*, mithin, was die Verknüpfung des Mannigfaltigen in denselben betrifft, den reinen Verstandesbegriffen *a priori* gemäß (als Schemate) gegeben werden können. Hingegen ist das sittlich Gute etwas dem Objecte nach Übersinnliches, für das also in keiner sinnlichen Anschauung etwas Correspondirendes gefunden werden kann, und die Urtheilskraft unter Gesetzen der reinen praktischen Vernunft scheint daher besonderen Schwierigkeiten unterworfen zu sein, die darauf beruhen, daß ein Gesetz der Freiheit auf

Handlungen als Begebenheiten, die in der Sinnenwelt geschehen und also so fern zur Natur gehören, angewandt werden soll.

Allein hier eröffnet sich doch wieder eine günstige Aussicht für die reine praktische Urtheilskraft. Es ist bei der Subsumtion einer mir in der Sinnenwelt möglichen Handlung unter einem reinen praktischen Gesetze nicht um die Möglichkeit der Handlung als einer Begebenheit in der Sinnenwelt zu thun; denn die gehört für die Beurtheilung des theoretischen Gebrauchs der Vernunft nach dem Gesetze der Causalität, eines reinen Verstandesbegriffs, für den sie ein Schema in der sinnlichen Anschauung hat. Die physische Causalität, oder die Bedingung, unter der sie stattfindet, gehört unter die Naturbegriffe, deren Schema transscendentale Einbildungskraft entwirft. Hier aber ist es nicht um das Schema eines Falles nach Gesetzen, sondern um das Schema (wenn dieses Wort hier schicklich ist) eines Gesetzes selbst zu thun, weil die Willensbestimmung (nicht die Handlung in Beziehung auf ihren Erfolg) durchs Gesetz allein, ohne einen anderen Bestimmungsgrund, den Begriff der Causalität an ganz andere Bedingungen bindet, als diejenige sind, welche die Naturverknüpfung ausmachen.

Dem Naturgesetze als Gesetze, welchem die Gegenstände sinnlicher Anschauung als solche unterworfen sind, muß ein Schema, d.i. ein allgemeines Verfahren der Einbildungskraft (den reinen Verstandesbegriff, den das Gesetz bestimmt, den Sinnen *a priori* darzustellen), correspondiren. Aber dem Gesetze der Freiheit (als einer gar nicht sinnlich bedingten Causalität) mithin auch dem Begriffe des unbedingt Guten kann keine Anschauung, mithin kein Schema zum Behuf seiner Anwendung *in concreto* untergelegt werden. Folglich hat das Sittengesetz kein anderes die Anwendung desselben auf Gegenstände der Natur vermittelndes Erkenntnißvermögen, als den Verstand (nicht die Einbildungskraft), welcher einer Idee der Vernunft nicht ein Schema der Sinnlichkeit, sondern ein Gesetz, aber doch ein solches, das an Gegenständen der Sinne *in concreto* dargestellt werden kann, mithin ein Naturgesetz, aber nur seiner Form nach, als Gesetz zum Behuf der Urtheilskraft unterlegen kann, und dieses können wir daher den Typus des Sittengesetzes nennen.

Die Regel der Urtheilskraft unter Gesetzen der reinen praktischen Vernunft ist diese: Frage dich selbst, ob die Handlung, die du vorhast, wenn sie nach einem Gesetze der Natur, von der du selbst ein Theil wärest, geschehen sollte, sie du wohl als durch deinen Willen möglich ansehen könntest. Nach dieser Regel beurtheilt in der That jedermann Handlungen, ob sie sittlich gut oder böse sind. So sagt man: Wie, wenn ein jeder, | wo er seinen Vortheil zu schaffen glaubt, sich erlaubte, zu betrügen, oder befugt hielte, sich das

Leben abzukürzen, so bald ihn ein völliger Überdruß desselben befällt, oder anderer Noth mit völliger Gleichgültigkeit ansähe, und du gehörtest mit zu einer solchen Ordnung der Dinge, würdest du darin wohl mit Einstimmung deines Willens sein? Nun weiß ein jeder wohl: daß, wenn er sich ingeheim Betrug erlaubt, darum eben nicht jedermann es auch thue, oder, wenn er unbemerkt lieblos ist, nicht sofort jedermann auch gegen ihn es sein würde; daher ist diese Vergleichung der Maxime seiner Handlungen mit einem allgemeinen Naturgesetze auch nicht der Bestimmungsgrund seines Willens. Aber das letztere ist doch ein Typus der Beurtheilung der ersteren nach sittlichen Principien. Wenn die Maxime der Handlung nicht so beschaffen ist, daß sie an der Form eines |

5: 70 Naturgesetzes überhaupt die Probe hält, so ist sie sittlich unmöglich. So urtheilt selbst der gemeinste Verstand; denn das Naturgesetz liegt allen seinen gewöhnlichsten, selbst den Erfahrungsurtheilen immer zum Grunde. Er hat es also jederzeit bei Hand, nur daß er in Fällen, wo die Causalität aus Freiheit beurtheilt werden soll, jenes Naturgesetz blos zum Typus eines Gesetzes der Freiheit macht, weil er, ohne etwas, was er zum Beispiele im Erfahrungsfalle machen könnte, bei Hand zu haben, dem Gesetze einer reinen praktischen Vernunft nicht den Gebrauch in der Anwendung verschaffen könnte.

Es ist also auch erlaubt, die Natur der Sinnenwelt als Typus einer intelligibelen Natur zu brauchen, so lange ich nur nicht die Anschauungen, und was davon abhängig ist, auf diese übertrage, sondern blos die Form der Gesetzmäßigkeit überhaupt (deren Begriff auch im gemeinsten Vernunftgebrauche stattfindet, aber in keiner anderen Absicht, als blos zum reinen praktischen Gebrauche der Vernunft *a priori* bestimmt erkannt werden kann) darauf beziehe. Denn Gesetze als solche sind so fern einerlei, sie mögen ihre Bestimmungsgründe hernehmen, woher sie wollen.

Übrigens, da von allem Intelligibelen schlechterdings nichts als (vermittelst des moralischen Gesetzes) die Freiheit und auch diese nur, so fern sie eine von jenem unzertrennliche Voraussetzung ist, und ferner alle intelligibele Gegenstände, auf welche uns die Vernunft nach Anleitung jenes Gesetzes etwa noch führen möchte, wiederum für uns keine Realität weiter haben, als zum Behuf desselben Gesetzes und des Gebrauches der reinen praktischen Vernunft, diese aber zum Typus der Urtheilskraft die Natur (der reinen Verstandesform derselben nach) zu gebrauchen berechtigt und auch benöthigt ist: so dient die gegenwärtige Anmerkung dazu, um zu verhüten, daß, was blos zur Typik der Begriffe gehört, nicht zu den Begriffen selbst gezählt werde. Diese also als Typik der Urtheilskraft bewahrt vor dem Empirism der praktischen Vernunft, der die praktischen Begriffe des Guten und Bösen blos in Erfahrungsfolgen (der sogenannten Glückseligkeit) setzt, obzwar diese und die unendlichen nützlichen Folgen eines durch Selbstliebe bestimmten Willens, wenn dieser sich selbst zugleich zum allgemeinen Naturgesetze machte, allerdings zum ganz angemessenen Typus für das sittlich Gute dienen kann, aber mit diesem doch nicht einerlei ist. Eben dieselbe Typik bewahrt auch vor dem Mysticism der praktischen Vernunft, welcher das, was nur zum Symbol diente, zum Schema macht, |

5: 71 d.i. wirkliche und doch nicht sinnliche Anschauungen (eines unsichtbaren Reichs Gottes) der Anwendung der moralischen Begriffe unterlegt und ins Überschwengliche hinausschweift. Dem Gebrauche der moralischen Begriffe ist blos der Rationalism der Urtheilskraft angemessen, der von der sinnlichen Natur nichts weiter nimmt, als was auch reine Vernunft für sich denken kann, d.i. die Gesetzmäßigkeit, und in die übersinnliche nichts hinein trägt, als was umgekehrt sich durch Handlungen in der Sinnenwelt nach der formalen Regel eines Naturgesetzes überhaupt wirklich darstellen läßt. Indessen ist die Verwahrung vor dem Empirism der praktischen Vernunft viel wichtiger und anrathungswürdiger, weil der Mysticism sich doch noch mit der Reinigkeit und Erhabenheit des moralischen Gesetzes zusammen verträgt und außerdem es nicht eben natürlich und der gemeinen Denkungsart angemessen ist, seine Einbildungskraft bis zu übersinnlichen Anschauungen anzuspannen, mithin auf dieser Seite die Gefahr nicht so allgemein ist; da hingegen der Empirism die Sittlichkeit in Gesinnungen (worin doch, und nicht blos in Handlungen, der hohe Werth besteht, den sich die Menschheit durch sie verschaffen kann und soll) mit der Wurzel ausrottet und ihr ganz etwas anderes, nämlich ein empirisches Interesse, womit die Neigungen überhaupt unter sich Verkehr treiben, statt der Pflicht unterschiebt, überdem auch eben darum mit allen Neigungen, die (sie mögen einen Zuschnitt bekommen, welchen sie wollen), wenn sie zur Würde eines obersten praktischen Princips erhoben werden, die Menschheit degradiren, und da sie gleichwohl der Sinnesart aller so günstig sind, aus der Ursache weit gefährlicher ist als alle Schwärmerei, die niemals einen daurenden Zustand vieler Menschen ausmachen kann.

Appendix II: English translation of the Typic chapter

On The Typic of *the* Pure Practical *Power of* Judgment
(*KpV* 5: 69–71; modified translation based on Kant 1996a)

5: 67 The concepts of good and evil first determine an object for the will. They themselves, however, stand under a practical rule of reason which, if it is pure reason, determines the will a priori with respect to its object. Now, whether an action possible for us in sensibility is or is not a case that stands under the rule **concerns** the practical **power of** judgment, by which what is said in the rule universally (*in abstracto*) is applied to an action *in concreto*. But a practical rule of reason *first*, as *practical*, concerns the existence of an object, and *second*, as a *practical rule* of pure reason, brings with it necessity with respect to the existence of an action and is thus a practical law, |

5: 68 not a natural law through empirical grounds of determination but a law of freedom in accordance with which the will is to be determinable independently of anything empirical (merely through the representation of a law in general and its form); however, all cases of possible actions that occur can only be empirical, that is, belong to experience and nature; hence, it seems absurd to want to find in the sensible world a case which, though as such it stands only under the laws of nature, yet **would admit** of the application to it of a law of freedom and to which there could be applied the supersensible **Idea** of the morally good, which is to be exhibited in it *in concreto*. Thus the power of judgment of pure practical reason is subject to the very same difficulties as those of pure theoretical reason, though the latter had means at hand **for getting out of** these difficulties, namely that with respect to its theoretical use it depended upon intuitions to which pure concepts of the understanding could be applied, and such intuitions (though only of objects of the senses) can be given a priori (as *schemata*) conformably with pure concepts of the understanding. On the other hand, the morally good as an object is something supersensible, so that nothing corresponding to it can be found in any sensible intuition; and **the power of judgment** under laws of pure practical reason seems, therefore, to be subject to special difficulties having their source in this: that a law of freedom is to [be] applied to actions **qua** events that take place in the sensible world and so, to this extent, belong to nature.
But here again a favourable prospect opens for **the** pure practical **power of**

judgment. Subsumption of an action possible to me in the sensible world under a *pure practical law* does not concern the possibility of the *action* as an event in the sensible world; for it belongs to the theoretical use of reason to appraise that possibility in accordance with the law of causality, a pure concept of the understanding for which reason has a *schema* in sensible intuition. Physical causality, or the condition under which it takes place, belongs among [the] concepts of nature, whose schema transcendental imagination sketches. Here, however, we have to do not with the schema of a case in accordance with laws but with the schema of a law itself (if the word 'schema' is appropriate here), |

5: 69 since the *determination of the will* (not the action with reference to its result) through the law alone without any other determining ground connects the concept of causality to conditions quite other than those which constitute natural connection.

To a natural law, as a law to which objects of sensible intuition as such are subject, there must correspond a schema, that is, a universal procedure of the imagination (by which it presents a priori to the senses the pure concept of the understanding which the law determines). **But no intuition, and hence no schema, can be put under the law of freedom (as that of a causality not at all sensibly conditioned), nor consequently under the concept of the unconditioned good, for their application *in concreto*.** Thus the moral law has no cognitive faculty other than the understanding (not the imagination) by means of which it can be applied to objects of nature, and what the understanding can put under an idea of reason is not a *schema* of sensibility but a law, such a law, however, as can be presented *in concreto* in objects of the senses and hence a law of nature, though only as to its form; this law is what the understanding can put under an idea of reason on behalf of **the power of** judgment, and we can, accordingly, call it the *type* of the moral law.

The rule of **the power of** judgment under laws of pure practical reason is this: *Ask yourself whether, if the action you propose were to take place by a law of the nature of which you were yourself a part, you could indeed regard it as possible through your will.* Everyone does, in fact, appraise actions as morally good or evil by this rule. Thus one says: if *everyone* permitted himself to deceive when he believed it to be to his advantage, or considered himself authorized to shorten his life as soon as he was thoroughly weary of it, or looked with complete indifference on the needs of others, and if you belonged to such an order of things, would you be in it with the assent of your will? Now everyone knows very well that if he permits himself to deceive secretly it does not follow that everyone else does so, or that if, unobserved, he is hard-hearted everyone would not straightaway be so toward him; accordingly, this comparison of the maxim of his actions with a universal law of nature is also not the determining ground of his will. Such a law is, nevertheless, a *type* for the appraisal of maxims in accordance with moral principles. If the maxim of the action is not so constituted that it can stand the test as to the form of a |

5: 70 law of nature in general, then it is morally impossible. This is how even the most common understanding judges; for the law of nature always lies at the basis of its most **ordinary judgments**,[494] even those of experience. Thus it has the law of nature always at hand, only that in cases where causality from freedom is to be appraised it makes that *law of nature* merely the type of a *law of freedom*, because without having at hand something which it could make an example in a case of experience, it could not provide use in application for the law of a pure practical reason.

Hence it is also permitted to use *the nature of the sensible world* as the *type* of an *intelligible nature*, provided that I do not carry over into the latter intuitions and what depends on them but refer to it **merely** the *form of lawfulness* in general (the concept of which occurs even in the most common use of reason, although it cannot be determinately cognized a priori for any purpose other than **merely** the pure practical use of reason). For to this extent laws as such are the same, no matter **where** they derive their determining grounds **from.**

Furthermore, since of all the intelligible **absolutely** nothing **is cognized** except freedom (by means of the moral law), and even this only insofar as it is a presupposition inseparable from that law; and since, moreover, all intelligible objects to which reason might lead us under the guidance of that law have in turn no reality for us except on behalf of that law and of the use of pure practical reason, although reason is entitled and even required to use nature (in the understanding's pure form of nature) as the *type* of judgment; the present remark will serve to prevent reckoning among concepts themselves that which belongs **merely** to the *typic* of concepts. This, then, as the typic of judgment, guards against *empiricism* of practical reason, which places the practical concepts of good and evil merely in experiential consequences (so-called happiness), although happiness and the endless useful consequences of a will determined by self-love, if this will at the same time made itself into a universal law of nature, can certainly serve as a quite suitable type for the morally good but is still not identical with it. The same

---

494 Deleted „ordinary ~~moral~~ judgments"

typic also guards against *mysticism* of practical reason, which makes what served only as a *symbol* into a *schema*, |
that is, puts under the application of moral concepts real but not sensible intuitions (of an invisible kingdom of God) and strays into the transcendent. Only *rationalism* of **the power of** judgment is suitable for the use of moral concepts, since it takes from sensible nature nothing more than what pure reason can also think for itself, that is, conformity with law, and transfers into the supersensible nothing but what can, conversely, be really exhibited by actions in the sensible world in accordance with a formal rule of a law of nature in general. However, it is much more important and advisable to guard against *empiricism* of practical reason, since *mysticism* is still compatible with the purity and sublimity of the moral law and, besides, it is not natural and not in keeping with the common way of thinking to strain one's imagination to supersensible intuitions, so that the danger from this side is not so general; empiricism, on the contrary, destroys at its root the morality of dispositions (in which, and not merely in actions, consists the high worth that humanity can and ought to procure for itself through morality), and substitutes for it something quite different, namely in place of duty an empirical interest, with which the inclinations generally are secretly leagued; and empiricism, moreover, being on this account allied with the inclinations, which (no matter what fashion they put on) degrade humanity when they are raised to the dignity of a supreme practical principle and which are, nevertheless, so favorable to everyone's way of feeling, is for that reason much more dangerous than any enthusiasm, which can never constitute a lasting condition of any great number of people.

Index of names

Adorno, Theodor   111, 118, 205
Aquinas, St. Thomas   16, 151, 181, 195–197, 225f.
Aristotle   25, 196, 200
Augustine, St.   166

Beck, Jacob Sigismund   4f., 11, 72, 113–115.

Cassirer, Ernst   3, 57, 71, 135f., 166, 174, 178f., 205, 208, 213, 231–233
Chomsky, Noam   123

Darwin, Charles   192

Euclid   188

Freud, Sigmund   134

Gadamer, Hans-Georg   176f., 198, 228, 230
Goethe, Johann Wolfgang von   179

Hegel, Georg Wilhelm Friedrich   104
Hölderlin, Johann Christian Friedrich   179

Humboldt, Wilhelm von   179
Hume, David   79, 186

Kosegarten, Gotthard Ludwig   3f., 19

Lessing, Gotthold Ephraim   157

Macbeth   163f., 168
Mendelssohn, Moses   155
Mill, John Stuart   92, 96–98, 218

Nicole, Pierre   166
Nietzsche, Friedrich   177

Pinker, Steven   180
Plato   169f.

Rawls, John   3, 5, 77, 80, 83f., 86, 88, 105–113, 115, 205, 212, 219, 228
Rousseau, Jean-Jacques   118, 169f.

Schiller, Johann Christoph Friedrich von   179
Schlösser, Johann Georg   134
Schopenhauer, Arthur   118, 234
Shakespeare, William   163
Swedenborg, Emmanuel   132f., 153–155, 229

Subject index

Absolute 1, 16, 142, 146, 160, 180, 182–185, 191, 193, 197, 199–201, 203f., 210, 212, 214, 224–226, 257
Aesthetic idea 140, 156, 173, 175–178, 224, 230
Algebra 157, 188
Analogy
– and mystical symbolism 152–156, 228f.
– and the Schematism 13, 51f., 68, 141, 143–146, 217
– and symbolic anthropomorphism 16, 182–204, 208–210, 224–227, 229f.
– and symbolic hypotyposis 16, 70, 143–146, 149–152, 159–162, 171, 175–177, 199–203, 208, 214, 223, 226, 230f.
– and the Typic 2, 6, 14–16, 61f., 68, 70–72, 81f., 87, 90, 101, 115, 120–123, 136, 143–146, 149–152, 159–162, 171, 204–210, 213f., 217f., 220–227, 230f., 235f.
– analogy of attribution 151, 195–198, 225f.
– analogy of proportionality 195–197, 225f.
– inductive analogy 186
– mathematical analogy 188f.
– philosophical analogy 186, 189, 198, 207, 225f.
Art 39, 57, 64, 118, 122, 128, 134, 142, 151, 156f., 177f.
Artisan example 183f., 189, 191, 202, 225
As if (*als ob*) 3, 69, 74, 82, 84–86, 90f., 99, 107f., 111–113, 117, 183–185, 189, 191f., 202, 212, 224f., 230
Aufklärung 134, 156, 165, 236
Autonomy 63, 65, 111, 129, 135, 202

Beauty 6, 11, 140, 142, 151, 174–176, 199, 231
Body with a soul example 146, 199, 201

Canon of moral appraisal 14, 76–78, 81, 83, 85, 88, 105, 218
Casuistry 149
Catechism 149, 156

Categorical Imperative (*see also* 'Moral law') 22, 36, 77f., 83, 90–92, 96f., 99, 102, 106–113, 116, 124, 141, 145, 147, 206, 219
– CI-Procedure 106–113
Causality
– free/supersensible 1, 28–31, 33f., 42, 48–50, 61, 117, 120–122, 205–207, 219f., 235, 256f.
– natural/physical 1, 13, 28–31, 33f., 47–50, 54f., 57f., 60f., 65, 81, 99, 103, 120–122, 126f., 161, 190, 205–209, 212, 216f., 219f., 222–224, 235, 256f.
– specific (teleological or mechanical) 99, 146, 160f., 199–203, 223, 225
Cognition
– faculties 24, 38f., 53–55, 67, 95, 119
– moral/practical 123f., 203f.
– theoretical 37–39, 50f., 53, 73, 121–123, 128, 157, 181–186, 190–194, 201, 203, 216
– other kinds 123, 153, 172, 194f., 195–198, 229
Common understanding 2, 15, 38, 68, 112, 117–124, 128, 136, 147, 167–170, 212, 220, 222, 224, 226, 235, 257
Communicability 165, 221, 236
Consequentialist interpretation 96–99, 104, 218
Contradiction in conception 77, 86–88, 103f., 109, 111, 125, 219
Contradiction in volition (contradiction in the will) 77, 86–88, 103, 109f., 125
Counterfactual – *see under* 'Nature'
Courtier example 114f.
Creed 156

Deed 48f., 79, 135, 163f., 216
Deism 182
Deposit example 103f., 129
Despotic state example 146, 160, 199f., 202
Dogmatism 191, 193, 211, 225, 227
– dogmatic anthropomorphism 150, 182, 190, 193, 224

Dualism 2, 232f.
Duty 24, 77f., 80, 90, 101–104, 114, 119, 123, 128f., 135, 141, 165–167, 175, 258

Empiricism 2, 15, 21, 68, 99, 111, 125–127, 129–131, 133, 165, 193f., 211–213, 219f., 225, 227, 233, 257f.
End(s) – *see under* 'Teleology'
Enthusiasm – *see 'Schwärmerei'*
Epistemology/epistemological 10, 119, 143, 181, 183–185, 192f., 196, 198, 204, 212, 225f.
Esotericism 134f., 155f., 230
Evil (*das sittlich Böse*) 1, 12, 19–27, 29f., 32, 50, 59, 75–77, 81f., 85, 88f., 92f., 95f., 109f., 117, 119, 126f., 129f., 135, 141, 148, 162f., 165, 167, 172, 206, 210, 212, 215, 220, 224, 227, 255–257
Example (*Beispiel*) 119–124, 168–170, 224
Exceptions 58, 78–82, 87f., 105, 115, 121f., 124f., 128, 152, 205f., 220, 227, 235f.

False negatives 113–115, 219
False positives 115, 219
False promise example 85–87, 98, 100, 108, 112f.,
False testimony example 87
Feeling
– affect 165–167
– apathy 166f.
– moral feeling – *see under* 'Morality'
– way of feeling (*Sinnesart*) 129f., 133, 258
Fiction (*see also* 'As if') 69, 74f., 165, 218
Finitude 1, 22, 26, 35, 38–43, 47f., 63, 65, 88, 130, 141, 149, 151, 183, 194f., 211, 214–216, 222
FLN (Formula of the Law of Nature/Law of Nature Formula) 5, 11, 90f., 104, 145, 204, 206, 218
Formalism (empty) 1, 35f., 44, 79f., 141, 150f., 174, 182
Formula of Humanity 36
Freedom (metaphysical) 28–32, 231–236
– Free causality – *see under* 'Causality'
– Law of freedom 14, 27–33, 42, 48–50, 72, 75, 117, 120, 122, 142, 148, 152, 161, 203–208, 212, 218, 235, 255–257

Generality (as opposed to universality) 78–80, 127
Genius 10, 134, 155, 176, 178
God 15, 40, 70f., 101, 131, 133, 135, 145, 150, 154f., 169, 175, 181–184, 189–193, 195–198, 202, 205, 209, 220, 225, 229, 233, 258
– invisible kingdom of 101, 131, 133, 154, 229, 258
Good (*das sittlich Gute*) 1, 12, 15, 19–30, 32, 41–43, 45f., 48, 50, 59, 65, 75–77, 81f, 85, 88f., 92f., 95f., 109f., 113, 117, 119f., 126f., 129–131, 141f., 148, 150f., 160, 165–167, 169, 171f., 174f., 209f., 212, 215f., 220f., 224, 231, 255–257
Grammar example 122f.

Handmill example 146, 160f., 199–202
Happiness 15, 96f., 99, 126–128, 130f., 135, 212, 219f., 233, 257
Heteronomy 15, 92, 98, 118, 129, 135, 166, 212, 220, 233
Heuristic 15, 89, 117, 124f., 129, 144, 162, 220

Ideas of reason 1f., 13–16, 27, 37–48, 52, 59, 61f., 65–68, 75, 91, 120f., 132–135, 140–144, 146, 149f., 160, 170, 173, 190, 194, 201, 209f., 213f., 216–218, 220–222, 227, 229f., 235, 255, 258
Idealism (absolute) 1
Ill-being (*das Übel*) 21, 126f.
Image (*Bild*) 1f., 44, 46, 69f., 75, 140f., 143, 145, 147, 153–157, 159f., 162, 167–171, 174f., 177f., 184, 189f., 197, 200f., 203, 213f., 218, 221, 223–225, 230, 232
Imagination 4, 13, 39, 45–49, 51–55, 59–61, 70, 130, 133, 141, 143, 147, 151f., 154f., 158–160, 162, 164f., 167f., 172–174, 176–178, 200, 209, 216, 223, 229–231, 256, 258
– moral imagination/mental theatre 141–143, 162–167, 172, 223
Indifference example 75, 82f., 87f., 107, 109f., 256
Infinity 121, 131, 173, 176, 195, 231f., 232, 235

Intellectual intuition   1, 39, 132, 183
Intelligible realm   39, 41, 66, 131, 194, 203, 208, 210, 212f., 225–227, 229

Kingdom of Ends – *see under* 'Teleology'
Kingdom of Nature – *see under* 'Teleology'

Lawfulness (*Gesetzmässigkeit*)   13f., 22, 36, 51f., 56–61, 66–68, 70, 72f., 75, 102, 115, 119, 136, 145, 207–210, 212f., 217f., 230, 234f., 257
Law
– law of freedom – *see under* 'Freedom' and 'Moral law'
– law of nature – *see under* 'Nature' and 'Type$_1$'
Logical interpretation   103–105, 112, 219
Lying example   23, 31, 47, 84, 92, 117, 120, 123, 176, 182f., 194, 201, 204, 257

Masturbation example   101
Maxim   2–4, 12, 14, 22f., 25, 34–37, 51f., 62, 69, 76–91, 93, 95, 97–106, 108–116, 120, 124f., 128, 130, 143, 147, 149f., 162–164, 167f., 170, 172, 179, 205f., 210, 212, 217–221, 224, 253, 257
Mediation   2, 13f., 26, 46, 50–52, 59, 61f., 65f., 68, 72f., 75, 89, 133, 143, 145, 152, 216–218, 221, 223, 230, 234f.
Mental theatre – *see under* 'Imagination'
Metaphor   145, 162, 172, 175, 181, 194, 200
Metaphysics   2, 5, 11, 28–31, 61, 101, 124, 131f., 147, 149, 153, 155, 169, 183, 192, 194, 197f., 206, 228f., 231f., 236
Morality   1, 6, 11f., 15, 22, 25, 43, 75, 79, 96, 98, 102f., 118, 125f., 129, 134f., 140, 142–145, 151, 162, 164f., 167, 169, 171, 174, 178, 199, 213, 216, 220–222, 228, 231–236, 258
– moral appraisal (*see also* 'practical judgment')   1f., 12–15, 19, 22–28, 30–34, 36, 38, 42–46, 48, 50–52, 59, 62, 69, 75–78, 80, 84f., 88–90, 94f., 99, 101f., 104f., 107, 109f., 118–129, 141f., 147, 151f., 160, 162, 164–172, 179, 205, 210–212, 215–220, 222–224, 226, 233, 235
– moral deliberation   148, 172
– moral didactics   149
– moral disposition   126, 150, 165, 212, 220
– moral feeling (respect)   78f., 86, 92, 135, 164–168
– moral law (*see also* 'Categorical Imperative')   1–4, 6, 12–15, 19–26, 28–36, 38, 41–43, 45f., 48, 51–53, 59–63, 69f., 72f., 76, 78–81, 86, 89–91, 95, 103, 113f., 118, 120–122, 132f., 140–145, 147f., 150, 152, 160–162, 166f., 169, 171–175, 179, 205–207, 209f., 215–217, 220–222, 224, 226f., 232–236, 256–258
– moral motivation   15, 135, 165f., 168, 221
– moral vocation   14, 63, 75
Mysticism (*see also* '*Schwärmerei*')   2, 4, 15, 40, 68, 118, 125, 129, 131–135, 153, 193f., 211, 213, 220, 225, 227, 229, 233, 254, 258

Nature
– actual/particular   113–116, 219
– counterfactual   2, 14, 62, 82f., 85–88, 91, 98, 107, 109, 218
– different senses of   56–58
– human nature   39, 99f., 133, 164, 232
– law of nature   2f., 6, 13–15, 27, 30, 36, 49f., 53, 56–63, 65, 68–70, 76f., 81–91, 95, 99–101, 103, 105, 107–109, 111–114, 116f., 120–123, 125, 130, 135, 142, 144f., 147, 159, 161, 167–169, 205–207, 209–212, 217, 219–224, 226f., 230, 234f., 255–258
– metaphysical relation to morality   28–32, 231–236
– *natura archetypa*   14, 51, 63–69, 75, 115, 136, 210f., 218, 227, 235
– *natura ectypa*   14, 63–68, 75, 136, 218
– *natura formaliter spectata*   13f., 56, 58, 60, 63, 65–69, 73, 75, 103, 123, 144, 206–208, 210, 217–219, 227, 235
– natural necessity   28f., 31–33, 215
– *natura materialiter spectata*   56, 61, 66f.
– unnaturalness   163
Normative-descriptive distinction   32–36

Subject index

Object of pure practical reason (*see also* 'Good' and 'Evil') 11f., 19–22, 32, 49, 59, 75, 89, 126, 148, 215
Ontology 2, 31, 43, 65, 142, 151, 154, 195, 197, 221f.

Pain 21, 126f., 129, 173
Pedagogy 25, 149
Phronêsis 25, 149, 222
Pleasure 126f., 129, 131, 166, 175, 212, 228
Poetry 16, 171, 175f., 178, 196, 200, 224
Politics 111, 135
Power of judgment
– determining power of judgment 16, 24f., 28, 42, 94f., 161, 169, 201, 203 223, 226
– practical power of judgment 1f., 3, 25, 11–13, 19, 23, 25, 27, 32–35, 37f., 42f., 46, 48–52, 59, 76, 89f., 127, 131, 136, 142f., 148, 151f., 204, 210f., 215–217, 222, 255f.
– reflecting power of judgment 16, 24f., 94f., 146, 148, 154f., 161, 168, 199, 201–203, 215, 218, 223, 226, 230
– theoretical power of judgment 13, 23, 34f., 37f., 43, 45, 48, 50f., 127, 143, 216
Protective functions
– of the typic 2, 125–136, 211–213, 220f., 225, 227, 232
– of symbolic anthropomorphism 180, 193–195

Rational agency interpretation 76, 98, 104–116, 124f., 218–220
Rational agents 20, 77, 104–116, 124f., 215, 218–220
Rationalism 2, 14–16, 75, 79, 127f., 131, 133, 135f., 169, 212–214, 218, 221, 225, 227–231, 234f., 254, 258
Reason
– practical 1, 3, 11f., 19–22, 27f., 33–35, 37, 42, 45, 49f., 75, 82, 87, 89, 92, 99, 120, 125f., 129–133, 136, 148f., 164, 166, 168, 172, 203, 205, 215, 219, 232–234, 255–258
– relation to finitude 26, 38–41, 183
– theoretical 37f., 45, 47–49, 127, 204, 211, 213, 227, 229, 233, 255f.

Receptivity (*see also* 'Sensibility') 39, 53, 165f.
Religion 4, 149f., 190, 193, 228f.
Representational mismatch 37–44
Respect – *see* 'Moral feeling'

Scepticism 193, 211f., 225, 227
Schematism 2, 4, 6, 11, 14, 37f., 45–48, 50–52, 58, 61f., 65, 122, 143f., 149, 152, 171f., 216f., 222f., 229
– 'schema of a law itself' 49–53, 60, 152, 217, 256
Schwärmerei (*see also* 'Mysticism') 39, 129, 132f., 136, 174, 194, 213f., 229, 233, 254
Scriptural exegesis 64, 70, 222
Sensibility (*see also* 'Receptivity') 1f., 23, 26, 34, 37–41, 46f., 53–56, 59f., 62, 73, 126, 133, 141, 147, 159, 166, 173, 177, 182, 190, 200, 208, 216, 255f.
Spirit 132, 152–155, 176, 218, 228f., 232, 236
Spontaneity 40, 47, 53f.
Sublime 16, 133, 140, 145, 156, 164, 170, 173f., 209, 224, 258
Subsumption 1, 12–14., 23f., 26–28, 34f., 37f., 42f., 45–52, 59, 88f., 95, 127, 150, 152, 210, 215–217, 256
Suicide example 83, 100
Supersensible
– subjective vs. objective senses 40f.
– supersensible representations – *see* 'Ideas of reason'
– supersensible intuition (*see also* 'intellectual intuition') 39, 48, 133, 194, 258
– supersensible nature – *see* 'Natura archetypa'
Symbolic anthropomorphism 4, 7, 10–12, 15f., 139, 158f., 180–185, 189–195, 198–205, 208–211, 213f., 224–227, 229f.
Symbolic hypotyposis 4–7, 10, 12, 15f., 139f., 146, 148–153, 155–161, 171–175, 177–181, 198–203, 208, 214, 221–224, 226, 230

Synthesis
- figurative synthesis   47, 52, 216
- intellectual synthesis   13, 39, 54 f., 60, 67, 70, 75, 159, 209, 217, 223

Teleology
- end(s)   7, 36 f., 49, 53, 71 f., 84–86, 100, 102–104, 106, 108 f., 111, 125, 128, 166, 173, 175, 219
- Kingdom of Ends   71, 101, 145, 205
- Kingdom of Nature   71, 145, 205
- teleological causality   201–203, 208
- teleological interpretation   14, 69, 71–73, 99–104, 111, 145, 208, 218 f.
Theism   182, 190, 193, 204
Thought experiment   2, 14, 62, 69, 81–89, 93, 97, 105–117, 124 f., 147, 162, 211, 217–220
Type (*Typus*)
- *túpos* (etymology)   9, 14, 64, 66, 69 f., 162, 218
- Type$_1$ (law of nature)   16, 59–63, 67 f., 103, 145, 159, 161, 207, 209 f., 219, 223, 227
- Type$_2$ (*natura formaliter spectata*)   14, 16, 63, 65–69, 71–75, 103, 115, 136, 145, 159, 161, 207–211, 218 f., 223, 227
- Type$_3$ (happiness)   15, 130 f., 145, 212, 220
Typic (*Typik*)
- Typic-procedure   14 f., 25, 75–78, 81–102, 104–108, 111–119, 124 f., 128, 136, 147, 162, 204 f., 208, 211 f., 218–220, 222 f., 226 f.
- Typification   14, 16, 61 f., 68, 91, 95, 101, 124, 140, 145–147, 152, 159–161, 163, 179, 204, 208, 217, 222 f., 227

Unconscious representations   120, 122 f., 220
Universality   1, 22, 44, 52, 61, 77–82, 87, 98, 104 f., 111, 114, 121, 125, 127, 130, 147, 168, 175, 207, 219, 220, 235
- aesthetic universality   121, 235
- strict/true universality   52, 80 f., 104 f., 121, 127
Universalizability   2, 14, 37, 62, 69, 76–81, 84 f., 100, 102, 104 f.,, 108, 115, 128, 167, 171, 210, 217 f., 224
- Universalization test (*see also* 'typic-procedure')   4, 6, 77, 86, 96–98, 100 f., 104, 115, 219
Utilitarianism   92, 96–98, 127

Versinnlichung (sensible rendering)   40, 51, 62, 68, 146 f., 159 f., 170, 199, 201, 223
Virtue   119, 131, 144, 150, 164, 166–170, 175, 178, 222

Well-being (*das Wohl*)   21, 111, 126 f.
Will/volition (*see also* 'contradiction in volition')   19–22, 26, 28–32, 88 f., 91–93, 102 f., 147
Windowpane example   121

www.ingramcontent.com/pod-product-compliance
Lightning Source LLC
Chambersburg PA
CBHW062006180426
43198CB00037B/2456